Autodesk Official Training Guide

Essentials

Autodesk® Inventor®

2010

Learning Autodesk® Inve

Hands-on exercises demonstrate fundamental principles of 3
part design, assembly design, and the creation of production

Autodesk Certification Preparation

Autodesk®

Published by: Autodesk, Inc.
111 McInnis Parkway
San Rafael, CA 94903, USA

Acknowledgements

Primary Author

The Autodesk Learning team wishes to thank everyone who participated in the development of this project, with special acknowledgement to the authoring contributions and subject matter expertise of Ron Myers and CrWare, LP.

CrWare, LP began publishing courseware for Autodesk® Inventor® in 2001. Since that time, the company has grown to include full-time curriculum developers, subject matter experts, technical writers, and graphics specialists, each with a unique set of industry experiences and talents that enables CrWare to create content that is both accurate and relevant to meeting the learning needs of its readers and customers.

The company's Founder and General Partner, Ron Myers, has been using Autodesk® products since 1989. During that time, Ron Myers worked in all disciplines of drafting and design, until 1996 when he began a career as an Applications Engineer, Instructor, and Author. Ron Myers has been creating courseware and other training material for Autodesk since 1996 and has written and created training material for AutoCAD®, Autodesk Inventor, AutoCAD® Mechanical, Mechanical Desktop®, and Autodesk® Impression.

Acknowledgements:

Cover Image

Cover and all similar images courtesy of Engineering Center LTD, Russia. Aircraft engine image courtesy of Adept Airmotive LTD. Wheelchair image courtesy of Magic Wheels, Inc. Grinding machine image courtesy of HTC Sweden AB.

Sr. Graphic Designer

Luke Pauw

Sr. Graphic/Production Designer

Diane Erlich

Special thanks go out to:

Travis Jones, Rodney Kerbyson, Willem Knibbe, Paul Mailhot, and Barbara Vezos.

Table of Contents

Chapter 03

Chapter 04

Chapter 05

Chapter 06

Chapter 07

Chapter 08

Chapter 09

Introduction

Welcome to the *Learning Autodesk Inventor 2010* training guide for use in Authorized
Training Center (ATC®) locations, corporate training settings, and other classroom settings.

Although this guide is designed for instructor-led courses, you can also use it for self-paced
learning. The guide encourages self-learning through the use of the Autodesk® Inventor® 2010
Help system.

This introduction covers the following topics:

- Course objectives
- Prerequisites
- Using this guide
- Completing the exercises
- Installing the exercise data files
- Projects
- Notes, tips, and warnings
- Feedback

This guide is complementary to the software documentation. For detailed explanations of features
and functionality, refer to the Help in the software.

Course Objectives

After completing this guide, you will be able to:

- Identify the main user interface components that are common to all Autodesk
  Inventor design environments and describe how to access different tools. Describe
  the characteristics and benefits of a parametric part model and how to view all
  aspects of your design by efficiently navigating around in 2D and 3D space.

- Use sketch tools to create 2D sketch geometry, apply geometric constraints to
  control sketch geometry, and add parametric dimensions to your sketch geometry.

- Create features using the Extrude and Revolve tools, use reference and
  construction geometry, use the browser and shortcut menus to edit parametric
  parts, use the 3D Grips tool to edit part geometry in the context of an assembly
  and in a stand-alone part, create, locate, and utilize work features to perform
  modeling tasks, and create swept shapes by sweeping a profile along a
  2D or 3D path.

- Create both chamfers and fillets on a part, use the Hole and Thread tools to place hole and thread features, create rectangular and circular patterns and mirror existing features, and create thin- walled parts.

- Describe the assembly modeling process, the Autodesk Inventor assembly modeling environment, and recommended assembly design workflows, and how to use Autodesk Inventor project files to manage design projects.

- Place components in an assembly, add constraints to components, use Content Center to place standard components in an assembly, and create new components in the context of an assembly.

- Use different tools and methods to identify, locate, and select components in an assembly, retrieve important analysis information from the parametric models and assemblies, and create animations of exploded views in a presentation file.

- Navigate the Autodesk Inventor user interface when creating and editing drawing sheets, create base and projected views of 3D parts and assemblies, create and edit section views, detail views, and cropped views, and manage drawing views.

- Dimension drawings with automated and manual techniques, create and edit hole and thread notes in drawings, add centerlines, center marks and symbols to your drawings, and configure, add, and edit revision tables and revision tags.

- View and edit bill of materials data, create and customize parts lists to document the components in your assembly, and review balloons and their purpose in the drawing annotation process.

- Set drafting standards to control the appearance of drawing features, use drawing resources to create multiple sheets and add borders and title blocks to your drawings.

Prerequisites

This course is designed for new Autodesk Inventor users who want to learn the essential tools and principles of 3D parametric part design, assembly design, and how to create production-ready part and assembly drawings using Autodesk Inventor 2010.

It is recommended that you have:

- A basic understanding of mechanical drafting or design.

- A working knowledge of Microsoft® Windows® XP, or Microsoft® Windows® Vista.

Using This Guide

The lessons are independent of each other. However, it is recommended that you complete these lessons in the order that they are presented unless you are familiar with the concepts and functionality described in those lessons.

Each chapter contains:

- **Lessons**
  Usually two or more lessons in each chapter.

- **Exercises**
  Practical, real-world examples for you to practice using the functionality you have just learned. Each exercise contains step-by-step procedures and graphics to help you complete the exercise successfully.

Installing the Exercise Data Files

To complete the exercises in this guide, you must download the data files from the following location and install them on your system.

To install the data files for the exercises:

1. Download the zip file from *www.sybex.com/go/learninginventor2010*.
2. Unzip the file *Setup.exe*.
3. Double-click *Setup.exe* and follow the onscreen instructions to install the files.
4. After the install is complete, you can delete Setup.exe from your system (optional).
Unless you specify a different folder, the exercise datasets are installed in the following folder:

C:\Autodesk Learning\Inventor 2010\Learning

Order a Trial Version of Autodesk Inventor

This guide was designed for use with Autodesk® Inventor® 2010 software. If you do not have Autodesk Inventor 2010 software installed on your system, you can order a trial version.

To order the latest trial version of the Autodesk Inventor software:

1. Navigate to *www.autodesk.com/autodeskinventortrial*.
2. Complete the registration and mailing information.
3. Submit the online form to receive a free** 30-day test drive DVD, which includes the Autodesk Inventor Software.
** This product is subject to the terms and conditions of the end-user license agreement that accompanies the software.

Completing the Exercises

You can complete the exercise in two ways: using the book or on screen.

- **Using the book**
  Follow the step-by-step exercises in the book.

- **On screen**
  Click the Learning Autodesk Inventor 2010 icon on your desktop, and follow the step-by-step exercises on screen. The onscreen exercises are the same as those in the book. The onscreen version has the advantage that you can concentrate on the screen without having to glance down at your book.

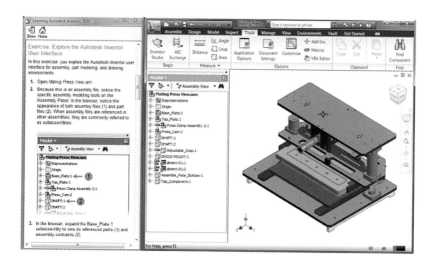

After launching the onscreen exercises, you might need to alter the size of your application window to align both windows.

Projects

Most engineers work on several projects at a time, and each project might consist of a number of files. You can use Autodesk Inventor projects to organize related files and maintain links between files. This guide has a project file that stores the paths to all the files that are related to the exercises. When you open a file, Autodesk Inventor uses the paths in the current project file to locate other required files. To work on a different project, you make a new project active in the Project Editor. Follow the instructions in the guide to locate the project file for the course and make it active.

Follow the instructions below to locate the Learning Autodesk Inventor 2010 project file for this guide and make it active.

1 Start Autodesk Inventor.

2 In the Application menu, click Manage > Projects.
   - In the Projects dialog box, click Browse.
   - In the Choose Project File dialog box, navigate to *C:\Autodesk Learning\Inventor 2010\ Learning*.
   - Select *Learning Autodesk Inventor 2010.ipj.*
   - Click Open.

3 In the Projects dialog box, double-click *Learning Autodesk Inventor 2010* to activate the project. Click Done.

> **Note**: *The check mark designates the active project.*

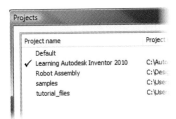

Notes, Tips, and Warnings

Throughout this guide, notes, tips, and warnings are called out for special attention.

  Notes contain guidelines, constraints, and other explanatory information.

  Tips provide information to enhance your productivity.

  Warnings provide information about actions that might result in the loss of data, system failures, or other serious consequences.

Feedback

We always welcome feedback on Autodesk Official Training Guides. After completing this course, if you have suggestions for improvements or if you want to report an error in the book , please send your comments to *learningtools@autodesk.com*.

Digital Prototyping

A digital prototype is created with Autodesk® Inventor® software and is a digital simulation of a product that can be used to test form, fit, and function. The digital prototype becomes more and more complete as all associated industrial, mechanical, and electrical design data are integrated. A complete digital prototype is a true digital representation of the entire end product and can be used to visualize and simulate a product to reduce the necessity of building expensive physical prototypes.

What is Digital Prototyping?

Digital Prototyping gives conceptual design, engineering, and manufacturing departments the ability to virtually explore a complete product before it becomes real. With Digital Prototyping, manufacturers can design, visualize, and simulate products from the conceptual design phase through the manufacturing process, boosting the level of communication with different stakeholders while getting more innovative products to market faster. By using a digital prototype created in Inventor, manufacturers can visualize and simulate the realworld performance of a design digitally, helping reduce their reliance on costly physical prototypes.

What is the Autodesk Solution for Digital Prototyping?

Autodesk Inventor software takes manufacturers beyond 3D to Digital Prototyping. With Inventor, you can create a single digital model that gives you the ability to design, visualize, and simulate your products:

- **Design**: Integrate all design data into a single digital model, streamlining the design process and increasing communication.

- **Visualize**: Create a virtual representation of the final product to review design intent, secure early customer validation, and market products before they're built.

- **Simulate**: Digitally simulate the real-world performance of your product, saving the time and money required to build multiple physical prototypes.

Inventor enables manufacturers to create a digital prototype, helping reduce reliance on costly physical prototypes and get more innovative products to market faster. The Autodesk® solution for Digital Prototyping brings together design data from all phases of the product development process into a single digital model created in Inventor.

What Pain Points Does Digital Prototyping Address?

The manufacturing product development process today is dominated by islands of competency, each presenting its own technical challenges:

- In the conceptual design phase, industrial designers and engineers often use paper based methods or digital formats that are incompatible with the digital information used in the engineering phase. A lack of digital data, compatible formats, and automation keeps this island separate from engineering—the conceptual design data must be recreated digitally downstream, resulting in lost time and money.

- In the engineering phase, mechanical and electrical engineers use different systems and formats, and a lack of automation makes it difficult to capture and rapidly respond to change requests from manufacturing. Another problem in the engineering phase: the geometric focus of typical 3D CAD software makes it difficult to create and use a digital prototype to validate and optimize products before they are built, making it necessary to build multiple costly physical prototypes.

- Manufacturing is at the downstream end of all the broken digital processes—the disconnection between the conceptual design phase, the engineering components, electrical, and mechanical— and they receive this analog information in the form of drawings. The result is a heavy reliance on physical prototypes and the subsequent impact on productivity and innovation.

- Disconnected product development processes make it difficult to bring customer and marketing requirements into the process early so customers can see exactly what the product will look like and validate how it will function before it is delivered. The inability to involve the customer early in the product development process means that the customer can't validate a design before the product goes to manufacturing. Customer requests for changes become exponentially more expensive to address the further along the product is in the manufacturing process. The result: companies have to build multiple physical prototypes for customer validation.

Hasn't the Concept of Digital Prototyping Been Around for Years?

Although there has been talk about the benefits of Digital Prototyping for years, the budget for the tools required to build and test a true digital prototype has been out of reach for most manufacturing companies. Digital Prototyping solutions are usually expensive, customized installations for large enterprises. Most out-of-the-box 3D modeling applications provide only part of the functionality needed to create a complete digital prototype.

What is Unique About the Autodesk Approach to Digital Prototyping?

Scalable: The Autodesk solution for Digital Prototyping is scalable, flexible, and easy to integrate into existing business processes. Using Inventor to create a single digital model, manufacturers can realize the benefits of Digital Prototyping at their own pace, with minimal disruption to existing productive workflows.

Attainable: The Autodesk solution for Digital Prototyping provides an easy to deploy and manage solution for mainstream manufacturers to create and maintain a single digital model that can be used in all stages of production.

Cost-effective: Delivering cost-effective software for design and manufacturing workgroups, an Inventor-based Digital Prototyping solution delivers the fastest path to ROI. Autodesk has a proven record of making powerful desktop technology available to mainstream manufacturers.

How Do the Autodesk Manufacturing Products and Technology Drive Digital Prototyping?

Inventor takes you beyond 3D to Digital Prototyping. The Autodesk solution for Digital Prototyping enables manufacturing workgroups to develop a single digital model, created in Inventor, that can be used in every stage of production—bridging the gaps that usually exist between conceptual design, engineering, and manufacturing teams. This single digital model simulates the complete product and gives engineers the ability to better design, visualize, and simulate their product with less reliance on costly physical prototypes—thereby improving time to market, and increasing competitive advantage. Autodesk provides the interoperable tools required to create a complete digital prototype from the conceptual phase of a project through manufacturing.

The **Autodesk® Alias®** product line enables you to work digitally from project outset using best-in- class industrial design tools. Capture ideas digitally—from initial sketches to 3D concept models using products in the Alias product line—then share those designs with the engineering team using a common file format, allowing a product's industrial design data to be incorporated into the digital prototype created in Inventor. Today, the look and feel of a machine or device is more important than ever for consumers, so industrial designers and engineers must share housing and user interfaces early in the process.

With **Autodesk® Showcase®** software, you can quickly evaluate multiple design variations by creating realistic, accurate, and compelling imagery from 3D CAD data—helping reduce the time, cost, and need for building physical prototypes. You can then interactively view the digital prototype in realistic environments, making it faster, easier, and less expensive to make design decisions.

Autodesk Inventor software moves engineers beyond 3D and enables them to develop complete digital prototypes of their products. The Autodesk Inventor family of software provides the powerful —yet cost-effective and easy to learn—desktop technology engineers need to take advantage of Digital Prototyping. Autodesk Inventor software enables engineers to integrate AutoCAD drawings and 3D data into a single digital model, creating a virtual representation of the final product. Using this single digital model, you can design, visualize, and simulate products digitally. The model serves as a digital prototype that is refined and used to validate design functions, helping to reduce reliance on physical prototypes and minimize manufacturing costs.

- **Functional Design**: Autodesk Inventor software products combine an intuitive 3D mechanical design environment for creating parts and assemblies with functional design tools that enable engineers to focus on a design's function, not geometry creation—letting the software drive the automatic creation of intelligent components such as plastic parts, steel frames, rotating machinery, tube and pipe runs, and electrical cable and wire harnesses. Reducing the geometry burden helps engineers spend more time rapidly building and refining digital prototypes that validate design functions and help optimize manufacturing costs.

- **DWG™ Interoperability**: Inventor provides direct read and write of native DWG files while maintaining full associativity to the 3D model without risking inaccurate translations. (DWG from Autodesk is the original format for storing and sharing design data when working with AutoCAD software. With billions of DWG files circulating throughout every industry, it's one of the most commonly used design data formats.) This gives engineers the freedom to safely reuse valuable 2D DWG files to build accurate 3D part models, then communicate insights gained from Digital Prototyping with partners and suppliers that rely on AutoCAD software.

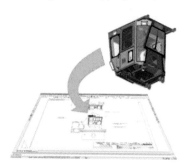

- **Dynamic simulation**: Autodesk Inventor delivers the best integrated simulation tools in the industry. Tightly integrated tools for calculation, stress, deflection, and motion simulation make it possible for engineers to optimize and validate a digital prototype before the product is built. Simulation is performed based on real-world constraints, so you know you can rely on the simulation results. The dynamic simulation tools in Inventor enable engineers to evaluate multiple potential solutions to a motion problem, making it possible to make the best design decisions and avoid costly mistakes.

- **Documentation**: Autodesk Inventor software includes comprehensive tools to generate engineering and manufacturing documentation directly from a validated 3D digital prototype, helping design teams communicate more effectively. Inventor combines the benefits of associative drawing views, so any changes made to the model are reflected in the drawing—with the power and widespread acceptance of the DWG format to help reduce errors and deliver the design in less time.

- **Routed Systems**: Inventor software's automated tools for designing routed systems, including complex tube and pipe runs, and electrical cable and harness design, allow you to create and validate a more complete digital prototype, which helps reduce errors and ECOs prior to manufacturing and get to market faster.

- **Tooling**: The tooling capabilities of Inventor software give designers and engineers intelligent tools and mold base catalogs to quickly and accurately generate mold designs directly from a digital prototype. Using the Inventor digital prototype, mold, tool, and die manufacturers can validate the form, fit, and function of a mold design before it's built, reducing errors and improving mold performance.

To help validate and optimize designs before manufacturing, you can use the broad range of finite element analysis (FEA) and simulation tools in Algor simulation software, which will enhance the Autodesk solution for Digital Prototyping.

AutoCAD® Mechanical software is built to help mechanical designers and drafters simplify complex mechanical design work, enhancing productivity. Quickly detail production drawings using industry- specific manufacturing tools, reducing errors and saving hours of time. AutoCAD, one of the world's leading design and professional drafting software, plays an important role in Digital Prototyping workflows. AutoCAD gives you the power and flexibility to explore, document, and communicate ideas. Both AutoCAD Mechanical and AutoCAD software enable engineers to accurately document digital prototypes created in Inventor, and communicate insights gained from Digital Prototyping with colleagues, partners, and suppliers that rely on AutoCAD software.

AutoCAD® Electrical software passes electrical design intent information for cables and conductors directly to Autodesk Inventor software, adding valuable electrical controls design data to the digital prototype created in Inventor. Inventor users can pass wire-connectivity information to AutoCAD Electrical and automatically create the corresponding 2D schematics. The smooth integration between Inventor and AutoCAD Electrical helps your electrical and mechanical teams work collaboratively and efficiently on 2D and 3D mechatronic product designs.

To optimize plastic part and injection mold designs, use **Autodesk® Moldflow®** injection molding simulation software.

Autodesk® 3ds Max® software enables you to leverage engineering data to create advanced software- rendered and -animated visualizations of digital prototypes created in Inventor. 3ds Max contains a complete suite of CAD data preparation, modeling, effects, and rendering tools to create the highest quality photorealistic and stylistic still and animated visualizations.

Autodesk® Navisworks® software for manufacturing enables manufacturing companies to visualize complete manufacturing facilities, industrial machinery, factory floor models, and production lines in a single environment. The software supports complete assembly visualization and optimization, and enables you to combine CAD data from various design systems regardless of file format or size.

Autodesk's data management tools allow design workgroups to manage and track all the design components for a digital prototype, helping you to better reuse design data, manage bills of material, and promote early collaboration with manufacturing teams and clients. With the Autodesk® Vault family of data management applications, design, engineering, and manufacturing workgroups can manage the Digital Prototyping process by helping reduce time organizing files, avoid costly mistakes, and more efficiently release and revise designs. You can further facilitate Digital Prototyping workflows with **Autodesk® Design Review** software, the all-digital way to review, measure, mark up, and track changes to designs—all without the original creation software.

What Can Customers Do with the Autodesk Solution for Digital Prototyping Today?

Industrial designers use Autodesk Alias products to digitally sketch design ideas and create 3D digital concept models for validation that then can be shared with engineering or manufacturing teams.

Engineers use Autodesk Inventor to explore ideas with simple, functional representations that help generate a digital prototype. Inventor software delivers the best bidirectional interoperability on the market between 2D and 3D mechanical and electrical design applications. Integrated stress analysis and motion simulation help engineers optimize and validate complete designs digitally and confirm that customer requirements are met even before a product is built.

Manufacturing teams benefit from accessing the most current and accurate data (release drawings, models, and BOMs)—avoiding mistakes caused by using outdated documents. They can provide expertise earlier in the engineering process by sharing the digital prototype with Autodesk's DWF™ (Design Web Format™) technology to communicate, mark up, and measure designs—moving one step closer to true paperless manufacturing processes.

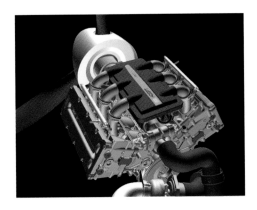

What Are the Business Benefits of Digital Prototyping?

According to an independent study by the Aberdeen Group, best-in-class manufacturers use Digital Prototyping to build half the number of physical prototypes as the average manufacturer, get to market 58 days faster than average, experience 48 percent lower prototyping costs, and ultimately drive greater innovation in their products. The Autodesk solution for Digital Prototyping helps customers achieve results like these.

How Does the Autodesk Solution for Digital Prototyping Help Get Customers to Best-in-Class?

By giving you the tools to develop a complete digital prototype, Autodesk helps you build fewer physical prototypes—and ultimately get to market ahead of the competition with more innovative products. Autodesk's position is that moving to 3D is only the first step in creating a digital prototype. In today's increasingly competitive global market, being best in class means using technology to stay ahead of the competition—incorporating Digital Prototyping into the product development process gives you that edge. Autodesk provides this functionality through a complete, easy-to-learn set of design applications and a wide range of partners for consultation regarding what is needed to make Digital Prototyping a reality.

Chapter 01
Getting Started

Autodesk® Inventor® has a context-sensitive user interface that provides you with the tools relevant to the tasks being performed. A comprehensive online help and tutorial system provides you with information to help you learn the application. This chapter introduces the tools and interface options that you use on a constant basis.

This chapter also introduces fundamental of parametric part design concepts that enable you to capture design intent and build intelligence into your designs.

Objectives

After completing this chapter, you will be able to:

- Identify the main user interface components that are common to all Autodesk Inventor design environments and describe how to access different tools.

- View all aspects of your design by efficiently navigating around in 2D and 3D space.

- Describe the characteristics and benefits of a parametric part model.

Lesson 01 | Autodesk Inventor User Interface

This lesson describes the application interface. You are introduced to the different file types (part, assembly, presentation, and drawing) you work with as you create and document your designs, and you examine the common user interface elements and view management tools in these environments.

As with all computer applications, the User Interface (UI) is what you use to interact with the program. While the Autodesk Inventor UI shares many common themes and elements with other Microsoft Windows applications, it also has some unique elements and functionalities that may be new to you, even as an experienced CAD user.

In the following illustration, the Autodesk Inventor User Interface is shown.

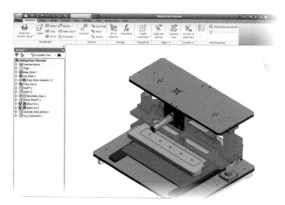

Objectives

After completing this lesson, you will be able to:

- Describe the multiple environments within Autodesk Inventor.

- Describe what project files are used for.

- Describe the types of files Autodesk Inventor creates and the kinds of information they store.

- Identify the major components of the Autodesk Inventor user interface.

- Identify the browser and panel bar in the assembly, part, presentation, and drawing environments.

- Identify and access various types of online help and tutorial resources.

About Multiple Environments

In order to provide the greatest design flexibility and reuse, each part, assembly, and drawing is stored in a separate file. Each part file is a stand-alone entity that can be used in different assembly files and drawing files. When you make a change to a part, the change is evident in each assembly or drawing that references that part. Assembly files can be referenced by other assembly files, presentation files, and drawing files. IDW and DWG files are now interchangeable. Depending on your workflow and need for use in downstream applications, you can create your production drawings with either file format.

The basic file references that exist in a typical 3D design are represented in the following illustration.

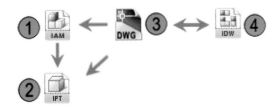

① **Assembly files:** IAM files reference part files and are referenced by drawing files.

② **Part files:** IPT files are referenced by assembly files and drawing files.

③ **Drawing files:** DWG files reference assembly files and part files.

④ **Inventor Drawing files:** IDW files are interchangeable with DWG files in Inventor and reference assembly and part files.

Using Template Files

Template files serve as the basis for all new files that you create. When you begin a file from a template file, you can control default settings such as units, snap spacing, and default tolerances in the new file.

The application offers template files for each type of file. Template files are categorized into two main groups: English for English units (inches and feet), and Metric for metric units (millimeters and meters).

The New File dialog box has three tabs: Default, English, and Metric. The Default tab presents templates based on the default unit that you select during installation, while the English and Metric tabs present template files in their respective units.

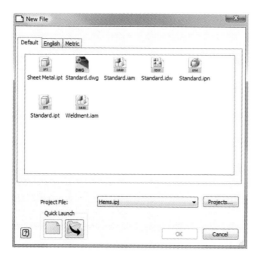

Part Modeling Environment

In the part modeling environment:

• You create and edit 3D part models.

• The interface adjusts automatically to present tools for your current task, for example, tools for sketching or tools to create 3D features.

The following illustration shows the user interface in the part modeling environment.

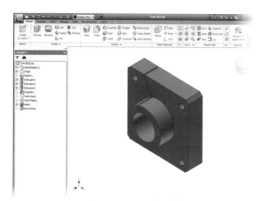

Assembly Modeling Environment

In the assembly modeling environment:

- You build and edit 3D assembly models. The components displayed in the system are references to external parts and subassemblies.

- You use assembly specific tools to position and build relationships between components.

- A common set of viewing tools is available.

The following illustration shows the user interface in the assembly modeling environment.

Presentation Environment

In the presentation environment:

- You create exploded assembly views.

- You can record an animation of an exploded view to help document your assembly.

- The presentation file references an existing assembly.

- A common set of viewing tools is available.

The following illustration shows the user interface in the presentation environment.

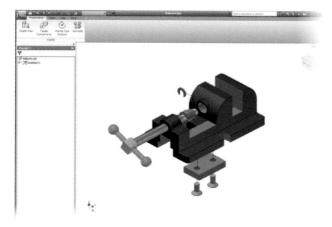

Drawing Environment

In the drawing environment:

- You create 2D drawings of parts and assemblies.

- A drawing file references one or more parts, assemblies, or presentation files. Changes to the part or assembly model update the associated drawing views and annotations.

The following illustration shows the user interface in the drawing environment.

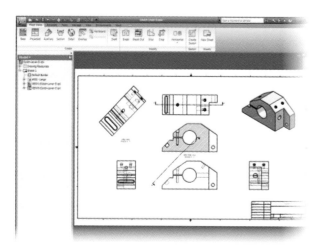

About Project Files

As you create designs in Autodesk Inventor, file dependencies are created between files of different types. For example, when you create a 3D assembly, a file dependency between the assembly and its part models is created. As your designs grow in complexity, these dependencies can become more complicated. Autodesk Inventor utilizes project files to locate the required files as they are needed. As a result of using the information contained in the project file, when you open that 3D assembly, Autodesk Inventor can locate the 3D part files and display them properly.

In the context of an introduction to the Autodesk Inventor user interface, all that is important to realize is that you must have an active project before you create any files. This is why the project file is listed in the New File dialog box. Autodesk Inventor installs several sample project files, but the default project is initially active.

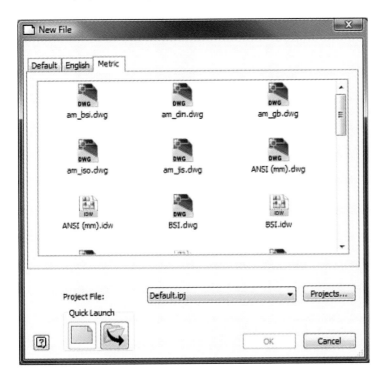

Inventor File Types

To maximize performance, Autodesk Inventor uses different file types for each type of file. Assembly files are stored in a different type of file than the parts that are used to create them. 2D drawing information can be stored in either the IDW file type that is unique to Autodesk Inventor, or the DWG format that is native to AutoCAD® and is an accepted industry standard.

In the following illustration, the New File dialog box illustrates the different types of files that you can create with Autodesk Inventor.

Part Files

 Part files (*.ipt) represent the foundation of all designs using Autodesk Inventor. You use the part file to describe the individual parts that make up an assembly.

Assembly Files

Assembly *(*.iam)* files consist of multiple part files assembled in a single file to represent your assembly. You use assembly constraints to constrain all the parts to each other. The assembly file contains references to all of its component files.

Presentation Files

You use presentation files *(*.ipn)* to create exploded views of the assembly. It is also possible to animate the exploded views to simulate how the assembly should be put together or taken apart.

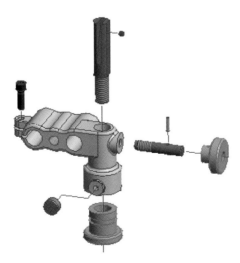

Drawing Files

You use drawing files *(*.idw)* to create the necessary 2D documentation of your design. Drawing files include dimensions, annotations, and views required for manufacturing. When you use a drawing file to create 2D views of an existing 3D model, the views are associative to the 3D model, and changes in model geometry are reflected in the drawing automatically. You can also use drawing files to create simple 2D drawings in much the same way that you use other 2D drawing programs.

Inventor drawing files can also be stored in the standard DWG format. If you use this format for your 2D drawings, they can be opened and saved in AutoCAD. This is a very useful option for users who must share their design data with others who use AutoCAD.

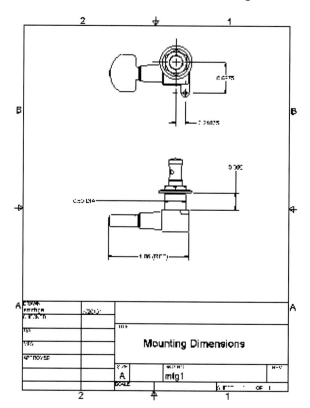

User Interface

All environments share a common layout for tabs on a single toolbar across the top of the application window called the ribbon. The ribbon contains tools and commands for specific tasks on separate tabs. Each environment, assembly, part, or drawing for example, displays tabs and tools specific to that environment. As you change tasks within a single environment, the ribbon adjusts to present the appropriate tabs and tools.

The following illustration shows the major components of the Autodesk Inventor user interface. The ribbon and tabs are displayed at the top of the application window.

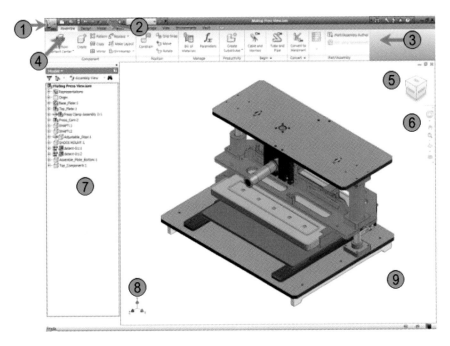

① Application Menu		⑥ Navigation Bar	
② Quick Access Toolbar		⑦ Browser	
③ Ribbon		⑧ 3D Indicator	
④ Ribbon Tabs		⑨ Graphics Window	
⑤ ViewCube			

Interface Structure

Autodesk Inventor uses a standard structure common in all Microsoft Windows applications. The structure is context-sensitive based on the environment and mode you are using.

As you are learning the application more thoroughly, you should take the time to familiarize yourself with the different options that are displayed on the ribbon in different work environments.

The following illustration shows the Assemble tab in the assembly modeling environment.

The following illustration shows the Model tab in the part modeling environment.

The following illustration shows the Place Views tab in the drawing environment.

Quick Access Toolbar

By default, a single Inventor standard toolbar is displayed in all environments and is called the Quick Access toolbar. When you change between environments, the Quick Access toolbar updates to present valid tools for the environment. The toolbar contains tools for file handling, settings, view manipulation, and model or document appearance.

A section of the Quick Access toolbar is displayed in the following illustration. It is organized into groups based on functionality. This area of the toolbar displays tools for standard file and modeling operations.

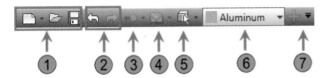

1. Standard file management tools
2. Undo and Redo
3. Environment navigation
4. Update document
5. Selection filters
6. Color List
7. Design Doctor

Context-Sensitive Tools

As you switch between environments or between tasks in a single environment, Autodesk Inventor displays the appropriate tools and information for the current task. The ribbon automatically presents tabs and tools for the current task. The browser displays information on the active environment.

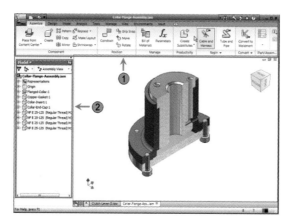

① The ribbon is your primary interface for accessing the tools available while you design. The context-sensitive design presents the relevant tools based on the current context of your design session. For example, when you switch from assembly modeling to part modeling, the ribbon switches automatically to display the correct tabs and tools for the context where you work.

② The browser is one of the main interface components. It is context-sensitive with the environment you use. For example, when you work on an assembly you use the browser to present information specific to the assembly environment. While you use the part modeling environment, the browser displays information that is relevant to part modeling.

Model Tab

When you are in the part modeling environment, the Model tab is displayed while you create and edit part models. You use these tools to create parametric features on the part.

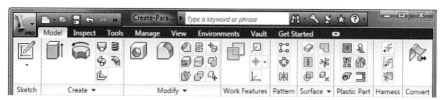

Sketch Tab

You use the Sketch tab in the modeling environment to create 2D parametric sketches, dimensions, and constraints. You use the same set of tools on the Assemble tab when creating a sketch in the assembly environment.

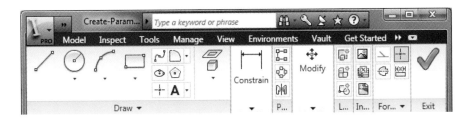

Part Modeling Browser

The browser displays all features you use to create the part. The features are listed in the order in which they are created. The browser also displays the Origin folder at the top of the list which contains the default *X*, *Y*, and *Z* planes, axes, and center point.

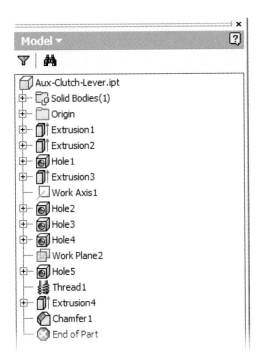

Assembly Modeling Environment

When you are in the assembly modeling environment, the browser displays all the parts you use in the assembly. It also lists the Origin folder containing the default *X*, *Y*, and *Z* planes, axes, and center point of the assembly.

If applied, nested under each part, you see the assembly constraints. If you select an assembly constraint, an edit box is displayed at the bottom of the browser, enabling you to edit the offset or angle value for the constraint.

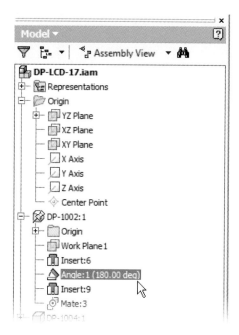

> **Tip** *In the assembly environment, you can use the Modeling View option in the Assembly View drop-down list to display the part features nested under the parts instead of the assembly constraints. This is useful when performing part modeling functions in the context of the assembly.*

In the following illustration, the Assemble tab is shown in the default Normal mode. In Normal mode, the tool icons and names are displayed.

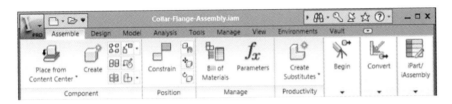

> **Tip** You can also choose to display tool icons without text by right-clicking anywhere on the ribbon and then clicking Ribbon Appearance → Text Off.

Design Accelerator

Clicking on the ribbon, Design tab displays the Design Accelerator tools.

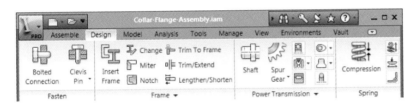

Presentation Tab

When you are in the presentation environment, you use the Presentation tab to create presentation views and tweaks, and to animate geometry in the presentation environment.

Presentation Browser

The browser displays the presentation views you create followed by the tweaks you use for the explosion. When you expand each tweak, you see the parts included in that tweak. You can also switch the browser mode from Tweak View to Sequence View or Assembly View.

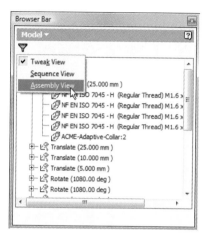

Drawing Environment

In the drawing environment, the browser displays the Drawing Resources folder containing sheet formats, borders, title blocks, and sketched symbols. It also displays each sheet in the drawing along with the views you create for each.

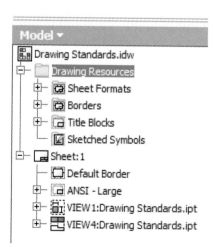

You use the Place Views tab in the drawing environment to create drawing views on the sheet.

You use the Annotate tab in the drawing environment to add reference dimensions and other annotation objects.

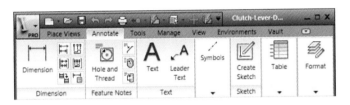

Keyboard Shortcuts

You can use keyboard shortcuts to access and begin tools and commands. For example, you can enter **P** for Place Component, or **N** for Create Component. Entering the keyboard shortcut is the same as clicking the tool on the tabs. When you hover the mouse over a tool on the ribbon, the tooltip will expand to reveal information about the tool. The keyboard shortcut (1) will be listed as shown in the following illustration.

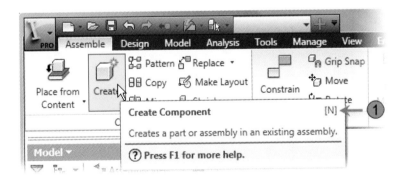

Note: **Access Shortcut Keys List** *You can access a complete list of the default shortcut keys from the Help menu. In the Info Center, click the arrow next to the Help icon > Shortcut/Alias Quick Reference.*

Condensed Ribbon

As you become more familiar with the tools in each environment, you can condense the ribbon by choosing to display tool icons without text. To switch, right-click anywhere on the ribbon and click Ribbon Appearance > Text Off. Clear the check mark to display icon text. In this mode, tools are displayed with icons only resulting in more area for the browser and graphics windows.

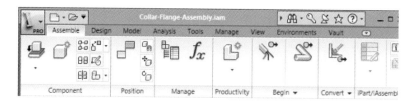

Alternative Ribbon and Browser Positions

In addition to the default positions, you can alter the location of the ribbon or browser by clicking and dragging the horizontal bars near the top of the element, or the title area when the element is floating. Both the ribbon and browser can be placed in a docked position on the left or right side of the screen, or in a floating position anywhere in the graphics window.

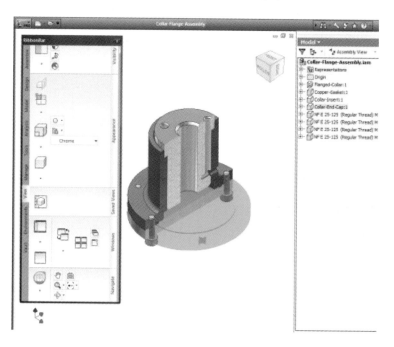

Online Help and Tutorials

Autodesk Inventor offers several types of online help, tutorial references, and other resources to assist in building your skill level. Standard Help files, context-sensitive how-to presentations, Show Me animations, and tutorials are available.

Setting Your User Type

The initial Help screen enables you to specify the user type that most closely matches your situation. The topics that are most relevant to the user type that you select are presented first on the initial help screen. By default, the option to Show Help on startup is enabled. This causes the Inventor Help system to launch each time you start Inventor and create a new file or open an existing file.

To access the Inventor Help System, press F1 or click Help menu > Help Topics.

Help for Returning and New Users

Returning and new users can find links to Help information that is most relevant for them.

Help for AutoCAD Users

AutoCAD users can use the Help topics designed specifically for them as they make the transition to Autodesk Inventor.

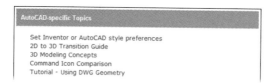

Shortcut/Alias Quick Reference

The Shortcut/Alias Quick Reference shows all of the default Shortcut/Alias keys along with the command names they execute.

Click Help menu > Shortcut/Alias Quick Reference to access the reference.

Show Me Animations

The Show Me animations present topic-specific information in animated presentations.

To access the Show Me animations, on the Info Center, click Help > Help Topics and select the Show Me Animations link. In the Show Me Animations dialog box, navigate to the topic of choice and the animation begins automatically.

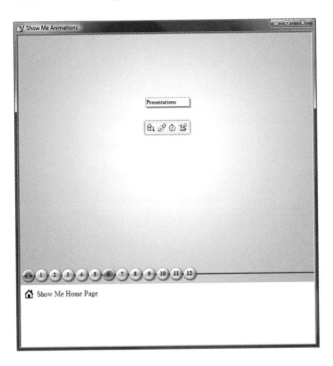

Tutorials

There are several tutorials available that cover a range of topics from Level 1 to Level 3. Click the tabs along the top of the page to view the tutorials for each level. On each tab, panels display tutorial titles and descriptions. From the main list of tutorials, select the topic of interest. The tutorials present step- by-step information on performing tasks in Autodesk Inventor.

You access these tutorials by clicking Help menu > Learning Tools > Tutorials, or by clicking Try It Tutorials on the main Help screen.

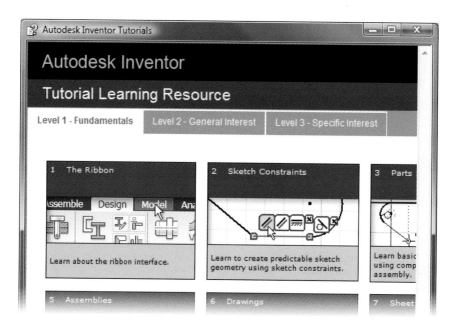

In the following illustration, the Introduction to the Ribbon Interface page of the Autodesk Inventor tutorial is displayed.

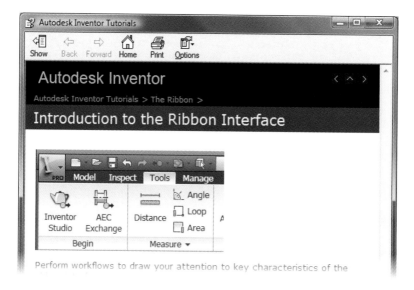

Exercise | Explore the Autodesk Inventor User Interface

In this exercise, you explore the Autodesk Inventor user interface for assembly, part modeling, and drawing environments.

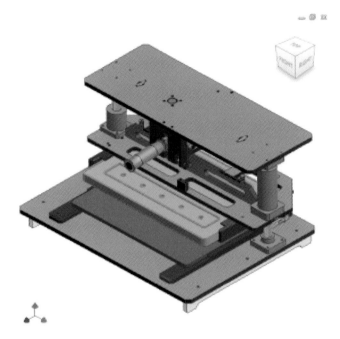

The completed exercise

Completing the Exercise:	*To complete the exercise, follow the steps in this book or in the onscreen exercise. In the onscreen list of chapters and exercises, click Chapter 1: Getting Started. Click Exercise: Explore the Autodesk Inventor User Interface.*

Exercise Setup

Before you can complete the exercises for the Learning Autodesk Inventor 2010 course, you must activate the Learning Autodesk Inventor 2010 project file.

1   Start Autodesk Inventor. If Autodesk Inventor is already running, close all files.

2   Click Get Started tab > Launch panel > Projects.

- If Learning Autodesk Inventor 2010 is displayed in the project list, double-click to make it active. A check mark appears next to the active project.
- If Learning Autodesk Inventor 2010 is not in the list, click Browse.
- Navigate to the installation folder of your student dataset files. By default, this location is *C:\Autodesk Learning\Inventor2010\Learning.*
- Double-click *Learning Autodesk Inventor 2010.ipj*. A check mark appears next to the active project.
- Click Done.

3   End of exercise setup. Continue to the exercise.

Explore the Autodesk Inventor User Interface

1   Open *Mating Press View.iam.*

2   Because this is an assembly file, notice the specific assembly modeling tools on the ribbon. In the browser, notice the appearance of both assembly files (1) and part files (2). When assembly files are referenced in other assemblies, they are commonly referred to as subassemblies.

3   In the browser, expand the Base_Plate:1 subassembly to view its referenced parts (1) and
     assembly constraints (2).

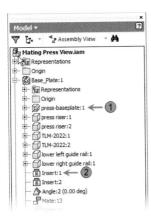

4   To activate a part in the context of the assembly:
     - In the browser, collapse the Base_Plate:1 subassembly node.
     - Double-click the Top_Component:1 part instance.
     - Notice the change in appearance in the browser, graphics window, and ribbon. In
       the browser, the area listing inactive components and subassemblies has a gray
       background. The ribbon changes to display tools specific to part modeling, and in the
       graphics window, all inactive components become transparent leaving only the active
       part opaque in color.

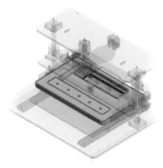

5   To return to the assembly, on the ribbon, click Return.
     Note: You could also double-click the assembly in the browser to return.

6   To open a part in its own window:

- In the browser, right-click the Top_Component:1 part. Click Open. The part opens in a separate window and any changes made to the part are reflected in the assembly.
- Notice how the part color is different than it appears in the assembly. This occurs because a part can be assigned a different color style in the context of the assembly.

7   To activate the sketch environment:

- In the browser, expand the Extrusion1 part feature.
- Double-click Sketch1.

The browser background color changes to indicate the active sketch, the part features are rolled-back, and the graphics window displays the sketch geometry.

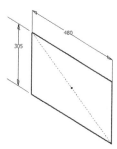

8   To exit the sketch, on the ribbon, click Finish Sketch

9   Close the part file and return to the assembly. If you are prompted to save changes, click No.

10   To open an Inventor drawing file:

- On the Quick Access toolbar, click Open.
- In the Open dialog box, select *m_Mating-Press-Drawing.idw* and click Open.
- The ribbon updates to show drawing related tasks and tools.

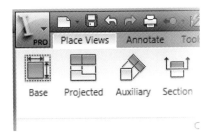

11   In the browser, expand the Drawing Resources node and View1: Mating Press View.iam node
      to reveal the nested resources, views, and assembly references.

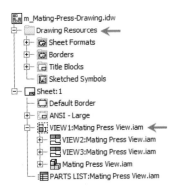

12   To explore the Help System resources:

   • Press F1.
   • If you are an experienced AutoCAD user, click the option for Users Transitioning from
     AutoCAD and explore the Help resources that are tailored for these users.
   • If you are new to Inventor and do not have AutoCAD experience, click the option for
     Returning / New Inventor Users and explore the Help resources that are tailored for
     these users.

13   Close the Help windows.

14   Close all files. Do not save.

Lesson 02 | View Manipulation

This lesson describes the use of the various view manipulation tools in the modeling and drawing environments.

You view all aspects of your 3D geometry by navigating around in 3D space. The view manipulation tools enable you to quickly perform these tasks in a manner that is intuitive and efficient.

In the following illustration, a constrained orbit is used to rotate the assembly and change the view orientation. The ViewCube, in the upper right corner of the graphics window, is shown with the compass displayed. The ViewCube rotates with the model and aids in the orientation of the model.

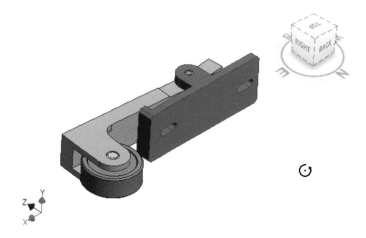

Objectives

After completing this lesson, you will be able to:

- Identify the tools that are available in the graphics window.

- Explain the behavior of the Free Orbit and Constrained Orbit tools.

- Explain the ViewCube options and how to access them.

- Describe how the ViewCube can be used to view part and assembly models and how to customize its appearance and behavior options.

- Explain the steps to define and restore the home view.

- Describe how to use various tools to restore previous views.

About the Graphics Window

Your 3D part and assembly models, presentations, and drawings are displayed in the graphics window. Many tools are available to manipulate the view and appearance of your model in the graphics window.

Viewing Tools

View manipulation is a key 2D drawing and 3D modeling skill. You are often required to view different areas of a design, and changing your view can help you visualize solutions for the current task. Many of the view manipulation tools are common to all environments.

The following illustration shows the view manipulation tools that are available on the Navigation bar.

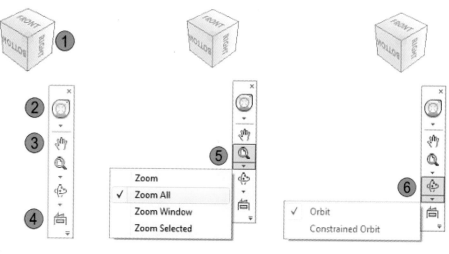

Navigation Bar

Zoom Options

Orbit Options

1 ViewCube

2 SteeringWheel

3 Pan

4 View Face

5 Zoom All

6 Free Orbit

You have different view manipulation tools available to you depending on how you want to change where you are viewing and to what magnification. To efficiently change your view to see exactly what you want or need to see, you need to know what view manipulation tools are available to you and how to use them.

Icon	View Tool	Description
	ViewCube	In the 3D environment the ViewCube tool displays as a default in the graphics window, enabling you to reorient your view of the model. In the 2D environment the ViewCube enables the definition of view orientations for a drawing view.
	Free Orbit	Enables you to freely rotate the view of your model on screen.
	Constrained Orbit	Constrained Orbit enables you to rotate around the vertical axis of a model in a manner similar to the rotation of a turntable.
	SteeringWheel	The SteeringWheel tool is designed to be a common tool for multiple Autodesk products. The SteeringWheel tool was implemented to provide many different levels and types of control over model and drawing navigation.

Tip: *You can use the mouse to accomplish most pan and zoom tasks.*

- *Roll the mouse wheel to zoom at the cursor location.*
- *Click and drag the mouse wheel to pan.*
- *SHIFT+click and drag the mouse wheel to free orbit.*
- *Double-click the mouse wheel to zoom all.*

Display Modes

This area of the toolbar displays appearance-related tools for controlling the appearance of your model. Select a render style from the list to change the color and texture of your model.

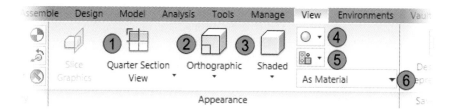

(1) Toggle the section views which graphically slice portions of an assembly so that you can visualize other features.

(2) Toggle between Orthographic and Perspective display modes.

(3) Toggle between Shaded, Shaded with Hidden Edge and Wireframe displays.

(4) Toggle between No Shadow, Ground Shadow, and X-Ray Shadow display modes.

(5) In an assembly file, toggle between Transparency On and Transparency Off display modes.

(6) Select a color/material to assign to a component.

3D Indicator

While using the assembly, part modeling, and presentation environments, the 3D Indicator is displayed in the lower-left area of the graphics window. The Indicator displays your current view orientation in relation to the X, Y, and Z axes of the coordinate system.

- **Red**: X-axis

- **Green**: Y-axis

- **Blue**: Z-axis

The 3D Indicator is positioned below and to the left of the assembly in this illustration.

Orbit Tools

You have two options to rotate the views of models and assemblies. The Free Orbit tool is used to rotate the model freely in screen space, while the Constrained Orbit tool is used to rotate the model about axes in model space.

In the following illustration, the functionality of the Constrained Orbit tool is compared to that of a globe. As you rotate a globe about the north-south axis, the angle at which you view the globe does not change. The Constrained Orbit tool is similar in behavior.

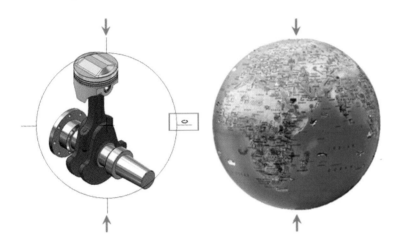

Access

Free Orbit

Navigation Bar: **Free Orbit**

Ribbon: **View tab > Navigate panel**

Access

Constrained Orbit

Navigation Bar: **Constrained Orbit**

Ribbon: **View tab > Navigate panel**

Free Orbit

The Free Orbit tool enables you to dynamically change your view of the model. It is important to remember that the model does not move, you change your viewing position with the Rotate tool.

The following illustration outlines the rotation modes available. The cursor provides feedback on the rotation mode available. You click and drag to rotate the view and you can set the center of rotation by clicking a location on the model.

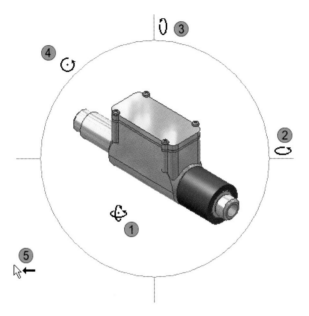

① Click and drag here to rotate the view about all axes.

② Click and drag here to rotate the view about a vertical axis.

③ Click and drag here to rotate the view about a horizontal axis.

④ Click and drag here to rotate the view about an axis normal to the screen.

⑤ Position and click here to exit.

Axis Orbiting with Free Orbit

The illustrations below display the behavior of the Free Orbit tool. When the model view is orbited using the horizontal cross hairs, the model rotates about an imaginary vertical axis based on the view. The model does not stay in the same view orientation. When the view is orbited without the use of the cross hairs, the rotation is about the center of the graphics area, or the center as assigned by the SteeringWheel.

In the following example, using the Free Orbit enables you to view the top and bottom of the assembly as it is orbited.

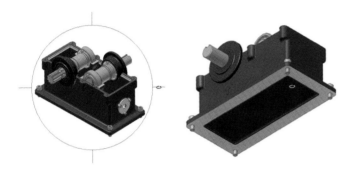

Axis Orbiting with Constrained Orbit

The Constrained Orbit tool places the axis of rotation on the vertical axis of the part or assembly. This functionality enables users to orbit around the vertical axis of their models as they would on a turntable.

In the following illustrations, the Constrained Orbit tool is started. The orbit starts from the right horizontal cross hair. As the assembly is orbited, you can see the sides of the assembly, but your view orientation remains the same.

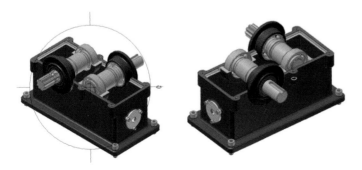

About the ViewCube

The ViewCube tool displays by default in the graphics window. The ViewCube enables you to be more efficient because it is accessible at all times, and provides intuitive access to multiple view orientations.

In the following illustration, the front view of the assembly is restored by clicking Front on the ViewCube.

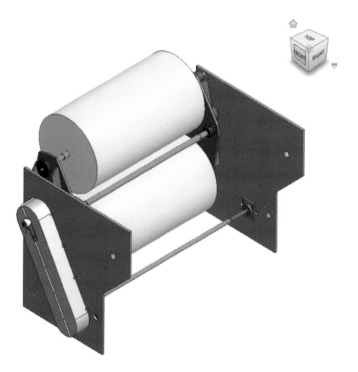

Definition of the ViewCube

The ViewCube is a view manipulation tool that enables you to efficiently and intuitively change the viewing angle of your parts and assemblies. The ViewCube uses faces, edges, and corners as selection options to define viewing angles.

ViewCube Example

In the following illustration, the view of the monitor arm assembly is changed from the current isometric view (1) to an angle view between the top and front views (3). The new view orientation was obtained by selecting the ViewCube edge (2) between the Top and Front panels on the ViewCube.

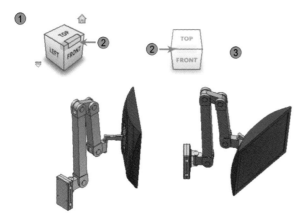

Using the ViewCube

You can access the ViewCube tools by selecting the face, edge, or corner of the ViewCube. Each face, edge, and corner of the ViewCube represents a different view orientation that corresponds to the model. The model rotates to the selected view orientation when the ViewCube is clicked.

In the following illustration, the ViewCube is used to reorient the view of the assembly.

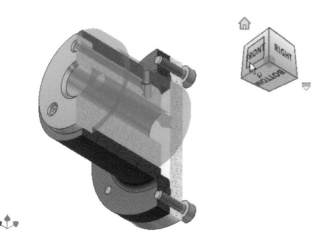

Access

ViewCube

Navigation Bar: **ViewCube**

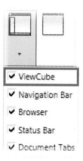

Ribbon: **View tab > Windows panel > Toggle Visibility of the User Interface Elements > ViewCube**

Access

ViewCube Options

Ribbon: **Tools tab > Application Options > ViewCube > Options**
Shortcut: **Right-click the ViewCube > Options**

Introduction to ViewCube Options

The ViewCube is displayed in the upper right corner of the graphics area of a new window by default. However, there are many options associated with the ViewCube that enable you to control both its appearance and behavior.

ViewCube Display Options

The following options control the display and appearance of the ViewCube.

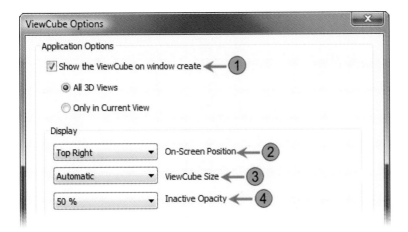

1. Use this option to display the ViewCube. To hide the ViewCube, clear the check mark in the box next to the Show the ViewCube on Window Create option. When a check is in the box for the ViewCube option, you can choose to display the ViewCube in all 3D views or only in the current view window.

2. Use this option to place the ViewCube in a corner of the graphics area. Options include: Top Right, Bottom Right, Top Left, and Bottom Left. The default location is Top Right.

3. Use this option to set the ViewCube size. Options include: Small, Normal, or Large. The default setting is Normal.

4. Use this option to control the ViewCube opacity. When the cursor is near the ViewCube, the ViewCube is fully opaque. When the cursor is away from the ViewCube, the opacity of ViewCube is reduced. Options include: 0%, 25%, 50%, 75%, and 100%. The default setting is 50%.

ViewCube Behavior Options

The following options control the behavior of the ViewCube.

1. Use this option to snap the ViewCube to a common view position when dragging the ViewCube through different view orientations.

2. When selecting a new view orientation using the ViewCube, use this option to fit the new view to the screen.

4. Use this option to create smooth transitions from the current view to the selected view.

4. Use this option to apply additional calculations for view orientation.

5. Use this option to set the default orientation of the ViewCube.

6. Use this option to display a compass with the ViewCube.

Procedure: Using the ViewCube to View Models

The following steps describe using the ViewCube to change the view orientation of your models and assemblies.

1   Select the panel on the ViewCube to change the view orientation.

2   Select the arrow to rotate the view orientation.

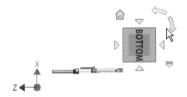

3   Select a corner to change the view orientation to an isometric view of the panel view. In this example, the Bottom view is shown.

4   An isometric view based on the Bottom view is displayed.

Procedure: Using the ViewCube to Orient Drawing Views

The following steps describe using the ViewCube to set the view orientation of your models and assemblies for drawing views.

1   Start the Base View tool. Click Place Views tab > Create panel > Base View.

2   Select to change the view orientation.

3   Select the desired ViewCube face.

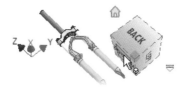

4   If necessary, rotate the model orientation.

5   Accept the changes and place the view.

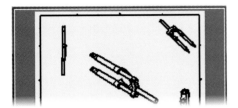

Procedure: Resetting the Current View as Front

The following steps describe resetting the current view orientation to the Front view.

1   Select the panel on the ViewCube to change the view orientation.

2   Right-click the ViewCube, click Set Current View as Front.

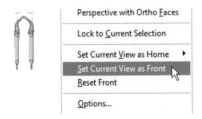

3   The ViewCube updates the orientation of the current view to Front.

Using Home View

Using the Home View tool, you can manipulate your model to any orientation, then specify that view as the home view. In addition to being able to quickly return to that view, the home view is also the view that is shown each time you open the file.

In the following illustrations, the view orientation of the assembly is restored to the home view when the Home View glyph next to the ViewCube is clicked.

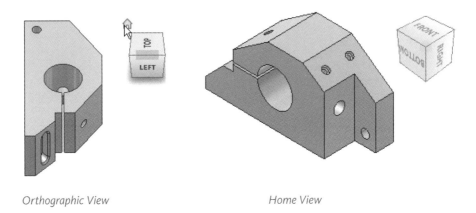

Orthographic View   Home View

Access

Home View

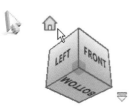

The Home View glyph displays as you move your cursor to the ViewCube.

> **Tip:** *In all modeling environments, you can quickly return to the home view using either of the following methods.*
> - *Right-click in the graphics window background.*
> - *Click Home View. Press the F6 function key.*

Home View Options

The following options control the model display when you use the Home View tool.

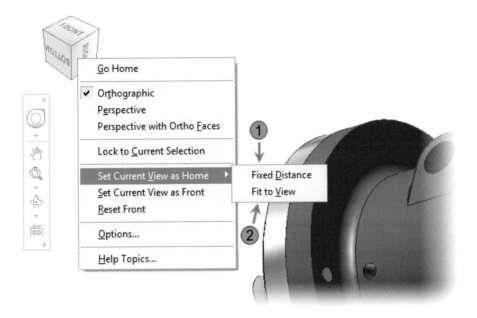

① Use to define the direction of the view and the zoom magnification.

② Use to define the direction of the view and automatically assign the zoom magnification as view all.

Procedure: Setting the Home View

The following steps describe how to set any view orientation to the home view.

1   Use any view manipulation tools to orient the model.

2   With the model in the desired orientation, right-click anywhere in the ViewCube. Click Set
    Current View as Home, and select Fixed Distance or Fit to View.

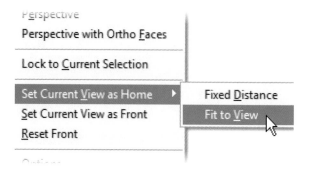

3   With the model in a different orientation, click the Home View glyph.

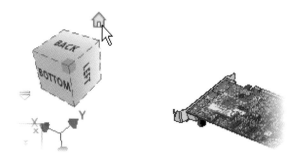

4   The view orientation returns to the specified home view.

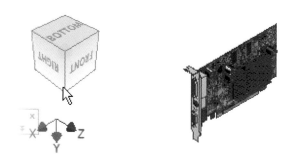

Restoring Your Views

As you manipulate the views in the graphics window, there will be times when you need to return to a previous view to reevaluate your design or to make additional edits. The Previous View tool, and the Rewind option of the SteeringWheels view manipulation tool, enable you to restore previous views. The Previous View tool enables you to return to the view previous to your current view, while the Rewind tool enables you to return directly to one of the previously defined views.

In the following illustration, the Rewind tool displays a filmstrip of previously visited views. As you move your mouse over the previews, the main view updates to reflect the view being selected on the filmstrip.

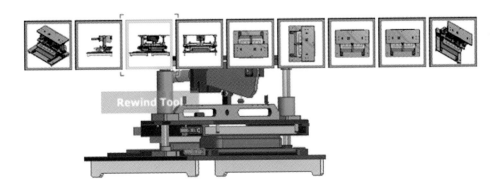

Access

SteeringWheel

Navigation Bar: **SteeringWheel**

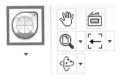

Ribbon: **View tab › Navigate panel**
Shortcut: **CTRL + W**

Access

Previous View

Ribbon: **View tab > Navigate panel**

Shortcut: **Right-click anywhere in the graphics window, click Previous View**
Shortcut: **F5**

Procedure: Restoring Views

The following steps describe the two main methods for restoring previous views.

1   To return to your previous view:

- Press F5. Each time that you press F5, you return to the view that was previous to the current view.

2   To return directly to a previous view that was active several views prior to your current view:

- Press CTRL+W to activate the SteeringWheel.
- Click Rewind.
- Drag the cursor through the slideshow ribbon that is displayed. When the desired view is reached, release the mouse button.

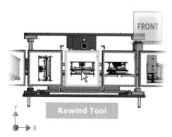

Exercise | Manipulate Your Model Views

In this exercise, you use the ViewCube and Home View tools to navigate through and restore different view orientations.

The completed Exercise

Completing the Exercise: *To complete the exercise, follow the steps in this book or in the onscreen exercise. In the onscreen list of chapters and exercises, click Chapter 1: Getting Started. Click Exercise: Manipulate Your Model Views.*

1   Open *3D Navigation.ipt*.

2   To switch to an isometric view, click the top left corner of the ViewCube.

Your view is displayed as shown.

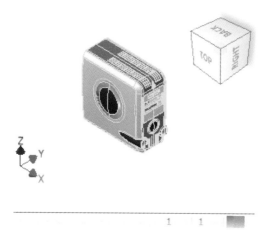

3   To view the current top view, on the ViewCube, click Top.

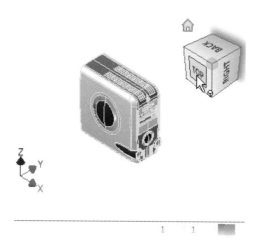

4   To rotate the view:

- On the ViewCube, click and hold Top.
- Drag the cursor toward the upper left corner of the ViewCube until the model is oriented as shown.

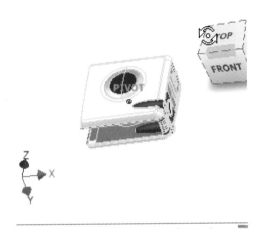

5   To return the view orientation to the original Home view:

- Move the cursor to the ViewCube.
- When the house image is displayed (1), click the image.

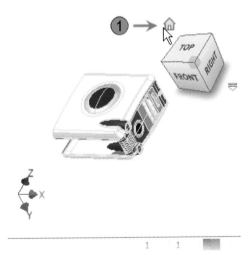

6   To redefine the current view as the Front view:

  • Move the cursor to the ViewCube.
  • Right-click the cube. Click Set Current View as Front.

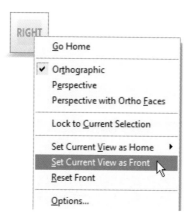

7   To view the model in an isometric view, click the upper left corner of the ViewCube.

8   To redefine the Home view to the current view:

  • Right-click the ViewCube.
  • Click Set Current View as Home > Fixed Distance.

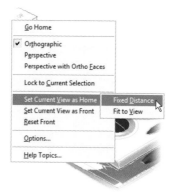

9 To edit the options of the ViewCube:

- Right-click the ViewCube. Click Options.
- In the ViewCube Options dialog box, under Document Settings, place a check in the box next to the Show the Compass Below the ViewCube option.
- Click OK.

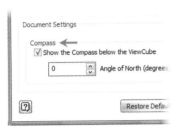

10 To orbit the model:

- Click View tab > Navigate panel > Free Orbit.
- Click the right quadrant line and drag the cursor to the left until you can see the bottom view of the computer housing.
- Right-click anywhere in the graphics window. Click Done.

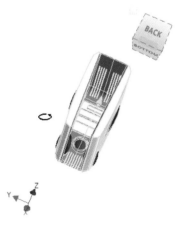

11   On the ViewCube, click Home View.

12   To constrain orbit the model:

- Start the Constrained Orbit tool.
- Click the right quadrant line and drag the cursor to the left.
- Right-click anywhere in the graphics window. Click Done.
  Notice that the orbit pivots about the axis.

13   To turn off the display of the ViewCube:

- Click View tab > Windows panel > Toggle Visibility drop-down > ViewCube.
- Click the option again to turn the ViewCube on.

14   To return to your previous view:

- Press F5.
- Your previous view is restored.
- Press F5 again to return the view previous to the current view.

15 To rewind to a specific view:

- Press CTRL+W to activate the SteeringWheel.
- Click Rewind and hold down the cursor.
- Drag your cursor over the views filmstrip and release the mouse button over the specific view you want to restore.
- Continue to use the Rewind tool to restore other views.

16 Close the SteeringWheel tool.

17 Close all files. Do not save.

Lesson 03 | Designing Parametric Parts

This lesson describes the characteristics of parametric part models and the overall process of their creation.

Familiarity with the basic characteristics of parametric models simplifies the process of learning and applying the tools to create such models.

A parametric part model is shown with dimensions displayed in the following illustration.

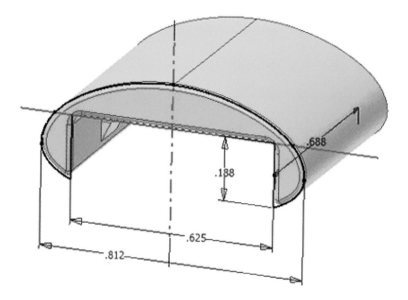

Objectives

After completing this lesson, you will be able to:

- Describe the characteristics of a parametric part model.

- Identify guidelines for capturing design intent.

- State the general workflow for creating parametric part models.

- State the characteristics of the ribbon and browser when in the part environment.

- Create a basic parametric part.

About Parametric Part Models

You can create and edit 3D geometry using parametrics. Parametrics use geometric and dimensional constraints to precisely control the shape and size of a 3D model.

A typical parametric part is shown in the following illustration, consisting of both 2D sketch geometry with dimensional constraints and the resulting 3D solid geometry.

Parametric Part Models

A parametric model is a 3D model that is controlled and driven by geometric relationships and dimensional values. You typically create parametric models from a combination of 2D sketches and 3D features. With a parametric part model, you can change a value of a feature and the part model is adjusted according to that value and any existing geometric constraints.

Sketched Features

Sketched features are features that add or remove material and are typically based on a 2D closed loop sketch. The sketch can be composed of lines, circles, and arcs.

Sketched features are shown in the following illustrations. After the sketch is used by a feature, it is considered consumed by the feature and is displayed nested below that feature in the browser.

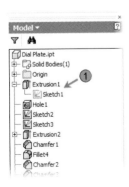

Placed Features

While sketched features start from a sketch, placed features have an internally defined shape for adding or removing material. You need to determine only where and at what size the feature should be created. Holes and fillets are two commonly used placed features.

Placed features are shown in the following illustration by the Fillet4 and Chamfer2 highlights.

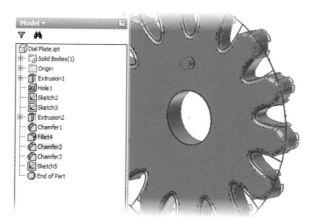

Base Features

The first feature that you create is typically a sketched feature. This first feature is also referred to as the base feature. All subsequent features either add material to or remove material from the part model.

Extrusion1 represents the base feature of the part in the following illustration.

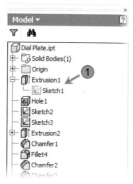

  Base sketch and base feature

Progression of a Parametric Model

A parametric model progresses through the stages of its creation in the following illustrations. The model is transformed after the size of the base feature is increased upon inclusion of sketched and placed features.

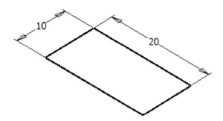

Initial sketch is created

Base feature is created

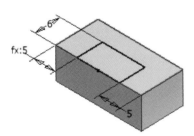

Secondary sketch is added

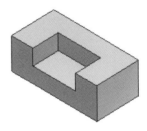

*Secondary feature is created
from secondary sketch*

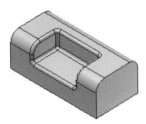

Fillets (placed features) are added

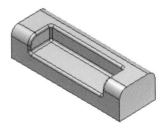

*Length is changed in initial sketch,
causing part to update*

Capturing Design Intent

Regardless of the type of design that you are creating, you should always aim to capture the intent of the design as early in the process as possible. It is common for a design to change as a result of inherent design problems or future revisions. The ability to capture design intent makes these potential changes much easier to implement.

Design intent has been captured in the following illustration by using a simple formula (2) to calculate the outside diameter of the part based on the inside diameter (1).

About Capturing Design Intent

When you capture your design intent, you add intelligence to your design. This intelligence can exist in several different forms. It can reside in a simple geometric constraint that forces two lines to be parallel or two circles to be concentric. Intelligence can also reside in dimensional constraints that force a feature's dimension to remain constant or enable the dimension to change based on a built-in formula.

Just as each part design is unique, so is the design intent for each part. Capturing this intent is a process in which you match the design intent with a feature or capability that makes it possible to create the design in the most efficient way while enabling you the maximum flexibility in making changes.

Different examples of design intent are shown in the following illustration being captured at the earliest stage of the design. The toolbars show constraint symbols (glyphs).

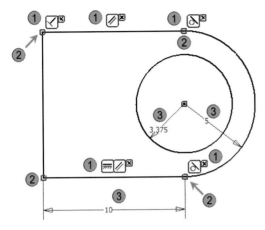

1. Toolbars displaying geometric constraints applied to the geometry. Each icon illustrates a specific type of geometric constraint that has been applied to the sketch, and as a result captures a portion of the design intent. For example, the right-most icon on the top toolbar indicates a tangent constraint between the top horizontal line and the arc on the right side of the sketch.

2. Coincident constraints are displayed by a yellow dot at the coincident point between two segments.

3. Dimensional constraints applied to the geometry. These types of constraints capture design intent by defining the size of objects in the sketch.

Guidelines for Capturing Design Intent

Consider the following guidelines when you begin a new part design. Each of the following points indicates an area in which design intent can be captured.

- Identify geometric relationships. For example, a feature's length may be directly related to its width, or the width or length of another feature.

- Identify areas of the design that may be prone to change as a result of design problems or revisions.

- Identify areas of symmetry or areas where features are duplicated or patterned.

Once you have identified the potential ways to capture your design intent, you can then match that intent with a specific Inventor tool or capability.

Example of a Part Design Capturing Design Intent

A simple parametric design of a plastic indexer is shown in the following illustrations. Each one reflects how a specific guideline of the design intent is captured and implemented into the design with a parametric feature.

Capturing Geometric Relationships in Design Intent

Design intent for the indexer part dictates that the outside diameter should be equal to twice the inside diameter in the following illustration. The design intent has been captured with the use of a simple formula in the dimension parameter.

1. Inside diameter of the indexer part.

2. Outside diameter is determined by a formula equal to twice the inside diameter.

Capturing Design Intent for Features That Are Prone to Change

Design intent has been captured to allow for potential design changes in the following illustration. As the thickness of the part changes, so does the depth of the slots. This result is achieved by setting the depth parameter for the slot to All, ensuring the slot always extrudes completely through the part.

① With a 3 mm part height, slot depth cuts though the entire part.

② With a change in part height from 3 mm to 6 mm, the slot depth continues to cut through the entire part.

Capturing Symmetry in Design Intent

Design intent for symmetry has been captured in the part design in the following illustration by using a parametric pattern feature. By capturing the design intent in this manner, you can easily change the number or angled spacing of slots by editing the feature.

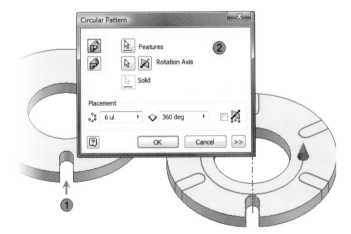

① Original slot feature.

② Circular pattern being created to duplicate the slot feature in a precise and easily editable manner.

Creating Parametric Part Models

The overall process for creating parametric part models is very flexible. With this flexibility, you can concentrate on your design, design intent, and essential design features instead of being limited by a rigid modeling process.

In the following illustration, what begins as a simple circle is transformed into a fully parametric model.

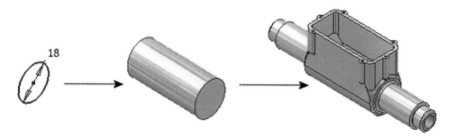

Process: Creating a Parametric Part

The following steps provide an overview of the process for creating a parametric part.

1   Create the initial sketch profile.

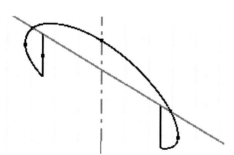

2   Capture the design intent by applying constraints and dimensions.

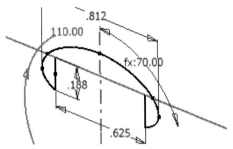

3   Use the part feature tools to create the base feature.

4   Continue to develop the design by creating additional sketched and placed features.

Part Design Considerations

When creating a parametric part model, try to determine the basic building blocks of the part; that is, how the part can be designed and built in stages. Also determine which aspects of the model are the critical aspects of the part. You create those aspects first in the order of their importance and relationship.

Part Design Workflow

The following steps represent the overall workflow for creating parts.

- Use one of the part templates provided to create a new part.

- All new parts you create have a blank sketch automatically placed. Create the profile of your geometry on the initial sketch.

- Use sketched features such as Extrude and Revolve to create your base feature.

- Create additional sketched and placed features as required to generate the necessary 3D geometry.

Part Design Environment

When you are editing a part file and the part environment is active, the ribbon and browser are displayed with the tools and information relevant to this environment.

The part design environment is shown in the following illustration.

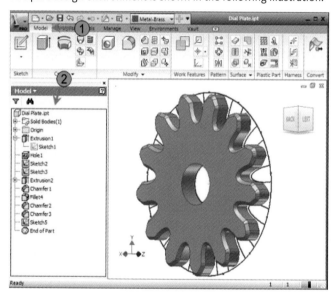

① **Part Features on Ribbon Model Tab:** Displays part modeling tools while in part modeling mode.

② **Browser:** Displays the feature history for the part or assembly

Model Tab

The Model tab is displayed when you are editing a part model. You use these tools to create sketched and placed features on the part.

Browser

When you use the browser in the part design environment, it displays the Origin folder containing the default X, Y, and Z planes, axes, and center point. It also lists all features you use to create the part. Features are listed in the order in which they are created.

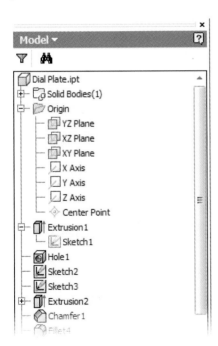

Exercise | Create a Parametric Part

In this exercise, you create a simple bracket by extruding the predefined sketch. You then edit the part by changing some of the parameters and add a fillet feature.

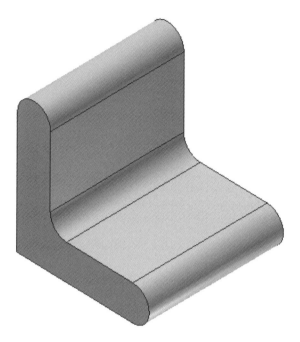

The completed exercise

Completing the Exercise:

To complete the exercise, follow the steps in this book or in the onscreen exercise. In the onscreen list of chapters and exercises, click Chapter 1: Getting Started. Click Exercise: Create a Parametric Part.

1   Open *Create-Parametric-Part.ipt*. The initial sketch profile has been created and constrained.

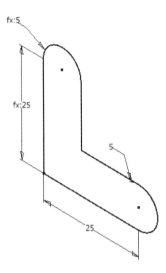

2   Click Model tab > Create panel > Extrude.

- For Distance, enter **25 mm**.
- Click OK.

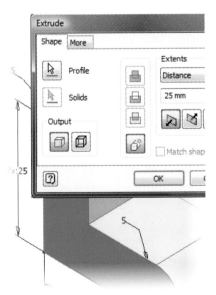

3   In the browser, expand the Extrusion feature.

- The initial sketch is consumed by the 3D extrusion feature.

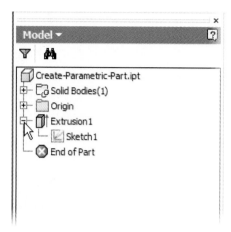

4   In the browser, double-click Sketch1.

- Double-click the 25 mm horizontal dimension.
- In the Edit Dimension dialog box, enter **35**.
- Press ENTER.
- On the Sketch tab, click Finish Sketch.
  The part is updated to reflect the new dimension value.

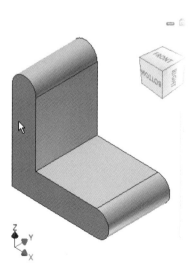

5   In the browser, right-click the Extrusion1 feature. Click Edit Feature.
    - For Distance, enter **40 mm**.
    - Click OK.
      The parametric part updates to reflect the new parameter value.

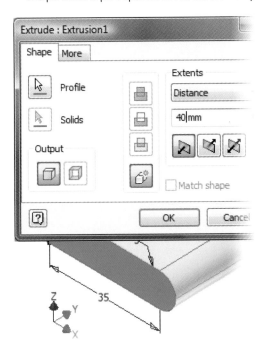

6   Click Model tab > Modify panel > Fillet.

- In the graphics window, select the inside edge.
- For Radius, enter **5 mm.**
- Click OK. The fillet feature is updated.

7   Close all files. Do not save.

Chapter Summary

By using the context-sensitive user interface and the tools that are available, you can quickly create basic parametric geometry. This chapter introduced you to the Autodesk Inventor user interface and concepts supporting parametric part design and capturing design intent.

Having completed this chapter, you can:

- Identify the main user interface components that are common to all Autodesk Inventor design environments and describe how to access different tools.

- View all aspects of your design by efficiently navigating around in 2D and 3D space.

- Describe the characteristics and benefits of a parametric part model.

Chapter 02
Basic Sketching Techniques

The majority of the features that you create on your parametric part models start with constrained 2D sketches. Intelligent and predictable part designs require a thorough understanding of how to create 2D sketches and how to capture design intent by applying geometric and dimensional constraints.

Objectives

After completing this chapter, you will be able to:

- Use sketch tools to create 2D sketch geometry.

- Use geometric constraints to control sketch geometry.

- Apply parametric dimensions to your sketch geometry.

Lesson 04 | Creating 2D Sketches

This lesson describes how to create 2D sketch geometry using sketch tools.

Nearly every parametric part begins with a 2D sketch, and every sketch you create defines a 2D plane on which your sketch geometry is created. These sketches not only form the foundation of each part, but are also used throughout the design process.

A basic parametric part for which several sketches were used to create its features is shown in the following illustration.

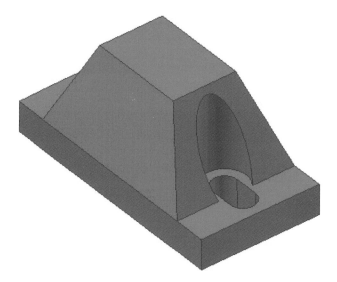

Objectives

After completing this lesson, you will be able to:

- Describe the differences between standard 2D sketching and 2D parametric sketches.
- Explain the options for aligning geometry in 2D sketches.
- Reorient the initial sketch to a different plane.
- Use sketch tools to create sketch geometry.
- Describe guidelines for creating successful sketches.

About Sketching

The sketch environment is where all 2D sketching takes place. When you create a new 2D sketch or edit an existing sketch, the sketch environment is activated.

The sketch environment is activated as the sketch is edited, as shown in the following illustration.

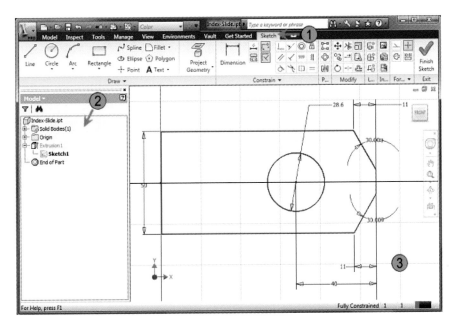

① When the sketch environment is active, the Sketch tab is displayed.

② The active sketch is highlighted in the browser while all other elements are dimmed.

③ When you activate the sketch environment, the grid lines and X and Y axes are displayed by default in the graphics window.

Parametric Sketching

A parametric sketch forms the base of each parametric part you create in Autodesk Inventor. Unlike 2D sketches that you can create in a nonparametric 2D application, when you create a sketch in Autodesk Inventor, you immediately begin to add intelligence to your part and capture design intent.

Constraints in Parametric Sketches

A parametric sketch consists of 2D geometry on which constraints are applied to control the size and potential behavior of the 2D geometry. There are two different types of constraints, geometric constraints and dimensional constraints. As you create geometry in Autodesk Inventor, some geometric constraints are applied automatically.

The symbols next to the geometry in the following illustrations are known as "glyphs" and represent 2D constraints. Glyphs are displayed while a sketch tool is active and you are sketching. The use of 2D constraints is one way in which design intent is automatically captured as you are creating your sketch geometry.

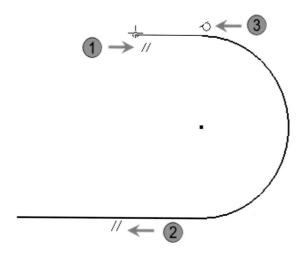

① Indicates a parallel constraint being applied to the bottom horizontal line.

② Indicates a parallel constraint with the top horizontal currently being drawn.

③ Indicates a tangent constraint between the arc and the horizontal line being drawn.

You must add dimensional constraints to each element of the sketch for which you need to specify a dimension. Both types of constraints applied to sketch geometry are shown in the following illustration.

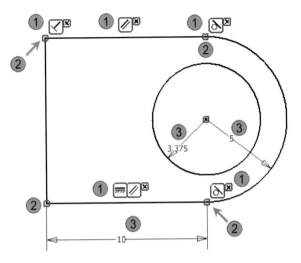

① Geometric Constraints

Geometric constraints, which are applied to geometry, are represented by the symbols on the following toolbar. Each type of constraint is represented with a unique symbol.

From left to right:

- Perpendicular constraint that forces the line to remain perpendicular to the left-side vertical line.

- Tangent constraint, forcing the line to be tangent to the arc.

- Parallel constraint indicating that the line must remain parallel to the lower horizontal line.

- Horizontal constraint that forces the bottom line to be parallel the X-Axis of the sketch.

② Coincident Constraints

These constraints force the endpoints of lines to remain coincident or connected.

③ Dimensional Constraints

These dimensions control the size of the objects. The diameter dimension controls the size of the circle, while the linear dimension controls the length of the horizontal line.

Parametric Sketches Versus Precise Sketches

Precise sketches created with AutoCAD®, by default have no parametric intelligence. A change in a dimension does not force the geometry to update to reflect the new dimension value. Parametric sketches in Inventor enable you to click and drag the geometry in directions allowed by the existing constraints while all conditions controlled by the constraints are maintained. For example, if you drag the outer arc to a different size, the horizontal lines remain tangent, horizontal, and one unit in length.

Example

The effect of 2D geometric constraints is shown in the following illustration, where an element of the sketch is dragged to reshape the geometry.

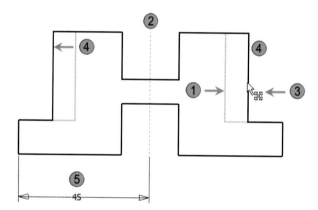

1. Original position of line element being moved.

2. Centerline element used with symmetry constraints.

3. Cursor dragging line to a new location.

4. New location of the line as it is being moved. Notice the same movement on the opposite side of the sketch.

5. Dimensional constraint positioning the edge of the part. A change in this dimension would be reflected on both sides of the centerline.

To achieve the same modifications in a nonparametric sketch, you would have to duplicate each edit on both sides of the centerline.

Fully Constrained Sketch Geometry

When you apply constraints to a sketch, each constraint removes degrees of freedom from the geometry. By removing degrees of freedom, you limit the direction or amount a given part of the sketch can be moved or resized. When a sketch has all degrees of freedom removed, it is considered to be fully constrained.

While it is not necessary to fully constrain a sketch before creating 3D features, it is recommended. A fully constrained sketch is predictable in the manner in which it can change, and reduces the number of errors as changes are made to the parametric part.

Identifying the Constraint Conditions

Once the sketch is fully constrained, the profile will be a single color.

Inventor uses color differences and numerical feedback to identify fully constrained as opposed to underconstrained geometry. Represented in the following illustration, the lighter colored geometry requires either geometric or dimensional constraints to fully constrain the sketch. You can use these colors to identify which elements still require constraints. At the bottom right of the interface, the application indicates "6 dimensions needed" to fully constrain the sketch geometry.

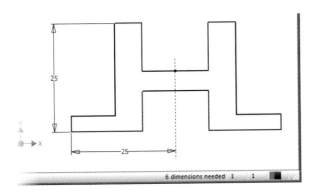

Colors used to show constraint conditions vary depending on your color configuration for Inventor. Color differences occurring while using the Presentation configuration (white background) are the least noticeable.

> **Note:** *As your sketch increases in complexity, the number of constraints or dimensions required to fully constrain the sketch also increases.*

Point Alignment

When you are creating sketch geometry and you want to align to a point projected from existing geometry, you have two different workflows you can follow depending on the current setting for point alignment. To utilize and benefit from automatic point alignment, you need to understand what point alignment is and where to toggle it on and off.

The following illustrations show different point alignments automatically occurring during the creation of sketch geometry.

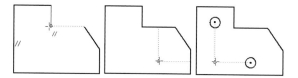

Point Alignment

The automatic alignment of points during sketch creation is an option that you can toggle on and off.

Point alignment during sketch geometry creation enables you to create your sketch geometry with the alignment you require as you create it. You can have the endpoints of the sketch geometry align to an extension, be perpendicular, or align to a virtual intersection of other sketch geometry. You achieve these point alignment locations by the position of the cursor. You do not need to scrub the cursor over the intended referencing geometry first.

The automatic point alignment option is set globally for the installation of Autodesk Inventor. You toggle on and off point alignment by selecting or clearing the Point Alignment On check box on the Sketch tab in the Application Options dialog box.

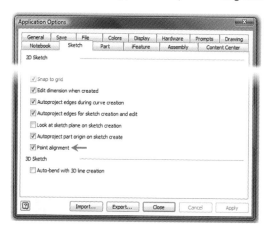

Reorienting the Initial Sketch

Each time you create a new part, the default configuration places a new sketch on the *XY* plane. In some cases you may want to begin sketching on a different plane. You can either delete the initial sketch and create a new one, or you can reorient the initial sketch including any geometry that might have been drawn.

The initial sketch of concentric circles has been reoriented from the *XY* plane to the *YZ* plane in the following illustration.

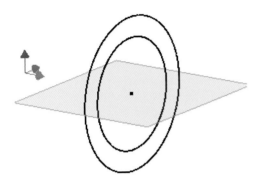

Procedure: Reorienting the Initial Sketch

The following steps describe how to reorient the initial sketch to a different plane.

1   If the sketch is active, exit the sketch environment.

2   In the browser, right-click the initial sketch and click Redefine.

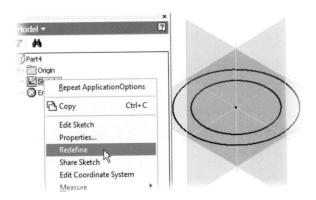

3   In the browser, expand the Origin node and select a plane to reorient the sketch.

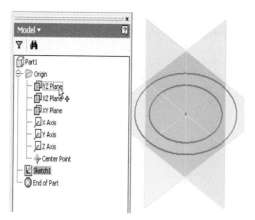

4   The sketch and any existing geometry are reoriented to the selected plane.

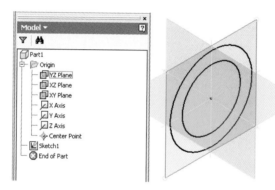

Basic Sketching Tools

A profile or path sketch can consist of objects such as points, lines, arcs, circles, and dimensional geometry. When the environment of a sketch plane is active, the ribbon switches to display the available sketch tools. The Sketch panel contains all the tools for creating, manipulating, and controlling sketch geometry.

Sketch Tool

By default, the first sketch in a new part is automatically created on the *XY* plane. If you require additional sketches, you use the Sketch tool to create them manually or to activate existing ones. The Sketch tool prompts you to select a plane to create a sketch, or to select an existing sketch to edit. You can select planes or sketches in the graphics window or in the browser. You can create a new sketch on a part face, origin plane, or work plane.

Access

Create 2D Sketch

Ribbon: **Model tab > Sketch panel**

Shortcut Menu: **Right-click a selected face or plane**

Exiting a Sketch

To exit the sketch, use one of the following methods:

- On the ribbon, click Finish Sketch.

- Right-click in the drawing area and click Finish Sketch.

Procedure: Creating Lines

The following steps describe how to create lines in your sketch.

1   Start the Line tool. Select a start point for the line segment.

2   Drag in the direction you want to draw the line. Notice that the constraint glyph (1) is displayed. This glyph indicates the type of constraint being applied to the line segments.

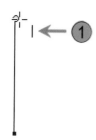

Select a point to end the line segment.

3   Drag in the direction of the next line segment, again noticing the constraint glyph indicating the automatic constraint.

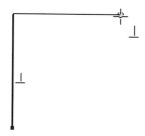

Select a point to end the line segment.

4   Continue drawing line segments as required.

If the constraint glyph represents a constraint that you would like to change, brush the cursor against the geometry on the sketch for which you want to apply the constraint and then continue drawing the line segment.

5   Continue drawing line segments as required.

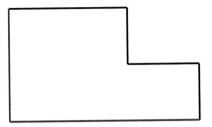

6   Right-click in the graphics window. Click Done.

Procedure: Creating Circles

The following steps describe how to create circles in your sketch.

1   To create a center point circle, start the Center Point Circle tool. Select the center point of the circle.

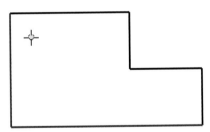

2   Drag to a location representing the outside perimeter of the circle. Select that point to create the circle.

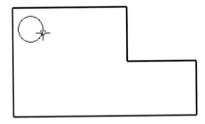

3   Right-click in the graphics window. Click Done.

4   To create a three-point tangent circle, start the Tangent Circle tool.

5   Select three parts of the geometry for the circle to be tangent to.

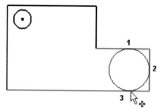

6   Right-click in the graphics window. Click Done.

Procedure: Creating Perpendicular or Tangent Arcs

The following steps describe how to create a perpendicular or tangent arc in your sketch using the Line tool.

1   Start the Line tool.

2   Click+drag the endpoint of an existing line or arc. Temporary tangent and perpendicular construction lines are displayed at the arc start point.

- To create a perpendicular arc, click+drag in the direction of the perpendicular construction line.

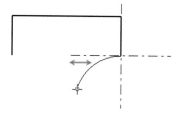

- To create a tangent arc, click+drag in the direction of the tangent construction line.

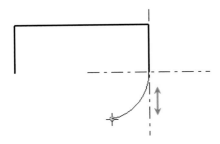

3   Continue to drag the endpoint to the final endpoint of the arc and release.

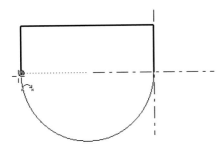

4   Right-click in the graphics window. Click Done.

Procedure: Creating Three Point Arcs

The following steps describe how to create three-point arcs in your sketch.

1   Start the Three Point Arc tool. Select the start point of the arc.

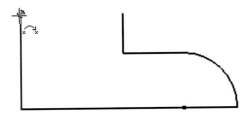

2   Select a point for the endpoint of the arc.

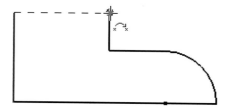

3   Drag to size the arc. Depending on existing geometry and arc size, constraint glyphs may be displayed.

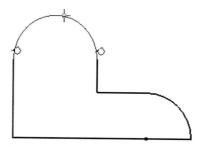

4   Right-click in the graphics window. Click Done.

Procedure: Creating a Two Point Rectangle

The following steps describe how to create a two point rectangle in your sketch.

1   Start the Two Point Rectangle tool.

2   Select a point representing the first corner of the rectangle.

3   Select a point representing the opposite corner of the rectangle.

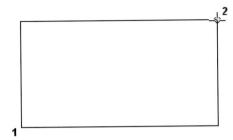

4   Right-click in the graphics window. Click Done.

Guidelines for Successful Sketches

You can use several methods to create closed shapes. You can use tools such as the rectangle, circle, or polygon, or you can constrain sketch geometry so that separate sketch elements come together to create a closed shape. At times you may need to create sketch geometry that is not closed, for example, a path for a sweep feature or to create a surface; however, these guidelines focus on creating closed profiles.

Sketch Guidelines

Follow these guidelines for successful sketching:

- Keep the sketch simple. Do not fillet the corners of a sketch if you can apply a fillet to the edges of the finished 3D feature and achieve the same effect. Complex sketch geometry can be difficult to manage as designs evolve.

- Repeat simple shapes to build more complex shapes.

- Draw the profile sketch roughly to size and shape.

- Use 2D constraints to stabilize sketch shape before setting size.

- Use closed loops for profiles.

Example of Sketching Guidelines

In the following illustration, the same part results from two different sketches. In the image on the left, the sketch contains no fillets. The fillet features are created on the 3D part as placed features.

In the image on the right, the fillet features were placed at the sketch level. While this results in the same part shape, this method complicates the sketch geometry.

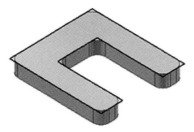

Correct: Sketch with no fillets

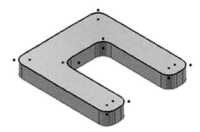

Incorrect: Sketch with fillets

Exercise | Create 2D Sketches

In this exercise, you create a simple Support Bracket extrusion using the basic sketching tools.

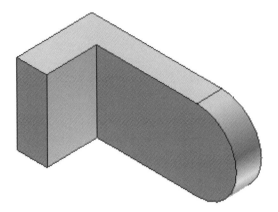

The completed exercise

Completing the Exercise :   *To complete the exercise, follow the steps in this book or in the onscreen exercise. In the onscreen list of chapters and exercises, click Chapter 2: Basic Sketching Techniques. Click Exercise: Create 2D Sketches.*

---

1   Create a new part using the Standard *(mm).ipt* template.

   - On the Quick Access toolbar, click New.
   - In the New File dialog box, click the Metric tab.
   - Select Standard (mm).ipt.
   - Click OK.

2   Create a basic shape.

   - Start the Line tool.
   - Select a point near the origin.
   - Drag the cursor to the right, making certain the horizontal constraint glyph appears near the cursor.
   - Select the second point of the line approximately 25 mm from the start point.

Note: The line length is displayed as it is drawn in the lower-right corner of the application window.

3   With the Line tool still active, create an inline arc segment.

- Drag the endpoint of the line segment to the right to define the direction of tangency for the arc.
- Release the left mouse button when the endpoint of the arc is directly above the start point. Use the grid spacing in the following illustration to define the size of the arc.

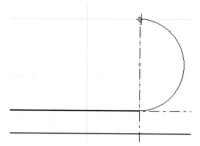

4   With the Line tool still active, draw another line segment to the left.

- Move the cursor to the left until it is positioned vertically above the start point of and parallel to the first line segment. Ensure that the constraint glyphs are displayed as shown in the following illustration.
- Click to create the line segment.

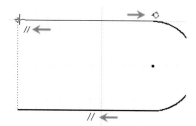

5   Complete the sketch by creating the last line segment as shown.

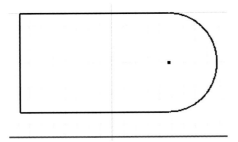

6   On the ribbon, click Finish Sketch to exit the sketch.

7   On the ViewCube, click the top-right corner to view the sketch in an isometric view.

8   Extrude the shape 5 mm.
   - Click Model tab > Create panel > Extrude.
   - In the Extrude dialog box, for distance, enter **5 mm**.
   - Click OK.

9   To create a new sketch on the front face of the part:
- Right-click the front face of the part.
- Click New Sketch.

10 Draw a rectangle on the top surface.
- Start the Two Point Rectangle tool.
- Select point 1 as shown.
- Select point 2 as shown.
  Note: When selecting the points for the rectangle, make sure the coincident constraint glyphs appear. Depending on how your Sketch Options are set, the edges on the face may not be projected and thus the coincident constraints will not appear. If this occurs, right-click in the graphics window while sketching the rectangle and select the AutoProject option.

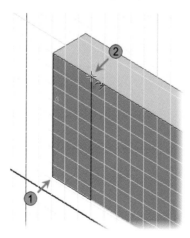

11   On the ribbon, click Finish Sketch to exit the sketch.

12   Extrude the new sketch a distance of 10 mm.
     - Start the Extrude tool.
     - Select a point inside the rectangle.
     - In the Extrude dialog box, enter **10 mm**.
     - Click OK.

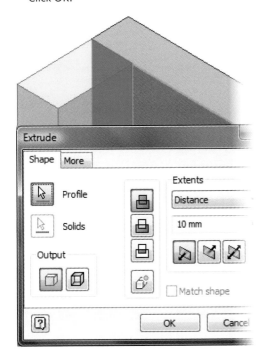

13   Close all files. Do not save.

Lesson 05 | Geometric Constraints

This lesson describes geometric constraints and how to apply them to sketch geometry. You use geometric constraints to control sketch geometry. For example, a vertical constraint applied to a line segment forces that line segment to be vertical. A tangent constraint added to an arc forces that arc to remain tangent to the geometry that has been constrained.

Geometric constraints represent the foundation of all parametric design. Using these objects, you can capture your design intent and force the geometry to follow the rules set by each constraint.

2D constraints on a part sketch are shown in the following illustration.

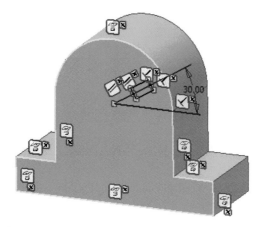

Objectives

After completing this lesson, you will be able to:

- Describe geometric constraints and their effects on geometry.

- Explain how constraint inference and persistence provide complete control over when, where, and which constraints are created in a sketch.

- Apply geometric constraints to sketch geometry.

- View and delete constraints using the Show Constraints tool.

- State key guidelines for successful constraining.

- Explain how to display sketch degrees of freedom and how they can assist in creating fully constrained sketches.

About Geometric Constraints

Several different types of constraints exist, each with a specific capability and purpose. The selection you choose depends largely on the design intent.

As you create sketches, some constraints are inferred (applied automatically). In most cases the inferred constraints are sufficient for your initial constraints. As you continue to develop the sketch, you may need to add additional constraints to properly stabilize the sketch geometry.

The effects of constraints on sketch geometry are shown in the following illustration. The sketch on the left was purposely drawn using only some of the inferred constraints. The sketch on the right is the result of adding additional constraints such as perpendicular, parallel, and collinear.

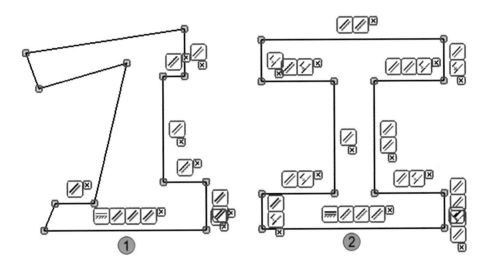

1 Initial inferred constraints only

2 After applying constraints

Definition of Geometric Constraints

Geometric constraints stabilize sketch geometry by placing limits on how the geometry can change when you attempt to drag or dimension it. For example, if a horizontal constraint is applied to a line, that line is forced to be horizontal at all times.

In the following illustration, the circle on the right is being resized. Tangent constraints have been applied to the lines. As the circle is resized, the lines remain tangent to both circles.

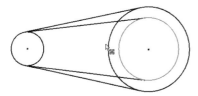

Constraint Types

You can use the following constraint types to constrain your sketches.

Constraint	Description	Before Constraint	After Constraint
	Tangent: Use to make selected elements tangent to one another.		
	Perpendicular: Use to make selected elements perpendicular to one another.		
	Parallel: Use to make selected elements parallel to one another.		
	Coincident: Use to make two points exist at the same point location.		
	Concentric: Use to force two arcs, circles, or ellipses to share the same center point.		

Constraint	Description	Before Constraint	After Constraint
	Collinear: Use to force two lines or ellipse axes to lie on the same line.		
	Horizontal: Use to force the element to be parallel to the X axis of the current sketch coordinate system.		
	Vertical: Use to force the element to be parallel to the Y axis of the current sketch coordinate system.		
	Equal: Use to force two elements to be of the same length. In the case of arcs or circles, the radius becomes equal.		
	Fix: Use to cause an element to be fixed in location to the current sketch coordinate system.		
	Symmetric: Use to cause the elements to be symmetrically constrained about a line.		
	Smooth: Use to cause a curvature continuous condition (G2) between a spline and another curve, line, arc or spline.		

Horizontal Constraint Example

In the following illustration, the application of a horizontal constraint is shown. The two circles are constrained to the endpoints of the line. The design intent requires these two circles to remain aligned. After the horizontal constraint is applied to the line, the line updates and the circle on the right side moves with the line.

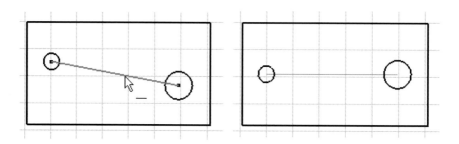

About Constraint Inference and Persistence

By default, when you create sketch geometry, that geometry can automatically have geometric constraints applied to it. To control when geometric constraints are automatically inferred and applied in a sketch, you must understand what it means to have constraints inferred and the meaning of persistence, and where and how to change their related settings.

In the following illustration, a sketch is shown being created alongside the completed sketch with its geometric constraints displayed. As the sketch geometry was being created, the geometric constraints were automatically added to the geometry.

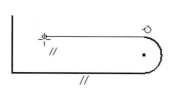
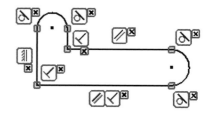

Definition of Constraint Inference and Persistence

As you are working in a sketch, several types of geometric constraints can be automatically applied to sketch geometry as it is created. This includes constraints such as perpendicular, parallel, coincident, horizontal, vertical, and tangent. The automatic application of geometric constraints is referred to as constraint inference and persistence.

When you are sketching geometry and a valid geometric constraint to another sketch geometry is identified, that constraint is said to be inferred. When a constraint is inferred, the constraint symbol for that geometric type displays. If you click to create the sketch geometry when the constraint symbol is displayed, and if the inferred geometric constraint is automatically applied to the sketch geometry, then that constraint is said to be persistent. Depending on your settings, that inferred constraint may or may not be automatically added to the sketch geometry.

The evaluation of sketch geometry for constraint inference occurs automatically based on the location and relationship of the geometry being sketched to the existing geometry around it. You can have a specific piece of sketch geometry inferred by passing the cursor back and forth over the geometry. Passing the cursor back and forth over the sketch geometry is referred to as scrubbing the geometry.

You can control the automatic application of geometric constraints through the use of the Constraint Inference and Constraint Options settings or the CTRL key.

By changing the Constraint Inference and Constraint Persistence options, you control whether constraints are automatically inferred and applied, only inferred but not applied, or neither inferred nor applied. When you press and hold CTRL as you create sketch geometry, no geometric constraints are inferred or applied.

Having geometric constraints automatically applied to the sketch geometry as you create it means you decrease the number of constraints required later to control the sketch geometry's shape, size, and position.

User-Controlled Constraint Inference and Persistence

As you create sketch geometry, the automatic inference of constraints is dependent on the setting of the Constraint Inference option, and the settings for the Constraint Options, as set in the Constraint Options dialog box. The actual creation of an inferred constraint in the sketch is dependent on the Constraint Persistence option.

Icon	Option	Description
	Constrain Inference	This setting controls whether or not sketch constraints are inferred.
	Constraint Persistence	This setting controls whether or not inferred sketch constraints are created.

You change the settings for the Constraint Inference and Constraint Persistence options on the Constrain panel of the ribbon. There are three different combinations of settings you can set for constraint inference and persistence. You can have both settings off, only the inference setting on, or both on. As you are creating sketch geometry, you can change the settings for Constraint Inference and Constraint Persistence to match your requirements for the sketch geometry you are about to create.

The following table illustrates the settings for Constraint Inference and Constraint Persistence and describes the various behaviors associated with these options.

Option	Description
	Both Off: As you create sketch geometry, you do not infer geometric constraints other than coincident constraints. Therefore, the sketch geometry does not automatically have geometric constraints like horizontal, parallel, or perpendicular applied to its geometry. Lines can still snap to horizontal and vertical, and point alignment can still occur if it is enabled.
	Inference Only: As you create sketch geometry, you can infer geometric constraints like parallel, perpendicular, and tangent. However, the only geometric constraints automatically applied to the sketch are coincident constraints. Use this setting to get the initial sketch geometry aligned and positioned as you require without adding initial geometric constraints.
	Both On: As you create sketch geometry, you can infer geometric constraints such as parallel, perpendicular, and tangent. Any inferred constraint is automatically added and applied to that sketch geometry.

Constraint Inference Options

You access the Constraint Options dialog box by clicking Constraint Options in the shortcut menu when a sketch is active for editing. Within the Constraint Options dialog box, there are two areas for setting constraint inference: Selection for Constraint Inference and Scope of Constraint Inference.

In the Selection for Constraint Inference area, you select which geometric constraints you want to infer as you are creating new sketch geometry. For these options to be selectable, the Constraint Inference option must already be on.

In the Scope of Constraint Inference area, you set either to automatically evaluate all sketch geometry to infer constraints from, or to use only the sketch geometry you preselect.

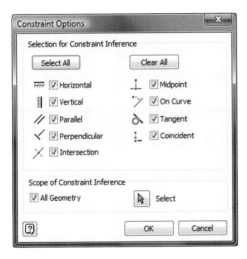

Example Settings and Uses for Constraint Inference and Persistence

The way you set the Constraint Inference and Constraint Persistence options depends on the sketch geometry you are creating and the workflow you want to follow. For example:

- If you are sketching geometry that needs to be at varying angles other than horizontal, vertical, parallel, and perpendicular to other geometry, you should have both settings off so the geometry does not align in that manner nor have geometric constraints applied.

- If you want to create the sketch geometry and manually apply each geometric constraint so it has a specific constraint scheme, then you should have both settings off or have only the Constraint Inference option on.

- If you want to infer constraints and apply the constraints to the sketch geometry as you create it, then you should have both settings on.

In the following illustration, the progressive steps used to create the sketch are shown along the top. The settings that were used for constraint inference and constraint persistence are shown at the bottom with their respective constraint results.

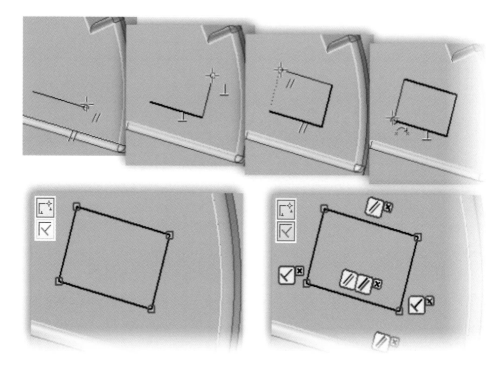

Applying Geometric Constraints

Each type of constraint can be applied to certain types of geometry and in certain situations. Some constraints such as perpendicular are relational constraints and must be applied to two elements in the sketch. A relational constraint defines a geometric relationship between two objects. Other constraints such as vertical can be applied to a single object or two points.

Accessing Constraint Tools

2D constraints are available on the ribbon, Sketch tab, Constrain panel.

Access

2D Constraints

Ribbon: **Sketch tab > Constrain panel**

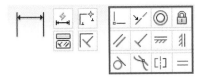

Procedure: Applying a Horizontal Constraint

The following steps give an overview for applying a horizontal constraint.

1   Click Sketch tab > Constrain panel > Horizontal.

2   Select the geometry to be constrained.

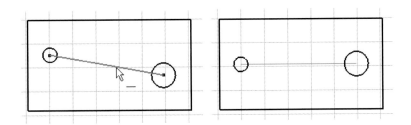

3   Add more horizontal constraints, or right-click and click Done.

Procedure: Applying a Horizontal Constraint Between Point and Midpoint

The following steps give an overview for applying a horizontal constraint between two points.

1   Start the Horizontal constraint tool.

2   Select a point such as the endpoint of a line or center of a circle.

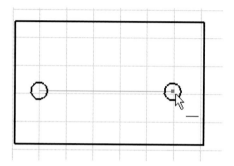

3   Select the midpoint of an existing line.

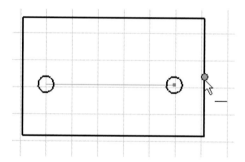

The geometry is now constrained horizontally based upon the two points selected.

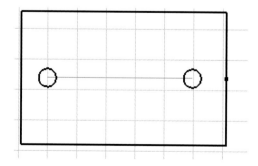

Procedure: Applying an Equal Constraint

The following steps give an overview for applying an equal constraint to two circles.

1   Click Sketch tab > Constrain panel > Equal.

2   Select a circle, line, or arc.

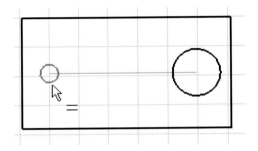

3   Select the circle, line, or arc to which you want to apply the equal constraint.

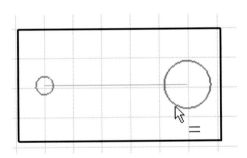

4   The selected geometry is now constrained to be equal in size.

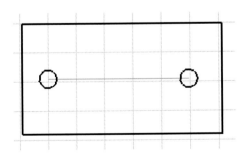

Procedure: Applying a Symmetrical Constraint

The following steps give an overview for applying a symmetrical constraint.

1   Click Sketch tab > Constrain panel > Symmetric.

2   Select the first sketch element for the constraint.

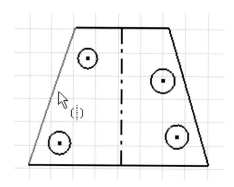

3   Select the second sketch element for the constraint.

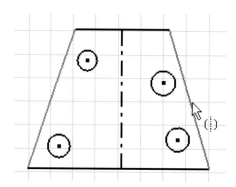

4   Select a sketch element to be used for the symmetry line.
     Note: You only need to select the symmetry line once during the current session.

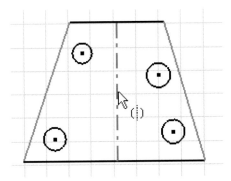

5   Continue selecting other sketch elements to apply the symmetric constraint.

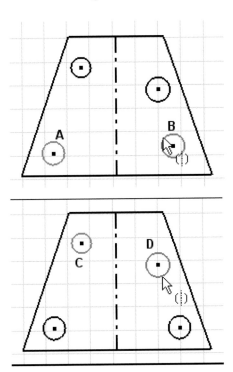

Showing and Deleting Constraints

As you create and constrain your 2D sketches, you may need to view and possibly delete some constraints. Using the Show Constraints tool, you can view the constraints applied to the selected geometry and if necessary, select the constraint(s) and delete them. You can also use the Show All Constraints tool to display the constraints on all the elements in your sketch.

The constraint glyphs for one piece of sketch geometry are shown in the following illustration. The illustration also shows that selecting a constraint glyph highlights the geometry it is associated with.

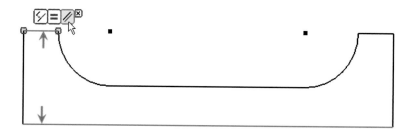

Showing Constraints on Multiple Objects

In the following illustration, the Show Constraints tool has been started. A selection window is used to select multiple objects in the sketch. The constraints for each object selected are displayed. The cursor is then moved to a single object to review the constraints related to that object.

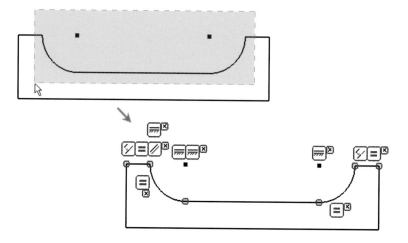

Constraint Glyph Features

You can use the Constraint Glyphs in the following ways.

Option	Method
Viewing constraints	Click the constraint glyph. The geometry referenced by the selected constraint glyph is highlighted.
Hide constraints	Right-click the constraint glyph, and click Hide.
Deleting constraints	Select the constraint glyph and press Delete, or right-click the selected constraint glyph and click Delete.

Show All Constraints

Using the Show All Constraints tool, you can see all constraints applied to the active sketch geometry. When you select the Show All Constraints tool, Show/Delete Constraint toolbars are displayed next to each sketch element. Pause over or select the constraint symbol to highlight the constrained geometry. Select the constraint symbol and press DELETE to delete the constraint.

Access

You can use the following methods to access the Show All Constraints tool.

Option	Method
Shortcut menu	Right-click in the graphics window and click Show All Constraints (sketch must be active)
Keyboard shortcut	**F8:** Show all constraints **F9:** Hide all constraints

The constraint toolbars are displayed next to each sketch element. Click and drag the bars on the toolbars to move them to another location.

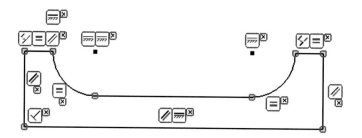

Guidelines for Successful Constraining

As you create sketch geometry, constraints are automatically applied. However, those constraints do not always completely represent your design intent. Therefore, you must add constraints or delete existing constraints.

Constraint Guidelines

The following list represents some guidelines to consider when you are placing constraints.

- **Determine sketch dependencies**: During the sketch creation process, determine how sketch elements relate to each other and apply the appropriate sketch constraints.

- **Analyze automatically applied constraints:** As you create sketch geometry, some constraints are automatically applied. After the sketch is created, you should determine whether any degrees of freedom remain on the sketch. If required, delete the automatically applied constraints and apply constraints to remove the degrees of freedom.

- **Use only needed constraints:** When you apply constraints to your sketch geometry, take into account the design intent and the degrees of freedom remaining on the sketch. It is not necessary to fully constrain sketch geometry in order to create 3D features. In some situations you may be required to leave sketch geometry underconstrained. You can use the constraint-drag technique to see the remaining degrees of freedom on the sketch.

- **Stabilize shape before size:** Before you place dimensions on your sketch elements, you should constrain the sketch to prevent the geometry from distorting. As you place the parametric dimensions, the sketch elements update to reflect the correct size. By stabilizing the geometry with constraints, you are able to predict the effect the dimensions have on the sketch geometry. If necessary, use the fix constraint to fix portions of the sketch.

- **Identify sketch elements that might change size:** When constraining sketches, take into account features that may change as the design evolves. When you identify sketch features that may change, leave those features underconstrained. When a feature is left unconstrained, the feature can change as the design evolves.

Guideline Examples

The following list illustrates and describes some basic constraint guidelines.

Determine sketch dependencies: In this illustration, the two short vertical line segments must remain perpendicular to the centerline, and the two diagonals must remain parallel to each other.

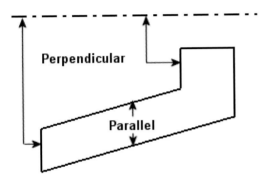

Analyze automatically applied constraints: In this illustration, the automatically applied constraints on the right-side vertical line and the lower diagonal line are being analyzed. The symbols (glyphs) on the toolbars indicate the types of constraints that have been applied. In this illustration the perpendicular and parallel constraints are highlighted.

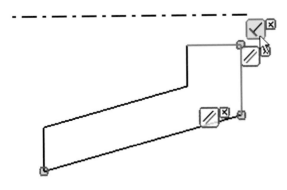

Use only needed constraints: In this illustration, the horizontal line has been intentionally left underconstrained. This enables the designer to adjust the position between the horizontal line and the centerline.

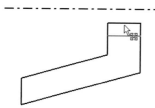

Stabilize shape before size: In this illustration, constraints are shown but no dimensions appear on this sketch. The constraints have been added to stabilize the sketch shape before dimensions are applied to control its size.

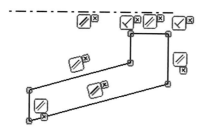

Identify sketch elements that might change size: In this illustration, the dimensions complete the constraint requirements. Notice how the short horizontal line below the centerline is not dimensioned for its position away from the centerline. This line's position has been identified as an element that may need to change, and thus is intentionally not dimensioned.

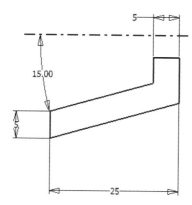

Toggling Sketch Degrees of Freedom Glyph Display

When you are constraining a sketch, if you understand how sketch geometry is free to move and rotate, it makes it easier to figure out your strategy for applying geometry and dimensional constraints. By understanding the purpose of sketch degree of freedom glyphs and how to display them, you will find that it is much easier to constrain the sketch geometry as you require.

In the following illustration, a sketch has all of its degrees of freedom glyphs being displayed for its sketch geometry. Based on these glyphs, you get a visual understanding of how each object or endpoint can move or rotate.

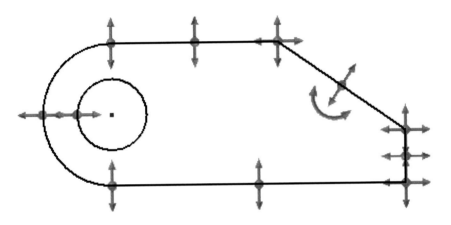

Sketch Degrees of Freedom

To visually identify how sketch geometry is underconstrained, you can have degrees of freedom (DOF) glyphs appear for all or selected geometry in a sketch. As you constrain the sketch, the visible DOF glyphs dynamically update to reflect the open degrees of freedom.

You toggle on and off the display of sketch geometry degrees of freedom glyphs in the active sketch by clicking the corresponding option in the shortcut menu. When there is no sketch geometry selected, the shortcut menu options are Hide All Degrees of Freedom and Show All Degrees of Freedom. These options toggle on and off the DOF glyph display for all geometry in the active sketch. If sketch geometry is selected when you right-click in the graphics window, you are then able to toggle on and off the display of the degrees of freedom glyph for just that geometry by clicking the Display Degrees of Freedom shortcut menu option.

In the following illustration, the same sketch is shown with sketch degrees of freedom glyphs before and after adding three dimensions. After adding the three highlighted dimensions, much of the geometry in the sketch had its degrees of freedom locked down. Degrees of freedom glyphs appear only for the geometry that still has open freedom. The degree of freedom glyphs that are displayed update to show just the open freedom for the geometry.

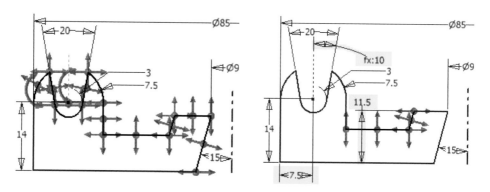

Procedure: Toggling Sketch Degrees of Freedom Glyph Display

The following steps give an overview of toggling on or off the display of all sketch degree of freedom glyphs in an active sketch.

1   Right-click in an open area in the graphics window.

2   In the shortcut menu, click Hide All Degrees of Freedom or Show All Degrees of Freedom.

Exercise | Constrain Sketches

In this exercise, you create and constrain sketch geometry. Using the concepts and procedures learned in this lesson, you create the slots on the Pillow Block component.

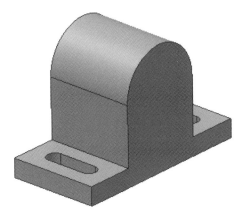

The completed exercise

Completing the Exercise: *To complete the exercise, follow the steps in this book or in the onscreen exercise. In the onscreen list of chapters and exercises, click Chapter 2: Basic Sketching Techniques. Click Exercise: Constrain Sketches.*

1   Open *Pillow-Block.ipt.*

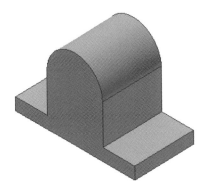

2   The Model tab is active. Click Sketch panel > Create 2D Sketch. Select the face on the part as shown.

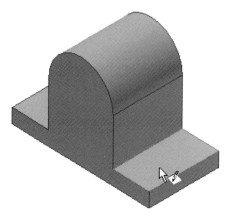

3   Start the Two Point Rectangle tool. Sketch a rectangle on the face as shown. Press ESC to exit the tool.
Note: The XYZ Indicator has its text turned off in the following image.

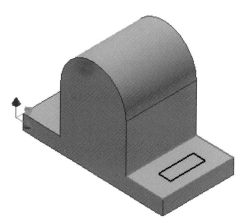

4   Start the Centerpoint Circle tool and create circles centered on the edge of the rectangle and coincident to the corners. Right-click in the graphics window and click Done when finished drawing.

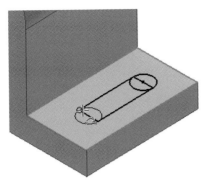

5   Start the Vertical Constraint tool and select the midpoint of the left edge and the centerpoint on the circle.

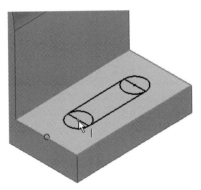

6   Start the Horizontal Constraint tool and select the midpoint of the face and the midpoint of the slot sketch.

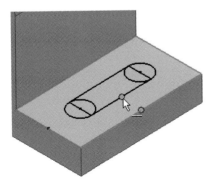

The slot sketch is now centered on the face.

7   Press ESC to exit the Horizontal Constraint tool.

8   Right-click anywhere in the graphics window, select Show All Degrees of Freedom. Observe that while the slot is constrained centered on the face, there are many degrees of freedom remaining.
Note: The material is set to glass in the following illustration to better display the DOF symbols.

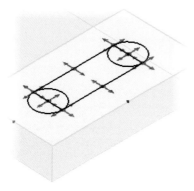

9   Right-click anywhere in the graphics window, select Hide All Degrees of Freedom.

10 On the ribbon, click Finish Sketch to exit the sketch.

11 Start the Extrude tool and select inside each circle and the rectangle area of the sketch. Adjust the options in the dialog box as shown. Click OK.

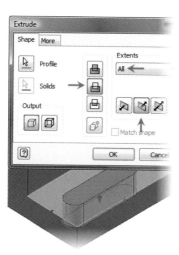

12   On the ViewCube, select the upper left corner of the cube as shown.

13   Start the Create 2D Sketch tool and select the face on the part as shown.

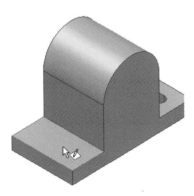

14   Repeat steps 3 through 11 to create a slot on this face of the part.

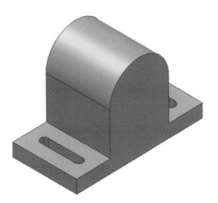

15   Close all files. Do not save.

Lesson 06 | Dimensioning Sketches

This lesson describes how to create and use various types of dimensions for your 2D sketch geometry.

Using dimensions for your sketches is a major aspect of constraining 2D geometry. While geometric constraints stabilize the sketch and make it predictable, dimensions size the sketch according to your design intent.

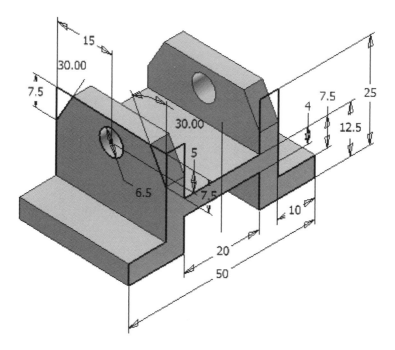

Objectives

After completing this lesson, you will be able to:

- Describe the function and properties of parametric dimensions.

- Create linear, radial, angular, and aligned dimensional constraints.

- Use additional options when applying dimensions.

- Describe best practices for dimensioning your sketch.

About Dimensional Constraints

You create dimensional constraints by adding parametric dimensions to your sketch. This is the final step in fully constraining your sketch geometry. When you apply a parametric dimension to a sketch element, the sketch element changes size to reflect the value of the dimension.

Various types of dimensions that you can apply to sketch geometry are shown in the following illustration.

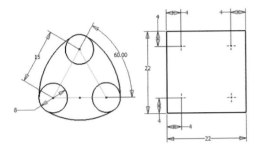

Definition of Parametric Dimensions

A parametric dimension is a dimension that, when placed on sketch geometry, determines the size, angle, or position of the geometry. Associative dimensions in nonparametric applications report the size, angle, or position of an object, whereas changes to parametric dimensions affect the object's size, angle, or position.

In the following illustration, when the dimension is placed, the initial value is 47.232. When the value is changed to 50 in the Edit Dimension dialog box, the width of the shape updates to reflect the new value. Note the do text in the title area of the Edit Dimension dialog box. This is the parameter name. Each time you place a parametric dimension, a unique parameter name is automatically assigned.

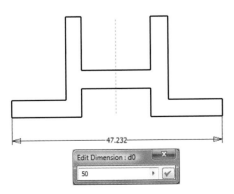

Unlike 2D CAD applications in which dimensions are simply numeric representations of the size of the geometry, in a parametric 3D modeling application, dimensions are used to drive the size of the geometry. With this technology, you can quickly change a dimension and immediately see how the change affects the geometry.

Example

Several types of parametric dimensions are available, but only one dimension tool is used to create them. The application places the appropriate type of dimension based on the geometry that you select. When you are placing dimensions, the shortcut menu displays additional options for placing the dimension.

Parametric Dimensions

The following illustration displays horizontal and vertical parametric dimensions and the shortcut menu, which enables you to choose the type of dimension to place.

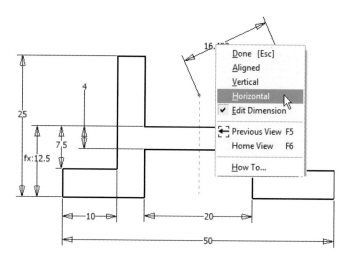

Creating Dimensional Constraints

You use the General Dimension tool to place dimensions on your sketch. You can produce linear, aligned, angular, radial, and diameter dimensions with this single tool.

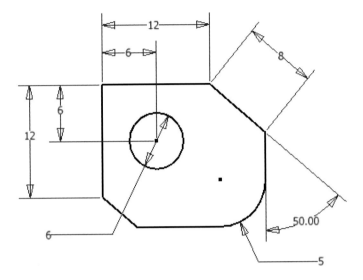

Access

General Dimension

Ribbon: **Sketch tab > Constrain panel**

Keyboard Shortcut: **D**

Procedure: Applying Linear Dimensions

The following steps describe how to apply a linear parametric dimension.

1   Click Sketch tab > Constrain panel > General Dimension.

2   Select the sketch element for the linear dimension and place the dimension.

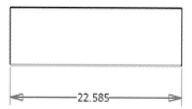

3   Select the dimension and enter a new value.

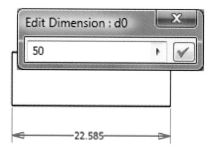

4   Press ENTER or click the green check mark on the Edit Dimension dialog box to have the geometry change to reflect the new dimension.

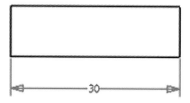

5   Right-click in the graphics window and click Done on the shortcut menu or continue placing additional dimensions.

Procedure: Applying Radial/Diameter Dimensions

The following steps describe how to apply radial or diameter parametric dimensions.

1   Start the General Dimension tool.

2   Select the sketch element for the radial/diameter dimension and place the dimension.

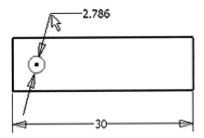

3   Select the dimension and enter a new value.

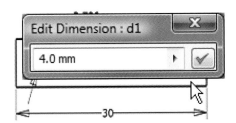

4   Press ENTER or click the green check mark on the Edit Dimension dialog box to have the geometry change to reflect the new dimension.

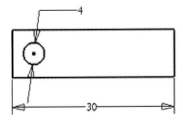

5   Right-click in the graphics window and click Done on the shortcut menu or continue placing additional dimensions.

Procedure: Applying Angular Dimensions

The following steps describe how to apply an angular parametric dimension.

1 Start the General Dimension tool.

2 Select each element for the angular dimension and place the dimension.
   Note: Select each element at any location other than their endpoints.

3 Select the dimension and enter a new value.

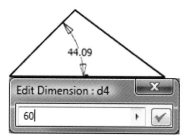

4 Press ENTER or click the green check mark on the Edit Dimension dialog box to have the geometry change to reflect the new dimension.

5 Right-click in the graphics window and click Done on the shortcut menu or continue placing additional dimensions.

Procedure: Creating Aligned Dimensions

The following steps describe how to apply an aligned parametric dimension.

1   Start the General Dimension tool.

2   Select the sketch element for the aligned dimension. Position the cursor near the geometry.
     Click when the Aligned Dimension icon is displayed.

3   Place the dimension.

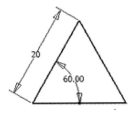

4   Select the dimension and enter a new value.

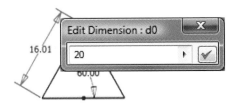

5   Press ENTER or click the green check mark on the Edit Dimension dialog box to have the
     geometry change to reflect the new dimension.

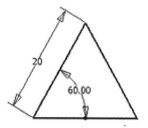

6   Right-click in the graphics window and click Done on the shortcut menu or continue placing
     additional dimensions.

Tip: *Instead of positioning your cursor near the geometry to cause the Aligned Dimension
            icon to be displayed, you can also select the element as you do when creating a linear
            dimension. Before positioning the dimension, right-click and set the dimension type
            as an aligned dimension by clicking Aligned on the shortcut menu.*

Dimension Values and Units

You click a dimension to define its value. If required, you can include specific units of measurement
such as millimeter, centimeter, meter, inch, and foot. It is not necessary to enter the suffix of the
default unit.

If your part consists of multiple units of measurement you must enter the nondefault unit suffixes.
For example, if the default unit of measurement is millimeters, you would enter a value of **50**
millimeters as 50 with no suffix. To specify a value of 50 centimeters in the same part, you would
enter **50 cm**.

The application evaluates the values as you enter them. Values shown in red indicate an improper
value or format, while values shown in black are considered to be valid.

Unit suffixes and parameters are case-sensitive. When you enter a unit suffix, it must be entered in
lowercase. For example, 50 cm would be evaluated correctly, while 50 CM is not valid.

Edit Dimension Flyout Menu Options

When applying parametric dimensions, the following options are available in the Edit
Dimension flyout.

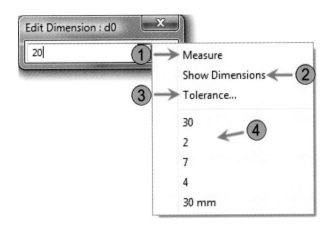

	Option	Description
1	**Measure**	Use to measure another sketch element or 3D feature. The resulting value is placed in the Edit Dimension dialog box.
2	**Show Dimensions**	Use to select a feature on the 3D part to display the underlying dimensions. After the dimensions are displayed, you can select a dimension for use in the existing dimension. The dimension being referenced can be used alone or in a formula.
3	**Tolerance**	Displays the Tolerance dialog box, which you can use to assign a tolerance to the parametric dimension.
4	**Recently Used Values**	Displays a list of recently used values. Select any value for use in the current dimension.

Additional Dimension Options

The following list represents additional options available on the shortcut menu when you place dimensions.

Option	Description
Edit Dimension	While placing a dimension, right-click in the graphics window, and on the shortcut menu click Edit Dimension. With this option set, the Edit Dimension dialog box is displayed automatically after each dimension is placed. 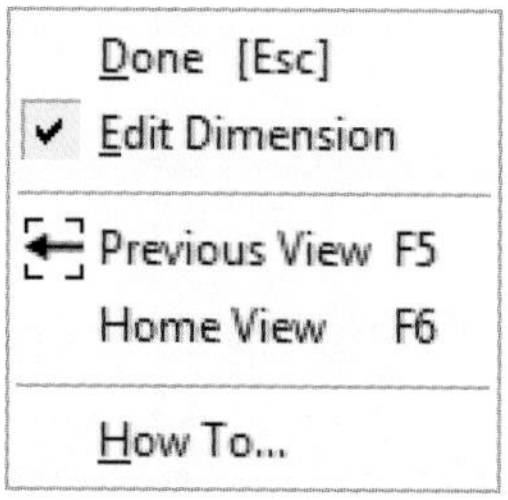
Radial/Diameter Dimension Options	When you place a dimension on an arc or circle, right-click in the graphics window and on the shortcut menu click Diameter or Radius to switch the default mode of the current dimension. When dimensioning an arc, the default mode is Radius. When dimensioning a circle, the default mode is Diameter. 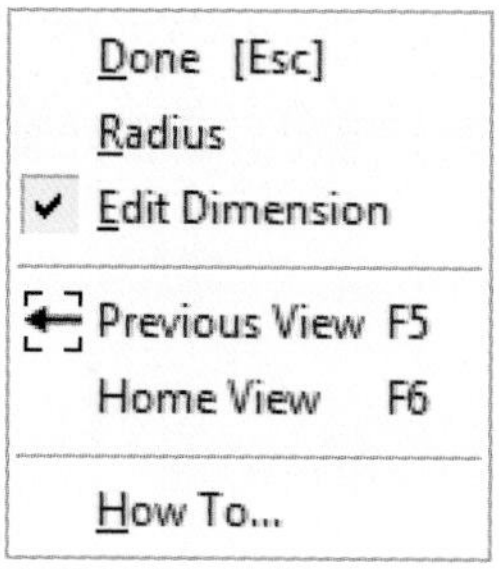 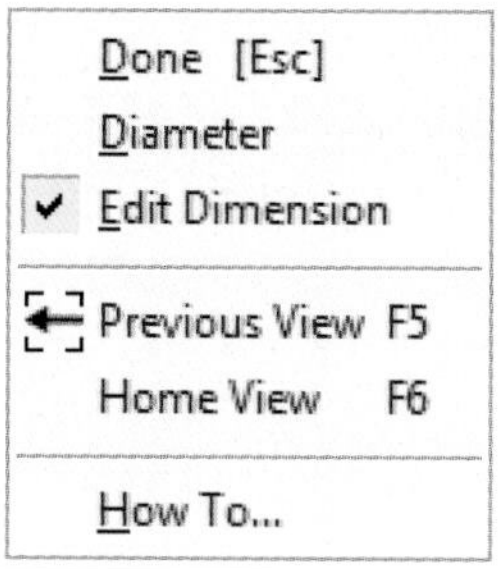

Option	Description
Linear Dimension Options	When you place a linear dimension to a line or two points at an angle, right-click in the graphics window, and on the shortcut menu click the desired dimension type. 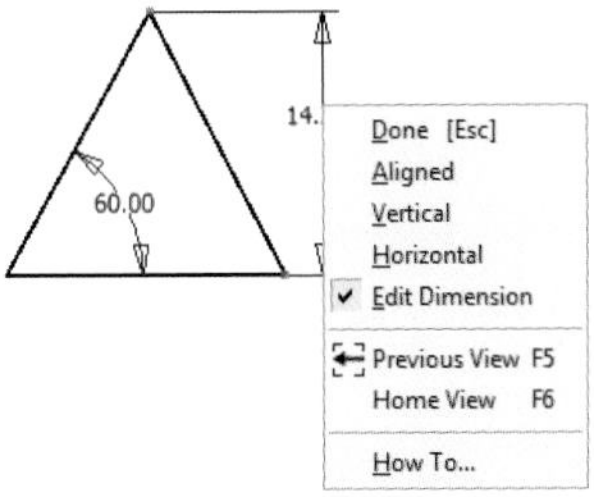 14. 60.00 Done [Esc] Aligned Vertical Horizontal ✔ Edit Dimension Previous View F5 Home View F6 How To...
Dimensioning to Quadrants	When you need to place a dimension to the quadrant of a circle, place the cursor near the quadrant and look for the quadrant dimension glyph. Select the arc or circle at the point where the glyph is displayed. 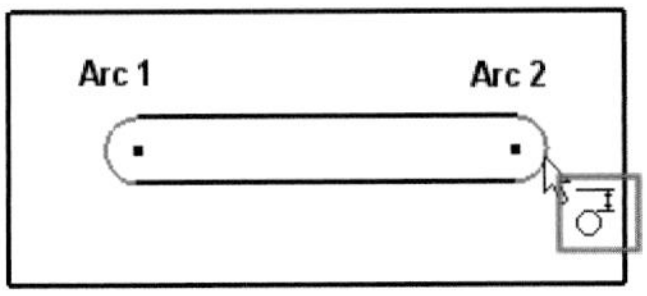 Arc 1 Arc 2

About Dimension Display and Relationships

When you apply dimensions to your sketch elements additional options are available that you can use to control the display of the dimensions. Also available are tools designed to assist you in creating dimensions referenced from other features and/or dimensions.

Dimension Display

After you apply dimensions to your geometry, you can control the visibility of all dimensions in the sketch and control the visual formatting of the displayed dimensions.

Being able to turn on and off the display of dimensions in a sketch means you have the flexibility when working with complex sketch geometry to decide how much information you see. Turning off the display of dimensions makes it easier to select the sketch geometry and review its general shape. When dimensions are not displayed and you make a sketch invisible, the dimensions remain off when you make the sketch visible again.

Using the optional display formats of Value, Name, Expression, Tolerance, and Precise Value can help you evaluate the structure of equations in relational dimensions, toleranced dimensions, and dimensions that contain equations.

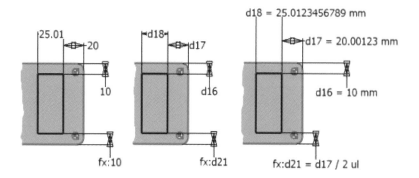

Option	Description
Value	The default mode. Displays the current value of the dimension at the precision specified in the Document Settings dialog box.
Name	Displays dimension names only. Dimension names are assigned automatically, or you can specify them in the Parameters dialog box.

Option	Description
Expression	Displays the dimensions as expressions. An expression can be as simple as d0 = 26.4375; or a formula can be used, such as d0 = d1/2. 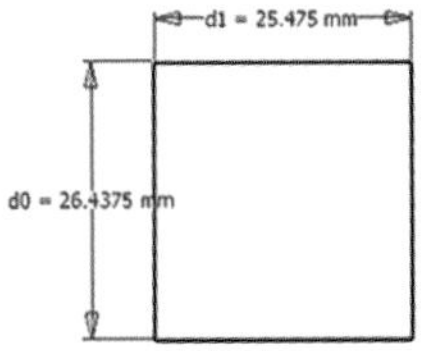
Tolerance	Displays the dimensions in a format associated with the specific type of tolerance applied. If a tolerance has not been applied to the dimension, there is no effect on the dimension display. 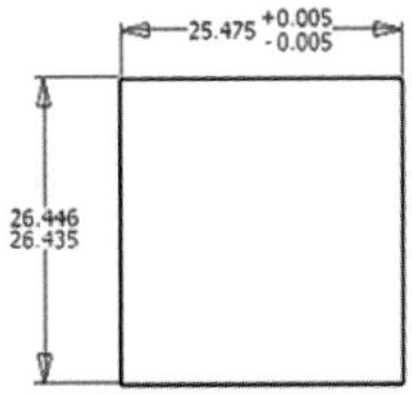
Precise Value	Displays the dimension using its exact numeric value, regardless of the Precision setting in the Document Settings dialog box. 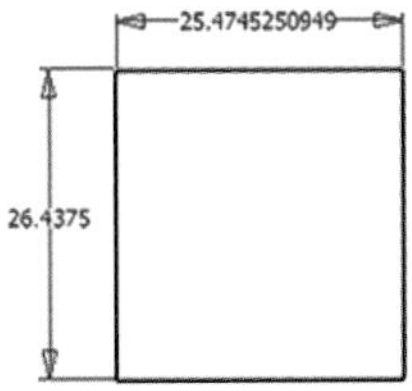

Procedure: Selecting the Dimension Display Mode

The following steps describe how to select the mode for displaying model dimensions.

1   With nothing selected, right-click in the browser or graphic window.

2   On the shortcut menu, click Dimension Display and then click the desired option on the cascading menu.

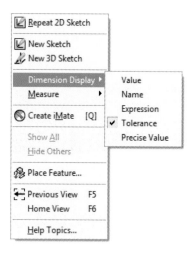

Referencing Other Dimensions

When you define the value of a dimension, you can reference an existing dimension by selecting the dimension in the graphics window. The dimension parameter name is automatically entered in the Edit Dimension dialog box.

The illustration shows dimension d18 being created equal to dimension d17. When you want to reference other dimensions in a new dimension, with the Edit Dimension dialog box open, select an existing dimension to reference. Your cursor changes to indicate that you are referencing an existing dimension. When you select the existing dimension, the parameter name of the dimension you selected is entered in the Edit Dimension dialog box. A dimension that references another dimension has fx: preceding its value.

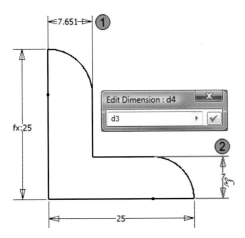

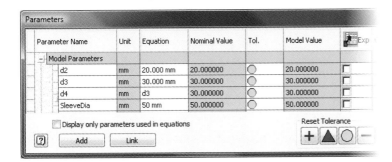

(1) Dimension being created.

(2) Dimension being referenced.

Dimensions Stored as Parameters

Each dimension you create is automatically named and stored as a parameter in the current part file. Selecting the Parameters tool on the ribbon, Manage tab, displays the Parameters dialog box which lists the model parameters.

Parameter Name	Unit	Equation	Nominal Value	Tol.	Model Value	
− Model Parameters						
d2	mm	20.000 mm	20.000000	○	20.000000	□
d3	mm	30.000 mm	30.000000	○	30.000000	□
d4	mm	d3	30.000000	○	30.000000	□
SleeveDia	mm	50 mm	50.000000	○	50.000000	□

Notice the parameter names d0 and d1. These names are generated each time a dimension is placed. If you delete a dimension, its parameter is also deleted and the original dimension name is not used again in the current part file. You can rename the default dimension names and modify their values in the Parameters dialog box. In the previous illustration the parameter d2 is renamed to SleeveDia.

Tip: **Quickly Change Parameters** *You can change parameters on the fly to improve your productivity. While creating dimensions, for example, you can enter* **Length=20** *and the current parameter is renamed to Length and the value is set to 20.*

Guidelines for Dimensioning Sketches

Applying parametric dimensions is straightforward because you use a single command. Following these guidelines assures that dimensions are properly applied to your sketch.

Guidelines for Dimensioning Sketches

Consider the following guidelines when adding dimensions to your sketch:

- Use geometric constraints when possible. For example, place a perpendicular constraint instead of an angle dimension of 90 degrees.

- Place large dimensions before small ones.

- Incorporate relationships between dimensions. For example, if two dimensions are supposed to be the same value, reference one dimension to the other. With this relationship, if the first dimension changes, the other dimension changes as well.

- Consider both dimensional and geometric constraints to meet the overall design intent.

These guidelines are not presented in any particular order and you do not apply all of them on every sketch.

Example of Relationships Between Dimensions

Building relationships between dimensions captures your design intent. In this illustration, the intent is for the circle to always remain centered on the part. Building this dimensional relationship ensures that if the sketch width or length changes, the hole also moves in order to remain centered on the sketch. The dimension display is set to expression for clarity.

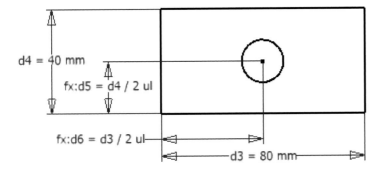

In the following illustration, the length is changed. Notice how the hole moved to maintain its centered position.

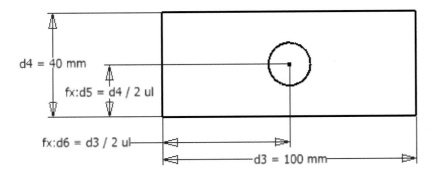

Without a dimensional relationship, a hole that was originally centered does not adjust if the length is changed.

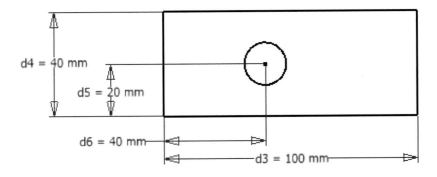

Exercise | Dimension Sketches

In this exercise, you apply dimensions to a sketch. Using the techniques learned in this lesson, you apply a variety of parametric dimensions to the sketch geometry.

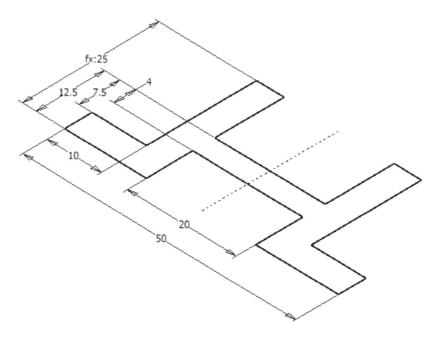

The completed exercise

| **Completing the Exercise** | *To complete the exercise, follow the steps in this book or in the onscreen exercise. In the onscreen list of chapters and exercises, click Chapter 2: Basic Sketching Techniques. Click Exercise: Dimension Sketches.* |

1   Open *m_Rod-Support.ipt*.

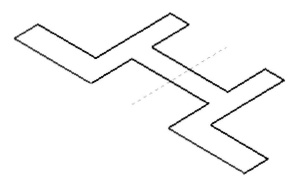

2   To rotate the view:

- On the ViewCube, click Front.
- Click the arrow to rotate the view counterclockwise 90 degrees.

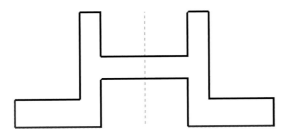

3   Constrain drag the sketch on various elements to examine the constraint conditions.

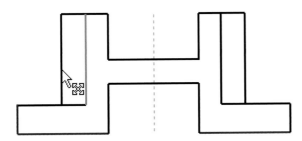

4   In the browser, double-click Sketch1 to activate the sketch.

5   Place an overall parametric dimension.
   - Start the General Dimension tool.
   - Select the lower left and right corners of the sketch.
   - Place the dimension and select it.
   - In the Edit Dimension dialog box, enter **50.**
   - Click the green check mark.

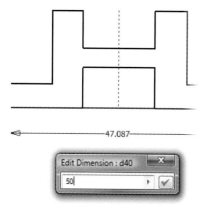

6   Set the Edit Dimension dialog box to automatic.
   - With the General Dimension tool still active, right-click in the graphics window.
   - Click Edit Dimension.
   - The Edit Dimension dialog box is displayed automatically as you place dimensions.

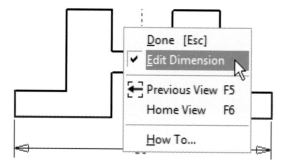

7   Add a vertical dimension in relation to the overall dimension just created.

- Select the lower-left and upper-left corners of the sketch.
- When the Edit Dimension dialog box is displayed, select the 50 mm horizontal dimension.
- In the Edit Dimension dialog box, enter **/2** after the dimension parameter name. The final dimension expression reads d40/2.
- Click the green check mark.

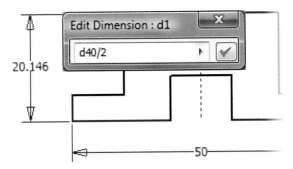

8   Add an interior horizontal dimension.

- Check to make sure that the General
- Dimension tool is still active.
- Select points as indicated.
- In the Edit Dimension dialog box, enter **20**.
- Click the green check mark.

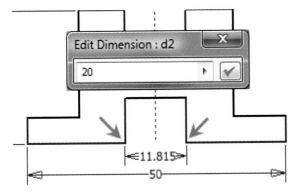

9   Add additional dimensions as shown. Do not be overly concerned with placement as you create the dimensions. You can drag the dimensions to locations after all of them have been created. Double-click each dimension and adjust its value to those in the following illustration if necessary.

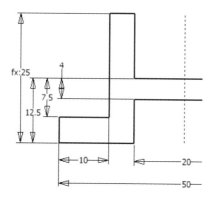

10   On the ribbon, click Finish Sketch to exit the sketch.

11   On the ViewCube, click the Home icon.

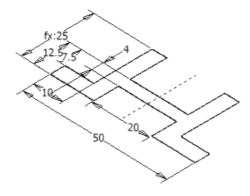

12   Close all files. Do not save.

Chapter Summary

Properly constrained 2D sketches are the fundamental building blocks of parametric parts. By being able to fully constrain the size and shape of your sketches, you can achieve the highest quality parametric part designs.

Having completed this chapter, you can:

- Use sketch tools to create 2D sketch geometry.
- Use geometric constraints to control sketch geometry.
- Apply parametric dimensions to your sketch geometry.

Chapter 03
Basic Shape Design

In earlier lessons, you learned how to create and constrain 2D sketches. In this chapter, you are introduced to the fundamentals of basic shape design by learning how to extrude, revolve, and sweep 2D sketches to create 3D features. This chapter also covers the proper techniques for adding multiple sketched features to your 3D design, creating more intelligent sketches by referencing existing part edges and using construction geometry, and modifying your parametric parts at any stage of the design process.

Objectives

After completing this chapter, you will be able to:

- Create features using the Extrude and Revolve tools.

- Use reference and construction geometry.

- Use the browser and shortcut menus to edit parametric parts.

- Use the 3D Grips tool to edit part geometry in the context of an assembly and in a stand-alone part.

- Create, locate, and utilize work features to perform modeling tasks.

- Create swept shapes by sweeping a profile along a 2D or 3D path.

Lesson 07 | Creating Basic Sketched Features

Two basic types of features exist: sketched features and placed features. The term *sketched feature* refers to a 3D feature that is based on a 2D sketch. The term *placed feature* refers to a 3D feature that you place on the existing faces and edges of the part, and which does not require a sketch. This lesson describes sketched features and how to create them using the Extrude and Revolve tools.

Because most 3D models include some combination of extruded and revolved features, a basic understanding of how to create them is essential to successful model creation.

The following illustration shows a 3D model that was created using multiple extrusion features.

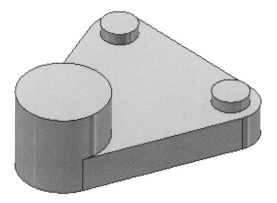

Objectives

After completing this lesson, you will be able to:

- Define sketched features and their attributes.

- Use the Extrude tool to create extruded features.

- Use the Revolve tool to create revolved features.

- Use the Operation and Extent termination options when adding 3D features.

- Orient sketch planes based on other planes or faces.

About Sketched Features

You create most 3D models by combining multiple extruded and revolved features. You start by creating a 2D sketch that represents the basic shape of the part and then use different feature creation tools to turn that 2D sketch into a 3D feature.

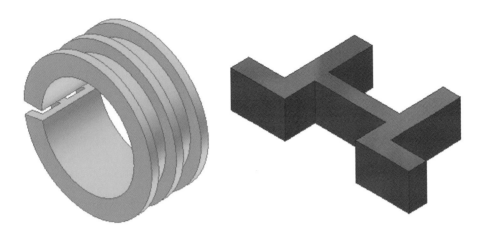

Definition of Sketched Features

Sketched features are 3D features that are created from an existing 2D sketch. These features serve as the basis for most of your designs. When you create a sketched feature, you begin by first creating the sketch or profile for the 3D feature. For simple sketched features, this profile usually represents a 2D section of the 3D feature being created. For more complex sketched features, multiple sketches can be created and used within one sketched feature.

The first sketch feature you create is considered the base feature. After you create the base feature, additional sketched and/or placed features are added to the 3D model. As you add the additional sketched features, options are available that control whether the secondary sketched features add or remove material from the existing 3D geometry.

Sketched Feature Attributes

The key attributes of sketched features include the following:

- An unconsumed sketch is required (not used by another feature).

- Sketches can be used for both base and secondary features.

- The result of the sketched feature can add or remove mass from the 3D geometry.

Consumed and Unconsumed Sketches

When you create a new part, the initial sketch is used as the basis of your 3D geometry. After the sketch is created, you can create a sketched feature, an extrusion for example, to create 3D geometry from the initial sketch. When you create the 3D sketched feature, the sketch itself becomes consumed by the 3D sketched feature. Prior to this time, the sketch is considered unconsumed and can be used for any sketched feature.

Unconsumed Sketch

The following illustration shows the initial sketch before it is consumed by the sketched feature.

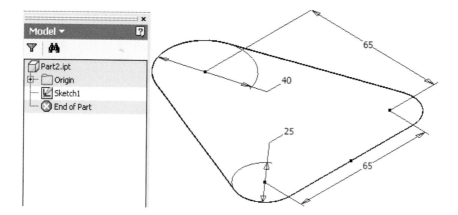

Consumed Sketches

The following illustration shows sketches consumed by the sketched features. In the browser, the sketches are nested below the sketched feature in which they were used.

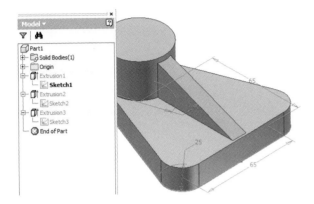

Typical Sketched Feature Creation

This illustration represents a typical workflow for creating a 3D part based upon sketched features. The base sketch is created, which is used to create the base feature. Secondary sketches and features are then added to the 3D model.

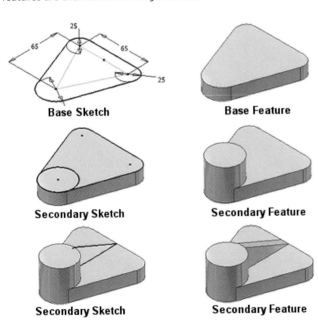

Base Sketch

Base Feature

Secondary Sketch

Secondary Feature

Secondary Sketch

Secondary Feature

Creating Extruded Features

You use the Extrude tool to create extruded features from existing sketch profiles. Considered sketched features, extruded features require an unconsumed and visible sketch to be available. If the sketch contains a single closed profile, that profile is selected automatically when you start the Extrude tool. If the sketch contains more than one profile, you are required to select the profiles to be included in the extruded feature.

Examples of Simple Extruded Profiles

In this example, the sketch contains multiple closed loop profiles selected to form a single extruded feature.

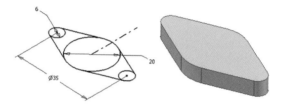

n this example, the sketch contains multiple closed loop profiles selected to form a single extruded feature with holes.

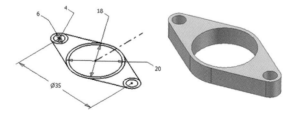

Access

Extrude

Ribbon: **Model tab > Create panel**

Toolbar: **Part Features**
Keyboard Shortcut: **E**

Extrude Options

The Extrude dialog box is displayed when you start the Extrude tool.

The following features and options are available in the Extrude dialog box:

Dialog Box Access	Option	Description
	Profile	Use to select geometry to be included in the extrusion. A red arrow indicates that no profiles have been selected for the extrusion feature.
	Solids	The Solids selection tool is only active when the part contains more than one solid body. Use to determine to which solid body the feature is going to be applied.
Output	**Output**	Use to specify the desired output option, Solid or Surface.

Dialog Box Access	Option	Description
	Direction	Select the direction icon or click and drag the preview of the extrusion in the desired direction.
	Operation	Use to create an initial feature or add volume to models with Join. Remove volume from models with Cut. Create a new feature from shared volume of two features with Intersect.
	New Solid	Use to create the extruded feature as a new solid body instead of using boolean operations to join, cut, or intersect the feature with an existing solid body.

Extrude Sample

You can select a corner of your part and drag the distance setting, as shown in the following illustration.

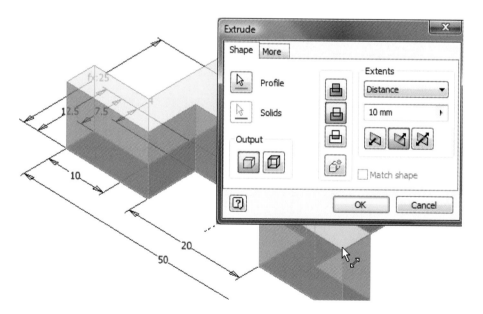

Procedure: Creating an Extruded Feature

The following steps describe how to create an extruded feature.

1   Create a new sketch.

2   Click Model tab > Create panel > Extrude.

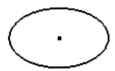

3   In the Extrude dialog box, adjust the options as required.

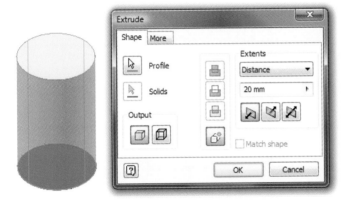

4   The extruded feature is created.

You use the Revolve tool to create revolved features from existing sketch profiles. You can revolve the profile at a full 360 degrees or at a specified angle. The Revolve tool requires an unconsumed and visible sketch to be available. When you start the Revolve tool, if the sketch contains a single closed profile, that profile is selected automatically.

Examples of Simple Revolved Profiles

In the following illustration, the sketch contains a closed profile and one centerline. When you start the Revolve tool, the centerline is automatically selected as the axis of revolution.

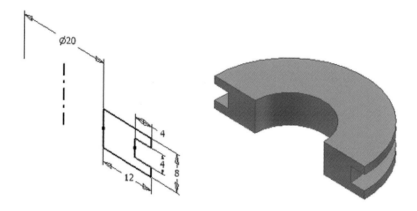

In the following illustration, the sketch contains a single closed loop profile, reference geometry, and one centerline. The profile is revolved with the Cut feature relationship.

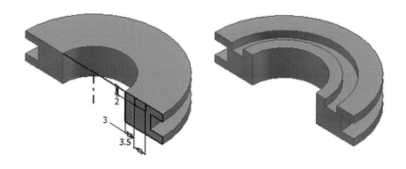

Access

Revolve

Ribbon: **Model tab > Create panel**

Toolbar: **Part Features**
Keyboard Shortcut: **R**

Revolve Options

The Revolve dialog box is displayed when you start the Revolve tool.

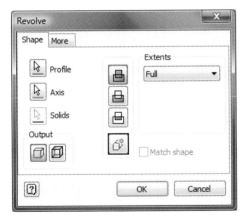

The following features and options are available in the Revolve dialog box:

Dialog Box Access	Option	Description
	Profile	Use to select geometry to include in the revolved feature. A red arrow indicates that no profiles have been selected for the revolved feature
	Axis	Use to select the line segment to use as the axis for the revolve feature. **Tip**: If the sketch contains a centerline, it is selected automatically as the axis.
	Solids	The Solids selection tool is only active when the part contains more than one solid body. Use to determine to which solid body the feature is going to be applied.
Output	**Output**	Use to specify the desired output option, Solid or Surface.
	New Solid	Use to create a new solid body from the revolved feature.
Extents Angle 90 deg	**Angle**	Use to specify an angle and direction for the revolution.
Extents Full	**Full**	Use to revolve the profile 360 degrees.

Facts About Revolved Features

- If the sketch contains a centerline, it is selected automatically as the axis for the revolved feature.

- If the sketch contains more than one profile, you are required to select the profiles to include in the feature.

- If the profile being revolved is closed, you can choose between a solid or surface for the result of the revolution.

- If the profile being revolved is open, the revolution results in a surface.

Procedure: Creating a Revolved Feature

The following steps describe how to create a revolved feature.

1   Create a new sketch containing a profile to revolve. If the profile is being revolved about a centerline, consider using the Centerline style on the line segment.

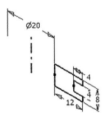

2   Click Model tab > Create panel > Revolve. In the Revolve dialog box, adjust the options as required.

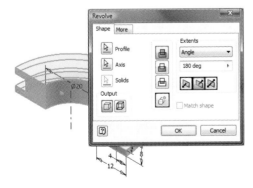

3   Create additional sketch geometry as required.

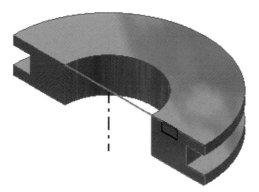

4   Start the Revolve tool. Select the geometry to be included in the revolved feature. Adjust the options as required.

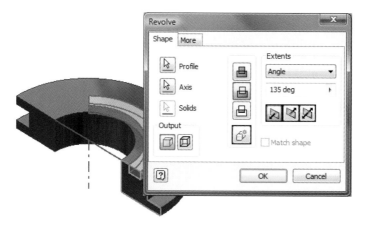

Specifying Operation and Extents

You use the Join, Cut, and Intersect operations to control how the feature you are creating affects existing features or Solid Bodies. By default, the Cut and Intersect operations are not available with base features and the New Solid button is automatically activated since the base feature will by default create a New Solid.

You use the Extents options to define the termination of a feature. For example, you can extrude a 2D sketch a specific distance or you can terminate the feature on an existing face of the model.

Example of Operation and Extents

In the following example, multiple sketched features with different operations and extents were used to define the shape of the part.

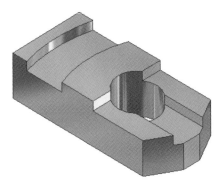

Specifying Operation: Join, Cut, and Intersect

When you create sketched and placed features, you can adjust operation options to control the effect of the current feature on existing features. These operations are not available for the first feature of the part.

The feature relationship options are available when using Extrude, Revolve, Loft, Sweep, and Coil. The following illustration shows an example of these options in the Extrude dialog box.

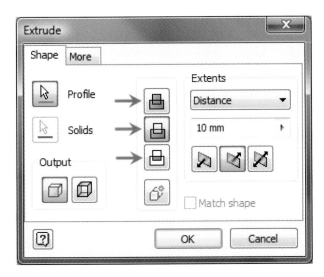

Use the following options with the extrude tool.

Dialog Box Access	Option	Description
	Join	This option joins the result of the extruded feature being created to existing part geometry. Using this option results in material being added to the existing part. A green preview indicates material is being added.
	Cut	This option cuts the result of the extruded feature being created from the existing part. Using this option results in material being removed from the existing part. A red preview indicates material is being removed.
	Intersect	This option removes material from the existing part by comparing the volume of the existing features and the feature being created and leaving only the volume shared between the existing features and the new feature. A blue preview indicates an Intersect relationship.

Note: **New Solid** *Using the New Solid option will create a new solid body from the feature definition. Solid Bodies are beyond the scope of this course and are not covered in this lesson.*

Specifying Extents

When you create extruded and revolved features, you can specify termination options for the feature in the dialog box. Depending on the option you choose, different interface options are available. By specifying termination options, you can control where the feature starts and ends.

The following illustration shows the Extents options that are available in the Extrude dialog box.

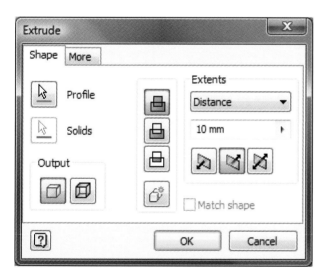

Option	Description
Distance Extents Distance 10 mm ▱ ▱ ▱	This option extrudes the profile according to the distance specified.

Option	Description
To Next Extents To Next Terminator	This option extrudes the profile to the next possible face or plane. Use the Terminator icon to select a solid or surface on which to terminate the extrusion. 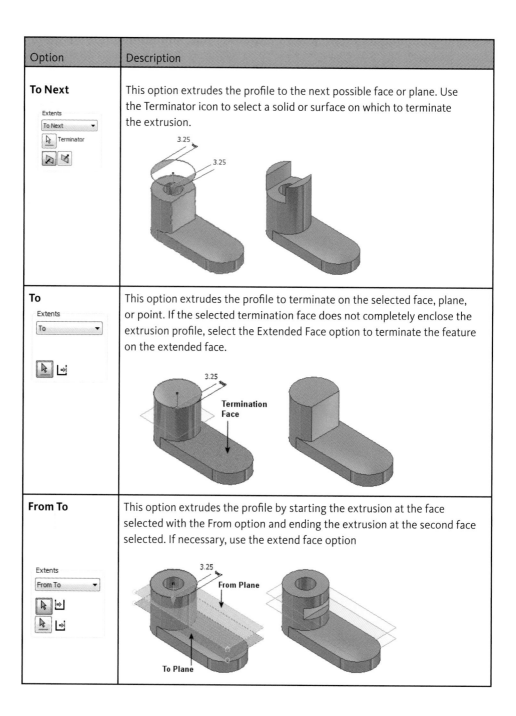
To Extents To	This option extrudes the profile to terminate on the selected face, plane, or point. If the selected termination face does not completely enclose the extrusion profile, select the Extended Face option to terminate the feature on the extended face.
From To Extents From To	This option extrudes the profile by starting the extrusion at the face selected with the From option and ending the extrusion at the second face selected. If necessary, use the extend face option

Option	Description
All 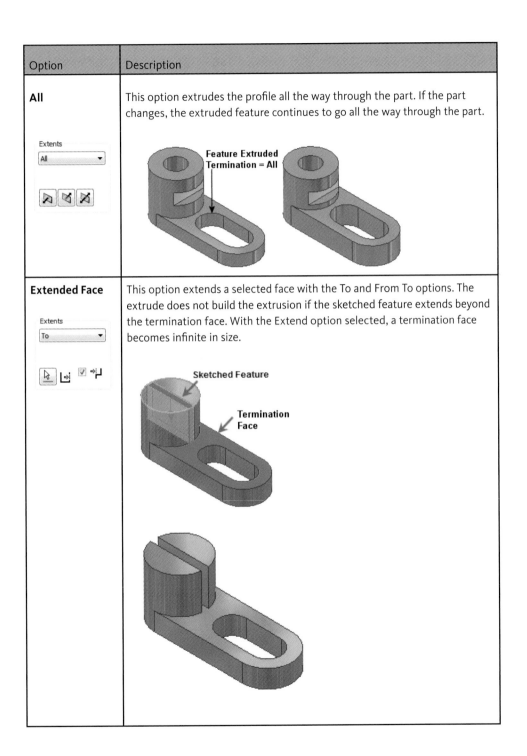	This option extrudes the profile all the way through the part. If the part changes, the extruded feature continues to go all the way through the part.
Extended Face	This option extends a selected face with the To and From To options. The extrude does not build the extrusion if the sketched feature extends beyond the termination face. With the Extend option selected, a termination face becomes infinite in size.

Additional Extents Options for Revolve

The following options are available for the Revolve tool.

Option	Description
Full Extents Full 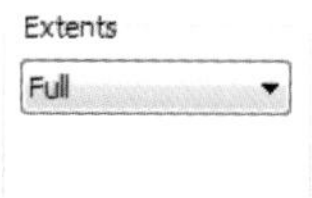	This option revolves the profile a complete revolution around a specified axis. If the part changes, the revolved feature continues to go all the way around the part. 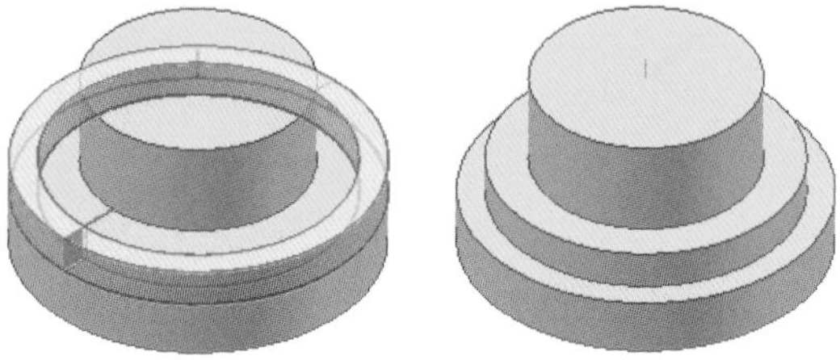
Angle 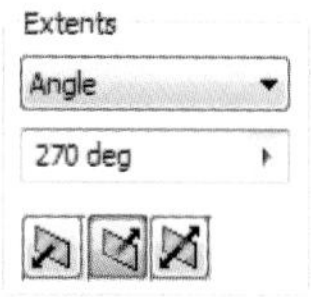 Extents Angle 270 deg	This option revolves the profile a specified number of degrees around an axis. 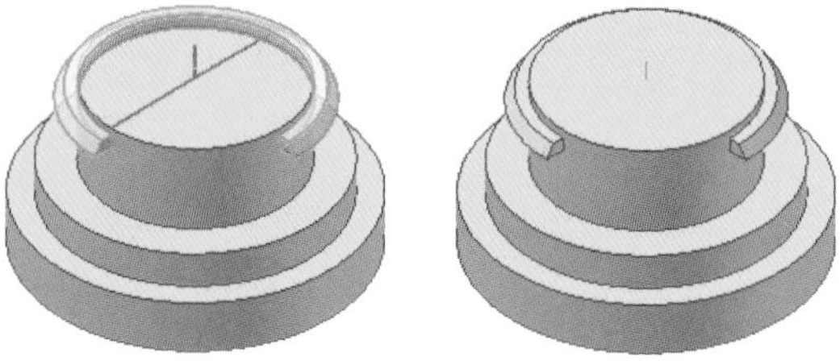

Procedure: Specifying Operations

The following steps describe how to specify operations.

1   Create additional sketch geometry on an existing feature.

2   Start the Extrude tool.

3   In the Extrude dialog box, adjust the operations as required. In this example, Join is selected.

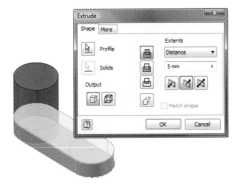

4   The additional extruded feature is added to the part.

Procedure: Specifying Extents

The following steps describe how to specify extents.

1   Create additional sketch geometry on existing features as required.

2   Start the Extrude tool.

3   In the Extrude dialog box, adjust the options as required. In this example, All is selected.

4   The additional extruded feature is added to the part.

Orienting Sketches

When you create the first sketch for the base feature of your part, you usually use the default *XY* origin plane. However, the sketches that you create to add new features to the part often need to be oriented to other part faces.

The sketch plane has been oriented to the selected part face in the following illustration.

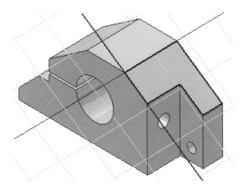

Procedure: Creating Sketch Planes on a Part Face

The following steps describe how to create a new sketch plane aligned to a selected face.

1   Right-click in a face of the part. Click New Sketch.

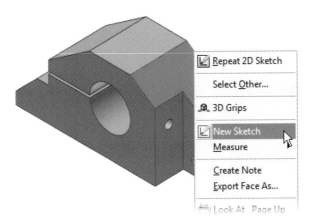

2   The sketch plane is created on the selected face.

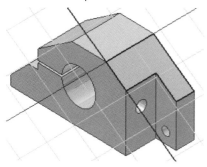

Procedure: Creating Sketch Planes Offset from a Part Face

The following steps describe how to create a new sketch plane offset from a selected face.

1   Start the Create 2D Sketch tool.

2   Click in the face and drag the sketch plane away from the selected face.

3   In the Offset dialog box, enter a value for the offset and click the green check mark. The sketch plane is created offset from the selected face at the distance you specified.

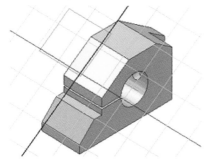

Exercise | Create Extruded Features

In this exercise, you build an Index Slide part file using several extruded features. Some initial geometry has been created, but you are required to create other sketch geometry.

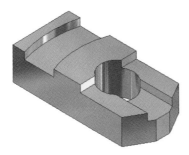

The completed exercise

Completing the Exercise	To complete the exercise, follow the steps in this book or in the onscreen exercise. In the onscreen list of chapters and exercises, click Chapter 3: Basic Shape Design. Click Exercise: Create Extruded Features.

Create Extruded Features Specific Distances

In this portion of the exercise, you extrude an existing sketch to create a base feature. Then you create a new sketch and extrude it a specific distance to create another sketched feature.

1   Open *Index-Slide.ipt*.

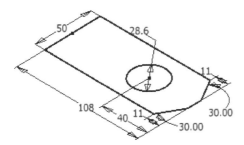

2   Extrude the sketch 28 mm.

  • Start the Extrude tool.
  • Select the profile as shown.
  • For Distance, enter **28 mm.**
  • Click OK.

3   On the Quick Access toolbar, select Nickel (Bright).

4   Right-click the face on the end of the part. Click New Sketch.

5 Change your view to look normal to your sketch plane.

   - On the Navigation bar, click View Face.
   - Select the same face on the part.

6 Use the ViewCube tool to change your display orientation.

   - In the upper left corner of your drawing, move the cursor to the ViewCube.
   - Select the clockwise arrow to rotate the view 90 degrees.

7 Verify that your view looks like the following illustration.

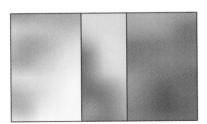

8   Use the Project tool to create geometry for the sketched feature.

- On the ribbon, click Project Geometry.
- Select the edges marked (A), (B), (C), (D), and (E).
  Note: Some edges may have been automatically projected when you created the sketch. If so, delete those edges and project only the edges shown.

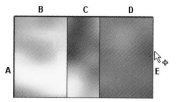

9   Using the Line tool, sketch the line segments for the profile as shown.

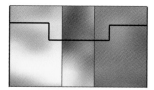

10   Apply a colinear constraint to the two lines marked (A) and (B).

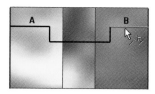

11   Apply a horizontal constraint to the midpoint of line (C) and the midpoint of the bottom edge (D).

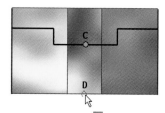

12   Apply parametric dimensions to the sketch.

- Start the General Dimension tool.
- Place dimensions as shown here.
- Right-click anywhere in the graphics window. Click Done.

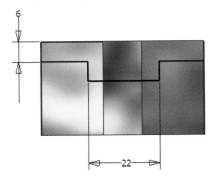

13   Right-click anywhere in the graphics window. Click Home View.

14   On the ribbon, click Finish Sketch to exit the sketch.

15   Extrude the new sketch and remove material from the part.

- Start the Extrude tool.
- In the graphics window, select the profile shown.
- For Distance, enter **48 mm**.
- Select Cut and make certain the extrude direction is as shown.
- Click OK.

16   Close all files. Do not save.

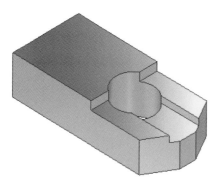

Create Extruded Features to Existing Geometry

In this portion of the exercise, you create a new sketch and extrude it to a point on the part to create a sketched feature.

1   Open *Index-Slide2.ipt*.

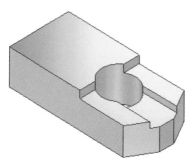

2   Turn on the Autoproject Edges option for sketching.
   • Click Tools tab > Options panel > Application Options.
   • In the Options dialog box, Sketch tab, select the Autoproject Edges for Sketch Creation and Edit option.
   • If this option is already checked, leave it as is.
   • Click Close.

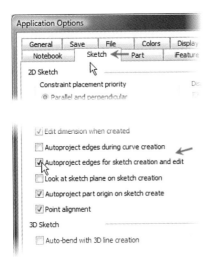

3 Right-click the top face of the part. Click New Sketch.

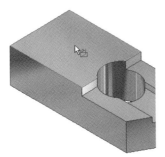

4 Change your view to look normal to the sketch plane.
 • On the Navigation bar, click View Face.
 • Select the top face of the part.

5   Using the Center Point circle tool, create two concentric circles.

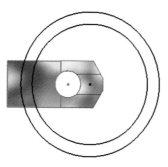

6   Apply a horizontal constraint to the sketched circles.
   • Start the Horizontal constraint tool.
   • Select the centerpoints marked (A) and (B).
   • Right-click anywhere in the graphics window.
   • Click Done.

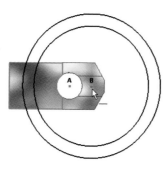

7   Remove a portion of the sketched circles.
   • On the Sketch tab, click Modify panel > Trim.
   • Select the circles at a point outside of the boundary of the part.

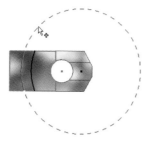

8   Use the General Dimension tool to locate and size the sketch.

- Start the General Dimension tool.
- Place dimensions on the arcs and center point as shown.

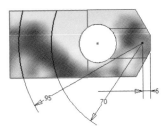

9   Return to the home view.

10   On the ribbon, click Finish Sketch to exit the sketch.

11   To extrude the new sketch to a specific point on the part, start the Extrude tool.

- Select the profile created by the two arcs (1).
- In the Extents list, select To.
- Select the corner vertex point (2) for the To point.
- Click the Cut operation option. Click OK.

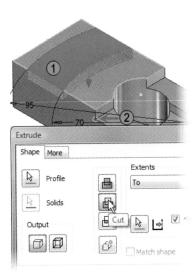

12 Close all files. Do not save.

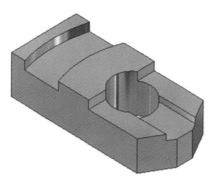

Exercise | Create Revolved Features

In this exercise, you create a simple Indexer part file using the Revolve tool. The origin Z axis is projected on the first sketch and changed to a centerline. You use the Project Geometry and Project Cut Edges tools to create different profiles to be revolved.

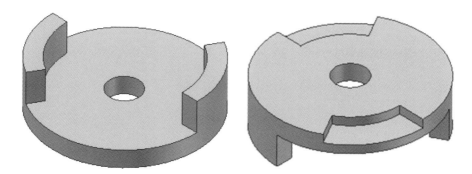

The completed exercise

Completing the Exercise:

To complete the exercise, follow the steps in this book or in the onscreen exercise. In the onscreen list of chapters and exercises, click Chapter 3: Basic Shape Design. Click Exercise: Create Revolved Features.

Create Revolved Features that Add Material to the Part

In this portion of the exercise, you create a sketch and revolve it into the base feature. You create another sketch and revolve it, creating another sketched feature that adds material to the part.

1   Open *Indexer.ipt.*

2   In the browser, double-click Sketch1.

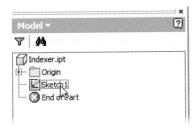

3   Change your display to a view that is normal to the sketch.
- On the Navigation bar, click View Face.
- In the browser, select Sketch1.

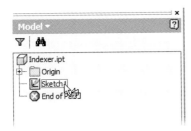

4   Use the Two Point Rectangle tool and sketch a rectangle similar to the following illustration.

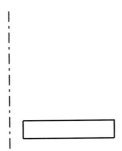

5   Use the General Dimension tool to dimension the sketch as shown here.

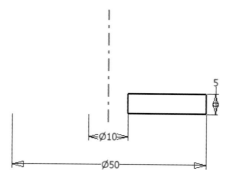

6   Switch to the home view.

7   On the ribbon, click Finish Sketch to exit the sketch.

8   Start the Revolve tool.
- The profile is selected automatically because it is the only closed profile on the sketch.
- The centerline is also selected automatically as the axis.
- Click OK to accept the default settings.

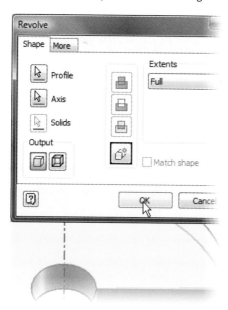

9   Create a new sketch using the default XZ plane.

  - Start the Create 2D Sketch tool.
  - In the browser, expand the origin folder.
  - Select the XZ Plane.

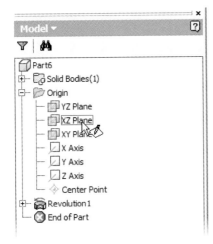

10   Press F7 to activate the Slice Graphics mode. This viewing mode slices the graphics at the location of the current sketch. It is available only in sketch mode.

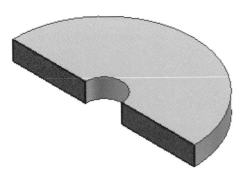

11 Start the Project Cut Edges tool. Reference geometry is created based on the location of the current sketch as it passes through the part.

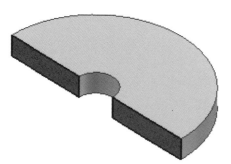

12 Use the Project Geometry tool to create an axis for the Revolve feature.

- Start the Project Geometry tool.
- In the browser, select the Z axis. This projects the origin Z axis onto the current sketch.

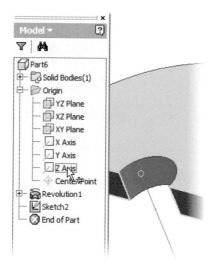

13 Create new sketch geometry.

- Start the Two Point Rectangle tool.
- Sketch two rectangles as shown.

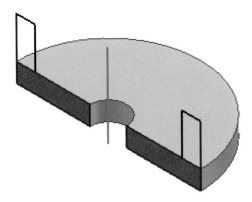

14 Apply a colinear constraint to the edges marked (A) and (B).

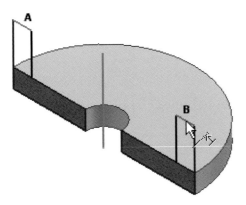

15 Complete the sketch by adding dimension constraints.

- Start General Dimension.
- Dimension the sketch geometry as shown.

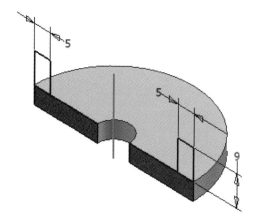

16 On the ribbon, click Finish Sketch to exit the sketch.

17 To revolve the new sketch, start the Revolve tool.

- Select the profiles as shown.
- Click Axis. Select the line created from the projection of the Z axis.

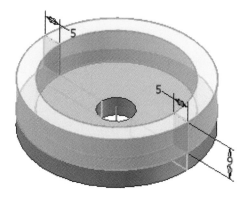

18   Complete the settings for the revolved feature.

  - From the Extents list, select Angle.
  - For Angle, enter **60 deg**.
  - Select Flip Direction if required to match the following illustration.
  - Click OK.

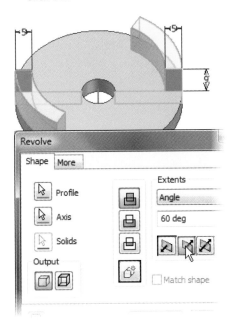

19   Close all files. Do not save.

Create Revolved Features that Remove Material from the Part

In this portion of the exercise, you use Revolve to create an additional sketched feature that removes material from the part.

1   Open *Indexer.ipt*.

2   Begin a sketch by using the YZ plane in the browser.
   - Start the Create 2D Sketch tool.
   - In the browser, expand the Origin node and select the YZ plane.

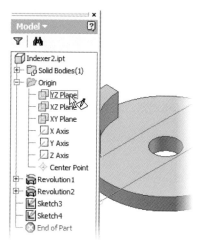

3   Press F7 to switch to Slice Graphics mode.

4   Start the Project Cut Edges tool.

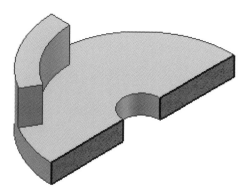

5   Sketch and constrain two rectangles.

- Start the Two Point Rectangle tool.
- Sketch two rectangles as shown.
- Use the General Dimension tool to apply the dimensions as shown.

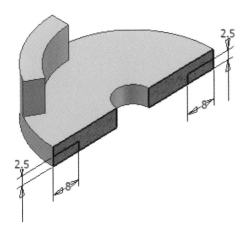

6   Project the Z axis for use in the Revolve operation.

- Start the Project Geometry tool.
- In the browser, select the Z axis.

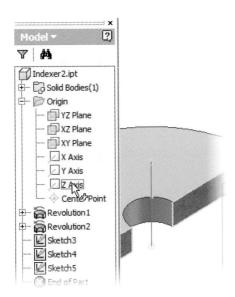

7 Right-click in the graphics window. Click Done.

8 Revolve the two rectangles to remove material from the part.

- Right-click in the graphics window. Click Create Feature > Revolve.
- Select the two profiles as shown.
- Click Axis.
- Select the line that was projected from the Z axis.

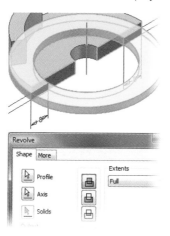

9 Complete the settings for the revolved feature.

- From the Extents list, select Angle.
- In the Angle field, enter **60**.
- Click Cut Feature Relationship.
- Click OK.

10 Change your display by using Orbit.

- On the Navigation bar, click Orbit.
- Rotate your part to view the cuts on the bottom of the part.

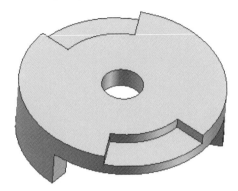

11 Close all files. Do not save.

Lesson 08 | Intermediate Sketching

This lesson describes the use of reference and construction geometry to add design intelligence to sketches on your parts. As your part progresses, you add multiple sketched features. Each sketch may require the use of reference and construction geometry to fully constrain your sketches.

In the following illustration, reference geometry and construction lines are used to constrain the rectangle geometry on the face of the part.

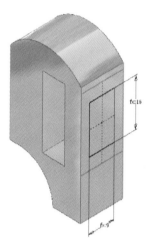

Objectives

After completing this lesson, you will be able to:

- Describe sketch linetypes and their behavior.

- Use the 2D sketch tools to create construction geometry.

- Project part edges onto a sketch plane.

About Sketch Linetypes

As your part design progresses, you need additional sketching tools to capture design intent within your sketch and to establish parametric relationships to existing faces and edges on your 3D part. As you create 2D sketch geometry, such as lines, arcs, circles, and prismatic shapes, you can use different linetypes for different purposes.

In the following example, several linetypes are used to define, position, and constrain geometry on the part.

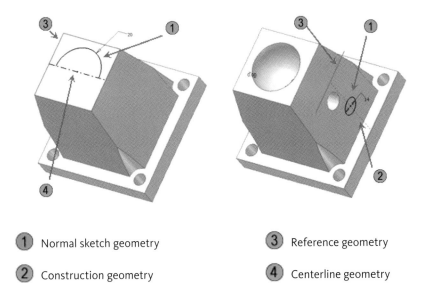

① Normal sketch geometry

② Construction geometry

③ Reference geometry

④ Centerline geometry

Definition of Sketch Linetypes

The following illustration shows the appearance of the different linetypes. Different linetypes display in different colors in the sketch environment; however the exact color is based on the color scheme you have selected. In the following illustration, using the Presentation scheme, lines 2 and 3 are displayed orange, while the reference geometry (4) is green. The reference geometry consists of projected edges of the solid model (arrows).

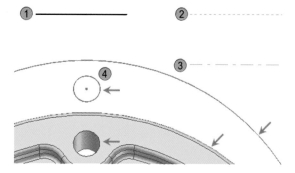

Sketch Linetypes

The following are the different linetypes and how they are used.

	Linetype	Description
1	**Normal**	This is the default linetype in a sketch. Normal lines define the profile or path that is used to define the shape of a sketched feature.
2	**Construction**	Construction lines are used to aid in constructing and constraining normal geometry. You use construction lines when you need additional geometry to constrain a sketch but do not want that additional geometry to participate in defining the profile for the feature.
3	**Centerline**	The Centerline linetype is another type of Construction linetype. It can be used to define the centerline about which to revolve a profile to create a revolved feature. When you add dimensions between centerlines and other sketch geometry, they are treated as diameter dimensions.
4	**Reference**	Reference geometry is geometry that is projected onto your sketch from existing part vertices, edges, and faces. You use reference geometry to constrain normal sketch geometry to existing features on the part. Reference geometry remains associative to the original part vertices, edges, and faces. You can also use reference geometry to define the profile or path for a sketched feature.

Normal Linetype Example

The notched rectangle sketch on the left, consumed in the block feature on the right, has been created with the Normal linetype. While sketching, normal lines are represented as solid lines.

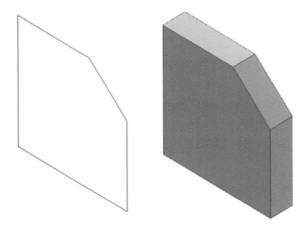

Construction Linetype Example

In the following example, the diagonal dotted line in the left image is a construction line. The endpoints of the construction line are constrained to the opposite corners of the face. The midpoint of the construction line is used to orient the center of the circle, which is defined with a normal linetype. The circle is then extruded with the Cut option to define a shaft opening in this block.

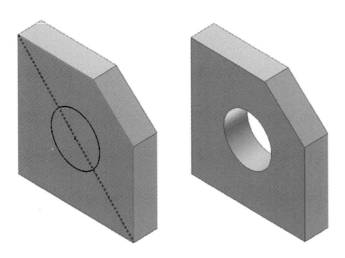

Reference Geometry Example

The current sketch plane in this example is coplanar with the side of the base of the part. Reference geometry is projected to the sketch plane from the perimeter of the part, from the hole through the part, and from the spherical cutout on the top.

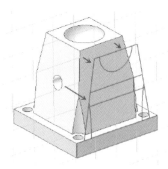

Centerline Linetype Example

The dashdot line on the left is a centerline. The circle is revolved around the centerline to create the torus feature on the right.

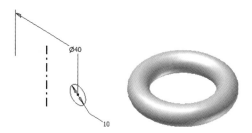

Creating and Using Construction Geometry

You can use construction geometry to help you control and define a sketch by using geometric construction techniques rather than complex dimensions and formulas. You can constrain and dimension construction geometry like any other 2D sketch geometry. You can use construction geometry as a reference for dimensions to other normal sketch geometry, as well as to constrain normal sketch geometry.

In the following illustration, construction lines (1) are used to position the slot from the center of the circle and along the angled construction line.

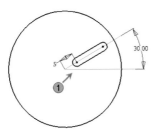

Tools for Creating Construction and Centerline Geometry

The ribbon contains two buttons for creating construction and centerline geometry. Unlike other toolbar buttons, these buttons also indicate the current status of the selected geometry or drawing mode. When you click a button, you activate that specific mode. The selected mode remains active until you click the button again.

Access

Construction Geometry

Ribbon: **Sketch tab > Format panel**

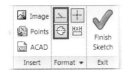

You can use the following buttons to create or change existing geometry types.

Icon	Option	Description
	Construction Geometry	When this button is selected, all 2D geometry drawn is construction geometry. To change existing geometry to construction, select the geometry, then click this button.
	Centerline Geometry	When this button is selected, all 2D geometry drawn is centerline geometry. To change existing geometry to centerline, select the geometry, then click this button.

> **Tip:** *To convert normal geometry or dimensions, select the geometry or dimension and then click the appropriate button on the ribbon.*

Procedure: Creating Construction Geometry

The following steps outline the procedure for creating construction geometry.

1   On the ribbon, click the Construction tool.

2   Using standard sketching tools, create the required 2D geometry. In the following example, a construction line was sketched between the opposite corners of a rectangle. The lines defining the rectangle are normal sketch lines.

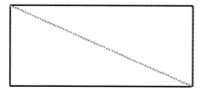

3   Click the Construction tool again to return to creating normal sketch geometry.

Procedure: Converting Existing Geometry to Construction Geometry

The following steps outline the procedure for converting existing sketch geometry to construction geometry.

1   To change existing geometry to construction geometry, select the geometry in the graphics window. In the following example, a circle was selected.

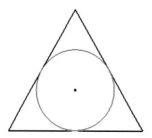

2   On the ribbon, click the Construction button. The selected geometry is changed to construction geometry.

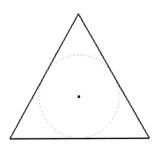

Procedure: Creating Centerline Geometry

The following steps outline the procedure for creating centerline geometry.

1   On the ribbon, click the Centerline tool.

2   Using standard sketching tools, create the required 2D geometry. In the following example, a vertical centerline was sketched to the left of the normal sketch geometry.

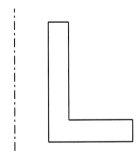

3   Click the Centerline tool again to return to creating normal sketch geometry.

Procedure: Converting Existing Geometry to Centerline Geometry

The following steps outline the procedure for converting existing sketch geometry to centerline geometry.

1   To change existing geometry to centerline geometry, select the geometry in the graphics window.
    In the following example, a horizontal line that bisects the slot shape is selected.

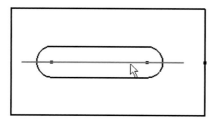

2   On the ribbon, click the Centerline button. The selected geometry is changed to centerline geometry.

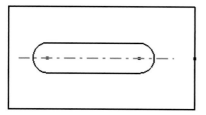

Creating and Using Reference Geometry

Reference geometry is geometry that is created when existing vertices and edges of the part are projected onto the active sketch plane. Reference geometry is not drawn; rather it is created when you define a new sketch plane on a planar face of the part or by using the Project Geometry tool. Without reference geometry, you cannot dimension or constrain sketch geometry to the existing features on the 3D part.

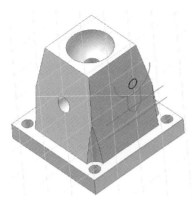

New Sketches and Reference Geometry

When you create new sketches on a planar face of the part, the edges of the selected face are automatically projected onto the sketch as reference geometry. You can use this reference geometry:

- To dimension to other sketch geometry.

- For relational constraints to other sketch geometry.

- As the basis for defining the path or profile for a sketched feature.

The example on the following page demonstrates how reference geometry is created and used when defining a new sketch on an existing part face.

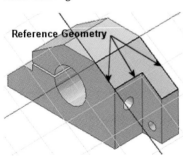

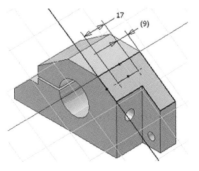

A new sketch is created on an existing part face. The coplanar edges of the existing part face are automatically projected onto the new sketch.

Create additional sketch geometry and use the projected reference geometry for dimensions or constraints.

Project Geometry Tool

You use the Project Geometry tool to project additional part vertices and edges that are not coplanar to the sketch plane onto the sketch as reference geometry. When you use the Project Geometry tool, you are prompted to select geometry to project onto the current sketch plane. As you select the geometry, it is projected onto the current sketch plane as reference geometry and is always associative to the original source geometry. This means that if the source geometry changes, the reference geometry also changes. However, after a reference geometry linetype is changed to another linetype, it loses its associativity.

Projecting Part Edges

Following are some key attributes for projecting part edges:

- Can be used as the basis for dimensions to new sketch geometry

- Can be used to apply relational constraints to new sketch geometry

- Cannot be dimensioned

- Cannot be trimmed

- Can be mirrored

- Cannot be drawn; can only be created by using Project Geometry tool or by selecting the Autoproject Edges option

Access

Project Geometry

Ribbon: **Sketch tab › Draw panel**

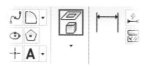

Toolbar: **2D Sketch Panel**

Autoproject Options

You can use the Autoproject functionality to speed projection of geometry to the sketch plane.

Autoproject for Sketch Creation

When you place a check in the box next to the Autoproject Edges for Sketch Creation and Edit option on the Sketch tab in the Application Options dialog box, the edges of the selected planar face are automatically projected onto the new sketch when you create a new sketch plane on an existing face.

Autoproject Edges

When the Autoproject Edges During Curve Creation option is selected, you can autoproject geometry by hovering the pointer over the geometry to be projected while sketching.

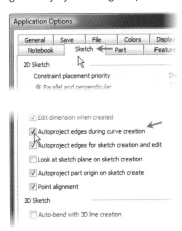

Sketching Shortcut Menu

While sketching, right-click in the drawing area and click AutoProject. This enables you to hover over geometry to automatically project onto the current sketch plane.

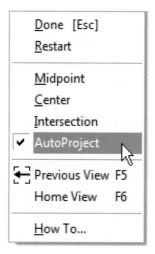

Procedure: Referencing Model Edge Geometry

The following steps outline how to create reference geometry during curve creation in a sketch by autoprojecting model edge geometry.

1   Create a new sketch on the existing part.

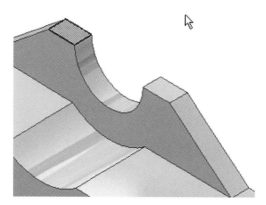

2 Begin sketching the required geometry. Right-click in the graphics window and click
   AutoProject on the shortcut menu.

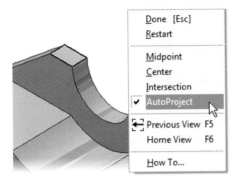

3 Hover over the geometry to project. It is automatically projected to the current sketch plane.

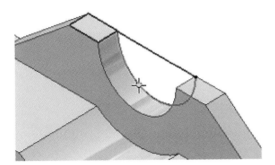

4 Continue sketching the required geometry as required.
   Tip: You may consider turning off the AutoProject option until it is needed again. This action
   prevents the accidental projection of geometry while sketching over existing part features.

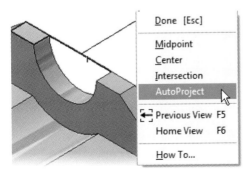

Exercise | Create a Part Using Construction and Reference Geometry

In this exercise, you apply the Construction and Center line attributes to sketch geometry. You also project and use reference geometry to create and constrain sketch features.

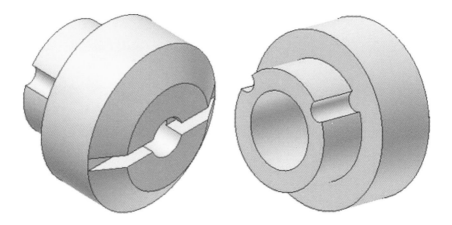

The completed exercise

Completing the Exercise:	*To complete the exercise, follow the steps in this book or in the onscreen exercise. In the onscreen list of chapters and exercises, click Chapter 3: Basic Shape Design. Click Exercise: Create a Part Using Construction and Reference Geometry.*

1 Create a new part using the *Standard (mm).ipt* template.

   - On the Quick Access toolbar, click New.
   - In the New File dialog box, click the Metric tab.
   - Select Standard (mm).ipt.
   - Click OK.

2 Click the Tools tab > Application Options.

   - On the Sketch tab, clear both of the options to autoproject edges.
   - Click OK or Close.

- [ ] Snap to grid
- [x] Edit dimension when created
- [ ] Autoproject edges during curve creation
- [ ] Autoproject edges for sketch creation and edit
- [ ] Look at sketch plane on sketch creation
- [x] Autoproject part origin on sketch create
- [x] Point alignment

3D Sketch
- [ ] Auto-bend with 3D line creation

3 Turn on the centerline linetype.

On the Sketch tab, click Centerline. The button is displayed with a blue background when active.

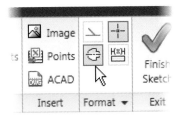

4 Start your sketch by creating a vertical centerline.

- Sketch a vertical line approximately **50 mm** long.
- Right-click and click Done.
- On the ribbon, click Centerline to turn off centerline. The button is displayed without a blue background when off.

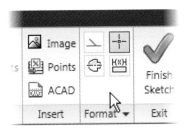

5   Sketch and constrain the remaining objects as shown.

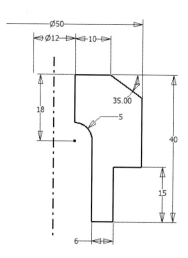

6   Right-click anywhere in the graphics window. Click Home View.

7   Revolve the sketch around the centerline using an Extents value of Full. Your profile and axis are selected automatically when you start the Revolve tool.

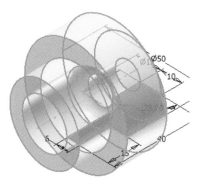

8   On the Quick Access toolbar, select Blue Pastel in the Color list.

9   Create a new sketch plane and project a circle as reference geometry.
   • Rotate your view as shown.
   • Create a sketch plane on the top of the part as shown.
   • On the Sketch tab, click Project Geometry. Select the large diameter to project it to the sketch plane.

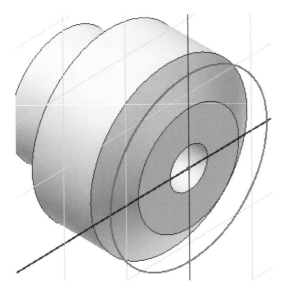

10 Sketch and constrain a rectangle using the projected reference geometry.

- Sketch a rectangle and add the 4 mm general dimension.
- Use a tangent constraint on each end of the rectangle to the reference circle.
- Use a horizontal constraint between the midpoint of the left side of the rectangle and the center point of the reference geometry to locate the rectangle centered on the part.

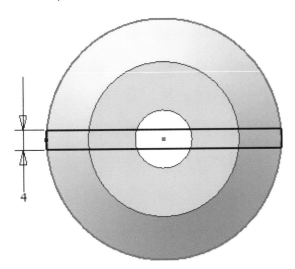

11   Extrude the rectangle sketch using the Cut option and a distance of 6.3 mm as shown.

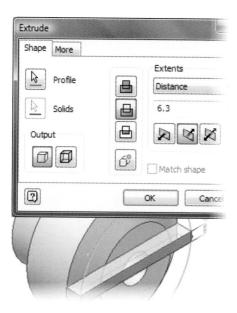

12   Create a new sketch plane on the bottom of the part.

- Create a new sketch plane on the bottom surface as shown.
- Use the Project Geometry tool and select the outside edge of the sketch face to project it as reference geometry.

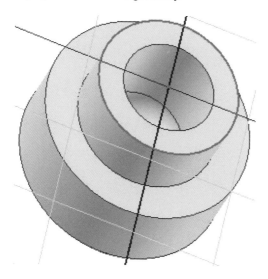

13   Create construction geometry that you use to locate a new sketch.

- On the ribbon, click Construction to turn on the Construction linetype.
- Sketch three separate lines (1) as shown.
  Tip: Right-click and click Restart to sketch separate lines.
- If necessary, use a coincident constraint to constrain the endpoints to the center of the circle (2).
- On the ribbon, click Construction to turn off the Construction linetype.

14   Add the following dimensions to the construction lines.

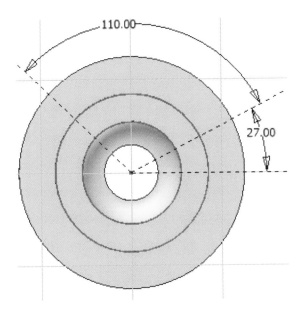

15 Add geometry constrained to the construction geometry and reference geometry.

- Draw two circles as shown.
- Use coincident constraints to constrain the circles to both the construction geometry (1) and the reference geometry (2).
- Dimension the circles as shown.

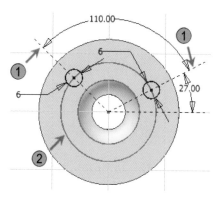

16 Complete the feature by extruding the new sketch with a cut operation.

- Start the Extrude tool.
- Select the two sketch circles for the profile and click the Cut option.
- For Extents select To. Select the circular face as shown. Click OK to create the extrusion.

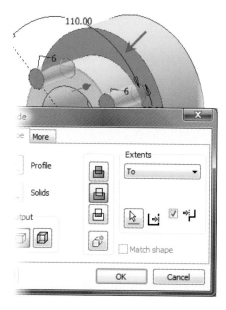

17   Your completed extrusion looks like the following illustration. Save your part with the name *Latch-Nut.ipt* and close all files.

Lesson 09 | Editing Parametric Parts

This lesson describes the various methods used to make changes to parametric part models. You can edit sketches, modify features, and create and use parameters while making modifications to your models.

Statistics show that designers spend more time making part modification and engineering changes than they spend creating new parts. You need to be able to modify your existing part models accurately and efficiently.

The following illustration shows a parametric part model before and after implementing changes to existing features.

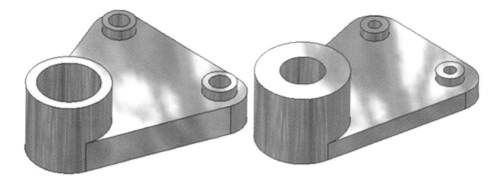

Objectives

After completing this lesson, you will be able to:

- Edit features from the browser.

- Edit sketches from the browser or toolbar.

- Create and modify parameters and equations.

Editing Features

After you create features on your parametric part, you can modify those features at any time. Sometimes all you need to change is the size of the feature. Other times you may need to make a more significant change. Autodesk Inventor provides multiple options for editing your designs.

The following illustration shows a part model before, and then after the extrusion distance was modified.

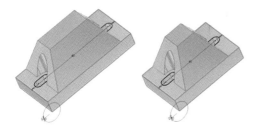

Options for Editing Features

There are three basic ways to modify features on your parametric parts. With both sketched and placed features, you can display and modify the dimensions to simply change the size of the feature, or you can access the feature dialog box to make a more significant change, like changing an operation, extrusion direction, or the extents of the feature. For sketched features you also have the option to modify the sketch geometry. For example, you can add and delete dimensions or constraints, or you can even modify the shape of the sketch by changing the sketch geometry.

In the following illustration, the left browser image shows the three options for editing a sketched feature. The browser image on the right shows the two options for editing placed features.

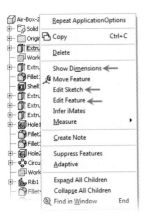 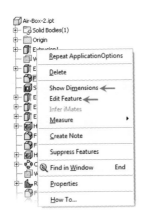

Editing Features Using Show Dimensions

If you want to change the size of a feature, you can use the Show Dimensions option to change the value of an existing dimension. All sketch dimensions are displayed as well as other dimensions that are used to define the feature size, such as extrusion depth, revolution angle, or taper value.

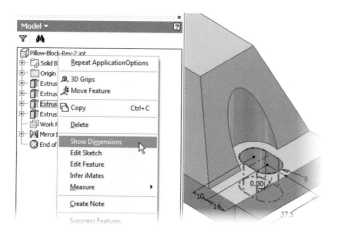

Editing Features Using Edit Feature

When you use the Edit Feature option to edit a feature, you are presented with the same dialog box that you used when you created the feature. You can change the parameters, such as distance, feature relationships, and termination options. You can also reselect geometry to be included in the feature.

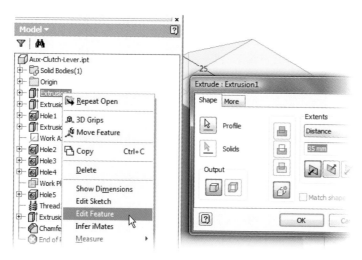

Access

Show Dimensions

Browser: **Double-click the feature**. **Note:** Dimensions are only visible on the underlying sketch while the feature is being edited.

Browser: **Right-click the feature > Show Dimensions.**

Access

Edit Feature

Browser: **Double-click the feature.**

Browser: **Right-click the feature > Edit Feature.**

Procedure: Modifying a Feature Using Show Dimensions

The following steps describe how to edit a feature using the Show Dimensions option.

1   Right-click the feature in the browser and click Show Dimensions. All the controlling dimensions are displayed on the feature in the graphics window.

2   Double-click the dimension to modify and enter a new value in the Edit Dimension dialog box.

3   Click Update on the Standard toolbar to apply the changes to the part.

Procedure: Modifying a Placed Feature Using Edit Feature

The following steps describe how to edit a placed feature using the Edit Feature option.

1   Right-click the feature in the browser and click Edit Feature. The dialog box used to create the feature is displayed.

2   Change the settings or values in the dialog box, then click OK. The part
     automatically updates.

Procedure: Editing Extruded Features

The following steps describe how to edit extruded features.

1   In the browser, right-click the feature. Click Edit Feature.

2   In the Extrude dialog box, adjust the options as required to edit the feature.

Procedure: Editing Revolved Features

The following steps describe how to edit revolved features.

1   In the browser, right-click the feature. Click Edit Feature.

2   In the Revolve dialog box, adjust the options as required.

Editing Sketches

As you build your parametric model, you create multiple sketches. When the sketch is used by a feature such as Extrude or Revolve, the sketch becomes consumed by the feature and is displayed under the feature in the browser. You can see each of the sketches in the browser by expanding the particular feature(s). Even though this sketch is consumed by the feature, it can still be modified.

The following illustration shows how sketches are consumed by the feature for which they are used.

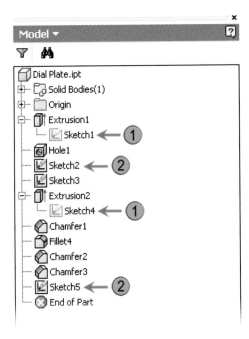

① The Extrusion1 feature has consumed Sketch1 and Extrusion2 has consumed Sketch4.

② Sketch2 and Sketch5 are unconsumed sketches

Editing Consumed Sketches

One powerful way to modify a feature is to edit the sketch. Editing the sketch places the model in a rolled-back state, where only the features existing at the time this sketch was created are visible. When you edit sketches, you are returned to the sketch environment and the panel bar changes, providing you with access to all the sketch tools initially used in creating the sketch. You can add, replace, or delete dimensions or constraints and even modify the sketch geometry. To return to the part modeling environment, click Return on the Standard toolbar.

In the following illustration, Sketch1 has been consumed by Extrusion1 in the browser. You can expand the Extrusion1 feature to expose and edit the consumed sketch. Notice the browser background color changes to indicate the active sketch.

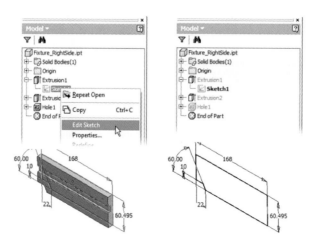

Access

Edit Sketch

Browser: **Double-click the sketch.**
Browser: **Right-click the feature > Edit Sketch.**
Toolbar**: Standard > Sketch > Select the sketch in the browser.**

Procedure: Editing Sketches

The following steps describe how to edit sketches.

1   In the browser, right-click the feature or sketch, and click Edit Sketch.

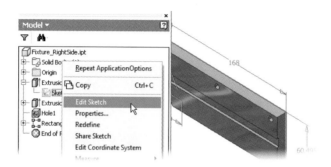

2   After the sketch has been activated for editing, you can make changes to geometry, dimensions, and constraints.

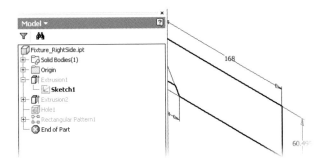

3   Continue to make edits to the sketch as required.

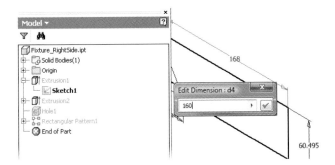

4   When you have finished editing the sketch, on the ribbon, click Finish Sketch to exit the sketch and return to the part model. The changes in the sketch are applied to the 3D features of the part.

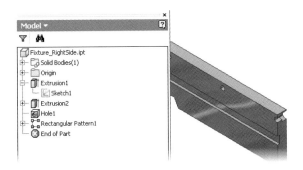

Using Parameters

When you establish a relationship between one dimension and another, you can incorporate basic design intent into your model and quickly modify a model. You can define and control complex relationships by creating mathematical equations in a dimension or user-defined parameter. Equations can range from simple equations to more complex equations that include complex internal parameters.

The Parameters dialog box is shown here. The User Parameters are expanded to show there are two user parameters for hole spacing and the space for each hole.

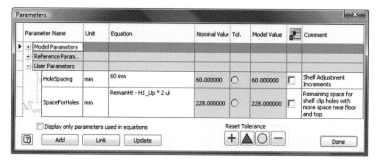

Access

Parameters

Ribbon: **Manage tab > Parameters panel**

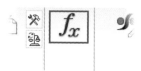

Note: *To establish a valid relationship to a parameter name, the spelling and capitalization must exactly match the name displayed in the Parameters dialog box. Select a custom parameter name from the list to ensure that spelling and capitalization match.*

Parameters Dialog Box

The Parameters dialog box is displayed when you start the Parameters tool.

The following illustration shows the Parameters dialog box with model, reference, and user parameters. Notice that some model parameters were renamed to clarify use and facilitate access. The equations in this example range from a single numeric value to more complex equations that use functions and parameters.

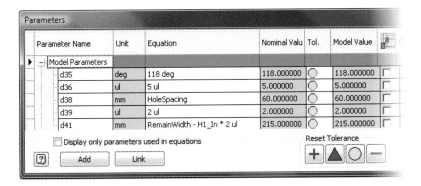

Managing Parameters

Every dimension that you add when you create or assemble parts is accessible in the Parameters dialog box. You can manage parameters in the Parameters dialog box to accomplish the following tasks:

- Create new user parameters.

- Change the name of model and user parameters to add meaning. For example, you can give model parameters a generic letter d and an incremental number (do, d1, d2, and so on).

- Change the unit of measure to match your design data. For example, you can create a user parameter to store a volume value and use it later in an equation to calculate the size of a part.

- Establish a mathematical equation to calculate a value.

- Add or adjust the tolerance or precision for a dimension.

- Adjust a dimension with tolerances at the maximum, minimum, median, or nominal value.

- Select a parameter to export to a custom iProperty value.

- Add a general comment to explain the function or purpose of a parameter.

List Parameters

You can select an existing custom parameter name for any dimension value. Right-click the value or click the arrow button on the right side of the value and click List Parameters to display a list of available custom parameter names.

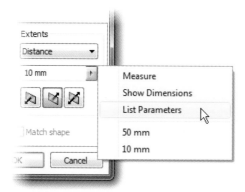

In this image, you right-click the value 10 or click List Parameters.

This image shows the Parameters list that opens when you click List Parameters.

Using Equations and Parameters

You can use equations wherever you can enter a numeric value. For example, you can write equations in the Edit Dimension dialog box, feature dialog boxes, and the Parameters dialog box. Equations can vary in complexity, and you can use them to calculate feature sizes, calculate assembly constraint offsets or angles, or simulate motion among several components.

Equations can be simple or contain many algebraic operators, prefixes, and functions. For example, here is a simple equation:

```
2 ul * (6 + 3)
```

The following complex equation uses internal parameters such as pi:

```
( PI rad /5 ul + (25 deg * PI rad / 180 deg ) )
```

Operator	Meaning
+	addition
-	subtraction
%	floating point modulo
*	multiplication
/	division
^	power
(	expression delimiter
)	expression delimiter
;	delimiter for multiargument functions

Supported Algebraic Operators

The following table lists the algebraic operators supported by Autodesk Inventor.

Prefix	Symbol	Value
exa	E	1.0e18
peta	P	1.0e15
tera	T	1.0e12
giga	G	1.0e9
mega	M	1.0e6
kilo	k	1.0e3
hecto	h	1.0e2

Prefix	Symbol	Value
deca	da	1.0e1
deci	d	1.0e-1
centi	c	1.0e-2
milli	m	1.0e-3
micro	micro	1.0e-6
nano	n	1.0e-9
pico	p	1.0e-12
femto	f	1.0e-15
atto	a	1.0e-18

When you use unit prefixes in an equation, enter the prefix symbol. Do not enter the prefix itself. For example, an equation that includes the unit *nanometer* might look like this: 3.5 ul * 2.6 nm.

When you add the unit prefix for nano to the meter unit, your equation is calculated based on the length of 2.6 nanometers.

Note: *Prefix symbols are case sensitive. You must enter them exactly as they appear in the previous table.*

Supported Functions

The following table lists the supported functions.

Syntax	Returns Unit Type	Expected Unit Type
cos(expr)	unitless	angle
sin(expr)	unitless	angle
tan(expr)	unitless	angle
acos(expr)	angle	unitless
asin(expr)	angle	unitless
atan(expr)	angle	unitless
cosh(expr)	unitless	angle
tanh(expr)	unitless	angle
acosh(expr)	angle	unitless
asinh(expr)	angle	unitless
sqrt(expr)	unit^1/2	any
sign(expr	unitless	any (Return 0 if negative, 1 if positive.)
exp(expr)	unitless	any (Return exponential power of expression; for example, return 2 for 100, 3 for 1000, and so on.)
floor(expr)	unitless	any (Return exponential power of expression; for example, return 2 for 100, 3 for 1000, and so on.)
ceil(expr)	unitless	unitless (Next highest whole number.)
abs(expr)	any	any

Syntax	Returns Unit Type	Expected Unit Type
max(expr1;expr2)	any	any
min(expr1;expr2)	any	any
ln(expr)	unitless	unitless
log(expr	unitless	unitless
pow(expr1;expr2)	unit^expr2	any and unitless, respectively
random(expr)	unitless	unitless
isolate(expr;unit;unit)	any	any

 Note: *Function names are case sensitive. You must enter them exactly as they appear in the previous table.*

Unit Types

The unit type that you use with an equation depends on the type of data that you are evaluating. For example, to evaluate a linear or angular value, you typically use a unit type of millimeters, inches, or degrees (mm, in, or deg).

Some equations must return a unitless value, for example, an equation to solve the number of occurrences in a pattern. You designate a unitless value with the characters ul. For example, 5 ul means that the equation has been evaluated and returned the number 5, as in the number of occurrences in a pattern.

Note: **Unit Types: Keep Them Consistent** *Keep units consistent within equations containing parameters that represent different unit types. You can do this using the Isolate function. For example, to calculate the number of occurrences for a pattern that is based on one occurrence for each unit of a parameter named Width, your linear equation would be:*

isolate(Width;mm;ul)

The Number of Occurrences value in a dialog box requires a unitless (ul) result, but you are referencing the unit width, which is a linear value. Therefore, you must convert the Width parameter to a unitless value.

The following illustration shows how to break down the equation.

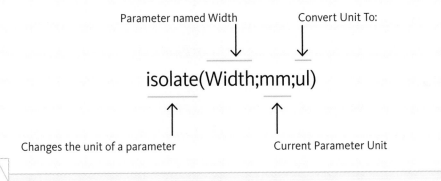

Order of Algebraic Operations

Equations are evaluated from the inside out, and evaluation precedence is given to functions. For example, in the equation **(15 * (25 + 3))**, 25+3 is evaluated first, and the sum is multiplied by 15. The result is 420.

The following table shows the algebraic operations in descending order.

Operation	Symbol	Example
parentheses	( )	(abs(5 * -2))
exponentiation	^	Length^2
negation	-	(-4.00 + Width)
multiplication or division	* or /	(Length * Width) or (Length / Width)
addition or subtraction	+ or -	(-5.00 + Length - 0.50 * Width)

 Tip: **Equation Color.** *When you create equations, the equation text is displayed in red until it is considered valid. At that point, the equation text turns black.*

Procedure: Using Equations in Dimensions

The following steps outline how to use equations in dimensions.

1   On the ribbon, click the General Dimension tool.

2   Select the geometry that you want to dimension.

3   Place the dimension.

4   In the Edit Dimension dialog box, enter the equation.

5   Click the check mark icon to accept the value.

Procedure: Using Equations in a Dialog Box

The following steps outline how to use equations in a dialog box.

1   On the ribbon, click the feature type that you want to create.

2   Select the geometry required for the feature.

3   Enter the equation in any text box that requires a numerical value.

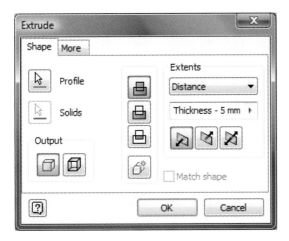

4   Click OK to create the feature and close the dialog box.

Exercise | Edit Parametric Parts

In this exercise, you implement changes to the clutch lever by editing sketches and features. You discover that changing one feature may create problems with other features that you will then need to edit as well.

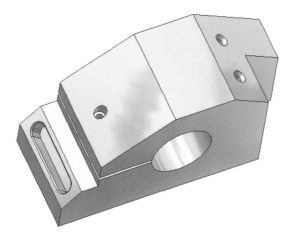

The completed exercise

Completing the Exercise: To complete the exercise, follow the steps in this book or in the onscreen exercise. In the onscreen list of chapters and exercises, click Chapter 3: Basic Shape Design. Click Exercise: Edit Parametric Parts.

1   Open *Aux-Clutch-Lever.ipt*.

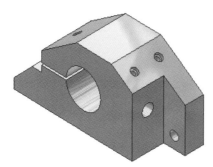

2   Display the dimensions on the original base sketch for editing:

   - In the browser, right-click Extrusion1.
   - Click Show Dimensions.

3   Modify the leftmost 25 mm dimension:

   - Double-click the leftmost 25 mm dimension and change it to **30 mm**.
   - On the Quick Access toolbar, click Update.

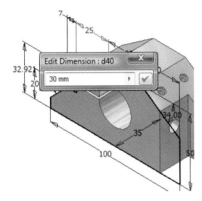

4   The previous edit caused a problem with Extrusion3. You now edit Extrusion3 to correct its size:

   - In the browser, right-click Extrusion3.
   - Click Edit Sketch.

5   Add a colinear constraint to control the left edge of the slot:

   - On the ribbon, click the Colinear constraint tool.
   - Select the left edge of the sketch and set it colinear to the left edge of the feature as shown.
   - On the ribbon, click Finish Sketch.

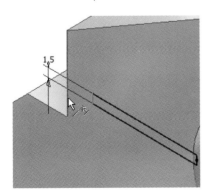

6   Change the counterbore holes to countersink clearance holes:

- In the browser, right-click Hole4. Click Edit Feature.
- In the Hole dialog box, set hole type to Countersink (1) and Clearance (2) by clicking the option button as shown.
- Under Fastener, for Standard, select Ansi Metric M Profile (3).
- For Fastener Type, select Flat Head Machine Screw (4).
- For Size, select M2.5 (5). Click OK.

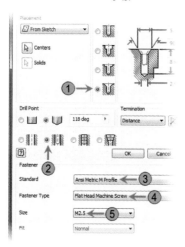

7   Modify the depth of the main extrusion:

- In the browser, double-click Extrusion1. The Extrude dialog box is displayed.
- Change the 35 mm depth dimension and change it to **40 mm** as shown.
- Click OK.

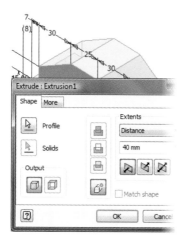

8   Modify the slot size of Extrusion4:

- In the browser, expand Extrusion4.
- Double-click Sketch10 to display its dimensions on the model.
- Using the ViewCube tool, reorient the part as shown.
- Double-click the 20 mm dimension and change it to **25 mm** as shown.
- On the Quick Access toolbar, click Return.

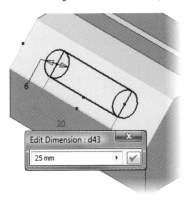

9   Change the size of the chamfer on the Extrusion4 slot:

- In the browser, right-click Chamfer1. Click Edit Feature.
- Change the Distance value to **0.5 mm**.
- Click OK to implement the change.

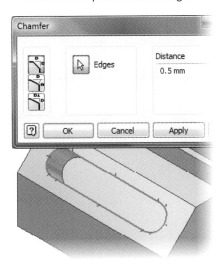

10 Close all files. Do not save.

Exercise | Create Parameters and Equations

In this exercise, you change the names of some of the existing dimensions to make them easier to identify and reference. You also create relational dimensions, dimensions that include both equations and parameters, and a user parameter.

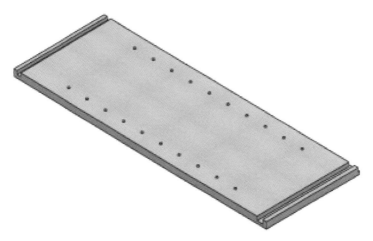

The completed exercise

Completing the Exercise : To complete the exercise, follow the steps in this book or in the onscreen exercise. In the onscreen list of chapters and exercises, click Chapter 3: Basic Shape Design. Click Exercise: Create Parameters and Equations.

1   Open *Wall-Cabinet-Side.ipt*.

2   On the ribbon, Manage tab, click Parameters.

   • In the Parameters dialog box, select the model parameter do. Change its name to
     Depth. Press ENTER.

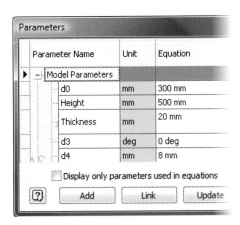

In the Parameters dialog box, review the existing model, reference, and user parameters.
Notice any custom parameter names or parameters with an existing equation instead of a
single numeric value.

   • Click Done.

3   In the browser, right-click the feature Hole1- Index. Click Show Dimensions.

4   Right-click in the graphics window. Click Dimension Display > Expression. Notice that all the
     dimensions have custom names. Also notice the use of reference dimensions to return a
     distance between sketch geometry.

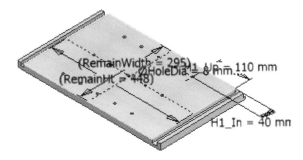

5   In the browser, right-click Extrusion1. Click Edit Sketch.

   - Change Height from 500 mm to **650 mm.**
   - On the Quick Access toolbar, click Update.

   The part looks like the following illustration. Notice that the number of holes did not automatically change when the height changed. You change this later in the exercise.

6   In the browser, right-click Extrusion1. Click Edit Sketch.

   - Change the dimension Depth from 300 mm to **200 mm**.
   - On the Quick Access toolbar, click Update. The part looks like the following illustration.

7   In the browser, right-click the feature Hole1- Index. Click Properties. Notice the conditional suppression. In this case, the value for the reference dimension RemainWidth is less than 250 mm, and the feature is automatically suppressed. Click Cancel.

8   In the browser, right-click the MidHole feature. Click Properties.
   - Under Suppress, select the If check box.
   - Select RemainWidth from the list of parameters.
   - Enter **300 mm** for the Less Than value.
   - Click OK.

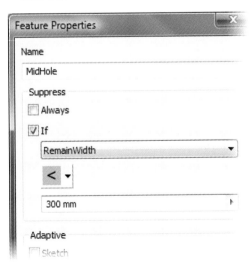

9   On the ribbon, Manage tab, click Parameters.

- In the row for the Depth model parameter, click the Equation column.
- Change its value to **400**. Press ENTER.

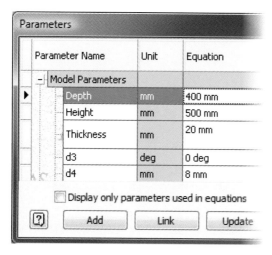

10   To add a user parameter:

- Click Add.
- Under User Parameters, enter **HolesPerColumn** for the parameter name for the new user parameter.
- Press TAB.

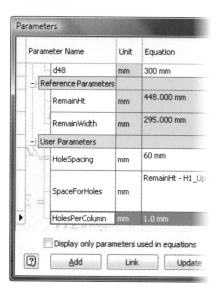

11   In the row for the new HolesPerColumn user parameter, click the Unit column.

- In the Unit Type dialog box, change the unit specification to **ul**.
- Click OK.

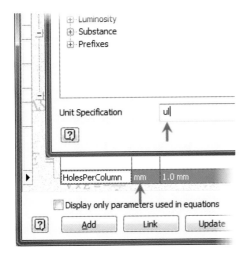

12   In the row for the new parameter, click the Equation column.

- Enter the following equation to calculate the number of spaces as a whole number that can fit in the remaining area.
  floor(SpaceForHoles/HoleSpacing) + 1
- Press ENTER. Click Done.

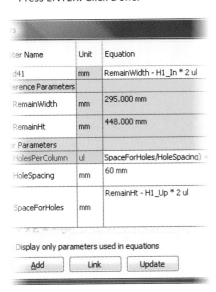

13   In the browser, right-click the feature Rectangular Pattern1. Click Unsuppress Features.

14   In the browser, right-click the feature Rectangular Pattern1. Click Edit Feature.

15   In the Rectangular Pattern dialog box:
- Delete the current value of 5 ul.
- Right-click the text box. Click List Parameters

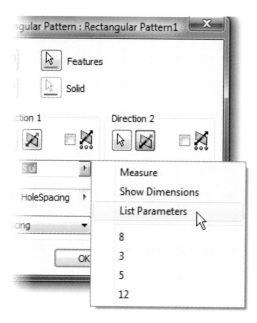

16   In the Parameters list, select HolesPerColumn. Click OK.

17 On the ribbon, click Parameters. Enter the following values in the Equations column for the corresponding parameters.

- Depth = **300 mm.** Press ENTER.
- Height = **820 mm.** Press ENTER.
- Click Done.
- On the Quick Access toolbar, click Update. The part looks like the following illustration.

18 Close all files. Do not save.

Lesson 10 | 3D Grip Editing

In this lesson, you learn how to use the 3D Grips tool to edit part geometry in the context of an assembly and in a stand-alone part environment.

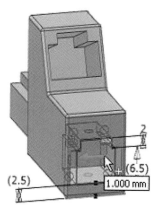

Instead of changing a parametric dimension value or adjusting sketch geometry to modify the size of a part, you can use the 3D Grips tool to resize a part by dynamically modifying its faces or edges.

Objectives

After completing this lesson, you will be able to:

- Describe 3D grip editing and its benefits.

- Utilize the 3D Grips tool and adjust the geometry a visual distance, a numeric distance, or to a specific geometric location.

About 3D Grip Editing

Modifying geometry with 3D Grips is a very fast and efficient way to adjust the geometry of your model. You can also adjust fully constrained geometry with 3D Grips, thereby eliminating the need to directly edit the dimension values that drive the feature.

Unlike the Edit Sketch and Edit Feature tools, with 3D grip editing, you can edit the geometry in a direct and dynamic way without first having to activate the sketch or feature.

In the following illustration, the Edit Offset tool is used to apply an offset distance to the selected face. The end result of this 3D grip edit directly affects the underlying sketch without having to activate it.

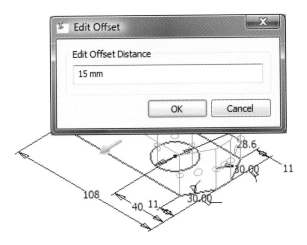

Definition of 3D Grip Editing

Editing with 3D Grips means quickly adjusting part geometry by selecting a face or edge, and then selecting a new location for it, or specifying a distance to change its location.

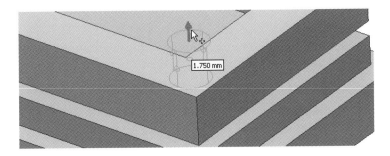

The following list summarizes basic benefits of using 3D Grips.

- Adjusting geometry with 3D Grips is useful during the conceptual design phase when the exact distances and part relationships are not known.

- You can use 3D Grips for sizing part geometry correctly within the context of the assembly.

3D Grip Edit Example

The following illustrations show the effects of grip editing a wrench component within the context of an assembly.

1   Before editing with 3D Grips.

2   The edit with 3D Grips.

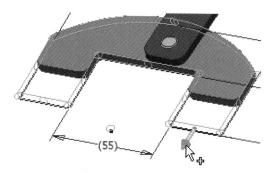

3   After editing with 3D Grips

Using the 3D Grips Tool

You use the 3D Grips tool to push or pull the faces of an extruded, revolved, or swept feature. You can use 3D Grips in the following ways:

- Drag the grip the desired distance.

- Select other geometry to adjust to.

- Enter a specific value.

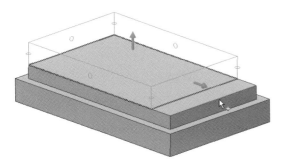

Tool Access

3D Grips

Shortcut Menu: **Right-click a grip-editable face. Click 3D Grips.**

Access to the 3D Grips tool is based on the following requirements:

- The 3D Grips tool is available only in assembly and part environments.

- The 3D Grips tool is available from the shortcut menu only after you select a feature, face, or sketch.

3D Grips Application Options

Application Options

Ribbon: **Tools tab > Options panel > Application Options > Part tab**

Application Options 3D Grip Settings

The following illustration shows the Application Options dialog box, Part tab, 3D Grips area.

```
3D grips
(1) ☑ Enable 3D grips
    (2) ☑ Display grips on selection
    Dimensional constraints (3)          Geometric constraints (4)
    ○ Never relax                         ● Never break
    ○ Relax if no equation                ○ Always break
    ● Always relax                        ○ Prompt
    ○ Prompt
```

(1) Choose to enable or disable 3D grips.

(2) Choose to display a grip when selecting the face or an edge of the part.

(3) Control how dimensional constraints are handled by 3D grip actions.

- **Never Relax:** Use this setting to prevent grip editing of a feature defined with a linear or angular dimension.
- **Relax if No Equation:** Use this setting to prevent grip editing of a feature defined with an equation.
- **Always Relax:** Use this setting to allow grip editing of a feature regardless of how it is defined.
- **Prompt:** Use this setting to receive a prompt, giving you the option to always relax when grip editing a feature defined with a dimension or equation.

(4) Control how geometric constraints are handled by 3D grip actions.

- **Never Break:** Use this setting to prevent grip editing of a feature controlled by a constraint.
- **Always Break:** Use this setting to allow grip editing of a feature regardless of constraints.

- **Prompt:** Use this setting to receive a prompt giving you the option to always break when grip editing a feature controlled with a constraint.

Restrictions for Using 3D Grips

Be aware of the following issues when editing with 3D Grips:

- When you modify a part from within an assembly environment, the model geometry is modified and saved within the individual part file.

- The 3D Grips tool can adjust only face geometry that is created from an extruded, revolved, or swept feature. Because the part file is manipulated, 3D Grips is not available for assembly-level features.

- Extruded and revolved features have grips positioned on the faces and the edges of the feature. For face grip editing, you can grip edit only the faces that are not in the plane of the original sketch.

- A sweep feature has grips available only for manipulating the profile sketch.

- When your 3D Grip options are set to allow it, during grip editing, any dimensional constraint is ignored and manipulated as if it were a reference dimension. When you finish the grip edit, the dimension value is updated to reflect the new distance or angle.

- You can select and change the value of any dimension that is displayed during a 3D grip edit in the same way that you can with the Edit Sketch command.

Note: **Dimensions with Formulas** *If a 3D grip edit changes the value for a parametric dimension and that parametric dimension contained a formula prior to the edit, the formula will be replaced by the exact measurement value.*

Editing with the 3D Grips Tool

You can edit 3D grips dynamically, by specifying a distance or angle, or by selecting another edge or face to align to.

Procedure: Grip Editing Dynamically

The following procedure shows how to access the 3D Grips tool and edit a feature or face dynamically.

1   Right-click the feature, face, or sketch to be edited. Click 3D Grips.

2   Place the cursor over the desired grip circle to display a vector normal arrow or edge line. Left- click and drag the arrow or line indicator the desired distance.

3   Continue to select and edit additional grips as required. Right-click anywhere in the graphics window. Click Done.

Procedure: Grip Editing a Specific Distance or Angle

The following procedure shows how to use 3D Grips to adjust geometry by a specific distance or angle.

1   Right-click the feature, face, or sketch to be edited. Click 3D Grips.

2   Place the cursor over the grip circle of the face to edit, so the vector normal arrow is displayed. Right-click the arrow. Click Edit Dimension, Edit Offset, or Edit Extent.

3   In the appropriate dialog box, change the numeric value.

4   Right-click the feature, face, or sketch. Click Done.

Procedure: Grip Editing to Selected Geometry

The following procedure shows how to use 3D Grips to adjust geometry to an existing edge, face, or vertex.

1   Right-click the feature, face, or sketch to be edited. Click 3D Grips.

2   Place the cursor over the desired grip circle, so a vector normal arrow or edge line is displayed. Left-click the arrow or edge line.

3   Click on the vertex, edge, or face of the geometry to align with.

4   The feature preview is updated to reflect the new position.

5   Right-click the feature, face, or sketch. Click Done.

Exercise | Edit with 3D Grips

In this exercise, you use the 3D Grips tool to dynamically lengthen the ends of a wrench, adjust their width a set distance, and adjust the opening in the handle so that it aligns with other geometry.

The completed exercise

Completing the Exercise:	*To complete the exercise, follow the steps in this book or in the onscreen exercise. In the onscreen list of chapters and exercises, click Chapter 3: Basic Shape Design. Click Exercise: Edit with 3D Grips.*

1   Open the file *AlignmentWrench.iam*.

2 Set selection priority to Faces and Edges.

- On the Quick Access toolbar, click Select > Select Faces and Edges.
- Select the face on the top of the wrench head.

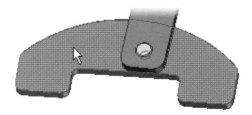

3 Right-click the wrench head. Click 3D Grips.

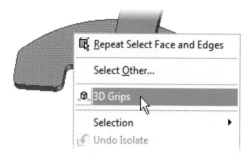

4 Notice the dimensional equation *fx:d3 = d2 / 3 ul* in the top illustration. As you grip edit the part, because of the equation, the entire part changes shape. Right-click anywhere in the graphics window. Click Cancel.

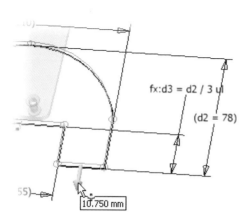

5   Change a 3D grip setting:
    - Click Tools tab > Options panel > Application Options.
    - Click the Part tab.
    - Under 3D Grips, for Dimensional Constraints, select Always Relax.
    - Click OK.

6   Repeat step 3 to start 3D Grips editing again.

7   Click and drag the face grip for the end of the wrench head to lengthen it to approximately 30 mm.

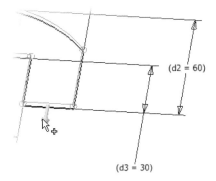

8   Move a face a specific distance:
    - Position the cursor over the right-side face grip and the subsequently displayed arrow.
    - Right-click the grip arrow.
    - Click Edit Offset.

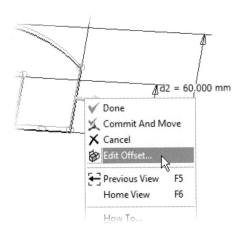

9   In the Edit Offset dialog box, for Edit Offset Distance, enter **15 mm**. Click OK.

10   Right-click in the graphics window. Click Done to accept your edits.

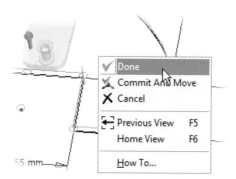

11   Set your selection priority to Features and select a feature:

- SHIFT+right-click anywhere in the graphics window. Click Feature Priority.
- Select the open slot in the handle.
- Right-click the selected feature. Click 3D Grips.

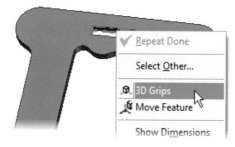

12 Click the side-face grip arrow (1). Click the straight left edge of the handle (2).

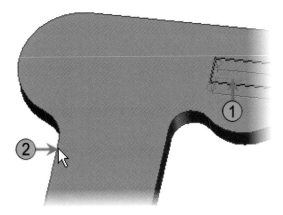

13 Right-click in the graphics window. Click Done.

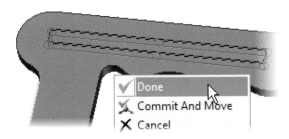

14 The slot is increased.

15 Close all files. Do not save.

Lesson 11 | Creating Work Features

In this lesson, you learn to create and use work planes, work axes, and work points. You use these work features to assist in creating geometry, placing constraints, and completing other modeling tasks.

The construction of most part models requires the use of work features to complete. The more complex your parts, the more work features you will likely use while creating it.

The following illustration shows how work planes, axes, and points are displayed in your parts.

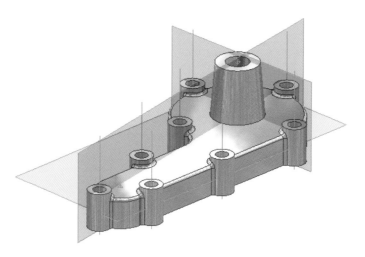

Objectives

After completing this lesson, you will be able to:

- Locate, display, and use the default work features and create new work features on a part.

- Use the Work Plane tool to create work planes on a part.

- Use the Work Axis tool to create work axes on a part.

- Use the Work Point tool to create work points on a part.

About Work Features

Every part contains a default set of work planes, work axes, and a center point. These default work features are located in the Origin folder of the Part browser. You use these default work features to define the initial orientation of your part design. You can use these default objects for the basis of new sketches, for feature termination options, and as the basis for creating new work features. As your part design progresses, you may need to create additional work plane, work axis, and work point features that are based on faces, edges, and vertices of your part.

The following illustration shows the default work planes, axes, and center point located in the Origin folder of the browser.

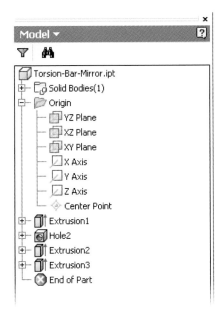

Definition of Default Work Features

There are three default work planes, each representing a different coordinate plane. The three planes represented are the *YZ* plane, *XZ* plane, and *XY* plane. There are three default work axes, each representing a different coordinate axis. The three axes represented are the *X* axis, *Y* axis, and *Z* axis. There is a single Center Point work point, it represents the 0,0,0 coordinate. Work planes and work axes extend outward from this point.

When you create a new part file, the initial sketch is created on one of these default planes. You can create additional sketches or features using the model or the default work planes.

The following illustration shows the three default work planes and the center point.

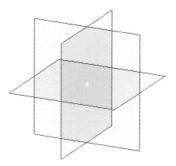

The following illustration shows the three default work axes and the center point.

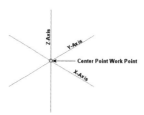

The default planes are not visible when starting a new part file. You can control their visibility in the browser. The following illustration shows all of the default work features selected in the browser. By clicking on Visibility, they will all become visible in the drawing.

Parametric Work Features

You create and use work features when physical geometry does not exist on the part for a specific task. For example, as you develop your part design, you typically orient sketches for your features on existing planar faces of the part. When a planar face does not exist, you can create one or more work features to define and orient a plane for that sketch.

Example of Parametric Work Features

In the following illustration, two work axes were used to create a centerline work plane. This work plane is then used to create a sketched feature on the end of the part.

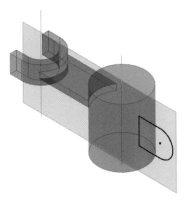

Browser Appearance of Parametric Work Features

The following illustration shows how work features are displayed in the browser.

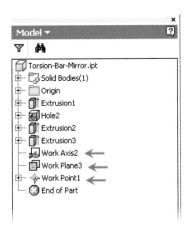

Work Feature Appearance

The appearance of work features is controlled in several different ways. You can turn on or turn off the appearance of work features individually or globally. To turn off the visibility of a single work feature, right-click it in the browser and click Visibility.

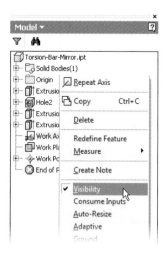

Controlling Global Visibility

On the ribbon, click View tab > Object Visibility to turn the visibility of work features and sketches on and off, as shown in the following image. Select the appropriate option. You can also use the keyboard shortcuts.

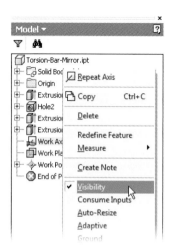

Creating Work Planes

You use the Work Plane tool to create work planes in the current part. Work planes are used to define planar surfaces when the existing geometry does not represent the required plane. When you create work planes, you select geometry and/or other work features. Each selection defines either orientation or position for the new work plane. Work planes are parametrically attached to the model geometry or default work planes. When you create a work plane using features of existing geometry, if the geometry changes, the work plane also changes. For example, if you create a work plane that is tangent to a cylindrical surface with a radius of 2 mm, and that radius later changes to 5 mm, the work plane moves to retain the tangent relationship with the cylinder.

Uses for Work Planes

The following list summarizes some potential uses for work planes:

- Basis for new sketches.

- Feature termination options.

- Basis for new work features.

In the following illustration, the work plane (1) is created at a 30-degree angle from a part face. The circular extrusion (2) is created from the work plane extruding to meet the part face. As the angle of the part face changes, the work plane updates to maintain the 30-degree angle, and the circular feature changes with the work plane.

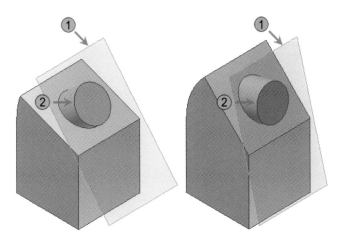

Access

Work Plane

Ribbon: **Model tab > Work Features panel**

Keyboard Shortcut: **]**

Creating Work Planes: Process Overview

When you create work planes, the type of work plane is based completely on the geometry you select. For example, there is no dialog box to create a planar offset work plane. All work planes are created based on two or three selections. Each selection represents either an orientation or position.

Follow these steps to create a work plane that is aligned with the Origin *XY* plane and tangent to the outside of the cylinder.

1 Select the feature or plane.

2   Select the second feature or plane.

The resulting work plane is created.

Procedures: Creating Work Planes

When you create work planes, the type of work plane is based completely on the geometry you select. For example, there is no dialog box to create a planar offset work plane. All work planes are created based on two or three selections. Each selection represents either an orientation or position.

Use the following approaches to create work planes.

Aligned to Origin Plane/Tangent to Cylindrical Surface

Selection 1 - Origin Work Plane

Selection 2 - Cylindrical Feature

Result

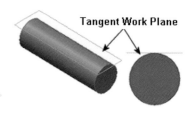

Aligned to Face/Midpoint Between Two Faces

Selection 1 - Part Face

Selection 2 - Part Face

Result

Offset from Plane or Surface

Selection 1 - Click and drag from plane or surface

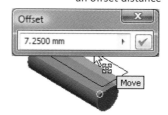

Selection 2 - Release the mouse and enter an offset distance

Result

Angle from Face/Along an Edge

Selection 1 - Edge on Part

Selection 2 - Planar Surface on Part, Enter Angle

Result

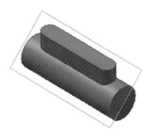

Work Plane on Three Points

Selection 1 - Vertex on Geometry

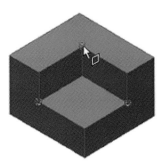

Selection 2 - Vertex on Geometry

Selection 3 - Vertex on Geometry

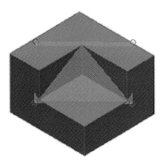

Result

Parallel to Face/Midpoint of Edge

Selection 1 - Plane/Face   **Selection 2** - Midpoint of Edge   **Result**

Procedure: Resizing Work Planes

Place your cursor over the corner of the work plane. When the resize indicator appears, click and drag the corner of the work plane to resize it.

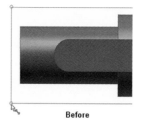 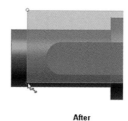

Before   **After**

Procedure: Moving Work Planes

Place your cursor over an edge of the work plane. When the move indicator appears, click and drag the work plane to a new location within that same plane. In the following illustration, the move indicator is displayed (1) and the work plane is moved to a new location (2).

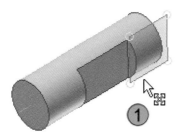 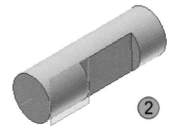

Creating Work Axes

The Work Axis tool is used to create work axes in the current part. Work axes are used to define an axis when the existing geometry does not represent the required axis. Work axes are parametrically attached to the model geometry and/or default work features. When you create a work axis using features of existing geometry, if the geometry changes, the work axis updates to reflect those changes.

Uses for Work Axes

The following are some potential uses for work axes:

- Axis of revolution for circular pattern.

- Basis for new work features.

- Representation of centerlines on sketches.

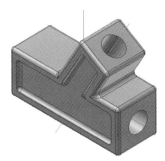

Access

Work Axis

Ribbon: **Model tab > Work Features panel**

Keyboard Shortcut: **/**

Procedure: Creating Work Axes

When you create a work axis, the type of work axis is based completely on the geometry you select. For example, there is no dialog box to create an axis at the intersection of two planes. All work axes are created by selecting existing geometric features or other work features. Follow these steps to create a work axis.

Procedures: Creating Work Axes

Use the following approaches to create work axes.

Work Axis at Center of Circular Feature

Selection 1 - Circular Feature   **Result**

Work Axis at Intersection of Two Planes

Selection 1 - Plane or Planar Surface   **Selection 2** - Plane or Planar Surface   **Result**

 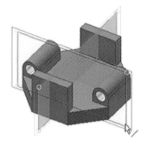 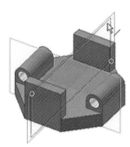

Work Axis Through Point/Normal to Plane

Selection 1 - Plane or Planar Surface   **Selection 2** - Point   **Result**

Work Axis Through Two Points

Selection 1 - Point or Midpoint   **Selection 2** - Point or Midpoint   **Result**

Creating Work Points

You use the Work Point tool to create parametric construction points on part features. Several methods are available for creating these work points. Each method creates a work point that is parametrically attached to the geometry or other work features. If this geometry changes, the work point changes accordingly.

Work points are used as construction geometry to assist in the creation of other geometry and features.

Grounded Work Points are fixed in space and have no association to other geometry. In part files, you place grounded work points at vertex points on the part. Once placed, you can modify the point using options found on the short cut menu.

Uses for Work Points

The following are some potential uses for work points:

- Projection onto sketches.

- Basis for new work features.

- Creation of 3D sketches by drawing lines between work points.

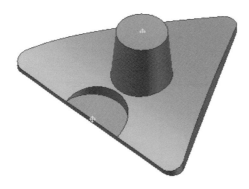

Access

Work Point

Ribbon: **Model tab > Work Features panel**

Keyboard Shortcut: **.**

Access

Grounded Work Point

Ribbon: **Model tab > Work Features panel**

Keyboard Shortcut: **;**

Procedures: Creating Work Points

Use the following approaches to create work points.

Creating a Work Point on a Vertex

1   On the panel bar, click the Work Point tool and select a vertex on the part.

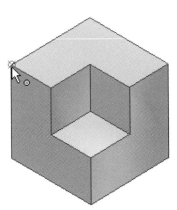

2   The work point is created on the selected vertex.

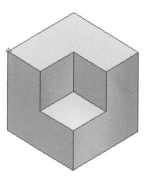

Creating a Work Point at the Midpoint of an Edge

1   On the panel bar, click the Work Point tool and select the midpoint of an edge.

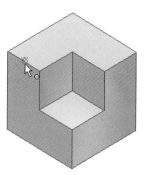

2   The work point is created on the midpoint of the selected edge.

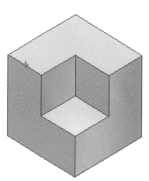

Creating a Work Point at the Intersection of an Edge and Plane

1   On the panel bar, click the Work Point tool and select an edge or axis.

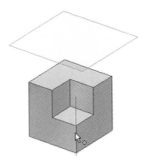

2   Select a plane or surface.

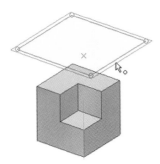

3   The work point is created at the intersection of the edge and plane.

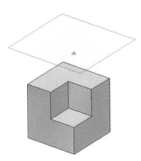

Work Point at the Intersection of a Line or Axis and a Surface

Selection 1: Line or Axis   **Selection 2:** Surface   **Result**

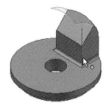 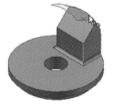 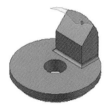

Work Point at the Intersection of a Plane and a Curve

Selection 1: Plane or Face   **Selection 2:** Curve   **Result**

Exercise | Create Work Planes

In this exercise, you create a cylindrical control valve using both origin planes and work planes.

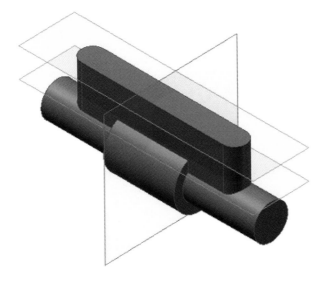

The completed exercise

Completing the Exercise:	To complete the exercise, follow the steps in this book or in the onscreen exercise. In the onscreen list of chapters and exercises, click *Chapter 3: Basic Shape Design.* Click *Exercise: Create Work Planes.*

1   Open *Control-Valve.ipt.*

2   Turn on the visibility of the default *YZ* plane.

- In the browser, expand the Origin folder.
- Right-click *YZ* Plane.
- Click Visibility.

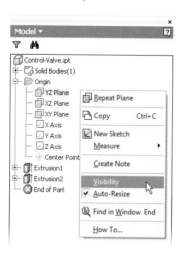

3   Mirror the new feature to the other side.

- On the ribbon, click the Mirror tool.
- Select the Extrusion2 feature.
- Click the Mirror Plane button.
- Select the YZ origin plane as shown here.
- Click OK.

4   In the graphics window, right-click the work plane. Click Visibility on the shortcut menu to
     turn off the work plane visibility.

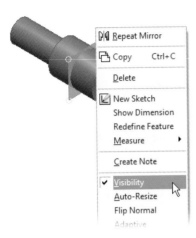

5   Create a new work plane tangent to the top of your part and parallel to the XY plane.

- On the ribbon, click the Work Plane tool.
- In the browser, select XY Plane.
- Select the top of the cylinder as shown here.

6   Create an offset plane to the plane just created.

- On the ribbon, click the Work Plane tool.
- Click and drag the work plane just created.
- In the Offset dialog box, enter **10.00 mm** and click the green check mark.

7   Turn off the visibility of Work Plane1.

- In the graphics window, right-click Work Plane1.
- Click Visibility on the shortcut menu to turn off the work plane visibility.

8   Create a new sketch using the offset work plane.

- On the ribbon, click the Create 2D Sketch tool.
- Select the work plane.

9　On the Navigation bar, click the View Face tool and select the work plane.

10　On the ribbon, click the Project Geometry tool and project the edges indicated.

11　Create a new sketch for an added feature.
- Using standard sketching tools, sketch, constrain, and dimension the geometry as shown here.
- Note the horizontal and vertical constraints on the geometry midpoints.

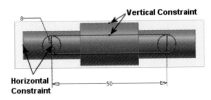

12　Right-click in the graphics window. Click Home View.

13　On the ribbon, click Finish Sketch to exit the sketch.

14　Extrude the new sketch to create the feature.
- On the ribbon, click the Extrude tool.
- Select the profile as shown.
- In the Extents list, select To Next. Click OK.

15   On the keyboard press ALT+] to toggle all user work planes off.

16   Close all files. Do not save.

Exercise | Create Work Axes

In this exercise, you use work axes to add features to an existing part. You utilize both origin work axes as well as new work axes to create the additional features required for the part.

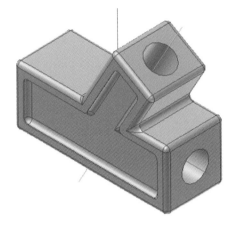

The completed exercise

Completing the Exercise: To complete the exercise, follow the steps in this book or in the onscreen exercise. In the onscreen list of chapters and exercises, click Chapter 3: Basic Shape Design. Click Exercise: Create Work Axes.

1 Open *Control-Block-45.ipt*.

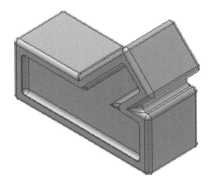

2   Turn on the visibility of default work features.

- In the browser, expand the origin folder.
- While pressing CTRL, select X Axis, Z Axis, and Center Point.
- Right-click one of the objects. Click Visibility.

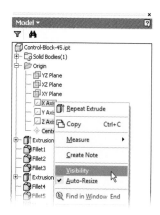

3   Activate an existing sketch using the browser.

- In the browser, expand Extrusion1.
- Right-click Sketch1.
- Click Edit Sketch.

4   Examine the sketch and dimensions. Notice how the sketch is constrained and dimensioned to origin features such as the Center Point and Work Axes.

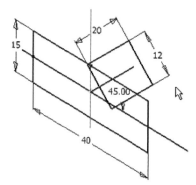

5   On the ribbon, click Finish Sketch to exit the sketch.

6   Turn off Autoproject Edges for Sketch Creation.

- Click Tools tab > Application Options.
- In the Options dialog box, select the Sketch tab.
- Clear the check mark for Autoproject Edges for Sketch Creation and Edit.
- Click OK.

7   Create a new sketch plane.

- Right-click the face of the part.
- On the shortcut menu, click New Sketch.

8   Project the default X axis to the new sketch plane.

- On the ribbon, click the Project Geometry tool.
- In the browser, select Origin X Axis.
- Right-click in the graphics window. Click Done.

9   On the ribbon, click Finish Sketch to exit the sketch.

10   Create a hole using the projected sketch point.

- On the ribbon, click the Hole tool.
- The point projected from the origin work axis should be automatically selected. If not, select the projected point.
- In the Termination list, select Through All.
- In the preview window of the Hole dialog box, enter **7 mm**.
- Click OK.

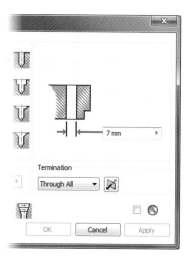

11 Create a new work axis using the center point and a part face.

- On the ribbon, click the Work Axis tool.
- In the browser, select the Origin Center Point object.
- Select the angled face of the part as shown here.

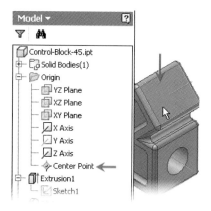

12 Verify the display of the work axis. If your work axis is not displayed, perform the following steps.

- In the browser, right-click Work Axis1.
- Click Auto-Resize. Your axis resizes and extends outside the part boundary.

13   Right-click the angled face of the part. Click New Sketch.

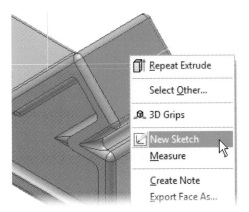

14   On the ribbon, click the Project Geometry tool. Select the work axis you created previously.

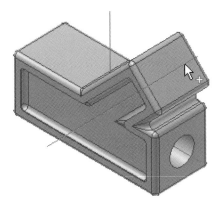

15   On the ribbon, click Finish Sketch to exit the sketch.

16 Create a new hole using the new projected point.

- On the ribbon, click the Hole tool.
- The point projected from the work axis should be automatically selected. If not, select the projected point.
- In the Termination list, select To. Select the inside face of the first hole you created.
- In the preview window of the Hole dialog box, enter **7 mm**, if required.
- Click OK.

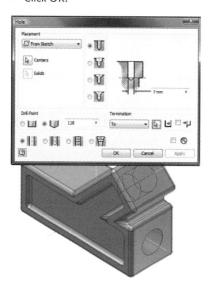

17 In the browser, double-click Sketch1 to edit the sketch.

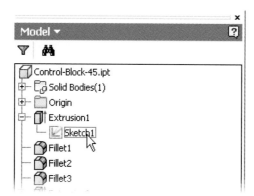

18 Edit the angle of the upper extrusion.

- Double-click the 45-degree angle dimension.
- In the Edit Dimension dialog box enter **60 deg**.
- Click the green check mark.

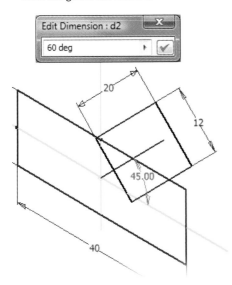

19 On the ribbon, click Finish Sketch to exit the sketch. Notice that the changes are applied to all affected features including the work axis and hole.

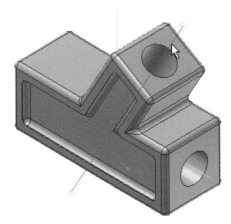

20 Close all files. Do not save.

Exercise | Create Work Points

In this exercise, you create a PC speaker base component by using sketched features and work points. To save time, the sketch geometry has already been created.

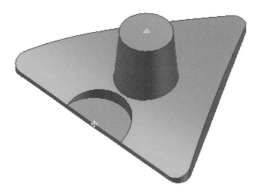

The completed exercise

Completing the Exercise:	To complete the exercise, follow the steps in this book or in the onscreen exercise. In the onscreen list of chapters and exercises, click Chapter 3: Basic Shape Design. Click Exercise: Create Work Points.

1   Open *Speaker-Base.ipt.*

2   On the ribbon, click the Work Point tool. Select the midpoint of the front edge of the
     Speaker- Base part.

3   Create a new work plane using the point projected previously.
     • On the ribbon, click the Work Plane tool.
     • In the browser, select Origin XY plane.
     • Select the Work Point1 feature previously created.

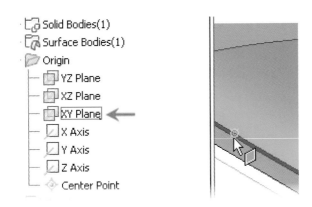

4   On the ribbon, click the Create 2D Sketch tool. Select the work plane previously created.

5   On the ribbon, click the Project Geometry tool. Select the work point as shown.

6   Sketch and dimension a circle from the projected work point as shown here.

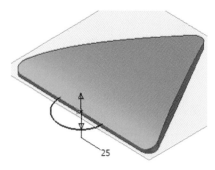

7   On the ribbon, click Finish Sketch to exit the sketch.

8   Extrude the sketch through all with a cut.

- On the ribbon, click the Extrude tool.
- Select the circle profile.
- In the Extrude dialog box, select the Cut feature relationship button.
- From the Extents list, select All.
- Click the direction button as shown. Click OK.

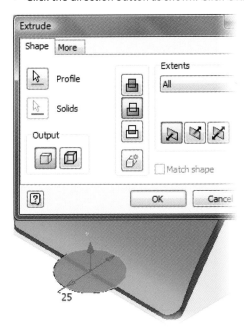

9   On the ribbon, click the Grounded Point tool. In the browser, expand the Origin folder and select the Center Point object.

10   Create a grounded work point offset up from the Center Point object.

- When the work point triad appears, select the Z axis arrow as indicated.
- Enter **25 mm** for Z.
- Click OK to create the work point.

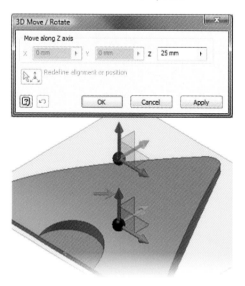

11   Create a new work plane parallel to the XY plane and through the grounded work point.

- On the ribbon, click Work Plane.
- In the browser, select the Origin XY plane.
- Select the Work Point 2 that you just created.

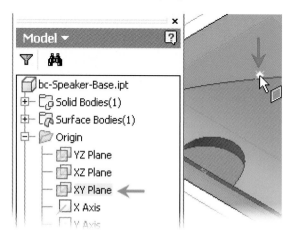

12   In the graphics window, right-click the work plane just created. Click New Sketch.

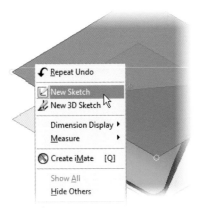

13   On the ribbon, click the Project Geometry tool and select the work point.

14   Sketch and dimension a circle from the projected work point as shown here.

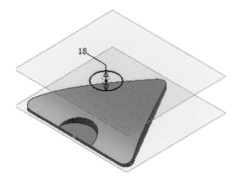

15 On the ribbon, click Finish Sketch to exit the sketch.

16 Extrude the sketched circle to the main body.
- On the ribbon, click Extrude.
- Select the circle profile.
- From the Extents list, click To Next.

17 Add a taper to the extrusion.
- In the Extrude dialog box, click the More tab.
- For Taper, enter **5**. Click OK.

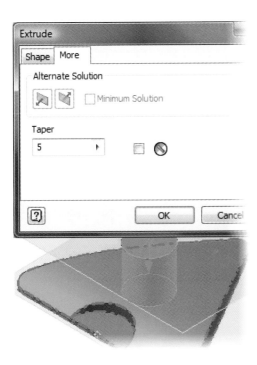

18　On the keyboard, press ALT+] to turn off all user work planes.

19　Close all files. Do not save.

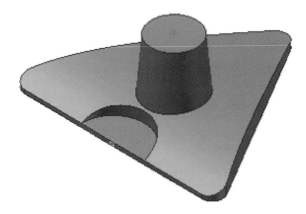

Lesson 12 | Creating Basic Swept Shapes

This lesson describes how to create basic swept shapes using the Sweep tool. The Sweep tool creates a sketched feature by sweeping a profile along a path.

When you need to create a shape that follows a predefined path, consider creating it as a sweep feature.

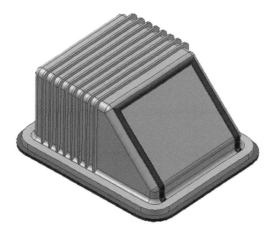

Objectives

After completing this lesson, you will be able to:

- Decide when to use a sweep feature.

- Use the Sweep tool to create sweep features that follow 2D and 3D paths.

- State the guidelines for creating sweeps.

About Swept Shapes

A swept feature is similar to an extrude feature, except that instead of extruding the profile to a specified or calculated distance, the profile is extruded or swept along a path. As the profile is swept along the path, it maintains the same cross section as the original profile, unless you use the Taper option. In that case, the taper angle is applied equally to all sides of the profile as it is swept along the path.

Sweep features can be used as base features (the first feature on the part) or secondary features used to cut, join, or intersect existing part geometry.

The following illustration shows the path sketch (2) and profile sketch (1) before and after executing the Sweep tool (3).

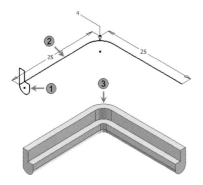

Definition of Sweep Features

You use sweep to create any nonlinear or nonperpendicular extrusions. Extrude always creates a feature that is perpendicular to the sketch plane. With sweep, you can define the extrusion path that is not perpendicular to the sketch plane, and the path can be 2D or 3D

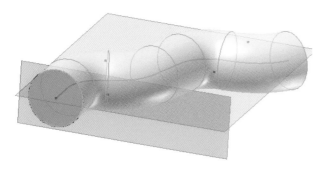

Example of a Sweep Feature

Many housings require a ledge around them to produce a seal with a lid that is made to cover the container in some way. The following illustration shows how a sweep feature produced the ledge on this simple housing.

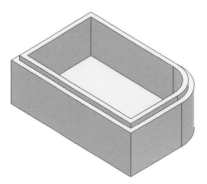

Creating Sweep Features

The process of creating a sweep feature is similar to using other sketched features, in that you must have a sketch profile. Where the sweep feature differs is that you must also have a sketched path for it to follow. Therefore, in order to create a sweep feature, you must have two unconsumed sketches, one for the path and one for the profile. The path can consist of lines, splines, and other sketch geometry, or it can be created using 3D sketch tools such as lines, splines, and bends.

Access

Sweep

Ribbon: **Model tab > Create panel**

Keyboard Shortcut: **CTRL + SHIFT + S**

Sweep Dialog Box

Use the Sweep dialog box to select the profile and path geometry and adjust the output options for the sweep feature.

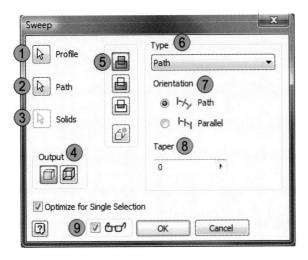

The following features and options are available in the Sweep dialog box:

	Option	Description
①	**Profile**	Click this button to select one or more profiles to sweep along the selected path. A red arrow indicates that no profiles have been selected for the sweep feature.
②	**Path**	Click this button to select the path along which the profile is swept. A red arrow indicates that no profiles have been selected for the sweep feature.
③	**Solids**	The Solids selection tool is only active when the part contains more than one solid body. You use this button to determine to which solid body the sweep feature is going to be applied.
④	**Output**	Specify the desired output option, Solid or Surface.
⑤	**Operation**	Select the appropriate icon for a join, cut, or intersect operation. Click New Solid to make the joined, cut, or intersected objects a new solid object.

	Option	Description
⑥	**Sweep Type**	Select from the following types of Sweeps:
		• **Path:** Create a sweep feature by sweeping a profile along a path.
		• **Path & Guide Rail:** Create a sweep feature by sweeping a profile along a path. The guide rail controls scale and twist of the swept profile.
		• **Path & Guide Surface:** Create a sweep feature by sweeping a profile along a path. The guide surface controls the twist of the swept profile.
⑦	**Orientation**	Path holds the swept profile constant to the sweep path while Parallel holds the swept profile parallel to the original profile.
⑧	**Taper**	Sets taper angle for sweeps normal to the sketch plane. The taper is not available for parallel orientation.
⑨	**Optimize for Single Selection**	Automatically advances to next selection after a single selection is made. Clear the check mark to make multiple selections.
⑨	**Preview**	Toggles the Preview feature on and off.

Procedure: Creating a Workplane Normal to a Path

The following steps describe how to create a work plane normal to a sketch path. The work plane can then be used to create a sketch profile that will be swept along the path.

1   Start by creating a sketch to use as the path for your sweep feature.

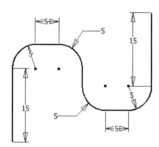

2   Start the Work Plane tool and select your path sketch as shown.

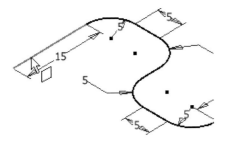

3   Select the point at the end of your sketched path as shown.

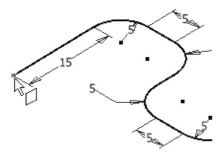

4   Create a new sketch on the work plane just created.

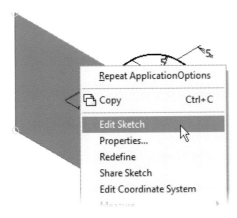

5   Sketch and constrain a profile for the sweep.

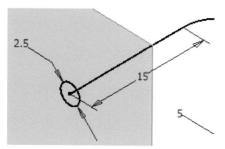

6   Create your sweep feature using the profile and path sketches.

Procedure: Creating Sweep Features

The following steps describe how to create sweep features.

1   Create and constrain the sketch geometry used for the path.

2   Create a new sketch, then create and constrain the geometry to be used for the profile. In the following illustration, a work plane was created that is coincident to the endpoint of the path and normal to the path. The work plane was then used to align the new sketch for the profile. This method ensures that the profile is normal to the path.

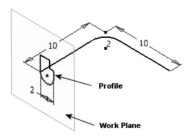

3   On the ribbon, click the Sweep tool and select the profile geometry. Click the Path button and select the path geometry.

4   If necessary, adjust the operation options for join, cut, or intersect. Optionally, enter a taper angle for the sweep feature.

5   The sweep feature is created according to the settings that you specified in the Sweep dialog box.

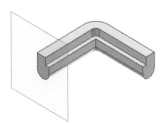

Guidelines for Creating Swept Shapes

There are several ways to create sweep features. Your path sketch can be either open or closed, and it can be either a 2D or 3D sketch. Your profile must be closed if creating a solid, but can be open if creating a surface. While it is not mandatory, creating your path and profile on perpendicular planes produces the best results.

Swept Shape Guidelines

Follow these guidelines for successful sweeps.

- Your path can be an open or closed loop, but it must pierce the profile plane.

- You must have two unconsumed sketches, the profile and path, to create a sweep.

- If Preview is enabled and the preview does not appear, it is likely that the sweep feature will not be created.

- Remember to avoid creating a profile that would self intersect when being swept along a path containing a bend.

- The taper creates sweeps normal to the sketch plane and is not available for parallel sweeps or closed paths.

- A positive taper angle increases the profile cross section while a negative angle decreases as the sweep moves away from the start point.

- Use a guide rail or guide surface to control twist and scale of the swept profile.

- An open profile cannot be used to create a solid base feature.

Example of a Sweep Feature

When creating a base feature sweep, it may be a good idea to use the default work planes for your path and profile sketches. In the following illustration, the path was created using the default *XY* plane, and the profile was created using the default *ZX* plane.

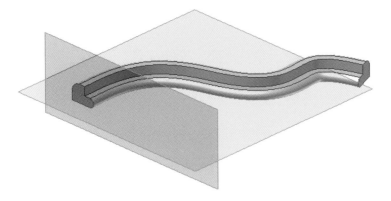

Relationship Between Path and Profile

When you create path and profile geometry, keep in mind that some items are optional, while others are crucial to achieving the desired results.

Intersecting Path and Profile

When you create a sweep feature, if the path and profile do not intersect, the following message is displayed. If you click Yes to continue, the application attempts to create the sweep. However, depending on the position of the profile and path, if errors do occur they can be difficult to diagnose.

Radius of Bends in Path

If the path includes bends, you must consider the radius of the bend compared to the furthest point on the profile from the path. As the profile is swept along the path, when it encounters a bend, if the radius is too tight, the swept geometry intersects itself as it changes direction. In that case, a message similar to the following is displayed.

The following illustration is an example of an incorrect positional relationship between the profile (2) and the path (1). Notice that the bend dimension (3) of 2 mm is less than the furthest distance (4) of the profile from the path. As the profile changes directions at the location of the bend, the resulting inside radius would be less than zero, and the geometry would be self-intersecting.

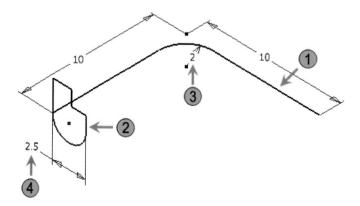

To correct this problem, the profile dimension would have to be less than or equal to the bend dimension. You can accomplish this by changing either the profile dimension or the bend dimension.

Exercise | Create Sweep Features

In this exercise, you use the Sweep tool to add a swept shape on the AirBox2component to allow the AirBox Lid component to seal. Instead of creating new geometry for the path, you use existing geometry on the part.

The completed exercise

Completing the Exercise:	*To complete the exercise, follow the steps in this book or in the onscreen exercise. In the onscreen list of chapters and exercises, click Chapter 3: Basic Shape Design. Click Exercise: Create Sweep Features.*

1   Open *Air-Box-2.ipt*.

2   Right-click the top face of the part. Click New Sketch.

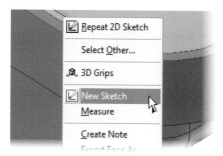

3   If the edges of the face are not automatically projected, use the Project Geometry tool to project the outside edges. These edges will be used as the path for the sweep profile.

4   On the ribbon, click Finish Sketch to exit the sketch.

5   Create a work plane using an edge and a point.
   - On the ribbon, click the Work Plane tool and select the edge (1) of the AirBox2 part.
   - Select the endpoint of the edge (2), as shown.

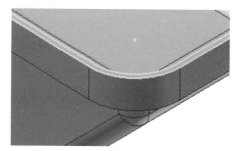

6   Right-click the work plane. Click New Sketch.

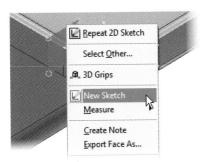

7   On the ribbon, click the Project Geometry tool and select the edge, as shown. This action creates a point that can be used to constrain your new geometry.

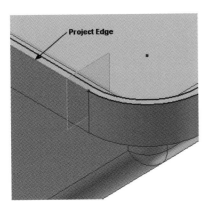

8   Using standard sketching tools, sketch and constrain the geometry, as shown.

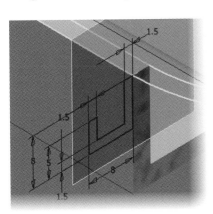

9   On the ribbon, click Finish Sketch to exit the sketch.

10   Create a sweep using the path and profile just created.
   • On the ribbon, click the Sweep tool and select the profile that you created previously.
   • For the path, select the outer edge of the part and click OK.

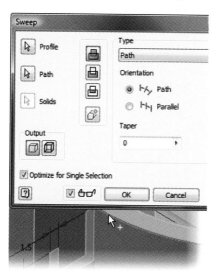

11   Notice that the profile is swept around the entire part.

12   Close all files. Do not save.

Chapter Summary

This chapter presented the tools and recommended workflows for basic shape design. Using these techniques, you can now create more complex 2D sketches at different locations on your part, combine multiple 3D features to create various shapes, and modify those shapes at any time during the design process.

Having completed this chapter, you can:

- Create features using the Extrude and Revolve tools.
- Use reference and construction geometry.
- Use the browser and shortcut menus to edit parametric parts.
- Use the 3D Grips tool to edit part geometry in the context of an assembly and in a stand-alone part.
- Create, locate, and utilize work features to perform modeling tasks.
- Create swept shapes by sweeping a profile along a 2D or 3D path.

Chapter 04
Detailed Shape Design

This chapter enhances your basic part modeling skills by providing additional tools and recommended workflows for detailed shape design. Common industry practice dictates the use of chamfers and fillets to break sharp corners and relieve stress. Holes and threaded features often must be added for fasteners. Some parts, such as stampings or molds, must be designed as thin-walled shapes. Additionally, most parts include some shapes or features that are patterned or mirrored.

The lessons in this chapter cover the tools required to meet each of these design requirements.

▶ **Objectives**

After completing this chapter, you will be able to:

- Create both chamfers and fillets on a part.

- Use the Hole and Thread tools to place hole and thread features on your part model.

- Create rectangular and circular patterns and mirror existing features.

- Create thin-walled parts using the Shell tool.

Lesson 13 | Creating Chamfers and Fillets

This lesson describes how to create both chamfers and fillets on your part. Fillets are commonly used on a part to reduce the potential of stress cracking, and for aesthetic reasons. Chamfers are used for angled faces, relief clearance, and also for aesthetic purposes.

Chamfer and fillet features are standard on most manufactured components and are among the most widely used placed features on any 3D part.

The following illustration shows a part where all sharp edges have been replaced with fillet or chamfer features.

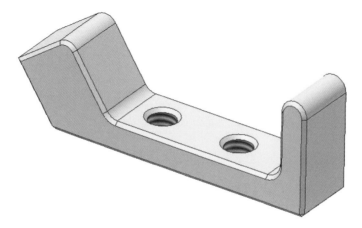

Objectives

After completing this lesson, you will be able to:

- Describe the difference between chamfers and fillets and give an example of how they are used.

- Use the Chamfer tool to create chamfers.

- Use the Fillet tool to create constant radius fillets.

- State the guidelines for creating chamfers and fillets.

About Chamfers and Fillets

A fillet creates a radius edge on an interior or exterior corner of your part, whereas a chamfer bevels an edge. Cast and molded parts rarely have true sharp edges. Chamfer and fillet features are applied to almost all the edges of your part designs. When completing a machined part on the shop floor, you always remove all sharp edges. You also apply this same principle to your parametric part designs.

The following illustration shows a cast part with fillets and rounds on edges and then chamfers placed on the holes to represent the machining process.

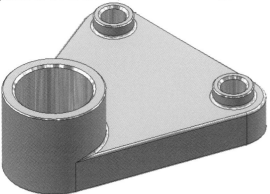

Definition of Fillets

A fillet is defined by a single constant radius, or in the case of a variable radius fillet, by more than one radius. Consider a fillet to be an interior shape, placed between faces of less than 180 degrees, which adds material to your part. A round is an exterior shape placed between faces of any angle, which removes material from your part when created.

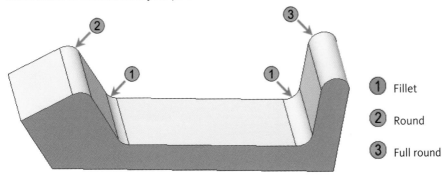

1. Fillet
2. Round
3. Full round

Definition of Chamfers

A chamfer is defined using equal distances, a distance and an angle, or two different distance values. Chamfers are used to break sharp edges and as lead-ins on holes or bosses. Most angles faces in parametric parts are created using chamfers.

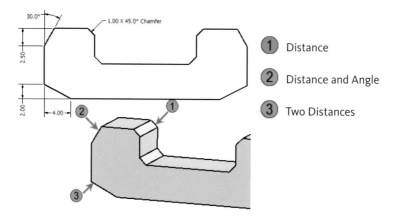

1. Distance

2. Distance and Angle

3. Two Distances

Example of Using Chamfer for a Lead-in

In most circumstances, placing a fastener into a hole is aided through the use of a chamfer. In the following illustration, it is easier to assemble the parts on the right that have a chamfer used as a lead-in.

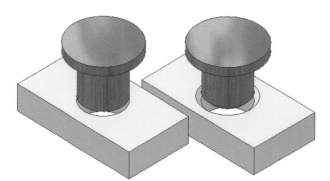

Creating Chamfers

You use the Chamfer tool to add chamfer features to edges on your part. These features, like other features, are fully parametric and easily editable after you create them. When you create chamfer features, you can choose from three different methods which determine how the chamfer is specified. With any of the methods, the end result is the replacement of the selected edge(s) with a face(s) at an angle specified either directly or indirectly through the use of distances.

The following illustration shows a part before and after adding chamfer features.

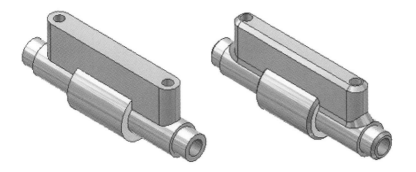

Access

Chamfer

Ribbon: **Model tab > Modify panel**

Keyboard Shortcut: **CTRL+SHIFT+K**

Chamfer Dialog Box

The Chamfer dialog box is displayed when you start the Chamfer tool.

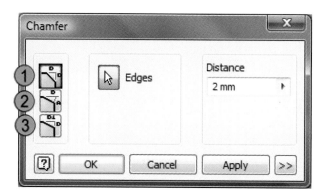

	Option	Description
(1)	**Distance**	Specify a distance for the chamfer. The distance is applied to both sides of the selected edge, resulting in a 45-degree chamfer.
(2)	**Distance and Angle**	Select a face adjacent to the edge you are chamfering. The angle is measured from this face. Select the edge(s) to be chamfered. This option is disabled until you select a face. The edge(s) selected must be adjacent to the selected face. Specify a distance for the chamfer. The distance is measured from the selected edge along the selected face. Enter an angle for the chamfer. The angle is measured from the selected face.
(3)	**Two Distances**	Select the edge to be chamfered. When you use this method, only one edge can be chamfered at a time. Specify the first distance of the chamfer. This distance is measured along one of the adjacent faces. Specify the second distance of the chamfer. This distance is measured along the opposite adjacent face.

Procedure: Creating Chamfers

The following steps describe how to create chamfer features.

1   On the ribbon, click the Chamfer tool.

2   In the Chamfer dialog box, select the desired method to create the chamfer.

- For a single distance chamfer, select the edge(s) to be chamfered. Enter a distance for the chamfer.

The resulting chamfer is created.

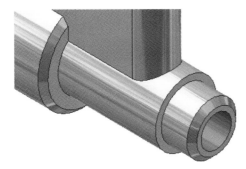

- For the distance and angle method, select the Distance and Angle option. Select the face, and then select the edge(s) to be chamfered. Enter a distance and angle for the chamfer.

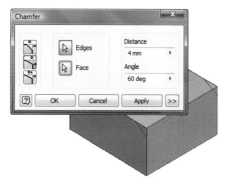

The resulting chamfer is created.

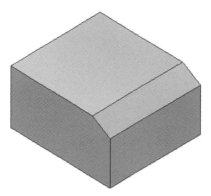

- For the two distances method, select the Two Distances option. Select the edge to be chamfered. Enter distance values in the Distance1 and Distance2 fields.

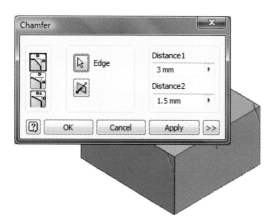

Click OK to create the chamfer. The resulting chamfer is created.

Creating Fillets

You use the Fillet tool to create fillets and rounds on existing 3D geometry. You can create both constant radius and variable radius fillets with the Fillet tool.

The following illustration shows a block before and after adding fillet features.

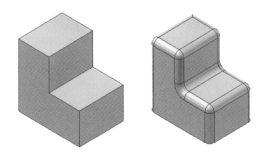

Access

Fillet

Ribbon: **Model tab > Modify panel**

Keyboard Shortcut: **F**

Constant Radius Fillet Options

The Fillet dialog box is displayed when you start the Fillet tool.

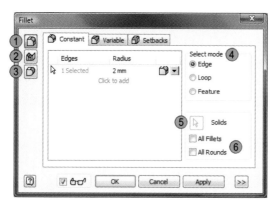

The following creation methods and options are available in the Fillet dialog box.

	Option	Description
1	**Edge**	Adds fillets or rounds to one or more edges of a part. All fillets and rounds created in a single operation become a single feature.
2	**Face**	Adds fillets or rounds between two selected face sets. The face sets do not need to share an edge.
3	**Full Round**	Adds fillets or rounds that are tangent to three adjacent faces. The center face is replaced by the fillet.
4	**Select Mode**	Mode selection enables easy selection of objects to fillet. Select Edge for edge selection priority; Loop for face selection priority; and Feature for feature priority selection.
5	**Solids**	This button is only available when multiple solid bodies exist in the part file. When this is the case, the user can click the solids button to select one or more solid bodies to use with the All Fillets and All Rounds selection options.
6	**Options**	Use the All Fillets or All Rounds check boxes to quickly select all fillet edges or all round edges on the part. Select them both to have all edges on the part selected.

Procedure: Creating Constant Radius Fillets

Follow these steps to create constant radius fillet features.

1 On the ribbon, click the Fillet tool.

2 With the Fillet dialog box displayed, in the graphics window, select the edges to be filleted and specify a radius for each edge set. Create an edge set for each different radius. In the following illustration, two edge sets have been created. The first edge set contains two edges to receive a 2 mm fillet and the second set contains three edges to receive a 1 mm fillet.

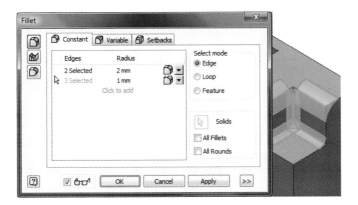

3 Click OK to create the fillet feature. Notice that in the browser only one fillet feature is displayed even though five edges were filleted in this example.

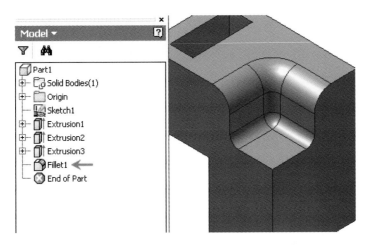

Guidelines for Creating Chamfers and Fillets

Although both fillets and chamfers are relatively simple shapes, they are often a challenge to create with consistency where multiple edges intersect. Following the guidelines presented here can improve your success in creating these features.

Chamfer and Fillet Creation Guidelines

- Avoid creating all of your fillets and chamfers with a single feature. You will have greater success creating and changing features with less edges selected.

- Create these features on parallel edges of a part first. When you create additional features, you can select the resulting face to complete the remaining edges at the same time.

- Remember that using the Two Distances option with the Chamfer tool limits you to creating the feature on one edge at a time.

- Pressing CTRL while clicking removes geometry from the selection.

- Because fillets and chamfers are considered finish features, consider creating them toward the end of the design process after all other features have been defined.

- Avoid including fillets and chamfers in your sketch geometry and instead create them as part features.

Example of Creating Separate Features

In the following example, by creating your side fillets first, you can select the continuously tangent edge as a single selection rather than having to select all the edges individually. Creating your fillet features in this way gives you more flexibility for possible changes to the part later.

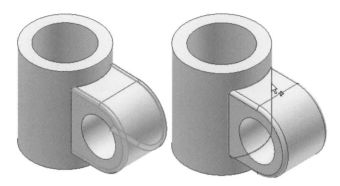

Exercise | Create Chamfers

In this exercise, you add chamfer features to an existing part.

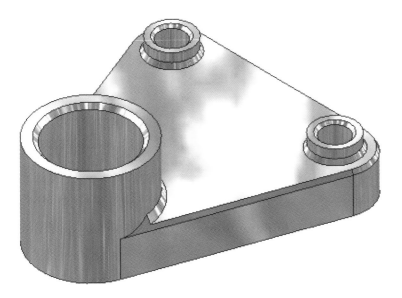

The completed exercise

Completing the Exercise:	*To complete the exercise, follow the steps in this book or in the onscreen exercise. In the onscreen list of chapters and exercises, click Chapter 4: Detailed Shape Design. Click Exercise: Create Chamfers.*

1   Open *Rod-Bearing-Mount.ipt*.

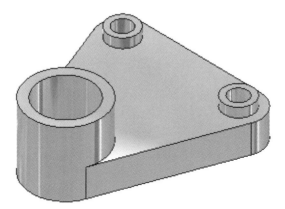

2   Create a chamfer on the inside edge of the large hole.

   • On the ribbon, click the Chamfer tool.
   • Select the inside edge of the large hole.
   • For Distance, enter **1.5 mm** . Click OK.

3 Create a 1.0 mm chamfer on the inside edge of the two small holes.

- Restart the Chamfer tool.
- Select the inside edges of the smaller holes.
- For Distance, enter **1.0 mm**. Click OK.

4 Create a chamfer around the top surface of the part.

- Restart the Chamfer tool. In the Chamfer dialog box, click the Distance and Angle option.
- Select the side face of part (1). Select the top edge of the part (2).
- For Distance, enter **1.5mm**. For Angle, enter **30 deg**. Click OK.

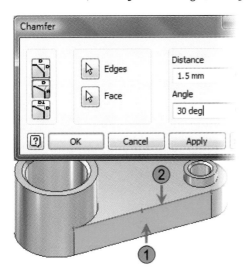

5   Add a chamfer between the cylinder and main face.

- Restart the Chamfer tool. Click the Two Distances method.
- Select the edge labeled (1) in the following illustration.
- For Distance1, enter **1.5 mm**. For Distance2, enter **2.5 mm**.
- Click OK.

6   Add a chamfer to the base of the two small bosses.

- Restart the Chamfer tool. Click the Distance and Angle method.
- Select the top face of the part (1). Select the two edges of the smaller bosses (2).
- For Distance, enter **1.0 mm**. For Angle, enter **60 deg.** Click OK.

7   Close all files. Do not save.

Exercise | Create Fillets

In this exercise, you create constant radius fillets on an existing part.

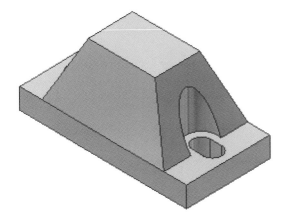

The completed exercise

Completing the Exercise: To complete the exercise, follow the steps in this book or in the onscreen exercise. In the onscreen list of chapters and exercises, click Chapter 4: Detailed Shape Design. Click Exercise: Create Fillets.

1   Open *Pillow-Block-Rev-2.ipt*.

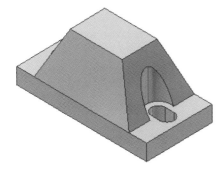

2　Create fillets from two edge sets on one end of the part.

- On the ribbon, click the Fillet tool.
- Select the geometry labeled (1). For Radius, enter **2 mm**.
- Click the Click To Add option and create a second edge set by selecting the geometry labeled (2). For Radius, enter **4 mm**.
- Click OK to create the feature.

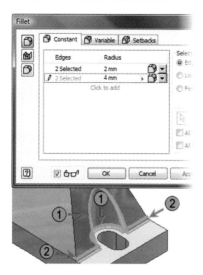

3　Repeat the previous steps to create the same fillets on the opposite side of the part.

- On the ViewCube, click the top-left corner to rotate the view until it appears as shown.
- On the keyboard, press F and create the same fillet feature as in step 2.

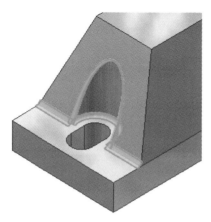

4   Create a fillet on the top edges.

- Click the Fillet tool.
- Select the two edges along the top of the part as shown in the following illustration.
- For the Radius, enter **20 mm.** Click OK.

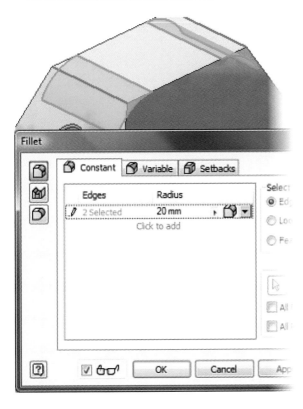

5   Create a fillet along each edge.

- On the ribbon, click the Fillet tool.
- Select the edges as shown in the following illustration. Notice that a single pick selects all the curves on a side due to the fillet created on the top face in the previous step.
- Set the Radius to **4 mm**. Click OK.

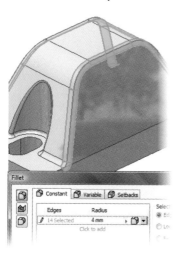

6   Create fillets on the remaining edges.

- Click the Fillet tool and select the edges shown here.
- For the Radius, enter **4 mm.** Click OK.

7   Create the same fillet features on the opposite side of the part as you did in the previous step.

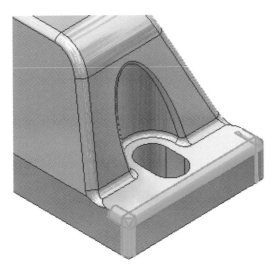

8   Close all files. Do not save.

Lesson 14 | Creating Holes and Threads

This lesson describes how to use the Hole tool to create parametric hole features and the Thread tool to create threads on existing model features. You use hole features to create parametric holes on parts. Although hole features are considered to be placed features, you can use unconsumed sketch geometry to represent the center point locations for the holes.

The most common method of joining two or more components together is with threaded fasteners. You should master the use of both the hole and thread features to produce the best models possible.

The following illustration shows a part that contains a combination of hole and thread features.

Objectives

After completing this lesson, you will be able to:

- Define a hole feature.

- Use the Hole tool to create holes on your part.

- Use the Thread tool to create external thread features.

About Hole Features

Hole features are parametrically created features that are placed on existing part geometry. You can create hole features with a number of different options, such as counterbore, countersink, flat bottom, spotface, threads, tapered threads, and fastener clearances.

The following illustration shows a part with various types of holes. The enlarged view (1) shows the bitmap thread representation.

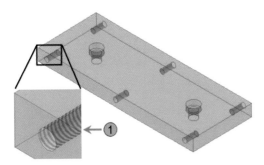

Definition of Parametric Holes

There are many different ways to fasten parts together and most require a hole. Although you can create holes by extruding a circle with a cut operation, the Hole tool provides greater flexibility in the variations and types of holes that you can create, such as counterbore, countersink, and threads. Using the Hole tool, you can create the various hole types in a single dialog box, rather than having to manually edit or create geometry.

A primary benefit of using the Hole tool is the ability to annotate holes in the drawing environment with the Hole Note and Hole Chart tools. A sample of the automatic hole note callout is shown in the following illustration.

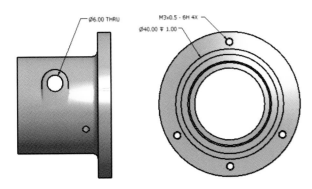

Example of Fastening Parts

Two metal components are often fastened together using a socket head cap screw. The following illustration shows the clearance hole for the screw in one part and the threaded hole in the mating part.

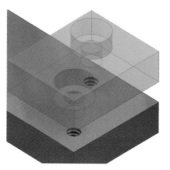

Benefits of the Hole Tool

Benefits of using the Hole tool include the following:

- You use a single tool to create holes with various options.
- You can annotate holes created with the Hole tool in the drawing with the Hole Note and Hole Chart tools.
- You can determine hole size by specifying the fastener thread type or clearance.
- Options such as the counterbore, countersink, and spotface enable you to add features in a single operation.

Creating Holes

When you use the Hole tool, different options are available for defining the location of the hole as well as for the type of hole to be created. You can define hole locations based on sketch geometry or existing planes, points, and edges on the part. You can create standard drilled holes, counterbored holes, and countersunk holes. Additional options are available for the drill point and thread options.

Access

Hole

Ribbon: **Model tab > Modify panel**

Keyboard Shortcut: **H**

Hole Dialog Box

The Hole dialog box is displayed when you start the Hole tool.

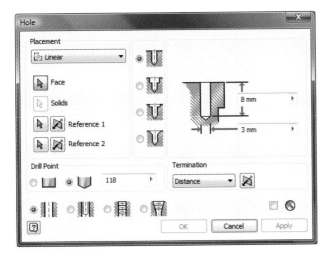

Hole Placement Options

You can use any of the following options in the Hole dialog box for placing a hole feature.

From Sketch

Select this option to create holes based on locations on a sketch. Hole locations can consist of Point/Hole Center objects, endpoints of lines or curves, or centers of projected circular geometry.

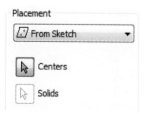

The following option is available when you select From Sketch placement.

Dialog Box Access	Option	Description
![]	**Centers**	Select the center points for the holes. Use this option to create a series of identical holes with one feature.
![]	**Solids**	This option is only available when the part contains multiple solid bodies. When available, you can use this option to select the solid body that the hole feature will apply to.

Linear

Select this option to position the hole relative to two selected edges.

The following options are available when you select Linear placement.

Dialog Box Access	Option	Description
	Face	Select a face on the part to orient the hole.
	Solids	This option is only available when the part contains multiple solid bodies. When available, you can use this option to select the solid body that the hole feature will apply to.
	Reference 1	Select a part edge as the first reference. A dimension is placed from the selected edge to the center of the hole. The dimension can be edited as a standard parametric dimension.
	Reference 2	Select a part edge as the second reference. A dimension is placed from the selected edge to the center of the hole.
	Flip Side	Select this option to position the hole on the opposite side of the selected edge.

Concentric

Select this option to position the hole concentric to another circular part edge.

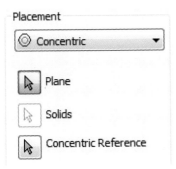

The following options are available when you select Concentric placement.

Dialog Box Access	Option	Description
[icon]	**Plane**	Select a part face to orient the hole.
[icon]	**Solids**	This option is only available when the part contains multiple solid bodies. When available, you can use this option to select the solid body that the hole feature will apply to.
[icon]	**Concentric Reference**	Select a circular edge or face to position the hole concentrically.

On Point

Select this option to position the hole on a work point.

The following options are available when you select On Point placement.

Dialog Box Access	Option	Description
[icon]	**Point**	Select a work point to position the hole.
[icon]	**Solids**	This option is only available when the part contains multiple solid bodies. When available, you can use this option to select the solid body that the hole feature will apply to.
[icon]	**Direction**	Select a plane, face, edge, or work axis to define the direction of the hole. If you select a plane, the hole direction is normal to the face or plane.

Hole Type and Size Options

You can use any of the following options in the Hole dialog box to define the type and size of the hole.

Hole Type

Use the following options to define a standard drilled hole, counterbore hole, spotface, or countersink hole.

Hole Parameters

Depending on the hole type selected, enter the hole parameters in each available field.

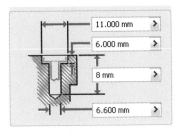

Drill Point

Select flat or angled drill point. If you select angled, either enter an angle for the drill point or accept the default value.

Termination

Select the termination option for the hole from the drop-down list.

Option	Description
Distance	The depth of the hole is based on the distance that you entered in the hole parameters area.
Through All	The hole is created through the entire part, even if the part depth at the location of the hole changes.
To	Select a face or plane to calculate the depth of the hole.

Additional Hole Type Options

Use the additional hole type options to define a simple hole, tapped hole, or clearance hole.

Option	Description
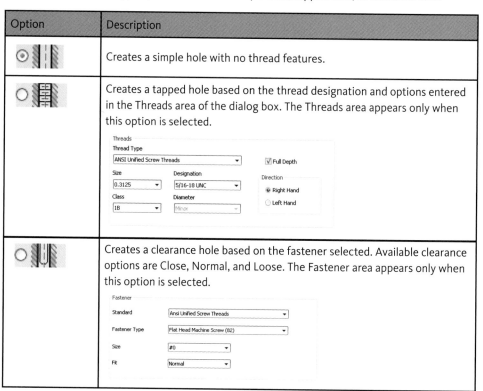	Creates a simple hole with no thread features.
	Creates a tapped hole based on the thread designation and options entered in the Threads area of the dialog box. The Threads area appears only when this option is selected.
	Creates a clearance hole based on the fastener selected. Available clearance options are Close, Normal, and Loose. The Fastener area appears only when this option is selected.

Option	Description
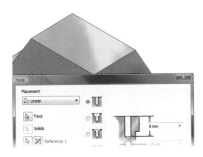	Creates an NPT tapped or Taper threaded hole based on the thread designation and options entered in the Threads area of the dialog box.

Procedure: Creating Hole Features Using the Linear Option

Follow these steps to create hole features using the Linear placement option of the Hole tool.

1   On the ribbon, click Hole and select Linear from the Placement list.

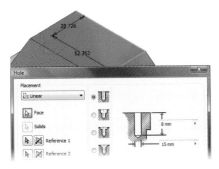

2   Select the face to orient the top of the hole, then select two reference edges to locate the hole. The edges that you select do not need to be on the same plane as the face that you select.

3 Select each dimension and enter its precise value in the Edit Dimension dialog box.

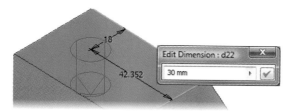

4 Adjust the options in the Hole dialog box. Click Apply to create the hole and continue placing other holes.

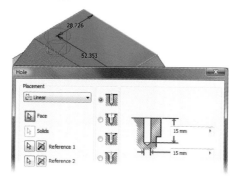

Procedure: Creating Hole Features Using the Concentric Option

Follow these steps to create hole features by using the Concentric placement option of the Hole tool.

1 On the ribbon, click Hole and select Concentric from the Placement list.

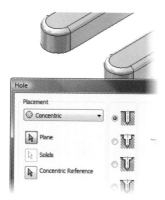

2   Select the plane or face (1) to orient the hole, then select a curved surface (2) as the
    concentric reference.

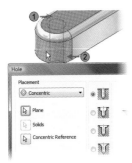

3   Adjust the options in the Hole dialog box. Click Apply to create the hole and continue placing
    other hole features.

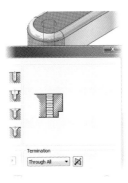

Procedure: Creating Hole Features Using the From Sketch Option

Follow these steps to create and edit holes using sketch geometry for the hole locations.

1   Create a new sketch that contains the center point location for the hole features.

2   On the ribbon, click Finish Sketch to exit the sketch.

3   On the ribbon, click Hole and select the From Sketch placement option. If you use the Point/ Hole Center sketch object, the hole centers are automatically selected. Adjust the options in the dialog box depending on the type of hole you need to create. Click OK to create the hole.

Procedure: Creating Hole Features Using the On Point Option

Follow these steps to create hole features using the On Point placement option of the Hole tool.

1   Create a work point (1) at the location of the hole.

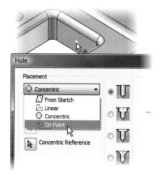

2   On the ribbon, click Hole. Select On Point from the Placement list and then select the work point.

3   Select a face, edge, or axis to define the direction of the hole. If you select a face or plane, the direction is normal to the face or plane.

4   Adjust the options in the Hole dialog box. Click Apply to create the hole and continue placing other holes, or click OK to create the hole and end the process.

Creating Threads

Using the Thread tool, you can create thread features on external and internal surfaces. Many of the options available for internal threads using the Hole tool are also available when you use the Thread tool. Threads are considered a placed feature, so the Thread tool does not require an unconsumed sketch. All that is required is existing cylindrical surfaces to apply the thread feature.

The following illustration shows external thread features (1).

About Thread Features

With the Thread tool, you can turn your cylindrical faces into threaded features. You should create your cylindrical diameters to the nominal size of the thread. The Thread tool automatically selects the correct thread for that diameter.

Your threaded features do not affect the mass property calculations. They do however work with the Hole Note callout in the drawing environment.

While in most cases you use the Hole command to produce internal threads, on occasion you need to use the Thread tool. This most often occurs when you produce an internal diameter with the Revolve Feature tool. The model in the following illustration was produced with the Revolve tool. Both the internal and external threads were produced using the Thread tool.

Access

Thread

Ribbon: **Model tab > Modify panel**

Toolbar: **Part Features**

Thread Options

The Thread dialog box is displayed when you start the Thread tool.

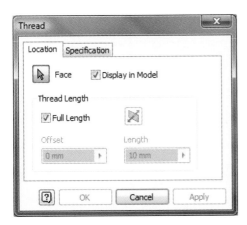

The Location tab in the Thread dialog box includes the following options and specifications.

Dialog Box Access	Option	Description
	Face	Click the icon to select the face(s) to apply thread features.
☑ Display in Model	Display in Model	Select this option to display the thread bitmaps on the model. If this option is not selected, the thread feature is created but is not displayed on the geometry.
Thread Length ☑ Full Length	Full Length	Select this option to apply the thread feature to the entire length of the selected face. When this option is not selected, the next three following options become available.
	Flip	Click this button to flip the direction of the thread feature.
Length 10 mm	Length	Specifies the length of the thread feature on the selected face.
Offset 0 mm	Offset	Specifies the distance from the start face of the thread feature.

The Specification tab in the Thread dialog box includes the following options and specifications.

Dialog Box Access	Option	Description
Thread Type ANSI Metric M Profile ANSI Unified Screw Threads ANSI Metric M Profile ISO Metric profile ISO Metric Trapezoidal Threads NPT for PVC Pipe and Fitting NPT ISO Pipe Threads ISO Taper Internal JIS Pipe Threads JIS Taper Internal Din Taper DIN Pipe Taper Internal DIN Pipe Threads BSP Pipe Threads BSP Taper Internal GB Metric profile GB Pipe Threads	**Thread Type**	Select the required thread type..
Size 7	**Size**	The nominal thread size is automatically selected based upon the diameter of the selected face. Selecting a nominal size other than the size automatically selected may result in an error when you click OK.
Designation M7x1	**Designation**	Select the appropriate thread pitch from the list.

Dialog Box Access	Option	Description
Class 6H	**Class**	Select the appropriate thread class from the list.
◉ Right hand ○ Left hand	**Right or Left Hand**	Select to designate your desired thread hand.

Procedure: Creating Thread Features

The following steps describe how to create external thread features using the Thread tool.

1   On the ribbon, click Thread and select a cylindrical face on the part. On the Location tab, adjust the Thread Length options as required.

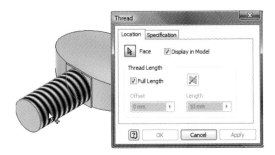

2   On the Specification tab, select the appropriate thread type and adjust the other settings as required.

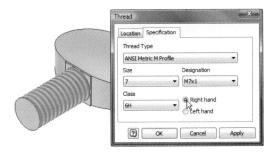

3   Click OK to create the thread feature. The thread feature is displayed on the model geometry as well as in the browser. Just like with other parametric features, you can right-click the thread feature and click Edit Feature to edit the feature using the same dialog box used in creating the feature.

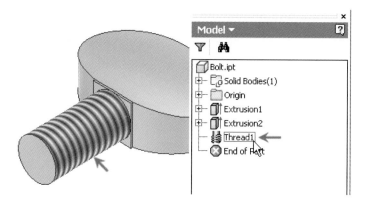

Exercise | Create Holes and Threads

In this exercise, you use the Hole tool with multiple placement options to create tapped, countersink, counterbore, and clearance holes. You also use the Thread tool to create an internal and external thread.

The completed exercise

Completing the Exercise:	*To complete the exercise, follow the steps in this book or in the onscreen exercise. In the onscreen list of chapters and exercises, click Chapter 4: Detailed Shape Design. Click Exercise: Create Holes and Threads.*

Create Holes

In this portion of the exercise, you use the Hole tool with multiple placement options to create tapped holes and a through hole using the On Point placement option.

1   Open *Hole_Thread_Features1.ipt*.

2   Create a tapped hole on the part face.

  • On the ribbon, click the Hole tool.
  • In the Hole dialog box, select Linear from the Placement list.
  • Click Face.

3   Select a location near the lower left corner on the front planar face.

4   Select the left edge as Reference 1. Select the bottom edge as Reference 2.

5   To locate the hole:

• Click the Reference 1 dimension.
• Enter a distance of **4 mm.**
• Click the Reference 2 dimension.
• Enter a distance of **4 mm.**

6   Finish selecting your settings and create the hole.

• Specify that the hole is M6 x 1 tapped with a 6 mm countersink and a depth of 10 mm (1).
• In the Threads area, select the Full Depth option (2).
• Click Apply to create the hole.

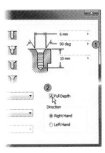

7   Repeat the previous steps to create a similar hole on the opposite side of the face.

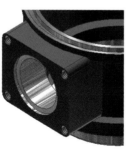

8   In the Hole dialog box, select Concentric from the Placement list.

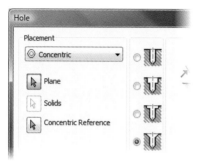

9   Select the top plane of the part that contains the three small machined flanges.

10   Create an M6 x 1 tapped hole through the flange.

- Select the circular edge of the machined flange to set the concentric reference. Holes can be placed concentric to a circular edge or a cylindrical face.
- Change the settings as needed to create an M6x1 tapped hole through all.
- Click Apply to create the hole.

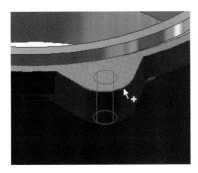

11   Repeat the previous steps to create two additional holes on the remaining small flanges. Close the Hole dialog box when done.

12   In the browser, right-click Work Axis3. Click Visibility. Rotate your view as shown.

13 Create a hole using the On Point option.

- Press H to start the Hole tool.
- In the Holes dialog box, select On Point from the Placement list.

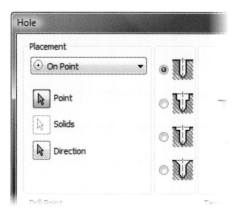

14 Select the point and specify direction for the On Point hole.

- In the graphics window, select Work Point3.
- Select Work Axis3 to define the direction of the hole.
  Note: Planes, axes, and edges can be used to define the direction of a hole. If the hole is previewed outside the part, it may be necessary to click the Flip Direction tool.

15 Finish the On Point hole.

- Change the hole diameter to **4 mm**.
- Set Termination to Through All.
- Click Apply to create the hole.

16 Close all files. Do not save.

Create Holes and Threads

In this portion of the exercise, you use the Hole tool with multiple placement options to create countersink, counterbore, and clearance holes. You also use the Thread tool to create an internal and external thread.

1   Open *Hole_Thread_Features2.ipt*.

2   Create a screw clearance hole.

- Start the Hole tool.
- For Placement, select On Point.
- For Hole Type, select Clearance Hole.

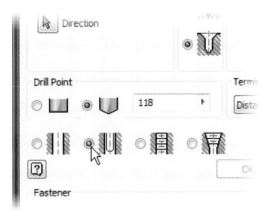

3   In the graphics window, select Work Point2 on the large flange.

4   In the graphics window, select the face on which the point exists to define the hole direction.

5   Complete the clearance hole as specified:

- Specify a loose fit clearance hole with counterbores for a 5 mm Ansi Metric Hex Head Cap Screw. The data used for clearance holes is stored in the *Clearance.xls* spreadsheet, located in the Design Data folder of the Inventor installation directory tree.

- Click Apply.

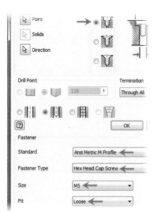

6   Repeat the previous steps to create a similar hole for the large flange on the opposite side of the part. Click Done to exit the Hole dialog box.

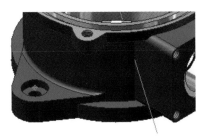

7   Add a thread feature to the underside of the part. Rotate your view as necessary to select the faces.

• On the ribbon, click the Thread tool.
• Select the outside face as shown.

8   Set the specification settings for the thread.

• In the Thread dialog box, click the Specification tab.
• Set Designation to M90x4. Click OK to create the thread.

9   Create a thread on an internal feature.

   • Start the Thread tool.
   • Select the inner face as shown.

10   Complete the thread by making the specification settings.

   • In the Thread dialog box, click the Specification tab.
   • Set the Designation to M30x2.5 and click Left Hand.
   • Click OK to create the thread.

11   Create a spotface threaded hole.

  • Start the Hole tool, Linear placement.
  • Select the Spotface and Taper Thread Hole options.
  • Select the face as shown.

12   To locate the hole:

  • For the first linear reference, select an edge along the front face. Enter **12**.
  • For the second linear reference, select the top or bottom face. Enter **22.5**.

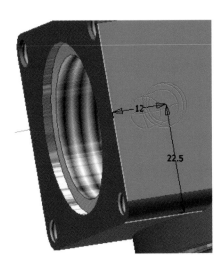

13   For the thread specification:

- For thread type, select DIN Taper.
- For size, select M5.

14   To define the hole:

- Enter **12** for the spotface diameter.
- Enter **1** for the spotface depth.
- Enter **15** for the drill depth.

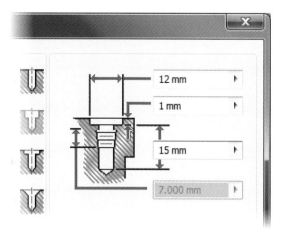

15   Click OK to create the spotface taper thread feature.

16   Close all files. Do not save.

Lesson 15 | Patterning and Mirroring Features

This lesson describes how to mirror features, and how to reuse existing features in rectangular and circular patterns. Mirroring and patterning can save you time in creating the geometry, as well as in editing the features when the design changes.

When you create patterns or mirror existing geometry, you reduce the need to manually draw and edit these duplicate features.

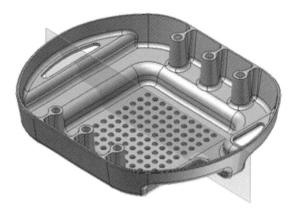

Objectives

After completing this lesson, you will be able to:

- Identify situations in which you should pattern or mirror part features instead of creating new ones.

- Use the Rectangular Pattern tool to create rectangular patterns.

- Use the Circular Pattern tool to create circular patterns.

- Use the Mirror tool to create symmetric features.

About Feature Reuse

Many designs require patterns of features or geometry that consist of features that are symmetric about a given plane. Instead of creating these features independently, you can use the Pattern and Mirror tools to populate your parts with existing features.

Definition of Patterns

You use patterns to duplicate existing geometry according to parameters that you specify. When you create patterns, occurrences of the original features are created. You can create these occurrences in a circular or a rectangular pattern. When you create these patterns, the occurrences are associative to the original feature, so any changes in the original feature are automatically reflected in the pattern occurrences.

Definition of Mirroring Part Features

Parts often include features that can be considered symmetric about a plane of symmetry to other features on the part. You can use the Mirror tool to mirror this geometry.

In the following illustration, Rectangular (1) and Circular (2) patterns have been created based on individual features.

Features That Can Be Reused

The following features can be patterned or mirrored:

- Most sketched and placed features
- Entire solids
- Work features

Benefits of Reusing Features

Benefits associated with patterning and mirroring features include the following:

- You need to create only one of the patterned or symmetric features.
- Changes that you make to the original feature are automatically applied to the patterned or mirrored features.

Appearance of Rectangular and Circular Patterns in the Browser

The way that patterns are displayed in the browser is different from the way that other features are displayed. When you expand a rectangular or circular pattern, the difference is immediately apparent. Any sketches used as a path, along with a folder containing the features used in the pattern, are displayed under the pattern feature. Beneath that is an Occurrence item for each occurrence in the pattern. The first Occurrence item represents the initial feature used in the pattern, followed by an Occurrence item for each occurrence created.

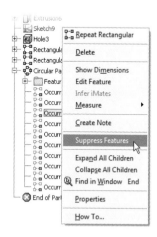

Right-click an occurrence and click Suppress on the shortcut menu to suppress the selected occurrence. This option is not available on the first occurrence.

Example of Mirrored Features

In the following illustration, the part consists of several features that are symmetric about a plane of symmetry. The symmetry planes are identified, along with the features that have been mirrored about them.

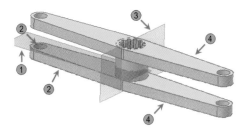

① Symmetry Plane A

② Features mirrored about Plane A

③ Symmetry Plane B

④ Features mirrored about Plane B

Creating Rectangular Patterns

You use the Rectangular Pattern tool to duplicate one or more features in a rectangular pattern. You can pattern a feature along one or two directions and/or paths, with options to control feature spacing.

Access

Rectangular Pattern

Ribbon: **Model tab > Pattern panel**

Keyboard Shortcut: **CTRL+SHIFT+R**

Rectangular Pattern Dialog Box

The Rectangular Pattern dialog box is displayed when you start the Rectangular Pattern tool.

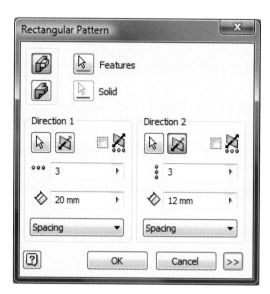

Pattern Type Options

The following pattern types are available in the Rectangular Pattern dialog box.

Dialog Box Access	Option	Description
	Individual Feature	Click this button to pattern individual features.
	Entire Solid	Click this button to pattern the entire solid.

When the Pattern Individual Features button is selected, you have the following selection options.

Dialog Box Access	Option	Description
	Features	Select one or more features to be patterned.
	Solid	This button is only available when multiple solid bodies exist. You use this button to determine to which solid body the feature is going to be applied.

When the Pattern Entire Solid button is selected, you have the following selection option.

Dialog Box Access	Option	Description
	Include Work/ Surface Features	Select the work features to include in the pattern.
	Solid	This button is only available when multiple solid bodies exist. You use this button to determine to which solid body the feature is going to be applied.

Direction Pattern Options

The following options are available in the Direction 1 and Direction 2 areas of the Rectangular Pattern dialog box.

Dialog Box Access	Option	Description
	Path	Select the path for Direction 1. This can be the edge of a part or a 2D sketch that represents the path for the pattern. Valid selections include 2D and 3D lines, arcs, splines, part edges, axes, and trimmed ellipses. Click the Flip button to flip the path direction.
	Mid Plane	Creates a pattern where the occurrences are distributed on both sides of the original feature.
2	Count	Enter the number of occurrences for the pattern. This number includes the original feature.
10 mm	Length	Enter a value for the pattern distance. This value represents either the total distance of the pattern or the spacing between the features.
Spacing / Spacing / Distance / Curve Length	Method	Specifies the total distance and direction of the pattern, the spacing between occurrences, or if the pattern is equally fitted to the length of the selected curve.

Compute Options

The following options are available in the Compute area of the Rectangular Pattern dialog box.

Dialog Box Access	Option	Description
Optimized	Optimized	For pattern occurrences of 50 or more, increases pattern performance.

Dialog Box Access	Option	Description
⦿ Identical	**Identical**	With this method, each occurrence uses an identical termination method, regardless of where it intersects other features.
⦿ Adjust	**Adjust**	Enables each occurrence termination to be calculated. This method requires more processing and can increase computational time on large patterns.

Orientation Pattern Options

The following options are available in the Orientation area of the Rectangular Pattern dialog box.

Dialog Box Access	Option	Description
⦿ Identical	**Identical**	Occurrence orientation is identical to that of the first feature.
⦿ Direction1 ◯ Direction2	**Adjust Direction**	Specifies which direction controls the position of patterned features. Rotates each occurrence so that it maintains its orientation to the 2D tangent vector of the path.

Procedure: Creating an Optimized Rectangular Pattern

Follow these steps to create an optimized rectangular pattern.

1   Create a part with one or more features to be patterned.

2   On the ribbon, click the Rectangular Pattern tool and select the feature to be patterned. Click the Path button under Direction 1 and select a path, part edge, or origin axis for the pattern. Enter the number of occurrences and distance values and adjust t10 link he spacing method as necessary. Optionally include information for Direction 2, then click OK.

3   As soon as the total number of occurrences is equal to or greater than 50, you are prompted to consider using the Optimized Compute option. Click OK to close the message box.

4   In the Rectangular Pattern dialog box, click the More button to expand the dialog box, and then select Optimized.

5   Click OK to create the optimized pattern.

Creating Circular Patterns

You use the Circular Pattern tool to duplicate one or more features in a circular pattern. When you start the Circular Pattern tool, you first choose to pattern individual features or the entire solid. You then select a rotation axis, which serves as the center of the pattern. Next you set the pattern properties, such as number of occurrences and angle. There are also options for controlling the creation method and positioning method.

The following illustration demonstrates a circular hole pattern being created.

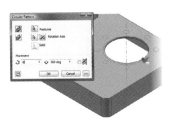

Access

Circular Pattern

Ribbon: **Model tab > Pattern panel**

Keyboard Shortcut: **CTRL+SHIFT+O**

Circular Pattern Dialog Box

The Circular Pattern dialog box is displayed when you start the Circular Pattern tool.

Pattern Type Options

The following pattern types are available in the Circular Pattern dialog box:

Dialog Box Access	Option	Description
	Individual Feature	Click this button to pattern individual features.
	Entire Solid	Click this button to pattern the entire solid.

Feature-Axis Selection

When the Pattern Individual Features button is selected, you have the following selection options.

Dialog Box Access	Option	Description
	Features	Select one or more features to be patterned.
	Rotation Axis	Specifies the axis, or pivot point, about which features are rotated. Click Flip to reverse the direction of the pattern.
	Solid	This button is only available when multiple solid bodies exist. You use this button to determine to which solid body the feature is going to be applied.

When the Pattern Entire Solid button is selected, you have the following selection option.

Dialog Box Access	Option	Description
	Include Work/ Surface Features	Select the work features to include in the pattern.
	Solid	This button is only available when multiple solid bodies exist. You use this button to determine to which solid body the feature is going to be applied.

Pattern Placement Options

The following placement options are available in the Circular Pattern dialog box:

Dialog Box Access	Option	Description
8	**Count**	Specify the number of occurrences for the pattern. This number includes the original feature.
360 deg	**Angle**	Specify the angle for the pattern. The result of this angle is based on the positioning method you select.
	Mid Plane	Creates a pattern where the occurrences are distributed on both sides of the original feature.

Creation Method Options

The following options are available in the Creation Method section of the Circular Pattern dialog box:

Dialog Box Access	Option	Description
⦿ Optimized	**Optimized**	For pattern occurrences of 50 or more, increases pattern performance.
⦿ Identical	**Identical**	With this method, each occurrence uses an identical termination method, regardless of where it intersects other features.

Dialog Box Access	Option	Description
⊙ Adjust	**Adjust**	Enables each occurrence termination to be calculated. This method requires more processing and can increase computational time on large patterns.

Positioning Method Options

The following options are available in the Positioning Method section of the Circular Pattern dialog box:

Dialog Box Access	Option	Description
⦿ Incremental	**Incremental**	Sets the angle value to represent the angle between occurrences.
⦿ Fitted	**Fitted**	Sets the angle value to represent the total rotational angle of the pattern.

Procedure: Creating Circular Patterns of the Entire Solid

The following steps describe to create circular patterns of the entire solid while including work features in the pattern.

1   Create a part that contains the feature or features to be patterned.

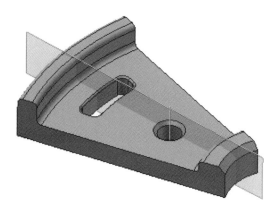

2   On the ribbon, click the Circular Pattern tool and click the Pattern the Entire Solid button.

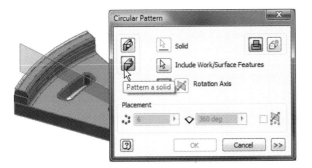

3   Click the Include Work/Surface Features button and select any work features to be included in the pattern. Select the Rotation Axis.

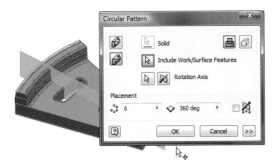

4   Specify the quantity placement information.

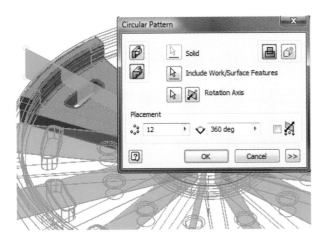

5   Click OK. The entire solid along with the selected work features is patterned.

Mirroring Features

When you mirror part features, you must first have the features to be mirrored and a plane to use as the symmetry plane. The symmetry plane can be any of the following:

*   An existing face on the part.

*   Any one of the origin work planes.

*   A new work plane.

With these conditions met, click the Mirror tool, select the features to be mirrored, then select the face or work plane to use as the mirror plane. The features are mirrored about the selected plane and displayed in the browser, with the included features and occurrences nested underneath the mirror feature.

The features to be mirrored are highlighted in the browser.

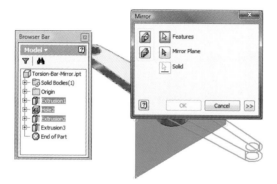

Access

Mirror

Ribbon: **Model tab > Pattern panel**

Keyboard Shortcut: **CTRL+SHIFT+M**

Mirror Dialog Box

The Mirror dialog box is displayed when you start the Mirror tool.

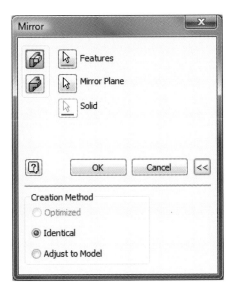

Mirror Type Options

The following mirror types are available in the Mirror dialog box:

Dialog Box Access	Option	Description
	Individual Feature	Click this button to mirror individual features.
	Entire Solid	Click this button to mirror the entire solid.

When the Mirror Individual Features button is selected, you have the following selection options.

Dialog Box Access	Option	Description
	Features	Select one or more features to be patterned.
	Mirror Plane	Select a face or work plane to be used as the plane of symmetry.
	Solid	This button is only available when multiple solid bodies exist. You use this button to determine to which solid body the feature is going to be applied.

When the Mirror Entire Solid button is selected, you have the following selection option.

Dialog Box Access	Option	Description
	Solid	This button is only available when multiple solid bodies exist. You use this button to determine to which solid body the feature is going to be applied.
	Include Work/ Surface Features	Select the work features to be included in the mirror.

Dialog Box Access	Option	Description
[cursor icon]	**Mirror Plane**	Select a face or work point to be used as the plane of symmetry.
☐ Remove Original	**Remove Original**	Placing a check in the box next to this option will delete the original solid that was originally used to pattern the feature.

Creation Method Options

The following options are available in the Creation Method area of the Mirror dialog box:

Dialog Box Access	Option	Description
⊙ Optimized	**Optimized**	Optimizes pattern performance.
⊙ Identical	**Identical**	The default; creates the mirrored occurrences identical to the original features.
⊙ Adjust	**Adjust to Model**	Enables the new mirrored occurrences to adjust to changes in model geometry. For example if you are mirroring a cut feature that extrudes through the part, using this option enables that cut feature to extrude the part on the opposite side, even if the part's thickness changes. **Note:** Use this option only when necessary, because additional processing resources are required to calculate the new occurrences.

Example: Creation Method = Identical

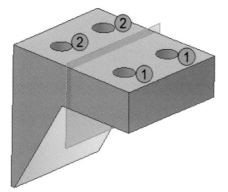

(1) Original hole features with through all termination option.

(2) Mirrored hole features

Example: Creation Method = Adjust to Model

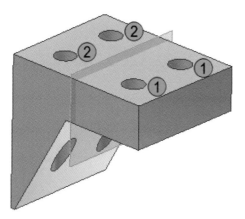

(1) Original hole features with through all termination option.

(2) Mirrored hole features.

Procedure: Mirroring Part Features

The following steps give an overview of mirroring part features.

1   Open or create a part that contains the geometry intended to be symmetric.

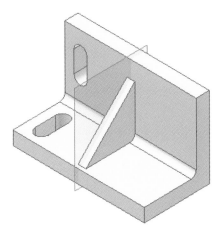

2   On the ribbon, click the Mirror Feature tool and select the features to be mirrored.

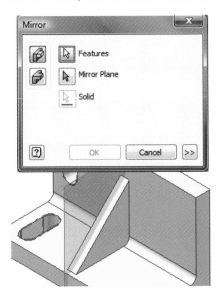

3   In the Mirror Pattern dialog box, click the Mirror Plane button and select a plane or face that represents the plane of symmetry for the mirrored features. Click OK.

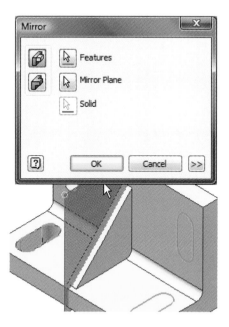

4   The mirrored features are created.

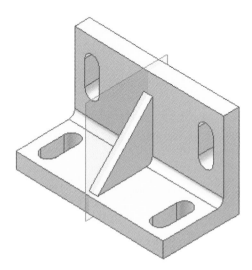

Exercise | Create Pattern Features

In this exercise, you open the face plate component and create both rectangular and circular patterned features. You then edit the patterned features to suppress occurrences within each.

The completed exercise

Completing the Exercise : To complete the exercise, follow the steps in this book or in the onscreen exercise. In the onscreen list of chapters and exercises, click Chapter 4: Detailed Shape Design. Click Exercise: Create Pattern Features.

1   Open *Receiver-Face-Plate.ipt*.

2   Create a rectangular pattern.

  • On the ribbon, click the Rectangular Pattern tool and select the Extrusion3 feature as shown in the following illustration. It may be easier to select the feature in the browser.
  • Under Direction 1, click the Path button and select the edge labeled 1 in the following illustration. If necessary, use the flip button to flip the path direction.
  • Under Direction 2, click the Path button and select the edge labeled 2 in the following illustration. If necessary use the flip button to flip the path direction.
  • Adjust the occurrence and distance options as shown and click OK.

3   Share a sketch to use as a pattern path.

  • The Hole3 feature was created on a sketch that can be used as the path for the next pattern. In the browser, expand the Hole3 feature to expose the Sketch9 feature.
  • Right-click the Sketch9 feature. Click Share Sketch. This action makes the sketch available for additional features.

4   Create a pattern using a sketch as a path.

- On the ribbon, click the Rectangular Pattern tool and in the browser select Hole3.
- In the Rectangular Pattern dialog box, under Direction 1, click the Path button.
- Select the shared sketch as shown in the following illustration.

5   Continue the pattern creation from the previous step.

- Under Direction 1, from the Spacing list, select Curve Length.
- In the Number of Occurrences box, enter **8**. Click OK.

6   In the browser, right-click Sketch9. Click Visibility on the shortcut menu to turn off the visibility of the shared sketch.

7   Create a circular pattern of a hole.

    • On the ribbon, click Circular Pattern.
    • Select the hole feature as shown in the following illustration.

8   In the Circular Pattern dialog box, click the Rotation Axis button and select the inside face of the large hole as shown.

9   In the Number of Occurrences field, enter **10**. Click OK.

10 Some of the occurrences that you just created are not required. You can suppress these occurrences by expanding the feature in the browser.

- In the browser, expand the Circular Pattern2 feature to expose the occurrences.
- While holding CTRL, select the occurrences as shown in the following illustration. Right- click one of the selected occurrences. Click Suppress.

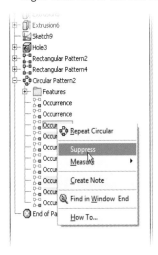

11 Close all files. Do not save.

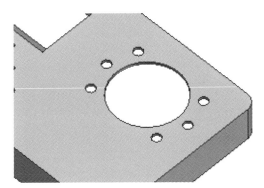

Exercise | Mirror Part Features

In this exercise, you create a torsion bar component that consists of multiple features that can be mirrored instead of recreated. You then create a new fillet feature and add that feature to the mirrored features.

The completed exercise

Completing the Exercise :	*To complete the exercise, follow the steps in this book or in the onscreen exercise. In the onscreen list of chapters and exercises, click Chapter 4: Detailed Shape Design. Click Exercise: Mirror Part Features.*

1   Open *Torsion-Bar-Mirror.ipt*

2   On the ribbon, click Mirror and select the Extrusion1, Hole2, and Extrusion2 features. Do not select the spline cut feature.

3   In the Mirror dialog box, click the Mirror Plane button. Select the bottom face of the part and click OK.

Notice that because the spline feature was not included in the mirror it does not extrude through the part.

4   In the browser, click and drag the Extrusion3 feature to move it under the Mirror3 feature.

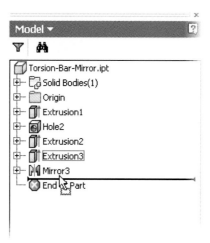

Because the extrusion was created using the Through All option, it now cuts through the part.

5   On the ribbon, click Mirror. In the browser, select the features as shown.

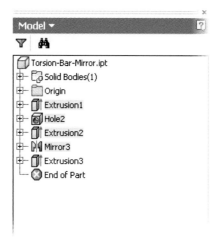

6   In the Mirror dialog box, click the Mirror Plane button. In the browser, expand the Origin
    folder and select YZ Plane, as shown.

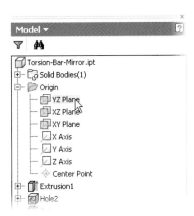

7   Click OK to create the mirror feature. The spline extrusion is no longer displayed because the
    results of the mirror feature override the extrusion feature.

8   In the browser, click and drag the Extrusion3 feature to drag it below the Mirror4 feature.
    Your part looks like the following illustration.

9   In the browser, click and drag the End of Part marker above the Mirror4 feature.

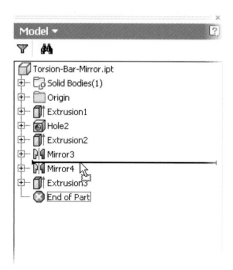

You do this so that you can create new features before the Mirror4 feature is considered. Dragging the End of Part marker enables you to roll back the model history and temporarily disregard all features below it.

10   Create a new sketch.

- Create a new sketch plane on the top surface.
- Draw and constrain the sketch as shown using the projected circle to locate it.

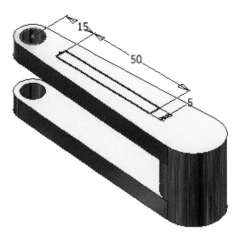

11   Extrude the new sketch to form a rib on the part:

- Start the Extrude tool.
- Select your sketched rectangle as the profile.
- For Extents, use From To.
- Select the two inside part faces as your surface to start and surface to end feature creation.
- Click OK to create the feature.

12   On the ribbon, click the Fillet tool and select all the edges around the web feature that you just created. Under Radius, enter **1 mm** and click OK.

13   In the browser, click and drag the End of Part marker below the Extrusion3 feature.

14   Edit the mirror feature to include the new extrusion and fillet.
   • In the browser, right-click the Mirror4 feature. Click Edit Feature.
   • In the Mirror Pattern dialog box, click the Features button and select the new extrusion and fillet features in the browser. This action adds the features to the mirror feature.
   • Click OK to save the changes to the mirror feature.

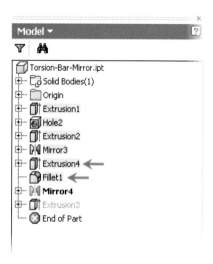

15   Confirm that your model looks like the following illustration.

16   In the browser, right-click the Hole2 feature. Click Edit Feature.

17   Change the hole diameter to **5 mm** and click OK. The original hole feature and all mirror
      occurrences are automatically changed to the new diameter.

18   Close all files. Do not save.

Lesson 16 | Creating Thin-Walled Parts

This lesson describes creating thin-walled parts using the Shell tool. You use shell features to remove material from existing solid features. By using shell features, you can create the overall shape of your part and then create a cavity in the part by specifying a wall thickness for the faces.

Objectives

After completing this lesson, you will be able to:

- Define a thin-walled part.

- Use the Shell tool to create shelled features.

About Thin-Walled Part Design

A thin-walled part is the result of offsetting existing faces to create new faces and then removing the remaining volume of the part. This process creates a hollow interior for the part.

While there is always more than one way to create parts, using the Shell tool to create thin-walled parts is generally the most efficient method. The following illustration demonstrates a solid both before and after applying a shell feature.

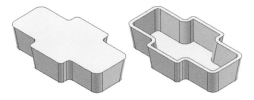

Definition of Thin-Walled Parts

You apply the Shell tool to existing part models to produce a shell. Objects like a drinking cup, cell phone case, and a computer casing can be considered thin-walled parts. These parts are originally created as complete solid models. You use the Shell tool to remove the unwanted material.

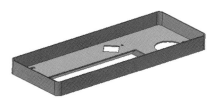

Example of Thin-Walled Parts

Plastic containers for consumer products, such as soda or cleaning solution bottles, are other examples of thin-walled containers. The following illustration of a plastic bottle is representative of these.

Creating Shell Features

You use the Shell tool to create shelled features on existing solid geometry. With the Shell tool, you can remove material from an existing part and create a cavity in the part by specifying a wall thickness for the faces. One key advantage to using the Shell tool is that you can create differing wall thickness for each face of the part. Generally, you select at least one face on the part to be removed from the shell feature leaving the remaining faces as the shell walls.

The following illustration shows the part before and after adding a shell feature.

Access

Shell

Ribbon: **Model tab > Modify panel**

Shell Options

The Shell dialog box is displayed when you start the Shell tool.

The following features and options are available in the Shell dialog box:

	Option	Description
(1)	**Inside**	The thickness is applied to the inside of the existing faces
(2)	**Outside**	The thickness is applied to the outside of the existing faces.
(3)	**Both**	Half of the thickness is applied to each side of the face.
(4)	**Remove Faces**	Click this icon to select the face(s) to remove from the shell feature. The remaining faces serve as walls for the shell feature. If you do not remove any faces from the shell feature, the result is a cavity in the part with no open faces.
(5)	**Automatic Face Chain**	When selected, all faces that are tangent to the selected face are selected. Clear this selection to prevent tangent faces from being automatically selected.
(6)	**Solids**	This button is only available when multiple solid bodies exist in the part file. When this is the case, the user can click the solids button to select one or more solid bodies to use the Shell tool on.
(7)	**Thickness**	Specify value for the wall thickness.

	Option	Description
⑧	**Unique Face Thickness - Thickness/ Select**	Enter a value to apply to the selected face(s). Select the face(s) to apply a unique wall thickness. This value overrides the default thickness for the selected face(s) only.
⑨	**Unique Face Thickness - Click to Add**	Click the Click to Add area of the dialog box to create unique face thicknesses for the shell feature.

Procedure: Creating Shell Features

The following steps describe how to create shell features.

1   Create a part representing the overall shape required.

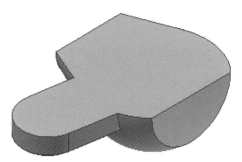

2   On the ribbon, click the Shell tool and select the faces to remove from the shell operation. Under Thickness, enter a wall thickness.

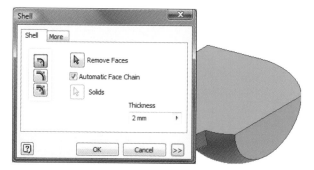

3   To assign unique wall thicknesses, click the [>>] button to expand the dialog box. Select the
    Click to Add area and select the face(s) to assign a unique wall thickness. Under Unique Face
    Thickness, specify a thickness for the selected face(s). Click OK to create the shell feature.

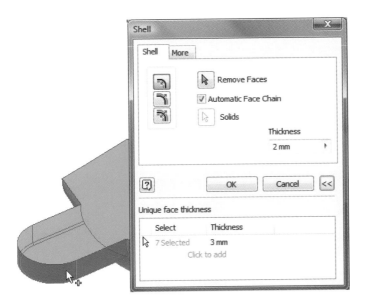

4   The shell feature is created.

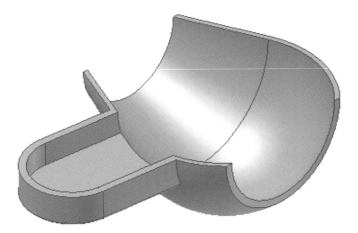

Exercise | Create and Edit Shell Features

In this exercise, you create a shell feature for the part applying a common wall thickness to all faces. You then edit the shell feature to include unique wall thicknesses on different features.

The completed exercise

Completing the Exercise:	*To complete the exercise, follow the steps in this book or in the onscreen exercise. In the onscreen list of chapters and exercises, click Chapter 4: Detailed Shape Design. Click Exercise: Create and Edit Shell Features.*

1   Open *Hair-Dryer-Housing.ipt*.

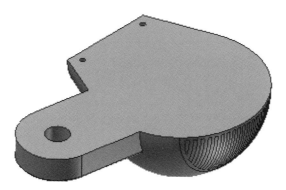

2   To create a shell feature:

- On the ribbon, click the Shell tool.
- Clear the Automatic Face Chain option.
- Select the faces indicated in the following illustration.
- In the Thickness box, enter **1 mm** and click OK.
  Note: The thickness is applied to all remaining faces on the part.

3   Notice that the shell feature is created as shown in the following illustration.

4   You now edit the feature to remove another face and create a unique wall thickness around the hole features.

  - In the browser, right-click the Shell5 feature.
  - Click Edit Feature.

5   Add another face to be removed from the shell:

  - In the Shell dialog box, click the Remove Faces button.
  - Select the opposite end of the component as shown in the following illustration.

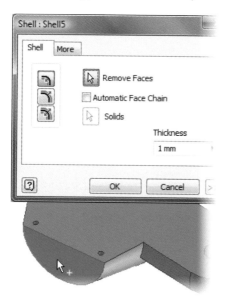

6   Add a unique thickness to the handle area of the part:

  - Select the Automatic Face Chain option.
  - Click the [»] button to expand the dialog box.
  - Select the Click to Add area and select the faces as shown below.
  - Under Unique Face Thickness, in the Thickness column, enter **2 mm**.

7. Add a unique thickness to the large hole:

- Select the Click to Add area.
- Select the inside face of the large hole. Under Unique Face Thickness, in the Thickness column, enter **2.5 mm.**

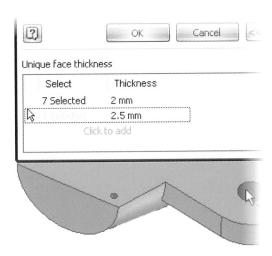

8 Add one more unique thickness to the two smaller holes:

- Select the Click to Add area.
- Select the inside surface of the two smaller holes.
- Under Unique Face Thickness, in the
- Thickness column, enter **1.5 mm**. Click OK.

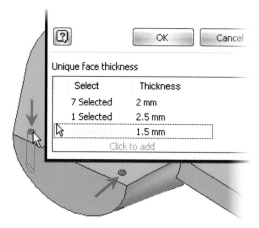

9 Notice that the shell feature is updated to reflect the additional removed face, as well as the unique wall thickness.

10 Close all files. Do not save.

Chapter Summary

This chapter enhanced your basic part modeling skills by providing additional tools and recommended workflows for detailed shape design. Understanding how to create chamfers and fillets, place hole and thread features, pattern and mirror features, and create thin-walled parts greatly extends your 3D part modeling capabilities to cover most part design requirements.

Having completed this chapter, you can:

- Create both chamfers and fillets on a part.
- Use the Hole and Thread tools to place hole and thread features on your part model.
- Create rectangular and circular patterns and mirror existing features.
- Create thin-walled parts using the Shell tool.

Chapter 05
Assembly Design Overview

In previous chapters, you learned the fundamental concepts and workflows for parametric part design. Because most products include more than one component, you need to understand how to work with multiple parts in a single design environment.

In this chapter, you are introduced to different approaches and workflows you can use to combine multiple 3D parts into an assembly design. Due to the number of unique and standard components included with all assembly designs, you also need to understand how to easily manage and organize multiple files using Inventor project files.

Objectives

After completing this chapter, you will be able to:

- Describe the assembly modeling process, the Autodesk Inventor assembly modeling environment, and recommended assembly design workflows.

- Describe how to use Autodesk Inventor project files to manage design projects.

Lesson 17 | Designing Assemblies

This lesson describes the assembly modeling process, the Autodesk Inventor assembly modeling environment, and recommended assembly design workflows.

Assembly models enable you to create fully parametric 3D representations of your design. You can use these models to validate design options and identify problem areas before a single part is manufactured. Assembly modeling can also reduce and in some cases eliminate the need for traditional prototypes.

The following illustration shows a typical assembly model comprised of multiple parts and fasteners.

Objectives

After completing this lesson, you will be able to:

- Describe assembly modeling and the procedures you use to create an assembly model.

- Describe the basic approaches to assembly modeling.

- Identify the key interface elements of the assembly design environment and their overall function.

- State the recommended assembly design workflow.

About Assembly Design

Using assembly modeling, you create or bring individual components into a common environment and use various tools to assemble them. You create new geometry, place existing parts or assemblies, and manage relationships among the parts in the assembly.

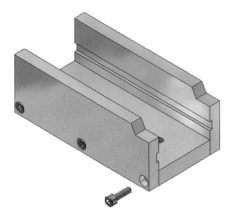

Definition of an Assembly Model

You create an assembly by combining multiple components and/or assemblies into a single environment. Parametric relationships are created between each component that determines component behavior in the assembly.

These relationships can range from simple constraint-based relationships that determine a component's position in the assembly, to advanced relationships such as adaptivity. Adaptivity enables a component to change size based upon its relationship to other components in the assembly.

Assembly Constraints

You use assembly constraints to create parametric relationships between parts in the assembly. Just as you use 2D constraints to control 2D geometry, you use 3D constraints in an assembly to position parts in relation to other parts. There are four basic assembly constraints, each with unique solutions and options.

Mate/Flush Constraint

Used to align part features such as faces, edges, or axis.

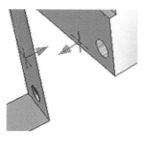

Before Mate Constraint

After Mate Constraint

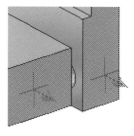

Before Flush Constraint

After Flush Constraint

Angle Constraint

Used to specify an angle between two parts. Applied to faces, edges, or axes.

Before Angle Constraint   **After Angle Constraint**

Tangent Constraint

Used to define a tangential relationship between two parts. Generally applied to circular faces and planar faces. One of the selected faces must be circular.

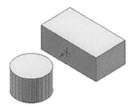

Before Tangent Constraint   **After Tangent Constraint**

Insert Constraint

Used to insert one component into another. This constraint effectively combines a mate axis/axis and a mate face/face constraint. Generally applied to bolts, or pins, or any part that needs to be inserted into a hole on another part. Applied by selecting a circular edge on each part.

Before Insert Constraint   **After Insert Constraint**

Assembly Design Approaches

Before you create assembly models, you must understand the three basic methods you use to create them and how to choose the correct assembly modeling approach.

- Using existing components

- Designing components in-place

- Grouping components using subassemblies

Regardless of which method you use to create the assembly, the part data resides in individual part files and is referenced into the assembly file.

Process: Using Existing Components

The following steps provide an overview of the process of using existing components in an assembly design. Individual components for an assembly are designed outside of the assembly where they are placed.

1   Each part file is designed separately from the assembly and other parts.

2   After you create the parts, they are placed into the assembly and constrained to other parts.

The following image illustrates how separate components are gathered together into a new assembly.

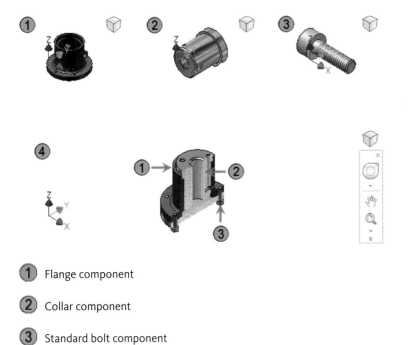

① Flange component

② Collar component

③ Standard bolt component

④ Assembly model

Process: Designing Components In-Place

The following steps provide an overview of the process of designing components in-place for an assembly. All assembly components are designed in the context of the assembly.

1 Create a new assembly and create a new component while in the context of the assembly.

2   Design each component while still in the assembly environment.

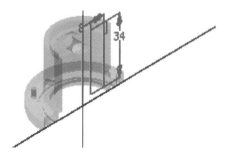

3   As you design each component, you are applying the required assembly constraints, and are making changes to parts based upon their relationships to other components in the assembly.

Subassemblies

You use subassemblies to organize large assemblies into smaller groups. A subassembly is essentially an assembly placed into another assembly. In the context of the overall assembly, the subassembly behaves as a single part. Components within the subassembly are constrained to each other, while the subassembly is constrained to the overall assembly as a single component. You must edit constraints within the assembly where they were created. To do this, you activate the subassembly by double-clicking the subassembly in the browser.

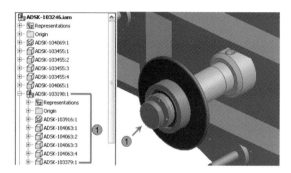

Guidelines

Keep the following general guidelines in mind for assembly design.

- You can use all three approaches to assembly design and switch between them at any time.

- You can begin the assembly using one method and change to a different one.

- As you become more proficient with the application, and understand the benefits of each modeling approach, you can choose the best approach for a given task.

Assembly Design Environment

The assembly environment in Autodesk Inventor is virtually the same as the part modeling environment, with the exception of tools that are unique to assembly modeling.

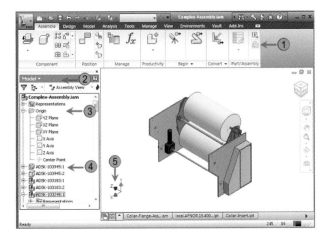

Autodesk Inventor Assembly Environment

A typical view of the Inventor assembly environment is shown in the following illustration.

(1) **Assembly Panel**: Contains tools specific to assembly modeling.

(2) **Assembly Browser**: Lists all parts and their constraints. When a part is activated for editing, the browser functions are identical to the part modeling environment.

(3) **Assembly Coordinate Elements**: Identical to the part environment, each assembly also contains an independent coordinate system. Expand the Origin folder to expose the origin planes, axes, and centerpoint.

④ **Assembly Coordinate Elements**: Each component in the assembly is listed. Expand the components to expose the assembly constraints that have been applied.

⑤ **3D Indicator**: Displays the current view orientation relative to the assembly coordinate system.

Assembly Ribbon

Similar to the Part Modeling ribbon, the Assembly ribbon contains the tools specific to assembly modeling. As you create your assembly model, the ribbon automatically switches among assembly, part, and sketch modes depending on the context you are using.

The Assembly ribbon is shown in the following illustration.

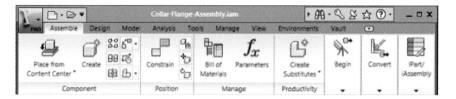

After you become familiar with the assembly tool icons, you can turn off the text display with icons. Right-click anywhere on the ribbon, select Ribbon Appearance > Text Off.

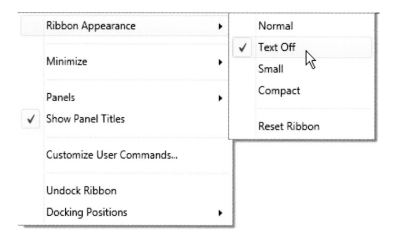

By turning off the text display with icons, you make more room available for the assembly or part browser.

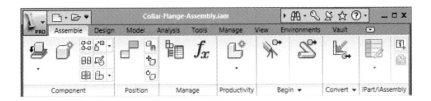

Assembly Browser

The assembly browser offers several options for working in the assembly environment and is your primary tool for interacting with assembly components and features.

When you open the browser in the assembly modeling environment, it displays the origin folder containing the default X, Y, and Z planes, axes, and center point. It also lists all parts that you use in the assembly.

Nested under each part, you see the assembly constraints. If you select an assembly constraint, an edit box is displayed at the bottom of the browser. This enables you to edit the offset or angle value for the constraint.

Note: If you select the Assembly View list, you can select Modeling View to switch the browser to display the part features nested under the parts instead of the assembly constraints. This result is useful when performing part modeling functions in the context of the assembly.

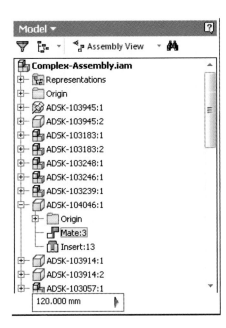

Recommended Assembly Design Workflow

When you create an assembly, the approach and process you utilize can and will vary depending on the design requirements.

Process: Creating Assemblies

The following steps represent the overall workflow for creating assemblies using Autodesk Inventor.

1. Create a new assembly using one of the assembly templates provided.

2. Place existing parts into the assembly or create new parts in the context of the assembly.

3. Use standard assembly constraints such as Mate, Angle, Tangent, and Insert to position and constrain the parts to other parts in the assembly.

4. Repeat the steps above until all components are added to the assembly.

Example of a Typical Assembly Design

The following illustration shows a typical assembly modeling workflow. The first part is created in the context of the assembly. The next part is then created in the context of the assembly. Additional components such as standard parts are also added to the assembly. How parts are created, whether in the context of the assembly or outside of the assembly as a separate part, has no effect on how the parts are constrained.

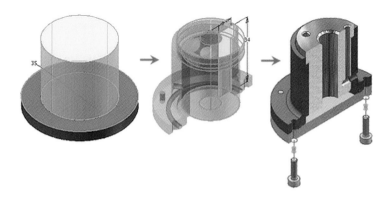

Exercise | Use the Assembly Environment

In this exercise, you open an assembly and explore the assembly modeling environment. You experiment with different interface objects in the assembly, part modeling, and sketching environments.

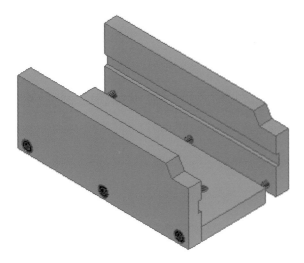

The completed exercise

Completing the Exercise:	*To complete the exercise, follow the steps in this book or in the onscreen exercise. In the onscreen list of chapters and exercises, click Chapter 5: Assembly Design Overview. Click Exercise: Use the Assembly Environment.*

1   Open *Fixture.iam*.

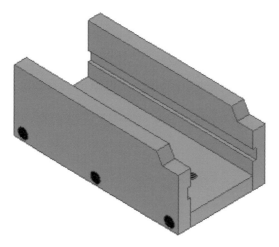

2   The Assembly ribbon is automatically loaded when you open an assembly file.

3   To edit an assembly constraint:
   • In the browser, expand Fixture_Base:1 and select the Insert:1 constraint.
   • At the bottom of the browser, in the edit box, enter **10.00** and press ENTER. The offset value of the insert constraint changes.

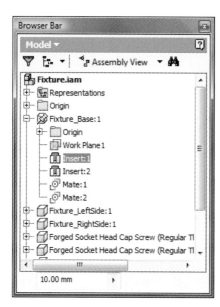

4   Compare the new position of the Fixture_RightSide:1 component with the
    following illustration.

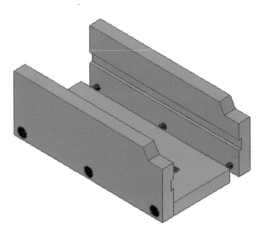

5   In the browser, on the Assembly View flyout, click Modeling View.
    The browser displays the part features instead of assembly constraints.

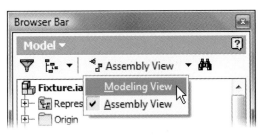

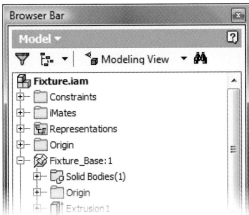

6   To edit a part feature:
    • In the browser, right-click Extrusion1.
    • Click Edit Feature.

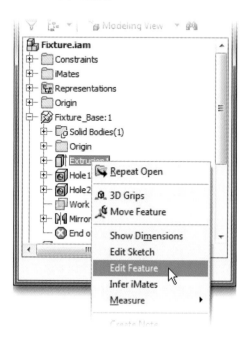

7   In the Extrude dialog box, click Cancel. The Part Modeling ribbon is displayed automatically.

8   On the ribbon, click Return to exit the part and return to the assembly.

9   To open a part in a separate window:
    • In the browser, right-click the Fixture_Base:1 component.
    • Click Open.

    The part is opened in a separate window and the ribbon switches automatically to display the Part Modeling ribbon.

10 In the browser, expand Extrusion1 and double- click Sketch1. The ribbon switches automatically to the 2D Sketch ribbon.

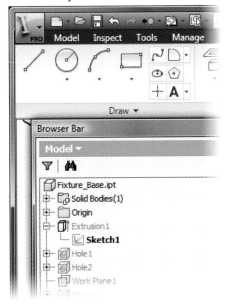

11 On the ribbon, click Finish Sketch to exit the sketch.

12 Close all files. Do not save.

Lesson 18 | Using Project Files in Assembly Designs

This lesson describes the characteristics and implementation of Autodesk Inventor project files. You use project files to resolve path locations. When an assembly file is loaded, the location of the part files must be resolved. The same is true when loading a drawing or presentation file.

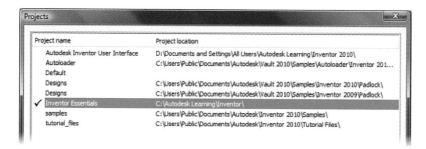

Objectives

After completing this lesson, you will be able to:

- Describe the characteristics and functions of project files.

- Set up projects.

- Create a project file for a single user.

- Edit project files.

- State some recommendations for setting up project files.

About Project Files

When you use Autodesk Inventor software to create designs, each one consists of multiple files and file types. The design and documentation of a single part file require at least two separate files: (a) a part file and (b) a drawing file. The design and documentation of assembly models require a minimum of three different file types: (a) assembly files, (b) part files, and (c) drawing files.

Using separate files for each file type is critical for performance and is common among most parametric modeling systems. By storing path information for each project, the application can search for the required files when opening an assembly, presentation, or drawing file. The need to search in different path locations for files is the primary purpose of project files.

The following illustration shows file dependencies in a typical assembly design.

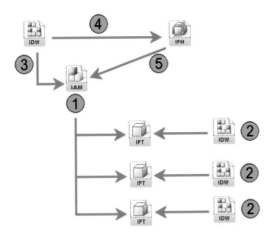

1. Assemblies reference parts.

2. Drawings reference parts.

3. Drawings reference assemblies.

4. Drawings reference presentations.

5. Presentations reference assemblies.

When you open an assembly, drawing, or presentation file, the active project file is used to resolve path locations to the referenced files.

Definition of Project Files

A project file is an ASCII text file that is stored with an *.ipj* file extension. The file contains information about paths and other options that enable Inventor to resolve the file references of other files when you open an assembly, presentation, or drawing file.

When you create designs you probably organize them in different folder locations. The same is true for Autodesk Inventor project files. You generally create one project file for each design you create. While there is no limit to the number of project files you can create, only one project can be active at a time.

In the following illustration, the active project is identified by the check mark.

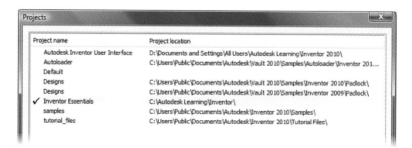

Example of a Project File

It is recommended that you store your project file in the upper level folder of your project design folders. This keeps your project file organized with your designs and simplifies portability issues.

The following illustration shows the folder structure for a project and where the project file is located.

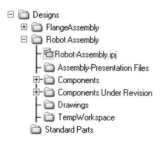

A typical project might have parts and assemblies unique to the project, standard components unique to your company, and off-the-shelf components such as fasteners, fittings, or electrical components.

To reduce the possibility of file resolution problems, set up a folder structure before you create a project and start saving files. To help organize your design files, it is a good idea to set up subfolders under your project workspace or workgroup folder. You can keep all your design files for a project in the subfolders, making it a logical way to organize the files used in a design project. Because references are stored as relative paths from project folders, if you change the folder structure, move, or rename files, you are likely to break file references.

Always save new files in the workspace or workgroup defined for your project or one of its subfolders.

Projects Folder Option

Because you can store your project files in several different locations, you need an efficient way of locating them. Rather than search every folder on your computer or network, Autodesk Inventor uses Microsoft Windows shortcuts to point to the project files that have been accessed on your computer.

Click Tools tab > Application Options, then click the Files tab in the Application Options dialog box. The default Projects Folder option is set to your Documents\Inventor folder. If you want to use a different path for your project files, enter or browse to a new location.

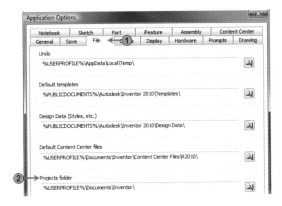

In the following illustration, the *Documents\Inventor* folder is selected to list all files. The Project file shortcuts in the right pane of the Explorer window are not the actual project files. They are Microsoft Windows shortcuts to the actual project files.

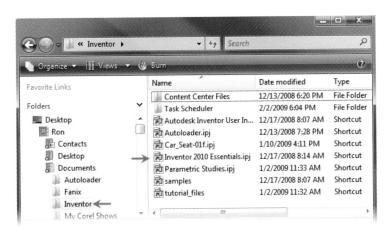

Project File Configuration

Each project file contains a series of categories and options. To successfully design a project file, you must understand how to use these categories and options, to ensure proper file referencing when you design assemblies.

Projects Dialog Box

You use the Projects dialog box to create, edit, or set a project file to current. The dialog box is divided into two panes. The top pane lists the currently available projects, while the lower pane shows the settings and configured options for the selected project.

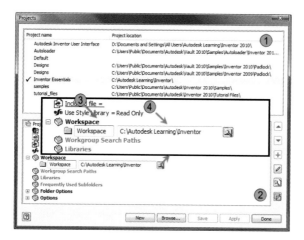

	Option	Description
1	**Select Project Pane**	Select a project to edit it, or double-click a project to make it active. *Note*: You cannot edit the active project or activate a different project if there are files open in Autodesk Inventor.

	Option	Description
②	**Edit Project Pane**	Select the category or right-click the option you want to change. When you edit search paths they are divided into two sections: (a) Named Shortcut and (b) Category Search Path.
③	**Named Shortcut**	Enter the shortcut name as you would like it to appear in the Open dialog box. This enables you to navigate easily to the search path.
④	**Category Search Path**	Enter the path name or click the browse button to define the path location.

Open Dialog Box: Location Shortcuts

When you open files, the Locations area of the dialog box displays all of the named shortcuts contained in the active project.

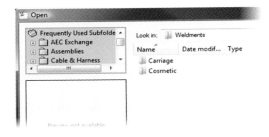

Project File Categories

Each project file is divided into separate categories in which you define different paths. A typical design makes use of some or all of these categories depending on the structure of your assembly and the environment in which you are working.

Category	Description
Type	Defines the type of project. Unless you also have Autodesk Vault installed, you only create single-user project files.
Location	Displays the physical location of the project file.
Use Style Libraries	Defines whether or not the project uses a style library. Options are Yes, Read Only, and No.
Workspace	A personal location where you edit your personal copy of design files. Only one designer should have access to the files in the folder called out in the workspace.
Workgroup Search Paths	Within this group you can define multiple search paths for accessing files. You do this when you want to add levels of organization to your design files or access files from another designer.
Libraries	You use this category to define search paths for part libraries. Part libraries can consist of standard off-the-shelf components that you use in your designs or can also include common parts that you design. Common factors in all libraries include that the path is considered by the application to be read-only, and parts stored within a library search path rarely, if ever, change. If library folders are defined, each needs a descriptive name that should not change. Because the library name is stored in the reference, changing the library name later breaks library references.
Frequently Used Subfolders	This group is used to define paths of frequently used subfolders within the project folder structure.
Folder Options	This group contains options for setting the folder locations of style libraries, templates, and Content Center files.
Options	You use these properties to set specific options for the project file.

Project Categories: Search Order

Knowing and remembering the category search order is critical to properly implementing and managing project files. The following illustration represents a typical project file with path locations defined in each category. When the application needs to locate referenced files, it searches for files using paths contained in each category using the following order.

1. Libraries

2. Workspace

3. Workgroup Search Paths

A simple way to remember the search order is to remember libraries first, and then the order that each category is displayed in the project window.

File Resolution

When examining this diagram, you see the assembly file is stored in a different location from the component files.

- Component files exist in the *Components* folder.

- Assembly files exist in the *Robot Assembly* folder.

Because the *Components* folder is a subfolder of the defined workspace, it is used to resolve the component locations. The Hex Cap Screw is stored in a folder defined as a Library category.

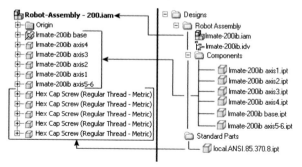

Relative Paths in Your Project Files

When you add paths to each category, the application stores only the relative path. The relative path is created by removing the project file location from the path text and leaving only the remaining path information. Using relative paths enables greater portability of your project files and data sets. When you view the paths under each category, the path settings begin with . followed by the folder location relative to the physical location of the project file. In the following example, the *Robot-Assembly.ipj* file is stored in the folder *C:\Designs\Robot Assembly*.

By storing only relative paths in your project file, it is possible to physically move the entire folder structure to another location or storage device. As long as the folders maintain their relative location to the storage location of the project file, the application can resolve the files as required.

① Location of project file

② Relative path

③ Full path

④ Full path

Frequently Used Subfolders

Projects have a Frequently Used Subfolders category that you can use to list commonly used subfolders for accessing Autodesk Inventor files. Adding subfolder locations to this category simplifies the task of navigating to these folders when opening files.

It is important to note the following:

- The folder specified must be a subfolder of an existing search path in the project being worked on.

- The folder entries have no effect on file resolution and are used only to aid in navigating when opening and saving files.

The following illustration represents a project file containing several paths in the Frequently Used Subfolders category.

The Open and Save dialog boxes display the Frequently Used Subfolder locations. Click the folder in the Locations list to navigate to the folder.

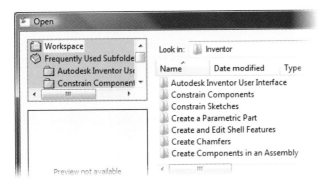

Project File Folder Options

Folder options identify where project level files such as templates and styles are stored.

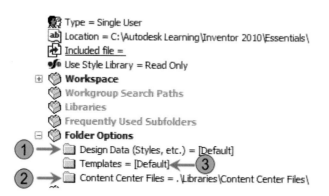

Option	Description
Design Data	Identifies where the project-specific style definitions are stored.
Templates	Specifies the location of the Autodesk Inventor document templates for the project.
Content Center Files	Specifies the location of the Content Center files used in the project.

Project Options

The following options can be set for each project.

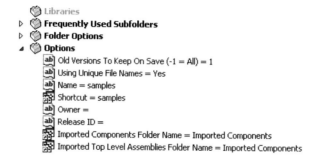

Option	Description
Old Versions to Keep on Save	Specifies the number of versions to keep when you save changes. Older versions of each file are stored in an Old Versions subfolder of the file location.
Using Unique File Names	Specifies whether all files in the project have unique file names. Not applicable for library locations.
	Yes: Indicates that no duplicate file names are used in the project. The application searches through all editable project locations to find the file name, even if it was last accessed from a different folder.
	No: Indicates that duplicate file names exist in the project. If duplicate file names are found when resolving files, the Resolve Files dialog box opens so you can browse to the correct file to manually reestablish the link.
Name	Indicates the name of the project file.
Shortcut	Indicates the name of the project file shortcut.
Owner	Identifies the project owner, typically the lead engineer or CAD administrator.
Release ID	Identifies the version of the released project data. If a project is used as a library by another project, the release ID may be useful in identifying which project to use.
Imported Components Folder Name	Identifies the name of the folder where imported components are stored.
Imported Top Level Assemblies Folder Name	Identifies the name of the folder where imported top level assembly data is stored.

Results of the search are listed in the Non-Unique Project File Names dialog box.

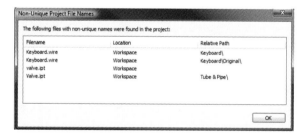

The use of unique file names within a project helps ensure that the correct files are always resolved when you open an assembly or other document that references other Autodesk Inventor files.

Vault Options

The following illustration represents vault options that are available. Autodesk Vault must be installed for these options to be displayed.

Creating a Project File

You begin to create project files through a wizard. You are prompted to fill in relevant information such as project name, workspace folder, and libraries to import from other projects. After the initial creation is complete, you proceed to add the required paths to the categories you will use.

Access

Create or Edit Projects

Ribbon: **Get Started tab > Launch panel**

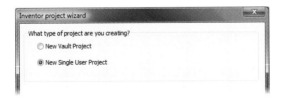

Open or New Dialog Boxes: **Projects**

Procedure: Creating a Single-User Project File

The following steps describe how to create a single-user project.

1   Access the Projects dialog box by clicking File menu > Projects.

2   Select the New Single User Project type and click Next.

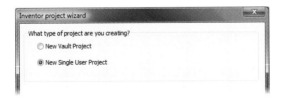

3   In the Name field, enter a name for the project. In the Project (Workspace) Folder field, enter
    a path location for storing the files for this project. Click Next.

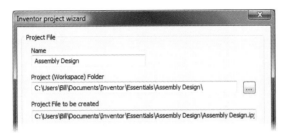

4   If you have any projects with libraries defined, they are displayed in this list. You can use this information to copy library paths from other project files.

- Click Finish to create the project.
- If you are prompted to create the path, click OK.

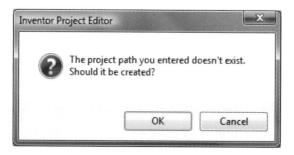

Editing Project Files

You can use the internal project editor or the stand-alone project editor located on the Microsoft Windows Start menu to edit projects. Under Select Project, select the project to edit. In the Edit Project area, select the category or option you need to edit. Depending on the item you edit, different options are available on both the shortcut menu and to the right of the Edit Project area.

Access

Edit Projects

Ribbon: **Get Started tab › Launch panel**

Windows Menu: **Start › All Programs › Autodesk › Autodesk Inventor 2010 › Tools › Project Editor**

Editing Projects

When editing projects, right-click a category or option to display the available editing tools in a shortcut menu.

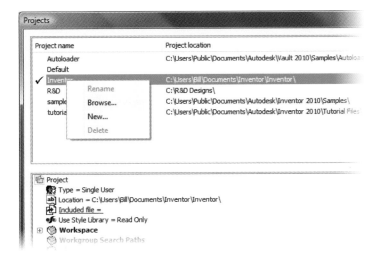

> **Note:** **Editing the Active Project** *You must close all files in Autodesk Inventor before attempting to edit the active project.*

Workspace and Library Category Options

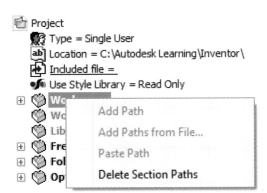

Option	Description
Add Path	This option adds a path to the workspace category. Enter a named shortcut and search path in the fields below the category.
Add Paths from File	This option adds the workspace path contained in another project file. A dialog box is displayed for you to select the project file.
Paste Path	This option pastes a path that was copied to the clipboard.
Delete Section Paths	This option deletes all paths from the category.

Workgroup Category Search Path Options

Option	Description
Add Path	This option adds a path to the workspace category.
Add Paths from File	This option adds the workspace paths contained in another project file. A dialog box is displayed for you to select the project file.
Add Paths from Directory	Select this option to add the path of a selected directory including all subdirectories.
Paste Path	Select this option to paste a path that was copied to the clipboard.
Delete Section Paths	Select this option to delete all paths from the category.

Edit and Position Buttons

Edit and position buttons are displayed on the right side of the Projects dialog box.

Button	Option	Description
▲	**Move Up**	Select this option to move the selected path up in the search order within its category.
▼	**Move Down**	Select this option to move the selected path down in the search order within its category.
+	**Add Path**	Select this option to add a path to the selected category.
✎	**Edit Path**	Select this option to edit the selected path.
>>	**Expand**	Click this button to display the Workspace and Workgroup categories. These categories are hidden by default.
🔍	**Find Duplicate Files**	Located in the Project Editor interface. You use the Find Duplicate Files button to search the current project for files with duplicate names within the editable search paths.
▦	**Configure Content Center Libraries**	Click this button to display the Configure Libraries dialog box and configure the Content Center libraries.

Recommendations for Project Files

Your project file design will depend largely upon the type of design project for which it is intended to be used. For example, if your current design task only involves 1 person, you would probably use a Single User project file. This could apply even if you are part of a larger design team or company. For example, you might be working on a small R&D project that only requires one designer. In this case, even though you are part of an engineering and design department of a large company, the R&D project requirements dictate a Single User project file.

On the other hand, you may, at the same time be required to collaborate with other designers on larger design/manufacturing projects. In this case, the recommended project type would be a Vault project. The Vault project type would enable all designers to interact with the design data at the same time without the fear of overwriting the work of others. This is because the Vault project type requires each user to check files out of the vault before they can be edited. Other files that are not being edited can still be referenced, as they remain in the vault.

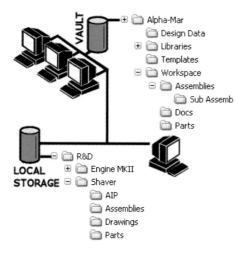

Guidelines for Creating Project Files

Consider the following guidelines when you design projects for simple design projects.

• When you create the project file, select the Single User project type.

• Store the physical project file at the root of your design folders. This will allow the data stored in subfolders to be stamped with a relative path designation. This makes your design project portable and will simplify the transition process if the design makes it through the R&D process into an actual design/manufacturing project where other designers may be required to collaborate.

• Add a path to common components as a Library path. This path is read-only and the components that are stored there, rarely, if-ever change.

• If additional paths are required, add them as Workgroup Search Paths.

Guidelines for Project Files Used in Complex Projects or Large Design Teams

Consider the following guidelines when designing project files for complex design projects, or when large design teams collaborate on design projects.

- When you create the project file, select the Vault project type. Autodesk Vault must be installed.

- For more information on Autodesk Vault, refer to the AOTC: Autodesk Vault Essentials courseware or inquire about training options with your local training center or reseller.

Examples of Project Types

The following illustrations show the differences between a project design for use by a single user and small amounts of design data, and a project designed for use by several users and large amounts of design data. In the single-user example, the design data is stored on a local drive or perhaps a network drive, but is generally edited by only one person at a time. In the Vault project the design data is stored in the Vault and is available to several designers at the same time. The Vault manages the data and prevents the users from overwriting each others' work, while at the same time offering other capabilities that would be required in a large design project.

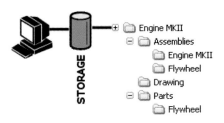

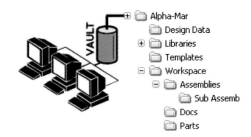

Single user project type

Vault project for larger complex designs and multiple users

Exercise | Create a Project File

In this exercise, you create a single-user project file with a workspace and library.

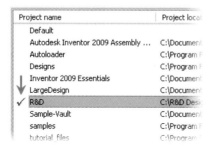

The completed exercise

 Completing the Exercise: *To complete the exercise, follow the steps in this book or in the onscreen exercise. In the onscreen list of chapters and exercises, click Chapter 5: Assembly Design Overview. Click Exercise: Create a Project File.*

1   Ensure that all files in Autodesk Inventor are closed.

2   To set up the exercise, you need to create some folders to simulate a theoretical design scenario.
    Using Windows Explorer, create the folders as shown to simulate a typical R&D Designs folder structure and a StandardParts folder for storing commonly used components.

3   Click the Get Started tab > Launch panel > Projects.

4   In the Projects dialog box:
    - Notice the name of the active project, identified by a check mark.
    - Click New.

5   To define the project as a single-user project:

- In the Inventor project wizard dialog box, verify that New Single User Project is selected.
- Click Next.

6   To name and locate the project file:

- For Name, enter **R&D**.
- Click the Browse button next to the Project (Workspace) Folder field and browse for the *C:\R&D Designs* folder.
- Select the folder and click OK.
- Click Finish.

7   To add a library path:

- In the Projects dialog box, right-click the Libraries category.
- Click Add Path.

8   To name and configure the library path:

- In the Name text box, enter **StandardParts**.
- In the Search Path text box, enter **C:\StandardParts.**
- Click Save.

9   To activate the project, double-click it in the Project dialog box. When it is activated, a check mark is displayed next to the project.
      Note: Your list of available projects differs from the list shown.

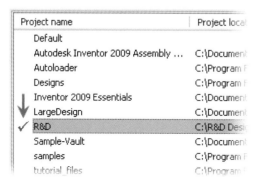

10   Click Done to close the dialog box.

11   To test the project:
     - Click Open.
     - In the Open dialog box, with the Workspace selected (1), make sure the R&D folders (2) that you created earlier are visible.
     - Select the StandardParts (3) library. Ensure that the Look In list changes to reflect the StandardParts folder that you created earlier.

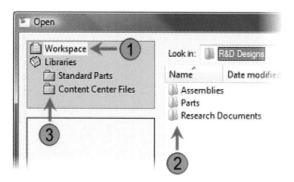

12   Click Cancel to close the Open dialog box.

13   Click Projects. Double-click the previously active project file.

14   Click Done.

Chapter Summary

With the information you learned in this chapter, you can make informed decisions about assembly design before you start a design project. With your understanding of the different approaches, workflow options, and the basics of assembly design, you can continue on to subsequent chapters that cover the individual tools and specific workflows that are available in the assembly design environment.

Having completed this chapter, you can:

- Describe the assembly modeling process, the Autodesk Inventor assembly modeling environment, and recommended assembly design workflows.
- Describe how to use Autodesk Inventor project files to manage design projects.

Chapter 06
Placing, Creating, and Constraining Components

This chapter covers the most common tasks in assembly design. One common task is to place components into an assembly and then define their orientation to one another. This includes components you have designed as well as industry-standard components. Another common task is to design a new part in the context of the assembly. Understanding the tools and workflows associated with both approaches provides the flexibility you need to create realistic and complete assembly designs.

Objectives

After completing this chapter, you will be able to:

- Place components in an assembly using the Place Component tool.

- Place assembly constraints on components in the assembly.

- Use the Content Center to place standard components into your assembly design.

- Create new components in the context of the assembly.

Lesson 19 | Placing Components in an Assembly

This lesson describes placing components into an assembly. As you create assemblies you place component geometry that represents the assembly's individual parts.

In the following illustration, the assembly was created by placing components into the assembly model.

A basic and critical aspect of any assembly design is the process of placing components in the assembly. While in some cases you are creating new components in the context of the assembly, in many other instances you need to use components that have already been designed. In order to use these components in the assembly, they must be placed.

Objectives

After completing this lesson, you will be able to:

- Describe the process of placing components in an assembly.

- Use the Place Component tool to place parts into an assembly.

About Placing Components in an Assembly

When you create an assembly model, there may be components that you are not designing in the context of the assembly. You must place these components into the assembly. A typical assembly model consists of components that were created in the context of the assembly and components that were created outside of the assembly.

In the following illustration, part files are being dragged from Windows Explorer to the assembly file. This is only one method with which you can place components in an assembly.

Definition of Placing Components in an Assembly

Placing components in an assembly is a process in which you add external part files or files from other sources to your assembly model. By doing so, you create a link between the assembly file and the part file. While the component's geometry is completely visible and can be manipulated and edited in the assembly environment, its definition is stored in a file that is separate from the assembly. This file link occurs, even though the component is created in the context of the assembly. All component file definitions are stored separately.

Because the component file exists outside of the assembly, it can be used in the other assemblies.

In the following illustration, the Design Assistant shows the file references that are created by placing components into the assembly. Each of the *.ipt* files represents the component file definitions.

Sources of Placed Components

As you use Autodesk® Inventor® software to build assemblies, you can use geometry from other applications as parts in your assembly. The following list details the supported formats that you can place into an assembly.

- Alias Files *(*.wire)*

- Autodesk Inventor Part and Assembly Files *(*.ipt, *.iam)*

- AutoCAD Drawing Files *(*.dwg)*

- CATIA V5 Files *(*.CATPart, *.CATProduct)*

- DWF Files *(*.dwf, *.dwfx)*

- DXF Files *(*.dxf)IDF Board Files (*.brd, *.emn, *.bdf, *.idb)*

- IGES Files *(*.igs, *.ige, *.iges)*

- JT Files *(*.jt)*

- Parasolid Binary and Text Files *(*.x_b, *.x_t)*

- Pro Engineer Files *(*.prt*, *.asm*, *.g, *.neu*)*

- SAT Files *(*.sat)* (ACIS/ShapeManager)

- STEP Files *(*.stp, *.ste, *.step)*

- SolidWorks Files *(*.prt, *.sldprt, *.asm, *.sldasm)*

- UGS NX Files *(*.prt)*

Different capabilities are available with each of these formats. Some formats are converted to Autodesk Inventor files when placed into an assembly, but others such as AutoCAD® Mechanical are linked to the assembly. Any changes in the AutoCAD Mechanical file are reflected in the assembly.

Supported File Types

In the Open dialog box, select the Files of Type drop-down list to display the supported file types.

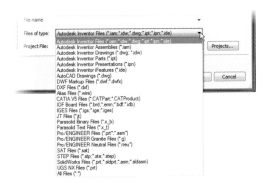

Example of Placing Components in an Assembly

In the following illustration, two assembly models are shown. Advancements in motor and power supply technology enable you to redesign the base with a slightly lower height profile. The design requirements dictate that you create these two different assemblies by using as many common components as possible. As you create the second assembly, you place components also used in the first assembly. You place a copy of the base component and modify it according to the lower height profile requirements.

(1) Original base component

(2) New lower-profile base component

Placing Components in an Assembly

You use the Place Component tool to place components into the assembly. Select this tool and the Place Component dialog box is displayed. The Place Component dialog box is similar to the Open dialog box in both style and function; however, the end result is that the selected file is placed into the assembly file instead of opened for editing.

The first component you place into the assembly is automatically placed at the assembly's origin point (o,o,o) and is grounded. Subsequent parts and subassemblies when placed are located by selecting screen locations, and need to be constrained to fix their positions.

Access

Place Component

Ribbon: **Assemble tab > Component panel**

Shortcut Menu: **Place Component**
Keyboard: **P**

Place Component Dialog Box

The Place Component dialog box is displayed when you start the Place Component Tool. Select the file to place into the assembly and click Open. To place files other than Autodesk Inventor files, select the file type in the Files of Type list.

Place Component Orientation

When adding a component to an assembly, the orientation of the component is either the way it is saved in its component file, or the way the last occurrence of that component is oriented in the assembly. You set which orientation you want to use, file or last occurrence, in the Application Options dialog box, Assembly tab.

By default, the option Use Last Occurrence Orientation for Component Placement is not selected. When this option is not selected, the orientation of placed components corresponds to their file orientation. When this option is selected, the orientation for placed components aligns with the orientation of the last occurrence for that component in the assembly.

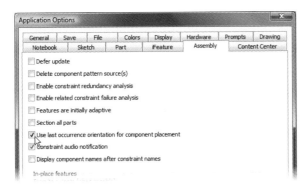

In the following illustration, the first (1) and second (2) placed components are identified. The second component placed has been constrained, causing the orientation of the last placed occurrence to be changed from the default orientation. When another component is placed in the assembly, the resulting orientation is based on how the option Use Last Occurrence Orientation for Component Placement is set. When it is not selected, the next placed component orientation is as shown in the middle image. When the option is selected, the next component's orientation is as shown on the right.

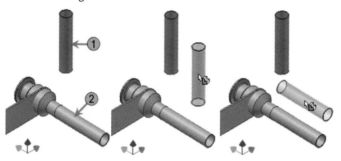

Assembly Coordinate System

Each assembly file contains an independent coordinate system. Default coordinate system elements are aligned with the 0,0,0 point in the assembly and can be used as you build the assembly. When you place the first part into the assembly, the origin point of the part file is matched to the origin point of the assembly file.

Note: This applies only if the first part in the assembly is placed into the assembly and not created in the context of the assembly. These components can be repositioned if required.

Grounded Components

By default, the first part in each assembly is grounded. All degrees of freedom are removed from the component and it cannot be moved. When you apply constraints to a grounded component, then on grounded component moves to validate the constraint, while the grounded component remains fixed in its position.

Although the first part is grounded, there is no limit to the number of grounded parts that you can have in an assembly. You can also remove the grounded property from the first part in the assembly.

When you ground parts, you can use them to mimic real-world situations where some parts are fixed in position, while others move relative to the parts to which they have been constrained.

Grounded components are displayed in the browser with the following icon:

In the browser or graphics window, right-click the part, and on the shortcut menu click Grounded. A check mark indicates that the component is grounded.

Procedure: Placing Components

The following steps describe how to place components into an assembly.

1   Open or create a new assembly file.

2   Start the Place Component tool.

3   In the Place Component dialog box, select the file you want to place into the assembly, and click Open.

4   The first component in the assembly is positioned automatically and is grounded, indicated by the push-pin icon. Optionally, place additional components by clicking other locations in the graphics window, or press ESC to cancel.

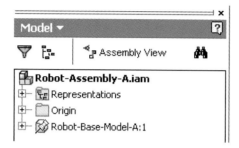

5   Click the Place Component tool and continue to place components into the assembly.

Exercise | Place Components in an Assembly

In this exercise, you use the techniques covered in this lesson to place components into a new assembly.

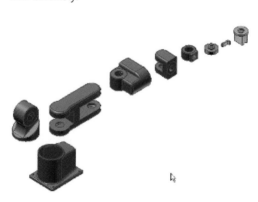

The completed exercise

Completing the Exercise:	*To complete the exercise, follow the steps in this book or in the onscreen exercise. In the onscreen list of chapters and exercises, click Chapter 6: Placing, Creating, and Constraining Components. Click Exercise: Place Components in an Assembly.*

1 Create a new assembly file based on the *Standard (mm).iam* template.

2 On the Quick Access toolbar, click Save to save the assembly. In the Save As dialog box, enter **Robot-Assembly-A.iam**. Click Save.

3 On the ribbon, click the Place Component tool. In the Place Component dialog box, double-click *Robot-Base-Model-A.ipt*.

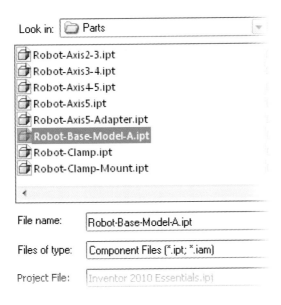

4 Press ESC to cancel the Place Component tool.
   - The first occurrence is automatically placed at the assembly origin.
   - In the browser, notice that the first component is automatically grounded.

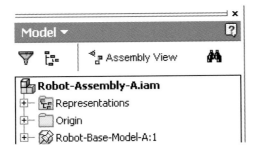

5   To place another component:

- On the keyboard press **P** then press ENTER to start the Place Component tool.
- In the Place Component dialog box, double- click *Robot-Axis1-2.ipt* and position the component as shown.
- Press ESC to cancel the command.

6   To drag components into an assembly:

- Open Windows Explorer and navigate to the folder where you installed the dataset for this exercise. The default location is *C:\Autodesk Learning\Inventor 2010\Learning\ Workspace\Parts.*
- Highlight the following part files and then click and drag them into the assembly window at the same time.
- *Robot-Axis2-3.ipt*
- *Robot-Axis3-4.ipt*
- *Robot-Axis4-5.ipt*
- *Robot-Axis5.ipt*
- *Robot-Axis5-Adapter.ipt*
- *Robot-Clamp.ipt*
- *Robot-Clamp-Mount.ipt*

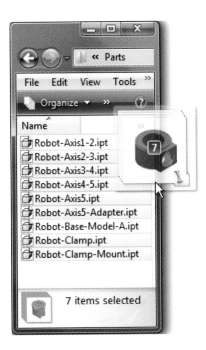

7   Notice how the components are spaced. The actual arrangement may differ on your screen depending on the order in which the components were selected.

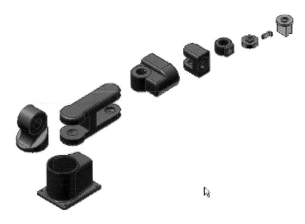

8   Close all files. Do not save.

Lesson 20 | Constraining Components

This lesson describes assembly constraints and how to apply, view, and edit them.

Constraining components is a vital part of the assembly design process. Using assembly constraints, you are able to accurately position the components and define their relationships with other components in the assembly.

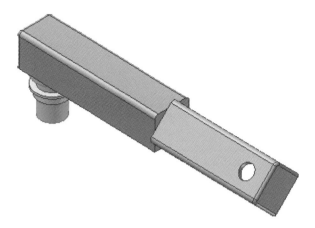

Objectives

After completing this lesson, you will be able to:

- Describe assembly constraints and their effect on components.

- Apply basic assembly constraints to parts in the assembly.

- Describe how assembly constraints affect individual parts in the assembly.

- Use different methods to view and edit assembly constraints.

- State some guidelines for proper constraining techniques.

About Assembly Constraints

When you build assemblies you define parametric relationships between the parts in the assembly. The relationships created between parts using assembly constraints realistically mimic real-world situations and operating conditions of the assembly components.

In the following illustration, an assembly constraint is used to align the center axes on each component.

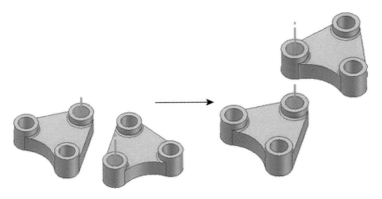

Definition of Assembly Constraints

As assembly constraint is a parametric relationship that you create between two components. There are different types of constraints, each designed to simulate real-world conditions between the components. For example, a mate constraint can be used to simulate two components positioned in a way that would cause their faces or edges to touch.

Except for the first component, which is grounded, each component, when placed in the assembly, has six available degrees of freedom; three translational and three rotational degrees of freedom. The sole purpose of assembly constraints is to reduce the available degrees of freedom for a component. You reduce available degrees of freedom to simulate the real-world condition for that component when it is manufactured and combined with other components in the assembly.

The following illustration shows the Degrees of Freedom symbol representing the six degrees of freedom.

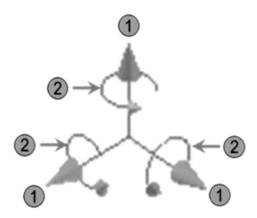

① **Translational degree of freedom**: the components can move along these axes.

② **Rotational degree of freedom**: the components can rotate about these axes.

Each assembly constraint you apply effectively reduces the degrees of freedom on the component. When you reduce the available degrees of freedom, you restrict the directions the component can move or rotate.

Initial degrees of freedom on a component in the assembly, with no assembly constraints being applied.

As you apply assembly constraints, the number of available degrees of freedom is reduced. In this example, there are three degrees of freedom remaining; two translational and one rotational.

In the following illustration, an angle constraint is used to define the angle between the two components. In this example, the angle is measured between the two selected faces, identified in the image on the left.

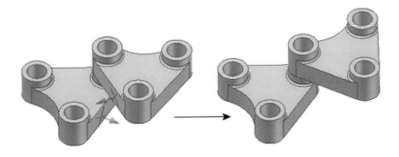

Example of Assembly Constraints

In the following illustration, the robot assembly consists of several components. Each component is designed to fit with the surrounding components and function within certain parameters. As each component is added to the assembly or designed in the context of the assembly, assembly constraints are used to define the relationships between each component.

After the constraints have been applied, the relationships between each component can be validated by dragging and manipulating the positions of various components. When the constraint conditions are valid, the connected components will move with the component being manipulated. This helps you to simulate the behavior of these components in a virtual environment.

The Constraint Tool

There are four basic assembly constraints. Each is designed to create a certain constraint condition between the components in the assembly. You use the Constraint tool to create all four types of basic assembly constraints.

Access

Place Constraint

Ribbon: **Position panel > Constrain**

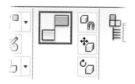

Toolbar: **Assembly panel**
Shortcut Menu: **Constraint**
Keyboard: **C**

Place Constraint Dialog Box

The Place Constraint dialog box is displayed when you start the Constraint tool.

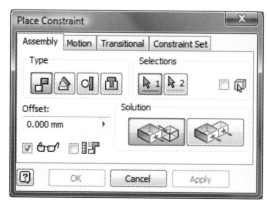

The following options are available in the Place Constraint dialog box.

Option	Dialog Box Access	Description
Type		Select the type of constraint to create.
Selections		As you select features, the selection1 and selection2 buttons are activated automatically. If you need to change a selected feature, click the appropriate selection button and reselect the geometry. The first selection previews with a blue highlight or shade while the second selection previews in a green highlight.
Pick Parts First		This option limits the feature selections to the selected part. You must first select the part, then select the feature for the constraint. This option is usually used in situations where the feature you are attempting to constrain is obstructed by other parts in the assembly.
Offset/Angle		The label for this field changes depending on the type of constraint you select. Enter a value for the offset or angle of the constraint.
Solution		Each constraint type offers different solutions. Select the flush or mate option.
Preview Constraint		This option previews the constraint before applying. The components move into position, enabling you to preview the constraint and confirm or change the constraint settings.
Predict Offset and Orientation		Only available for Mate and Angle constraints, this option inserts the angle or offset value automatically if the offset field is blank. The offset or angle value is calculated based upon the part's current position and is inserted into the offset/angle field. To override this setting, enter the offset/angle value manually. This functionality is useful when applying constraints without moving the geometry from its current position.

Mate Constraint

Constraint	Description
⊡	You use the mate constraint to mate selected geometry. Valid selections include faces, planes, axes, edges, and points. You can also enter an offset value to offset the geometry.

Option	Dialog Box Access	Description
Mate	⬛	Selected geometry is mated to each other.
Flush	⬛	Selected faces are coplanar.

The following illustrations show examples of using the mate constraint.

Mate Constraint/Mate Solution: Axis/Axis

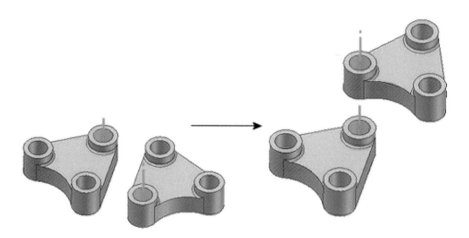

Mate Constraint/Mate Solution: Face/Face

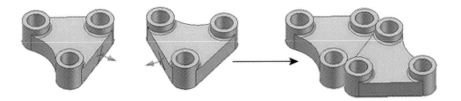

Mate Constraint/Mate Solution: Point/Point

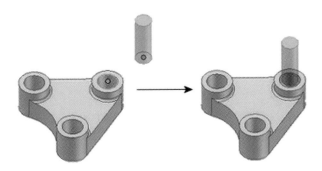

Mate Constraint/Flush Solution: Face/Face

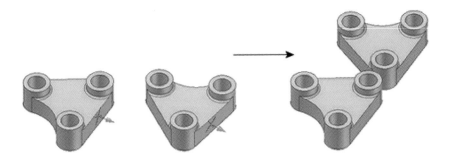

Constraint	Description
⬠	Use the angle constraint to specify an angle between face, planes, or lines.

Option	Dialog Box Access	Description
Directed Angle		Using this solution option, the angle is measured by using the right-hand rule.
Undirected Angle		This is the default solution, and it enables either orientation of the angle constraint. Using this option can resolve situations in which the component's orientation flips during a constraint drive or drag.
Explicit Reference Vector		This solution option enables you to select a third set of geometry that is used as a reference by the first two sets of selected geometry.

Angle Constraint: Face/Face

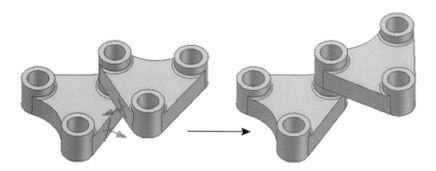

Explicit Reference Vector Constraint Example

In the following illustration, the position of one cover section is set at an angle relative to the other section. The Explicit Reference Angle constraint solution was used to ensure the relative position is maintained even if the first cover section rotates.

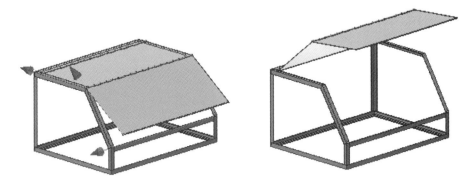

Tangent Constraint

Constraint	Description
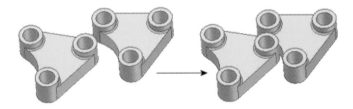	Use the tangent constraint to define a tangency condition between one circular feature and plane or face, or between two circular features.

Option	Dialog Box Access	Description
Inside		Creates an inside tangent solution.
Outside		Creates an outside tangent solution.

Tangent Constraint/Outside Solution: Circular Face/Circular Face

Insert Constraint

Constraint	Description
	Use the insert constraint to insert a circular part feature into another circular part feature. This requires the selection of two circular edges. The center point of the edge is calculated, and the result is a constraint in which the centerlines are aligned and the selected edges are made coplanar.

Option	Dialog Box Access	Description
Opposed		This solution forces the face normals to be opposed.
Aligned		This solution aligns the face normals.

Insert Constraint

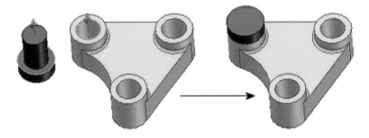

Placing Constraints

You apply each assembly constraint to either two components in the assembly or to one component and one assembly origin feature. When you start the Constraint tool, after you select the type of constraint, you select one feature on each part to apply it. The geometry that you choose is dependent upon the type of constraint you apply. The features to which the constraints are applied can be geometric part features, or work features (work planes, axes, or points) at the assembly or part level.

There are four types of assembly constraints that can be applied between parts: mate, angle, tangent, and insert. The constraint type chosen depends on the part features and the design intent.

The following illustration shows the cylindrical axes of two parts being constrained together.

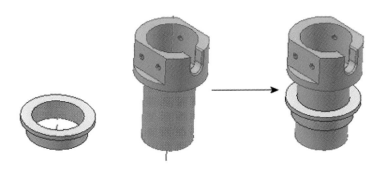

> **Tip**   **Placing Constraints on Obstructed Geometry** *When placing constraints on obstructed geometry or features, on the ribbon, Appearance panel, Shaded flyout, select the Hidden Edge Display option to display all edges on the parts.*

Process: Placing Constraints

Although each type of constraint creates a different result, the overall process of applying constraints is the same. The following steps provide an overview of how to place constraints.

1   Open or create an assembly.

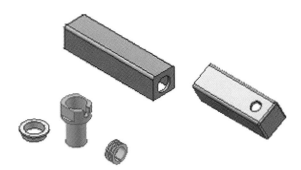

2   On the ribbon, click the Constraint tool and select the type of constraint to apply.

3   Select the features to apply the constraints. Depending on the type of constraint and the geometry chosen, you are given a preview of how the constraint will be applied.

4   If necessary, adjust the Solution option and enter an offset or angle value.

5   Click Apply to create the constraint and keep the Constraint tool active.

6   Add additional constraints.

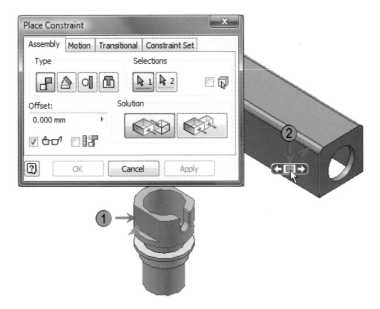

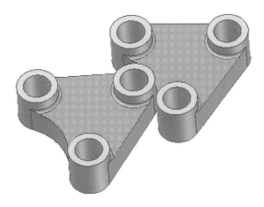

Viewing and Editing Constraints

After you create the assembly constraints you can view them in the browser different ways. If you select a constraint in the browser, it highlights the geometry referenced by the constraint.

Browser View Options

At the top of the browser, you can select a specific browser view option.

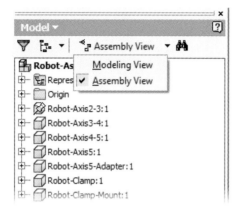

Browser: Assembly View

When you create assembly constraints, each part or origin feature is associated with one-half of the constraint, for example when the browser is in the default position view. Each constraint is listed twice in the browser.

The following illustration shows how the assembly constraint is displayed under each part to which it has been applied. If you need to edit, suppress, or delete a constraint, you can access the constraint under either part.

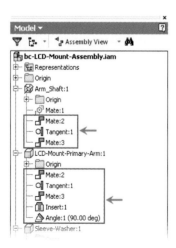

Browser: Modeling View

If you change the browser view to Modeling View, the constraints are displayed under the Constraints folder. You can expand the folder to access the constraints. Using this view places all the constraints in one location. However, it can be difficult to identify constraints on specific parts in larger assemblies.

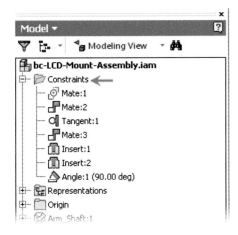

Component Names in Browser

You can display component names after the constraints in the browser as shown below. By default, this option is turned off. To turn this option on, on the ribbon, Tools tab, click Application Options. In the Application Options dialog box, Assembly tab, place a check mark next to the Display component names after constraint names option.

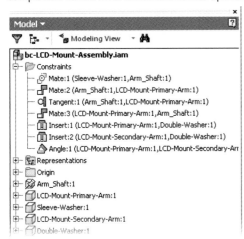

Shortcut Menu Options

In the browser, when you right-click a constraint the following shortcut menu is displayed.

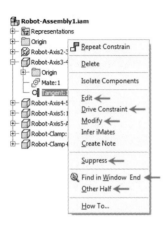

Option	Description
Edit	Select this option to display the Edit Constraint dialog box. You can completely redefine the assembly constraint.

Option	Description
Drive Constraint	Select the option to display the Drive Constraint dialog box and animate the component through valid constraint conditions.
Modify	Select the option to display the Edit Dimension dialog box. Use this dialog box to edit the constraint offset or angle values.
Suppress	Select this option to turn off the constraint. It still remains associated with the component, but its effect on available degrees of freedom is turned off.
Find in Window	Select this option to zoom the current view to geometry containing the selected constraint. This helps identify the constraint graphically.
Other Half	Select this option to highlight the other half of the constraint, by expanding the other component to which it has been applied and highlighting the constraint. This option helps identify which components the constraint has been applied to.

Procedure: Editing Constraints

The following steps describe how to edit assembly constraints.

1 Locate the constraint in the browser, then right-click the constraint and on the shortcut menu, click Edit.

2 When you edit a constraint, all edits are done in the same dialog box used to create the constraint.

- All options can be changed including the type of constraint.

- The geometry selected for the first selection highlights in blue (1), while the geometry selected for the second selection highlights in green (2), as shown in the following illustration.

- Make the required edits and click OK.

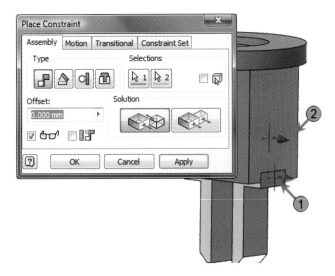

Changing the Constraint Offset/Angle Value

You can use two different methods to change the constraint offset/angle value without using the Edit Constraint dialog box.

Option	Description
Using the edit box at the bottom of the browser	Selecting a constraint causes the edit box to be displayed at the bottom of the browser. Enter a new offset/angle value for the constraint and press ENTER.

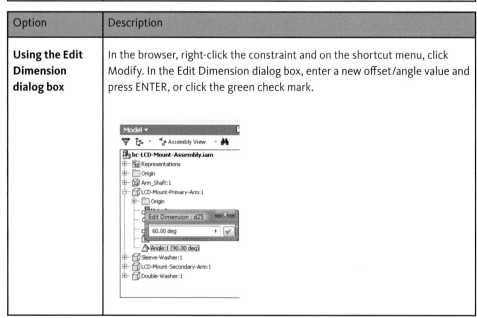

Option	Description
Using the Edit Dimension dialog box	In the browser, right-click the constraint and on the shortcut menu, click Modify. In the Edit Dimension dialog box, enter a new offset/angle value and press ENTER, or click the green check mark.

Procedure: Dragging Constrained Components

The following steps describe how to use constrained dragging components to validate existing assembly constraints.

1   With the assembly model in its current position, select any of its components.

2   Click and drag the component to validate existing constraints. The components move based upon the available degrees of freedom.

3   Continue to constrain-drag the components as required.

Proper Constraining Techniques

As you begin to create your assembly designs, you may discover that often there is more than one way to apply assembly constraints to components and achieve the same or similar results. When applying constraints, there are some techniques and guidelines that you can use to simplify the process and apply constraints in a predictable and uniform manner.

Constraining Technique Guidelines

- You should apply the constraints using the simplest approach possible while using constraint solutions that constrain the parts as completely as required by the design intent.

- You are not required to fully constrain parts in the assembly, but parts should not be left unconstrained, or with constraint conditions that do not fully represent the intended function of the part in the assembly. If a component in an assembly is not intended to be constrained to other components, then it should be grounded or constrained to assembly-level work features.

- As you plan the constraints, mimic the real world conditions of the parts in the assembly by using assembly constraint solutions that most closely resemble how the parts are assembled after manufacturing. With this approach, you can develop an assembly of parts that interact as intended with other parts in the assembly.

Example of Proper Constraining Techniques

In the following illustration, you could use a variety of different constraint solutions to assemble these two components. However, after analyzing how the components are put together, you use the proper constraint to mimic the real-world process of assembling the two components.

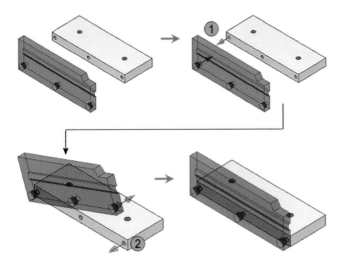

① Insert constraint simulates a bolted connection.

② Insert constraint simulates a bolted connection.

Exercise | Constrain Components

In this exercise, you use the concepts and techniques learned in this lesson to constrain components in the assembly. After you apply the constraints, you edit some constraints to see the effect on the assembly.

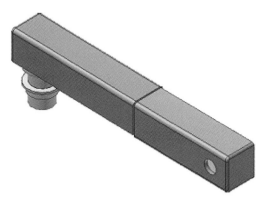

The completed exercise

Completing the Exercise :

To complete the exercise, follow the steps in this book or in the onscreen exercise. In the onscreen list of chapters and exercises, click Chapter 6: Placing, Creating, and Constraining Components. Click Exercise: Constrain Components.

1 Open *LCD-Mount-Assembly.iam.*

2   To create a Mate-Axis/Axis assembly constraint:

- On the ribbon, click Constrain.
- Select the inside surfaces (1 and 2) of the parts as shown.
- Click OK to create a Mate-Axis/Axis constraint and close the dialog box.

3   Constrain-drag the Sleeve-Washer:1 component as shown.

4   To apply a Mate-Face/Face assembly constraint:

- On the ribbon, click Constrain and select the face marked (1). Hover over the outside face (2) until the Select Other tool is displayed. You must keep your cursor on the Select Other tool, or else it is not displayed.
- Click the left or right arrow until the inside face (2) is highlighted. Click the center of the Select Other tool.
- Click OK to create the constraint and close the dialog box.

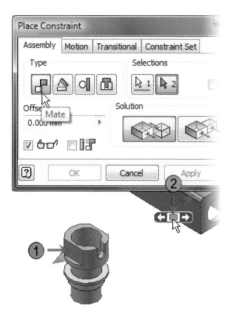

5   On the Navigation bar, click the Orbit tool and rotate the view as shown.

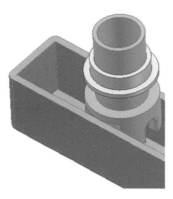

6   To apply a Tangent assembly constraint:

- On the ribbon, click Constrain and click the Tangent type.
- Select the faces marked (1) and (2) and make sure that the Outside solution is selected.
- Click OK.

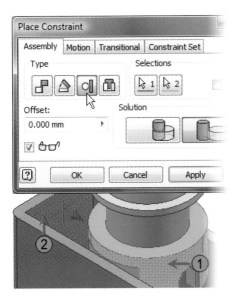

7   Press F6 to return to a home view.

8   Constrain-drag the LCD-Mount-Primary-Arm:1 component away from the Arm_Shaft:1 component.

9   On the Navigation bar, click the Orbit tool and rotate the view as shown.

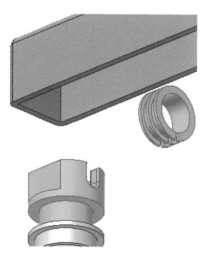

10   To use the ALT+Select method of applying assembly constraints:

- Press and hold the ALT key.
- Select the lower face of the LCD_Mount- Primary-Arm:1 component and drag it to the circular edge of the Arm_Shaft:1 component as shown.

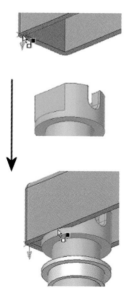

11   Press F6 to return to a home view.

12 To apply an Insert assembly constraint:

- On the ribbon, click Constrain.
- Click the Insert type and then select the edges marked (1) and (2), as shown in the following illustration.
- Click OK.

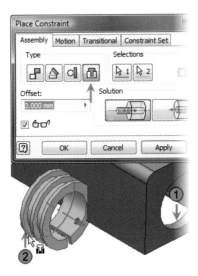

13 On the ribbon, click the Rotate Component tool. Select the LCD-Mount-Secondary-Arm:1 component and rotate it as shown.

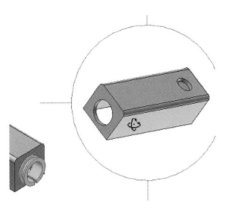

14 To place another Insert assembly constraint:

- Press C to start the Constraint tool.
- In the Place Constraint dialog box, select the Insert type.
- As shown in the following illustration, select the edges marked (1) and (2).
- Click Apply.

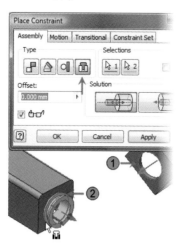

15 To apply an Angle assembly constraint:

- In the Place Constraint dialog box, select the Angle type and then select the faces shown.
- In the Angle field, enter **45 deg.**
- Click OK.

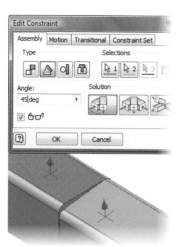

16 To edit a constraint value:

- In the browser, locate and expand the LCD- Mount-Secondary-Arm:1 component and select the Angle:1 constraint.
- In the Edit Box, enter **90** and press ENTER.

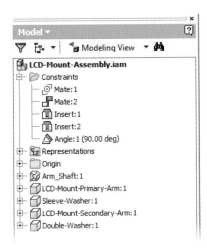

17 Switch the browser to Modeling View and expand the Constraints folder to view the constraints.

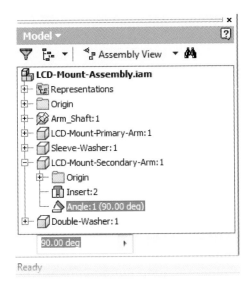

18 Close all files. Do not save.

Lesson 21 | Placing Standard Components Using the Content Center

This lesson describes the enhancements associated with placing components into an assembly from the Content Center.

Enhancements have been made to the Content Center to help you identify the properties of a family of content and to place components. By understanding these enhancements, you are able to easily view the columns of properties for the families in a category, place components from the Content Center's Table View pane, and place parts with custom size parameters as standard parts.

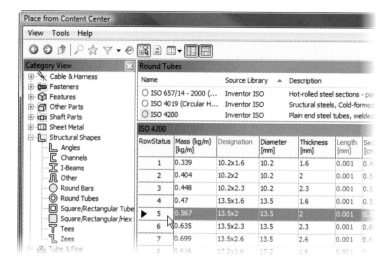

Objectives

After completing this lesson, you will be able to:

- Describe the purpose and functionality of the Content Center.

- Describe the Content Center consumer environment and what Content Center consumers can do.

- Use the Content Center consumer environment to place, change, and open Content Center components.

- Use the Supplier Content Center to access millions of native Autodesk Inventor models of purchased parts and standard components.

About the Content Center

The Content Center consists of multiple libraries of content that have been created based on industry standards. By accessing Content Center content, you save significant time researching possible sizes and modeling geometry to represent in your design. You can also create your own custom libraries and publish your own parts or features for reuse by yourself and other team members. When you publish your library content to the Content Center, everyone can reuse the custom geometry following the workflow for reusing supplied industry content.

In the following illustration, multiple categories of part content are listed in the Place from Content Center dialog box. In this case, a needle roller bearing has been selected for reuse. All of the defined variations for this part are listed in the family preview pane. By clicking OK, this part is created and ready for you to use.

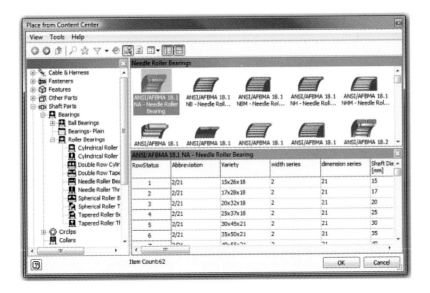

The Content Center

The Content Center has two environments for two distinct roles; consumer and editor. In the consumer environment, you access the libraries and use the parts or features within your design. In the editor environment, you define the categories and their required parameters within a library, publish parts or features to these categories, and define the iterations for the parts or features the consumer can select from when reusing the parts or features.

About Content Center Consumers

When you place parts or features from the Content Center into an assembly or part design, you are referred to as a consumer of that content. To replace or resize part content, you again interact with the Content Center as a consumer. You are also a consumer of the content when you open it from the Content Center. To be a Content Center consumer, you need to understand the different things you can do as a consumer.

In the following illustration, the tree view was expanded exposing the Rounded shaft machine key category. After selecting this category, you can then select different types of rounded shaft machine keys for reuse in your design.

Typical Tasks for Content Center Consumers

Being a Content Center consumer means you can:

- Directly open the content to save it in your library path or save it somewhere outside your library path so you can modify it.

- Place content into an assembly or part as custom or standard content.

- Edit content added to an assembly or part by changing its size or replacing it with other content.

For content that follows certain authoring and publishing criteria, you have special drag-and-drop capabilities to size and position the content. This special capability is referred to as AutoDrop. When you use AutoDrop-enabled components, the correct size is automatically determined by hovering the cursor over applicable geometry for that content being reused.

In the following illustration, the AutoDrop-configured plain bearing automatically determines the appropriate OD bearing size based on the highlighted ID edge of the housing about to be selected. Had an edge to the shaft been selected, the bearing would have been sized based on its ID values.

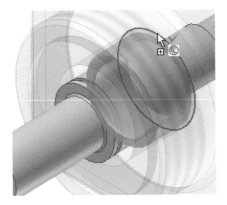

Placing Standard Components

By placing components from the Content Center you save time creating the digital prototype of your design while also ensuring you use industry and company standard parts. Being able to place the specific component member that you see in the Table View pane and place parts that have custom size parameters as standard parts means you are able to add exactly what you need.

Placement from the Table View

In the Place from Content Center dialog box > Table View pane you can select to insert a specific member from the table. Double-clicking the row for a member in the Table View pane or selecting the row and clicking OK initiates the placement of that content member. The placement process skips the Family dialog box and goes directly to the placement of the component if that library component does not require a user entered custom size parameter. If the component member requires a user entered value, like the length value for a structural shape, then the Family dialog box displays enabling you to enter the custom size parameter value prior to placing the part.

In the following illustration, an M6 x10 ISO 2009 slotted countersunk flat head screw is in the process of being double-clicked so it can be directly added to the digital prototype of an assembly design.

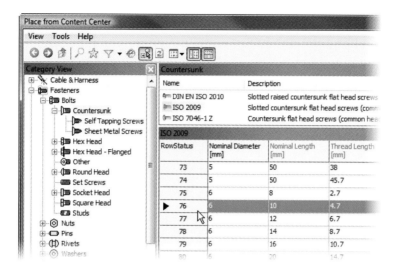

Content Center Dialog Box

As a Content Center consumer, you interact and select parts or features from the Place from Content Center dialog box. The following illustration shows the Place from Content Center dialog box with the optional display of the tree view, favorites, and family preview.

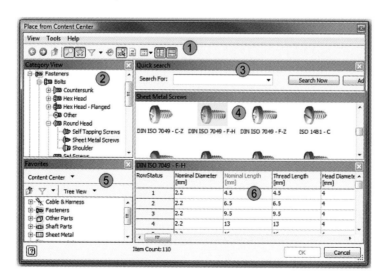

(1) Use the toolbar buttons to navigate, search, and filter through the content. Also change the display of the icons and which panes are displayed.

(2) When the Tree View button is activated, use this area to navigate and switch to different library categories.

(3) Use to search for Content Center components.

(4) The Categories and Family Collection pane. It is the main area of the Content Center where you select which part family or feature family you want to use.

(5) When the Favorites button is active, use to access content you have identified as favorites. Organize your favorites into groups of favorite content by having the group active prior to adding the content to favorites.

(6) Use to preview the different family members and their properties for the selected part or feature selected in area (4).

Configure Libraries in the Project File

To consume content from a library, your active project file must be configured to access the content in that library.

In the following illustration, the Configure Libraries dialog box is shown listing the libraries currently configured for a project called Exercises. You can use the content defined only within the libraries listed in this dialog box. This dialog box is displayed by clicking the Configure Content Center Libraries button (1) in the Projects dialog box.

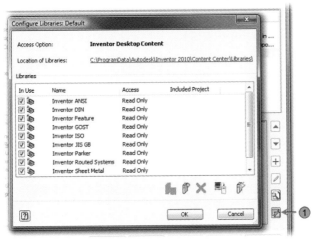

Placing Content

You have two types of content you can place directly into your designs. You can place parts into an assembly or you can place features into a part or part sketch. To place parts into an assembly, you use the Place from Content Center tool. To place features, you use the Place Features tool.

Because some content in the Content Center can be configured with AutoDrop capabilities and other parts require you to enter in distance values, the procedure for placing parts in an assembly can vary depending on the type of content you select.

If you double-click a part in the Content Center, regardless of whether it is configured with AutoDrop, you select and specify the size and other properties within a dialog box. When placing standard content, like bolts, washers, and bearings, this dialog box also has an option you can select to create the placed component as a custom part instead of a standard library part. If placing it as a custom part, you specify a name and location for the part to be created so you can modify it later.

If the part is AutoDrop enabled, click the part once in the Content Center to select it and then click OK to add it to the assembly. To set the size of the part, hover your cursor over geometry in the assembly that defines that part. The part automatically changes its size to match the geometry the cursor is hovering over. For example, when placing a bearing on a shaft, hovering over the different diameters of the shaft automatically changes the size of bearing to match. The match is dependent on the required size being already defined as a member of that part family.

Access

Place from Content Center

Ribbon: **Assemble tab › Component panel › Place from Content Center**

Access

Feature

Ribbon: **Manage tab > Insert panel > Feature**

Shortcut Menu: **Place Feature**

Procedure: Placing Content

The following steps describe how to place content from the Content Center.

1   Start the tool to place a part or feature from the Content Center.

2   In the Content Center dialog box, navigate to and select the part or feature family.

3   Insert the part or feature member into the active assembly or drawing file.

Changing Content

After placing part content into an assembly, you have different tools to access the Content Center data to either change the part's size or change the type of part. To make these changes, you use the Change Size tool or Replace from Content Center tool. For either of these tools to change a part, you must first select the part prior to accessing the tool. When changing the size, you make your modifications in the dialog box listing the sizes for the members of that part family. When replacing the part, the Content Center dialog box is displayed and you make your selection there.

When you place a feature into a part, you modify that feature by changing its parameter values or using 3D grips to resize or reposition the feature.

Access

Change Size

Shortcut Menu: **Change Size**

Access

Replace from Content Center

Shortcut Menu: **Replace from Content Center**

Procedure: Changing Content

The following steps describe how to change part content after placing it in an assembly.

1   In the drawing window or browser, select the part to change.

2   Start the tool to change the part's size or to replace it.

3   Select a new part type or size.

Opening Content

You directly open a part from the Content Center libraries using the Open from Content Center tool. You do this so you can save the part to a library path for use at a later time, or to save it to a path outside the library path. To save it outside the library path, perform a Save Copy As operation after opening the part. After it is saved in a path outside of a library path, you can modify and save the modifications. These modifications may be for a one-time variation, or to publish the modified part back to the library. Depending on the library, the part could be published back to the original to update the content, or it could be added as a new part with new part family members.

Access

Open from Content Center
Application Menu: **Open > Open from Content Center**

Procedure: Opening Content

The following steps describe how to directly open a library part without placing it in an assembly.

1   Start the Open from Content Center tool.

2   In the Content Center dialog box, navigate to and open the part family.

3   Click Save to save it within the library path. Click Save Copy As to save it to a path outside of the library.

Using the Manufacturing Community

The Manufacturing Community is an Internet portal that provides you with direct access to millions of standard components through the Supplier Content. With the Supplier Content Center, you have a common location to access native Autodesk Inventor models or other file formats of the purchased parts and components you may need in your assembly.

Access

Supplier Content Center

Ribbon: **Manage tab > Web panel > Supplier Content**

Procedure: Accessing the Supplier Content Center

The following steps describe how to access and use the Supplier Content Center.

1. Click Manage tab > Web panel > Supplier Content.

2. The first time you access the portal, you must create a user account.
    - After creating the account, you are sent an activation e-mail.
    - Use the link in the e-mail to activate the account.

3. After logging in to the account, you can search for parts from global suppliers or search member content.

4. After you have identified the components, download them to your system or network.

5. Depending on the file type downloaded, import or open them in Inventor.

Exercise | Use Content Center Data

In this exercise, you use content from the Content Center to add a machine key and bearing to help you complete a design.

The completed exercise

Completing the Exercise:	*To complete the exercise, follow the steps in this book or in the onscreen exercise. In the onscreen list of chapters and exercises, click Chapter6: Placing, Creating, and Constraining Components. Click Exercise: Use Content Center Data.*

1 Check to make sure the current project file is configured to access the Inventor ISO library.

- Click Get Started tab > Launch panel > Projects.
- Click Configure Content Center Libraries (1).
- In the Configure Libraries dialog box, review the list of libraries to ensure Inventor ISO is listed (2). Click Add Library to add the library if it is not listed.
- Click OK to close the Configure Libraries dialog box.
- Click Done to close the Projects dialog box.

2   Open *Content Center.iam*.

3   To begin to place a file from the Content Center, click Assemble tab > Component panel >
     Place from Content Center.

4   Create your own Content Center favorites group. In the Place from Content Center dialog
     box, on the toolbar, click Favorites.

5   Under Favorites, click the down arrow next to Content Center. Click Add New
     Favorites Group.

6   In the New Favorites Group dialog box:
    • Enter **Common Shaft Parts**.
    • Click OK. The Favorites pane is displayed as shown.

7   In the Category View tree, navigate to the rounded machine keys. Click the Filter button and make sure ISO is selected.

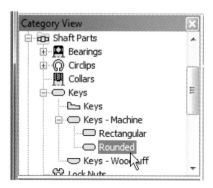

8   Add the rounded machine key ISO 2491 A to your favorites group.
    • In the Category and Family Collection area, right-click ISO 2491 A.
    • Click Add to Favorites. The Favorites pane for the Common Shaft Parts group is displayed as shown.

9   Add an occurrence of ISO 2491 A to the assembly. Under Favorites, double-click ISO 2491 A.

10 In the ISO 2491 A dialog box, on the Select tab, select the sizes for the key:
   - In the Shaft Diameter column, select 12-17.
   - In the Width X Height column, select 5x3.
   - In the Parallel Key Nominal Length column, select 25.
   - Click OK.

11 In the graphics window, click to add a single occurrence of this component. Right-click in the graphics window and click Done.

12 Change the color of the Handle Bearing Mount to Glass so that you can see the inside edges of it and the outside edges of the shaft:
   - Select the Handle Bearing Mount:1 component.
   - On the Quick Access toolbar, in the Color Override list, click Glass.

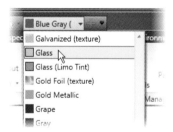

13 Add a plain bearing to the shaft:

- Click Assemble tab > Component panel > Place from Content Center.
- Navigate to the Bearings-Plain category and select ISO 4379 (Cylindrical).
- Click OK.

14 Size the bearing using the AutoDrop functionality:

- Hover the cursor over different cylindrical edges to see the bearing size automatically change according to that geometry, fitting to an inside or outside surface.
- Hover the cursor over the back circular edge of the hole where the shaft slips into the other part, as shown.
- With the green check mark displaying next to the cursor, click once.

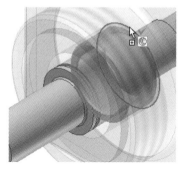

15 Click and drag the arrow as shown to change the bearing size.

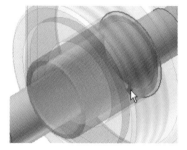

16   On the AutoDrop toolbar, click Done. In the Table dialog box, click OK.

17   Change the size of the bearing:

- In the graphics window, right-click the bearing. Click Change Size.
- In the ISO 4379 (Cylindrical) dialog box, from the list on the Select tab, click 20 x 26 x 20.
- Click OK.

18   Close all files. Do not save.

Lesson 22 | Basic Part Design in an Assembly

This lesson describes basic part design in the context of an assembly.

By creating components in an assembly, you can design parts in the context of the assembly in which they will reside. You can take advantage of other part features in the assembly to create new geometry and validate this new geometry based upon the design intent.

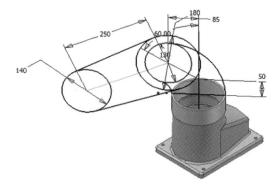

Objectives

After completing this lesson, you will be able to:

- Describe in-place assembly design and state some of its benefits.

- Describe how design intent can be captured while creating components in an assembly.

- Create components in an assembly.

- Edit components in the context of an assembly.

- State some guidelines for in-place component design.

About Designing and Editing in an Assembly

By designing in the context of the assembly, you can take advantage of other geometry in the assembly by referencing the features of other parts to assist in the creation of new parts. Commonly referred to as top-down assembly modeling, this approach allows you to design new parts in the assembly environment in which they will reside.

Definition of In-Place Design

In-place component design, sometimes referred to as top-down assembly modeling, is a process in which the individual components in the assembly are designed in the context of the assembly. As new components are required for the assembly, they are created while working in the assembly.

In the following illustration, a new component is being designed in the context of the assembly. The other components in the assembly can be used as references for new geometry. As the new component is created, you can immediately see how the design relates to other components in the assembly.

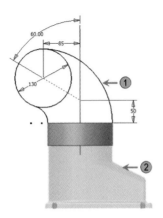

1. New component being designed in the assembly.

2. Existing component in the assembly.

Example of In-Place Design

In a typical design, the component responsible for connecting the primary and secondary axes of rotation on a desktop robot must be created. The base component that houses the primary motor and power supply has already been designed and is being reused from a different assembly. The new component must mate with the existing base component while adhering to the design parameters for the new robot. This is accomplished by using the existing base component to start the assembly and designing the additional components in the context of the assembly.

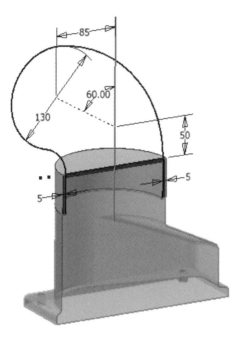

Benefits to Designing and Editing in an Assembly

The following are some benefits to creating parts in the context of the assembly.

- Ability to reference other parts in the assembly.

- Ability to validate function within the assembly.

- Ability to create adaptive relationships between parts.

- Presents a better picture of the overall design intent.

Capturing Design Intent

Designing components in the context of the assembly provides opportunities to capture design intent that might not otherwise be possible, or at minimum be very time consuming or difficult. For example, perhaps you are designing two components that must mate together. Each of them shares a common bolt-hole pattern as well as other features such as locator pins and holes that must align. While it is possible to design each of these components separately, it would be much easier to accomplish while working in the context of the assembly and referencing the key features on the other component.

In the following illustration, each matching callout indicates design intent that must be captured from one component and transferred to the other.

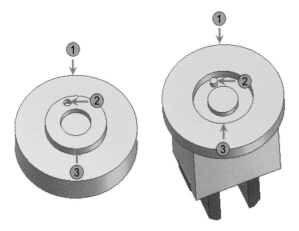

1. Outside diameters for both components are equal.

2. Drive pin and hole features must fit together.

3. Male and female feature diameters must fit together.

Definition of Capturing Design Intent

The definition of capturing design intent can differ depending on the context in which it is being described. In the context of part design in an assembly, the following list summarizes some examples of capturing design intent:

- Duplicating features on mating surfaces from one part to another.

- Enabling a component's feature to change as a result of changes occurring to mating features of other components.

- Using reference geometry on one part to position new geometry on another part.

- Using the appropriate assembly constraints to mimic real-world conditions and validate the design of each component with respect to other components in the assembly. How does one component's form and function affect the form and function of other components in the assembly?

You can think of capturing design intent as using the tools at your disposal to meet or automate a given set of design tasks or rules.

Example of Design Intent Captured

In the following illustration, design intent is being captured by projecting a cross section of the 3D Stand-Off component to design the Spacer component. The Spacer component requires a tab feature that fits in the slot feature of the Stand-Off component. By projecting the cross section of the Stand- Off component at the sketch plane, you can constrain the new sketch geometry to the cross section, ensuring a perfect fit.

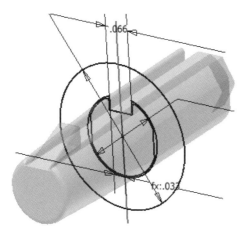

Creating Components in Place

When you design components in the context of the assembly, you use the Create Component tool to create the new parts or subassemblies. After the new component is created, the part modeling/sketch environment is automatically activated. All the tools you would use when doing standard part modeling are available and the modeling procedures are identical.

Access

Create Component

Ribbon: **Assemble tab › Component panel › Create Component**

Toolbar: **Assembly Panel**
Shortcut Menu: **Create Component**
Keyboard: **N**

Create In-Place Component Dialog Box

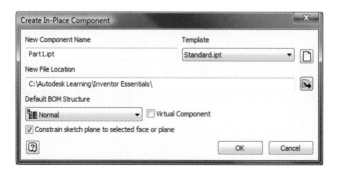

Option	Description
New Component Name	Enter a file name for the part of subassembly.
Template	Select a template to use for the new part or subassembly.
New File Location	Enter or browse to the location for the new part or subassembly.
Default BOM Structure	Select the way this part or subassembly is represented in the bill of materials (BOM). Select Normal, Inseparable, Purchased, Phantom, or Reference.
Virtual Component	Use this option to create representational components in the browser that do not require modeling geometry and do not require a file.

Procedure: Creating Parts in Place

The following steps describe how to create parts in place.

1   From within an assembly file, on the ribbon, click Create Component.

2   Enter the required values in the Create In-Place Component dialog box. Click OK to create the new part.

3   Select a face or plane to define the initial sketch plane on the new part

4   Use the sketching tools available to create new sketch geometry, or project geometry from other parts in the assembly.

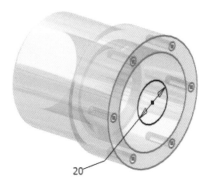

5   Use part modeling tools to create the 3D geometry.

Procedure: Creating Subassemblies in Place

The following steps describe how to create subassemblies in place.

1   From within an assembly file, on the ribbon, click Create Component.

2   Enter the required values in the Create In-Place Component dialog box. Click OK to create the new subassembly.

3   Select a face or plane to orient the new subassembly's origin.

4   The subassembly is activated automatically. You can now create new parts in the context of the subassembly or place components that have already been created.

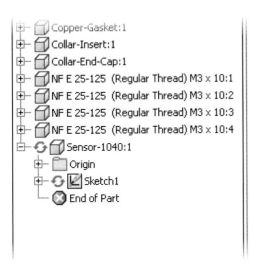

Editing Components in Place

As you design components in the assembly, you are constantly working at a different level of the assembly. As the design evolves, you may be performing assembly-level edits to constraints or other properties, then editing specific components in the assembly. To edit a component in the assembly, you must first activate the component. You can have only one active component in the assembly at any given time. When a component is active, you can edit only that component.

The following illustration shows an active component in the context of the assembly.

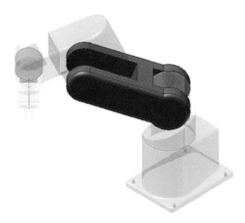

Effect of Activating Components in the Assembly Environment

When a component is activated in the context of the assembly, the assembly environment changes.

- In the browser, the background behind all other components is gray.

- In the browser, the component is automatically expanded to expose the component's features.

- The panel bar switches to display the modeling tools.

- In the graphics window, the nonactive components are dimmed.

The following illustration shows the browser when a component is active for in-place editing in an assembly.

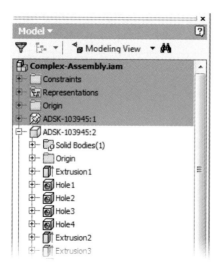

Activating Components in the Assembly

To edit a component in the context of the assembly, you must first activate the part. There are several options available for activating a component in the context of the assembly.

- In the browser or graphics window, double-click the part.

- In the browser or graphics window, right-click the part and on the shortcut menu click Edit.

- In the browser or graphics window, right-click the part and on the shortcut menu click Open. This option opens the part in a separate window. Any changes to the part are automatically reflected in the assembly.

Guidelines for In-Place Component Design

In-place component design provides you with the most flexible methods and tools to enable you to focus on your design and capture and implement as much design intent as possible. Some guidelines can help to ensure your success with this design methodology, while leveraging the functionality of the application.

In-Place Component Design Guidelines

- When you create a new component, the initial sketch of your new component is oriented to the face or plane you select on existing components or origin work features. Keep this in mind as you select that face or plane.

- Use existing geometry as a reference for creating new geometry. This is done by projecting edges or work features onto the new sketches.

- If you are projecting associative edges, turn off adaptivity for the component when you no longer require adaptive functionality.

- As the component design evolves and features are added, continue to add assembly constraints as required to simulate real-world assembly conditions.

- On complex assemblies it may be beneficial to open the component in a separate window. Right- click the component in the browser or graphics window and click Open.

- Use the Slice Graphics tool at the sketch level, or assembly section tools at the assembly level to reveal internal details as required.

Example of In-Place Component Design

In the following illustration, the Slice Graphics tool is being used while sketching to clarify internal features. In this example, you see how the offset profile compares with the inner profiles of the part.

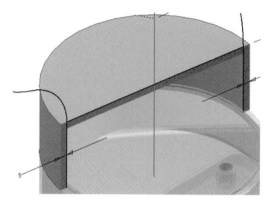

Exercise | Create Components in an Assembly

In this exercise, you open an assembly and create a new component using the techniques learned in this lesson.

The completed exercise

Create a New Component Based on an Existing Component

In this portion of the exercise, you open an assembly and create a new component in place based on an existing component

1   Open *Design-Robot.iam.*

2   To make sure you can project associative edges:

- On the ribbon, Tools tab, Options panel, click Application Options.
- In the Application Options dialog box, click the Assembly tab and make sure the Enable Associative Edge/Loop Geometry Projection During In-Place Modeling setting is selected.
- Click Close.

In-place features
From/to extents (when possible):

☐ Mate plane

☐ Adapt feature

Cross part geometry projection
☑ Enable associative edge/loop geometry projection during in-place modeling

↑

3   To create the new component:

  - On the ribbon, click the Create Component tool.
  - In the Create In-Place Component dialog box, for New Component Name, enter
    Design-Robot-Axis1-2.
  - If necessary, select the Metric\Standard (mm).ipt template. Confirm that the
    Constrain Sketch Plane to Selected Face or Plane option is selected. Click OK.

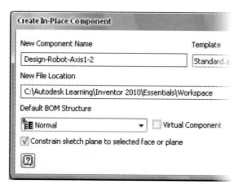

4   Select the face on the part as shown

5   To project geometry from the existing component to be used in the new component:

  - On the ribbon, click the Project Geometry tool and select the same face on the
    existing part.
  - You may need to zoom in to the part to select the face as shown.

6   Press ESC to end the command.

7   On the ribbon, click Finish Sketch to exit the sketch.

8   To extrude the profile:
   - On the ribbon, click the Extrude tool and select the profile you just projected.
   - In the Extrude dialog box, for Distance, enter **50 mm** and ensure that the extrusion direction is going upward.
   - Click OK.

9   To create a new sketch:

- On the ribbon, click Sketch.
- Select the top of the component, as shown.
- If the edges of the face are not automatically projected onto the sketch, use the Project Geometry tool to project them.

10 On the Quick Access toolbar, click Return or, on the ribbon, click Finish Sketch to exit the sketch.

11 To extrude the top surface of the component. On the ribbon, click Extrude.

- Select both the inner and outer profiles.
- For Distance, enter **5 mm**.
- Select the direction button as shown.
- Click OK.

12   On the Quick Access toolbar, click Save to save the new part file.

13   On the Quick Access toolbar, or on the ribbon, click Return to activate the assembly.

14   Save and close the assembly.

Create a New Component Based on a Sketch

In this portion of the exercise, you open an assembly and create a new component in place based on a sketch.

1   Open *Design-Robot.iam*. If your assembly does not match the one shown, open *Design-Robot-2.iam*.

2   In the browser, double-click *Design-Robot- Axis1-2*. If using *Design-Robot-2.iam, double- click Design-Robot-Axis1-2b*.

3   To create a new sketch on the YZ plane:

- On the ribbon, click Sketch.
- In the browser, expand the Origin folder of the current part and select YZ Plane.

4   To create a plan view of the new sketch:

    • On the Navigation bar, click View Face.

    • In the browser, select Sketch3.

5   Sketch a circle similar to the one shown.

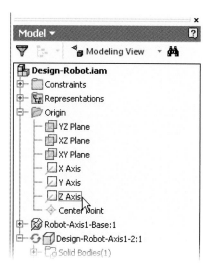

6   To project an axis on the component:

    • On the ribbon, click Project Geometry.

    • In the browser, select the Z axis origin of the current part.

7   To continue projecting edges:

  - Select the edges as shown in the following illustration.
  - Press ESC to end the command.

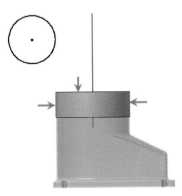

8   Using standard sketching tools, sketch and constrain the geometry as shown. The arcs should be constrained tangent to the circle and projected edges.

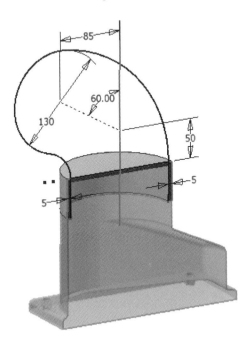

9   On the ribbon, click Finish Sketch to exit the sketch.

10 Use the Extrude tool to create a midplane extrusion 40 mm thick.

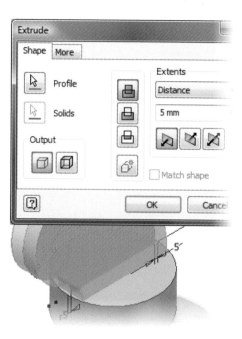

11 Sketch and extrude a circle 50 mm as shown.

Chapter 06 | Placing, Creating, and Constraining Components

12   To mirror the feature:

- On the ribbon, click Mirror.
- Select the extruded circle.
- Click the Mirror tool and select YZ plane in the browser.
- Click OK.

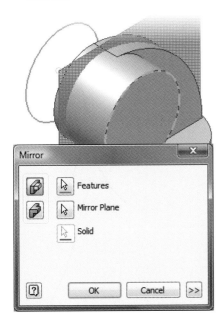

13   On the Quick Access toolbar, select Beige (Light) in the Color Style list.

14   In the browser, double-click *Design-Robot.iam* to return to the assembly.

15   To turn off Adaptivity:
   • In the browser, right-click the Design-Robot- Axis-1-2:1 component.
   • Click Adaptive to clear the check mark.

16   To apply a Mate-Axis/Axis constraint:
   • On the ribbon, click Constraint.
   • Select the circular surfaces of each component.
   • Click OK.

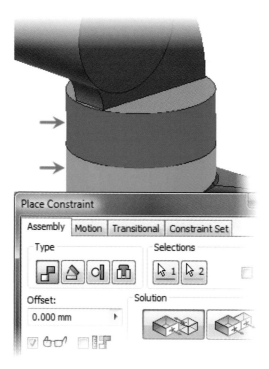

17   Close all files. Do not save.

Chapter Summary

This chapter covered the basics of assembly design, including the tools and workflows for placing and orienting components, and designing parts in the context of the assembly. With this understanding of how to create assembly designs, you continue to the next chapter where you learn how to interact with, analyze, and animate your assembly designs.

Having completed this chapter, you can:

- Place components in an assembly using the Place Component tool.
- Place assembly constraints on components in the assembly.
- Use the Content Center to place standard components into your assembly design.
- Create new components in the context of the assembly.

Image Gallery

Image courtesy of Engineering Center LTD, Russia

Images courtesy of Engineering Center LTD, Russia

Images courtesy of Adept Airmotive LTD

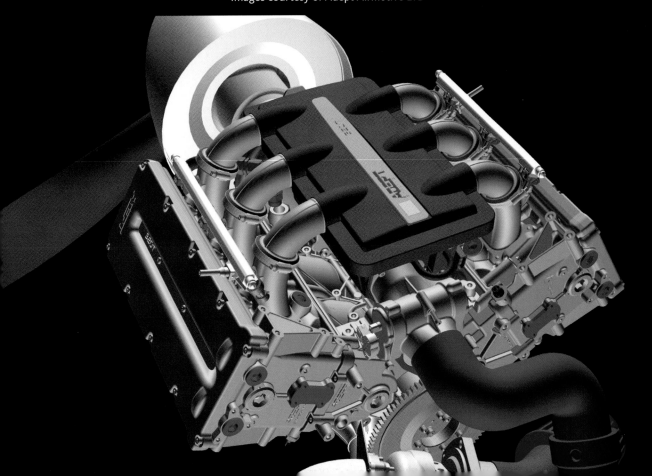

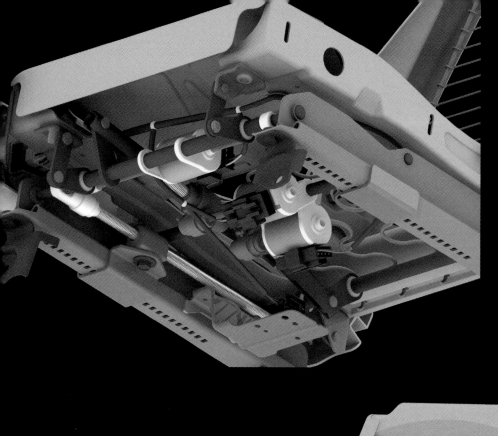

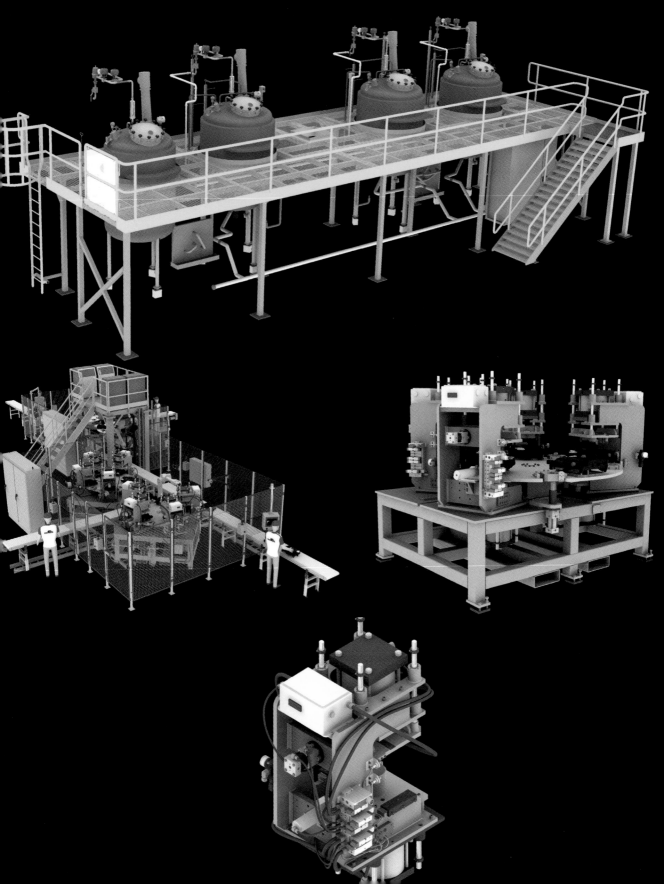

Images Courtesy of HTC Sweden AB

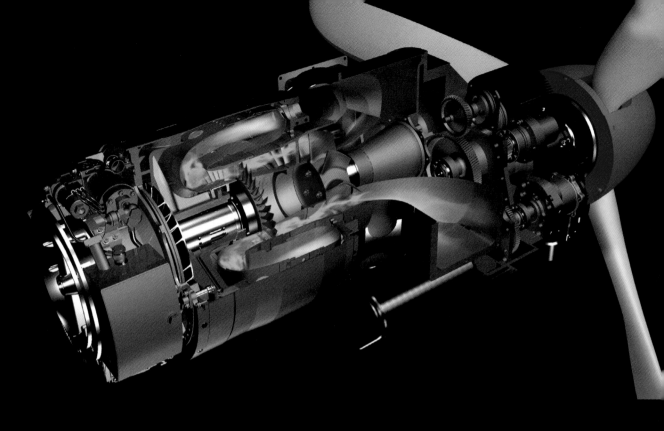

TP 100 engine gear box design and images courtesy of Prvni brnenska strojirna Velka Bites, a.s. (www.pbsvb.cz) Czech Republic, Vyzkumny a zkusebni letecky ustav, a.s. (www.vzlu.cz) Czech Republic.

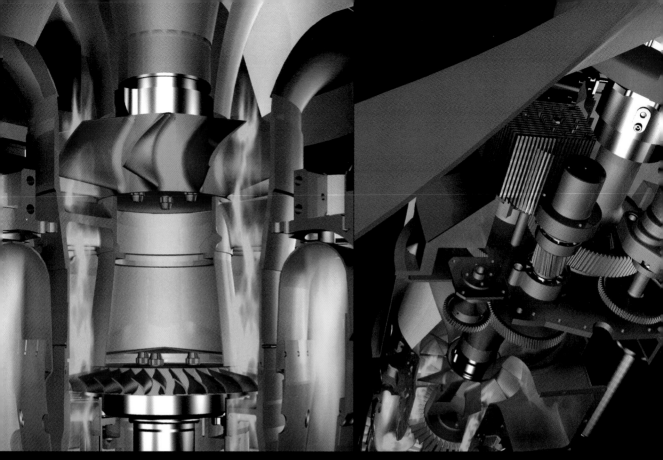

TP 100 engine gear box design and images courtesy of Prvni brnenska strojirna Velka Bites, a.s. (www.pbsvb.cz) Czech Republic,
Vyzkumny a zkusebni letecky ustav, a.s. (www.vzlu.cz) Czech Republic.

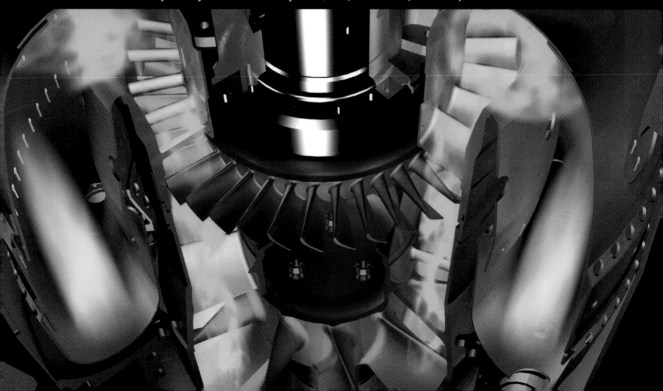

Images courtesy of Prensa Jundiai, Brazil

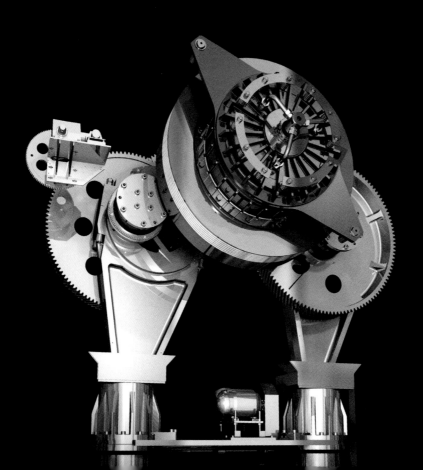

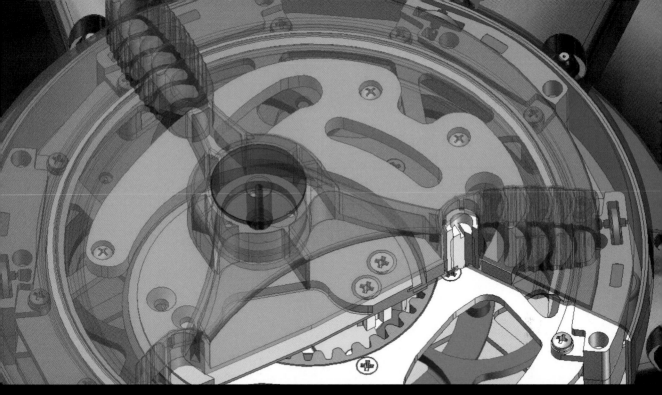

Chapter 07
Interacting with an Assembly

In this chapter, you learn how to interact with your assembly designs. Understanding how to quickly identify, locate, and select components during the assembly modeling process is essential to efficiency. Learning how to analyze your assemblies, obtain important physical properties, and check for interference between components helps to ensure the integrity of your designs. When your design is complete, you can represent your assembly with exploded views and animations that show others how to assemble or disassemble the components of your assembly.

Objectives

After completing this chapter, you will be able to:

- Use different tools and methods to identify, locate, and select components in an assembly.

- Retrieve important analysis information from the parametric models and assemblies.

- Create animations of exploded views in a presentation file.

Lesson 23 | Identifying Parts in an Assembly

This lesson describes the tools and methods you can use to identify, locate, and select components in an assembly.

As your assemblies grow in complexity, identifying specific components for editing or other procedures can become more challenging, especially if the assembly was created by someone else.

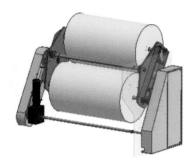

Objectives

After completing this lesson, you will be able to:

- Use the Selection Priority and Component Selection tools to simplify and enhance component selection.

- Use the Isolate tool to isolate components in the assembly.

- Describe browser filters and utilize them in an assembly.

- Quickly and easily locate components in the browser and graphics window.

- Create section views in the assembly environment.

Selecting Components

Traditional methods of selecting objects individually or with selection windows can be time consuming in medium to large or complex assemblies. The component selection options enable you to select components in the assembly using methods other than the traditional manual selection techniques.

In the following illustration, the Select by Plane option is being used to select all components on one side of the plane.

Access

Select Component Options

Quick Access Toolbar: **Component Priority Flyout › Select**
Shortcut Menu: **SHIFT+right-click**

Selection Priority

When you are working in the assembly environment, the Selection Priority menu contains settings that are not available or relevant to the part modeling environment.

The default setting is Component Priority. When this setting is used, you can select components that reside in the top-level assembly, but you cannot select components residing inside a subassembly in the graphics window unless the subassembly is first activated for editing. When the selection priority is set to Component Priority, selecting a component that resides inside the subassembly selects the entire subassembly, including all its components.

Selecting Part Priority enables you to select components that reside inside a subassembly without first activating the subassembly. This simplifies the process of selecting nested components.

The following illustrations show the effect of the selection priority settings. When Component Priority is the setting, selecting component (1) that resides in a subassembly, selects all components in the subassembly. When Part Priority is the setting, selecting component (1) selects only that component even though it resides in a subassembly.

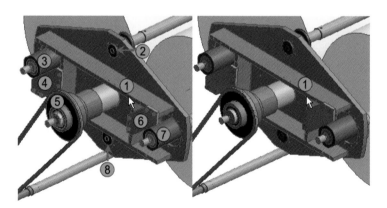

Component Priority   **Part Priority**

Note: Callout numbers indicate selected components.

Component Selection Tools

The Component Selection tools provide additional methods for selecting components in the assembly. You use these options when traditional methods of selecting components would be impractical.

The following list describes the component selection tools.

Option	Description
Select All Occurrences	Selects all occurrences of the component you select.
Constrained To	Selects all components that are constrained to the component you select.
Component Size	Selects components based on their size. You can enter a percentage value in the dialog box, in which case components are selected based on their percentage in relation to the largest component in the assembly. You can also select a component to use its size as the reference. Size is calculated by the diagonal length across the virtual bounding box of the part.
Component Offset	When you select a component, a bounding box around the component is drawn. Its size is based on the Offset value you enter in the dialog box. All components contained within the bounding box are selected.

Option	Description
Sphere Offset	When you select a component, a sphere around the component is drawn. Its size is based on the value you enter in the dialog box. All components contained within the sphere are selected.
Select by Plane	You use this option to select all components on one side of a plane or face.
External Components	You use this option to select all external components in the assembly. Adjust the Percentage Visible slider to achieve the desired result.
Internal Components	You use this option to select all internal (hidden) components in the assembly. Adjust the Percentage Visible slider to achieve the desired result.
All in Camera	You use this option to select components in the current view. Adjust the Percentage Visible slider to achieve the desired result.

Procedure: Selecting Components

The following steps describe how to use selection priority and component selection tools to select components in the assembly.

1   To set the selection priority to Part Priority:

- On the Quick Access toolbar, click Component Priority flyout > Select Part Priority.

2   To use a component selection tool:

• On the Quick Access toolbar, click Selection Priority flyout > Constrained To.

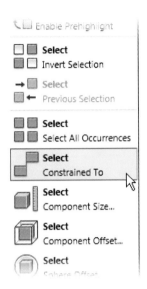

3   Select a component in the graphics window or browser.

4   Confirm the results of the selection set in the browser and graphics window.

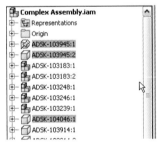

About Isolating Components

When you are editing large or complex assemblies, it can be helpful to isolate specific components in the view by turning off the visibility of other components that are not directly related to the edits you are making.

The Isolate tool enables you to turn off the visibility of all but the selected components. When you are ready to return to the previous visual state of the assembly, use the Undo Isolate tool. This action turns on the visibility status for each component that was turned off by the Isolate tool.

In the following illustration, the subassembly components are being isolated.

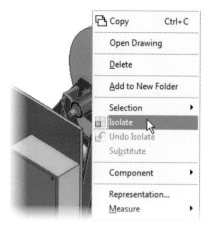

Subassembly selected for Isolate

All components except for subassembly are hidden

Access

Isolate

Shortcut Menu: **Right-click a selected component > Isolate**

Access

Undo Isolate

Shortcut Menu: **Right-click in the browser or graphics window > Undo Isolate**

 Note: *The Undo Isolate tool is available only after the Isolate tool has been used.*

About Browser Filters

You can filter the display of information in the browser by using browser filters. As your assembly grows in complexity, browser filters can assist you by streamlining its information. At the top of the assembly browser, click the Filter button and the Filter menu is displayed.

Browser Filters Access

Click the Filter button (funnel) on the browser to access browser filters. Any combination of the available filters can be turned on or off.

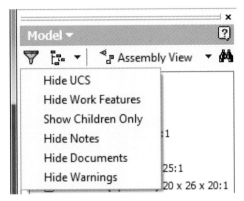

Option	Description
Hide UCS	Hides all UCS coordinates for parts in the assembly.
Hide Work Features	Hides all work features including the Origin folders.
Show Children Only	Displays only first-level children. Hides parts contained within a subassembly when the top-level assembly is active.
Hide Notes	Hides all notes attached to features.
Hide Documents	Hides inserted documents.
Hide Warnings	Hides warning symbols attached to constraints in the browser.

About Locating Components in the Browser and Graphics Window

As your assembly grows in complexity and number of components, it can be increasingly difficult to correlate what you see in the graphics window to the component reference in the browser. The same is true for correlating a component reference in the browser with the geometry in the graphics window.

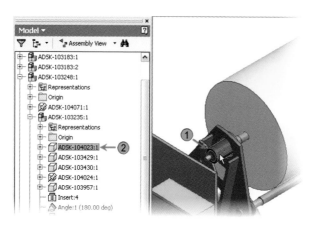

 Subassembly component selected in window.

 Using the Find in Browser tool, the subassembly is expanded and the component is identified.

Access

Find in Browser

Shortcut Menu: **Right-click a selected component in the graphics window.**

Access

Find in Window, Zoom Selected

Ribbon: View tab > **Navigate panel**

Keyboard: **END**
Shortcut Menu: **Right-click a selected component in the browser.**

Note: *When selecting components in a subassembly, to use the Find in Browser tool, you*
         must first set the selection priority to Part Priority.

Creating Assembly Sections

While working in the context of the assembly, it is possible to create sections of the assembly,
revealing internal components and features. There are three different types of assembly sections:
quarter section, half-section, and three-quarter section.

In the following illustrations, each type of assembly section view is shown.

Half-section view   **Quarter-section view**   **Three-quarter
                                                                    section view**

Access

Assembly Sections

Ribbon: **View tab > Appearance panel**

Toolbar: **Assembly Panel**

Section Menu Options

After selecting the plane or planes for the section view, right-click anywhere in the graphics window to access the following options.

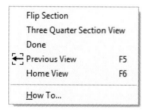

Quarter-section options

Half-section options

Three-quarter section options

Option	Description
Flip Section	Select this option to view the section from the opposite side of the section plane or planes.
Three Quarter Section View	Select this option to switch the quarter-section view to a three-quarter section view.

Option	Description
Quarter Section View	Select this option to switch the three-quarter section view to a quarter-section view.
Done	Select to accept the current section view.

Procedure: Creating Assembly Section Views

The following steps describe how to create assembly section views.

1   To create a quarter-section view:
   - On the ribbon, click Quarter Section View.
   - Select two planes or faces.

2   To switch to a three-quarter section view:
   - Right-click in the graphics window. Click Three Quarter Section View

3   To view the section from the opposite side of the plane:
    • Right-click anywhere in the graphics window. Click Flip Section.

4   Right-click anywhere in the graphics window. Click Done to accept the current section settings. ribbon, click End Section.

5   To turn off sectioning, on the ribbon, click End Section.

Exercise | Identify Parts in an Assembly

In this exercise, you use the tools and methods discussed in this lesson to locate and identify components, select them in the assembly, and create assembly section views

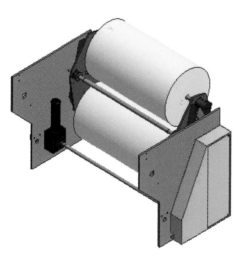

The completed exercise

1   Open *Complex-Assembly.iam*.

2   To isolate a component or subassembly:

- Right-click the subassembly indicated (1).
- Click Isolate.

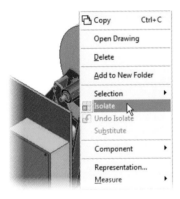

3   In the browser, notice that the visibility status for all other components and subassemblies has been turned off.

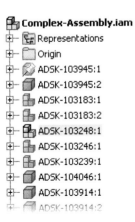

4   To use a browser filter:

  • Scroll to the bottom of the list and notice the appearance of the work features (2).
  • Click the Browser Filters button and select Hide Work Features (1).

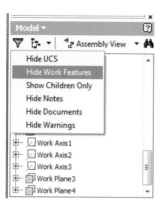

5   Scroll to the top of the browser list and expand the isolated subassembly ADSK-103248:1.

  • Notice the nested subassemblies and components.
  • On the Browser Filters menu, click Show Children Only.
    All nested components and subassemblies are filtered out of the browser list. While they are not displayed in the browser, they are still visible in the graphics window.

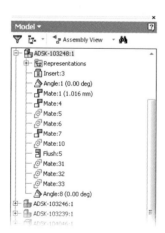

6   On the Browser Filters menu, clear the Hide Work Features and Show Children Only options to display all work features, components, and subassemblies.

7   In the graphics window, try to select any of the components in the subassembly. The entire subassembly is highlighted.

8   To set the selection priority:

- Press SHIFT+right-click anywhere in the graphics window.
- Click Select Part Priority.
- Select the component indicated.

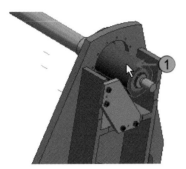

9   To locate the component reference in the browser, right-click the component in the graphics window. Click Find in Browser. The component is highlighted in the browser.

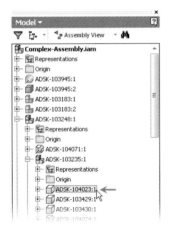

10   To select other occurrences of the component:

- Press SHIFT+right-click the selected component.
- Click Select All Occurrences.

11   In the browser, expand the subassemblies as shown. All occurrences of the component are selected in the browser and in the graphics window.

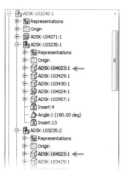

12   To undo the effects of the Isolate tool used in the beginning of the exercise, right-click anywhere in the graphics window. Click Undo Isolate. The visibility status of all components is returned to their previous state, prior to the Isolate tool being used.

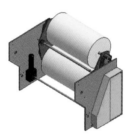

13   To create a half-section view:
   • Click View tab > Appearance panel > Quarter Section View flyout, Half Section View.
   • In the browser, scroll to the bottom of the list and select Work Plane3.
   • Right-click anywhere in the graphics window. Click Done.

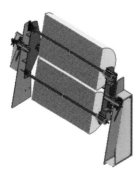

14 To create quarter-section and three-quarter- section views:

- Click View tab > Appearance panel > Quarter Section View flyout, Quarter Section View.
- In the browser, scroll to the bottom of the list. Select Work Plane3 and Work Plane4.
- Right-click anywhere in the graphics window. Click Three Quarter Section View.
- Notice the effect on the section view.

15 Right-click anywhere in the graphics window.

- Click Flip Section.
- Notice the effect on the section view.
- Continue flipping the section until the section view is displayed as shown.
- Right-click anywhere in the graphics window. Click Done.

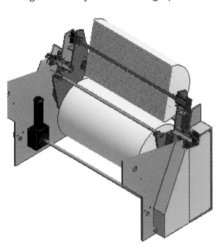

16 Click View tab > Appearance panel > End Section View.

17 Close all files. Do not save.

Lesson 24 | Analysis and Motion Tools

This lesson describes calculating physical properties, checking for interferences, and driving constraints for simple motion.

Part and assembly models are a fully parametric 3D representations of your design. You can use the information from your models to determine physical properties such as mass or center of gravity without creating a physical prototype. You can check your assemblies for interference between mating parts and display motion to identify potential problems. This capability is inherent when you create and assemble your models using standard tools found in the software.

Objectives

After completing this lesson, you will be able to:

- Calculate physical properties.

- Check for interference between components of an assembly.

- Animate components in an assembly by driving constraints

Calculating Physical Properties

The physical properties of your product design can show you how differences in material and analysis tolerances affect your model. Physical properties change whenever you modify a feature on a single part of your assembly or add or remove a component from your assembly. To calculate the properties of mass, volume, area, and inertial properties of your assembly, you use the iProperties dialog box. On the Physical tab, you click Update to calculate the properties. If you make a change to your assembly, you need to click Update each time you return to the Physical tab of the iProperties dialog box.

Based on the results of calculating the physical properties of your part, you can determine the amount of material required to produce it. In the example shown in the following illustration, you could use the Mass calculation to determine the shipping cost of the assembly.

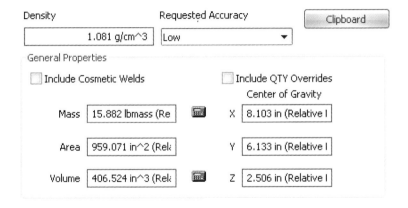

Access

iProperties

Application menu: **iProperties**
Shortcut Menu: **Properties or iProperties**

iProperties Dialog Box

The iProperties dialog box is displayed when you start the iProperties tool.

Physical Properties

When you click the Physical tab, you must click Update to calculate the assembly properties. You also must click Update after adding or removing components from your assembly or making a change to a part or a feature.

Material for Calculations

The material used for calculations is determined from the part files in the assembly. Based on the combined materials, the density is set. By default Low accuracy is set, but you can choose a greater level of accuracy as desired.

General Physical Properties

The physical properties for Mass, Area, and Volume are displayed in the General Properties area of the iProperties dialog box. The units used are determined from the template that was used to create the assembly. You also have the option to include cosmetic welds and quantity overrides from the bill of materials when you select these check boxes.

The following icons indicate whether an override value is applied.

Icon	Option	Description
	Calculated Value	This icon indicates a calculated value based on the part material settings.
	User Override Value	This icon represents a noncalculated override value.
	Calculated with Override(s) Value	This icon indicates that the value is calculated using one or more override values.
	Approximated Value	This icon is displayed when cosmetic welds are included.

Inertial Properties

You must select Principal, Global, or Center of Gravity to calculate inertial properties. The inertial properties do not include data from cosmetic welds or BOM quantity overrides.

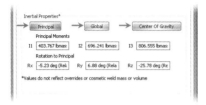

Procedure: Calculating Physical Properties

The following steps describe how to calculate the physical properties of an assembly.

1   In the browser, right-click the assembly. Click iProperties.

2   In the iProperties dialog box, Physical tab, click Update to calculate the assembly properties.

3   Review the general and inertial properties shown in the dialog box.

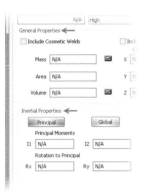

Checking for Interferences

You can check your assembly for interference between assembled components. If no interference is detected, you receive a message stating that no interferences are detected. When an interference is detected, the tool returns a report that describes the interfering components, their location, and the volume of the interfering body. In addition, the volume of the interference is temporarily displayed.

The following illustration shows the results of an interference between two assembled components.

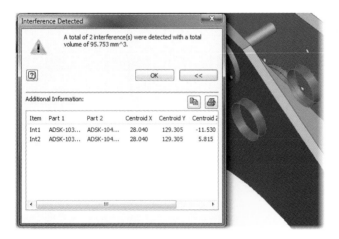

Access

Analyze Interference

Ribbon: **Analysis tab > Interference panel**

Interference Analysis Dialog Box

The Interference Analysis dialog box is displayed when you start the Analyze Interference tool.

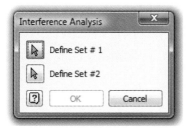

You have two ways to check your assembled components. In the first method, using Design Set # 1 only, you select two or more components or subassemblies to check against each other. You do not use Design Set # 2. This method analyzes all the components selected with each other to detect interference. Using the second method requires you to select one or more components for Define Set #1 and one or more components for Design Set # 2. This method analyzes all the components in the first set against all the components in the second set. This method does not detect interference between components selected in the same definition set.

No Interference Detected

The following message is displayed when no interference is detected between the components selected.

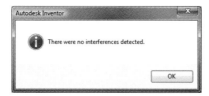

Interference Detected

The following illustration shows the information returned when a single interference is detected. The information includes a summary stating the total number of interferences detected and the total volume of that interference, followed by a table listing the parts involved, the centroid, and the volume of the interference. You also have the option to print the report, or to copy it to the clipboard and import it into a text editor or spreadsheet document.

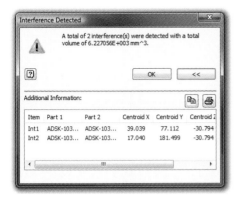

Procedure: Analyzing Interference

The following steps describe how to analyze for interference between components in an assembly.

1   Click Inspect tab > Interference panel > Analyze Interference.

2   In the dialog box, if Define Set #1 is not activated, click Define Set #1. In the graphics window or browser select the first component or components to analyze.

3   Click Define Set #2 and in the graphics window or browser, select the second component or components to analyze.

4   Click OK and view your results

Driving Constraints for Simple Motion and Analysis

One way to correct interference between parts in an assembly is to drive assembly constraints. By simulating the motion of components in an assembly, you can determine at what point or angle they interfere with each other. You can use driving assembly constraints to simulate motion by setting a start and end range for the assembly constraint offset or angle value.

The following illustration shows an angle constraint driven from 96 degrees to 62 degrees.

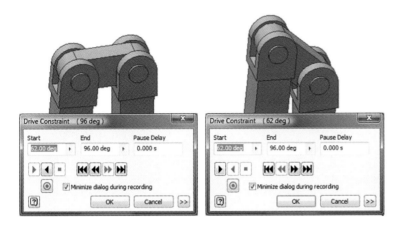

Access

Drive Constraint

Shortcut Menu: **Drive Constraint**

Start the Drive Constraint Tool

You start the Drive Constraint tool from the shortcut menu. Right-click a constraint in the browser and then click Drive Constraint.

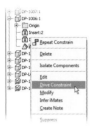

Drive Constraint Dialog Box

The Drive Constraint dialog box is displayed when you start the Drive Constraint tool. The following illustration shows the Drive Constraint dialog box in the expanded state.

The following options are available with the Drive Constraint command.

Icon	Option	Description
▶	**Play Forward**	Plays the set sequence from the start.
◀	**Play Reverse**	Plays the set sequence in reverse.
■	**Pause**	Temporarily stops the sequence at its current position.
◀◀	**Start Point**	Returns the set sequence to its start position.
◀◀	**Back**	Moves the set sequence back one step.

Icon	Option	Description
⏩	**Forward**	Moves the set sequence forward one step.
⏭	**End Point**	Returns the set sequence to its end position.
◉	**Record**	Records the sequence to an AVI or WMV file.

The following settings are available with the Drive Constraint command.

Option	Description
Start	Enter a value for the start position when driving the assembly constraint.
End	Enter a value for the end position when driving the assembly constraint.
Pause Delay	Enter a value in seconds for a pause between steps.
Drive Adaptivity	Enables adaptive parts to be updated while the constraint is being driven.
Collision Detection	Turns on collision detection while the constraint is being driven. Motion stops as soon as a collision is detected.
Increment	• **Amount of value**: Specifies that the increment is the value specified in the edit box. • **Total # of steps**: Divides the drive sequence into equal increments based on the number of steps entered in the edit box. • **Edit box**: Enter a value, measure, or parameter representing each increment, or the number of steps in the sequence.
Repetitions	• **Start/End:** Drives the sequence from the start position to the end position specified. • **Start/End/Start:** Drives the sequence from the start position to the end position and back to the start position. • **Edit box:** Enter a value representing the number of repetitions to drive the constraint.
Avi Rate	Specifies the increment at which a snapshot of the sequence is recorded to the animation file. A higher number creates a smoother animation but also increases the recording time and file size.

Procedure: Driving a Flush Constraint

The following steps describe how to use the Drive Constraint tool.

1. In the browser, right-click a constraint. Click Drive Constraint.

2. Set your start and end values.

3. Click the desired drive button.

4. Your component moves according to the sequence set.

Exercise | Calculate Properties and Analyze Interference

In this exercise, you calculate the physical properties of an assembly, modify the assembly, recalculate the properties, and check for interference between parts.

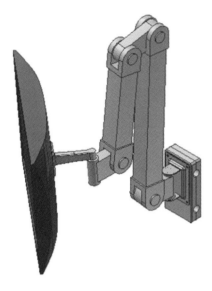

The completed exercise

Completing the Exercise:	*To complete the exercise, follow the steps in this book or in the onscreen exercise. In the onscreen list of chapters and exercises, click Chapter 7: Interacting with an Assembly. Click Exercise: Calculate Properties and Analyze Interference.*

1   Open *DP-LCD-17.iam*.

2   Calculate the physical properties of the assembly:
    - In the browser, right-click *DP-LCD-17.iam*. Click iProperties.
    - In the Properties dialog box, Physical tab, click Update.
    - Write down the calculated Mass, Area, and Volume. Click Close.

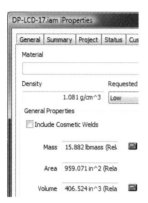

3   Activate a component and apply an override value to its mass:
    - In the browser, double-click DP-LCD-1600x1200-17:1 to activate the part.
    - In the browser, right-click DP-LCD-1600x1200-17:1. Click iProperties.
    - On the Physical tab, under General Properties, for Mass, enter **12.750.** Click Apply. Click Close.

4   Return to the assembly and update the properties calculation:

   - On the Quick Access toolbar, click Return.
   - In the browser, right-click *DP-LCD-17.iam*. Click iProperties.

5   Compare your new mass calculation to the original. The system used the override value from the DP-LCD-1600x1200-17:1 part file to calculate the mass for the assembly. Because the LCD is a purchased part, the part file is only a representation of the actual part, and therefore you keyed in the actual mass of the LCD. Click Close.

6   Select the first set of components to check for interference:

   - Click Inspect tab > Interference panel > Analyze Interference.
   - If the Define Set # 1 is not active, click Define Set # 1.
   - In the browser, click DP-1004:1, DP-1007:1, and DP-1006:1.

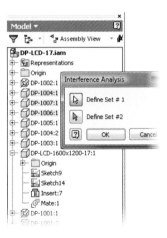

7 Select the second set of components to check for interference:

- Click Define Set # 2.
- In the browser, click DP-1005:1, DP-1004:2, and DP-1003:1.
- Click OK.

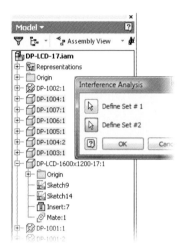

8 No interference is detected. Click OK.

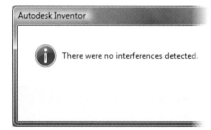

9   Check the components from set 1 against each other instead of set 2:

- Click Inspect tab > Interference panel > Analyze Interference.
- If Define Set # 1 is not active, click Define Set # 1.
- In the browser, click DP-1004:1, DP-1007:1, and DP-1006:1. Click OK.

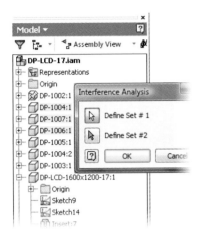

10 Evaluate the interference found:

- Click >> to display the additional interference information.
- Review the additional information regarding the interference. Notice that these three components were selected as set 1 in the previous interference analysis and no interference was detected.
- Observe the display of the volume of interference. The total volume of interference is shown in the summary and the volume of each interference in the expanded information section.

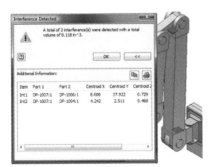

11 Click OK to close the Interference Detected dialog box.

12 At this point you would use the interference information to identify the problem and make corrections to your assembly or assembly components as needed.

13 Close all files. Do not save.

Exercise | Drive Constraints

In this exercise, you drive constraints to determine the location of interference with other components.

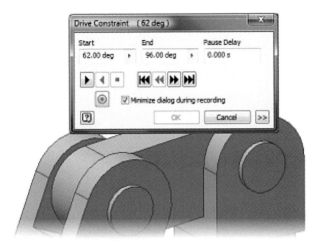

The completed exercise

Completing the Exercise: *To complete the exercise, follow the steps in this book or in the onscreen exercise. In the onscreen list of chapters and exercises, click Chapter 7: Interacting with an Assembly. Click Exercise: Drive Constraints*

1   *Open DP-LCD-17.iam.*

2   To place an angle constraint between components:
     - Click Assemble tab > Position panel > Constrain.
     - Under Type, click Angle.
     - Clear the Show Preview check box.
     - Click the Undirected Angle option.
     - For Angle, enter **-90.**

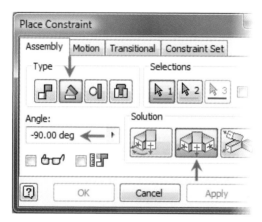

3   Select the components.
     - Select the inside surfaces of DP-1004:1 (1).
     - Select the inside surfaces of DP-1007:1 (2).
     - Click OK.

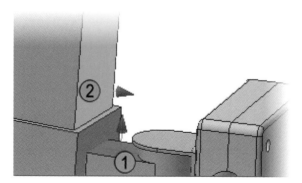

4   To place another angle constraint between components, start the Constrain tool.

- Under Type, click Angle.
- Ensure the Undirected Angle option is selected.
- Select the inside surfaces of DP-1006:1 and DP-1007:1 as shown.
- For Angle, enter **-90**. Click OK.

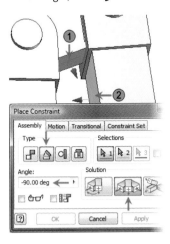

5   Drive the previous angle constraint to detect the collision angle between the components. Start the Drive Constraint tool and enter values and options:

- In the browser, under part DP-1006:1, right-click the Angle:3 (-90.00 deg) constraint. Click Drive Constraint.
- Click » to expand the Drive Constraint Dialog box. Select the Collision Detection check box.
- Enter **90** for the Start angle and **100** for the End angle.

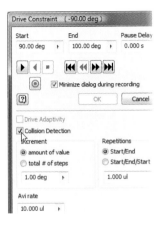

6   Complete the settings and drive the constraint:

- Under Increment, select the Amount of Value option button. Enter **.5** degrees.
- Click the Forward button to start the motion.
- Notice that a collision is detected and the title bar shows that it occurs at an angle of 97 degrees. Click OK.

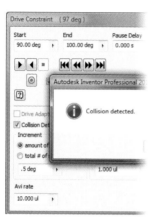

7   Modify the Start and End angles to determine the collision angle in the other direction:

- Enter **60** for the Start angle and **96** for the End angle.
- Leave the other setting the same.
- Click the Reverse button to drive the constraint.

8   Modify the Start angle so that no collision occurs:

- Notice that the collision angle in the title bar displays 61 degrees (collision angle may vary slightly). Click OK.
- Enter **62** for the Start angle.
- Under Repetitions, select the Start/End/ Start option button. For its value, enter **4**.

9   Drive the constraint with no collision detected:

- Click Forward to drive the constraint through its full range of motion.
- Notice that no collision occurs.
- Click OK to close the dialog box.

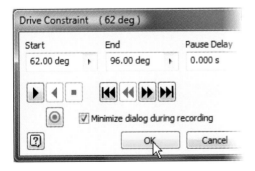

10   Close all files. Do not save.

Lesson 25 | Presenting Your Assembly

This lesson describes how to create presentation files based on your assemblies.

You use presentation files to create exploded views of an assembly. Exploded views created in a presentation file can be used to create exploded view drawings complete with balloons and a parts list.

Presentation files also enable you to create an animated explosion sequence and to visualize the components in the assembly moving into or out of their assembled positions. You can record the animation to a standard AVI format for use on other computers.

In the following illustration, an exploded view animation is ready for playback.

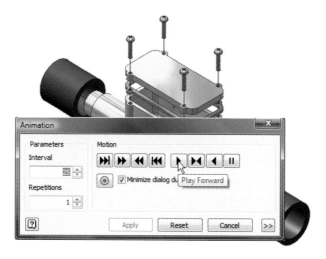

Objectives

After completing this lesson, you will be able to:

- Describe presentation files and their role in creating exploded drawing views.
- Create and manage presentation views.
- Create and edit tweaks and trails.
- Describe animated presentation views and their role in the assembly design process.
- Outline the steps required to create animations of presentation views.

About Presentations

Exploded drawing views are first developed as presentation views. You then use the presentation views to create exploded views in the drawing environment. These exploded views are used in the drawing environment for documentation and visualization. Because presentation views are based on an assembly, when changes are made to the assembly, the presentation views are updated automatically.

In the following illustration, an exploded view of an assembly is shown in a presentation file. This presentation view will be used to create an exploded drawing view.

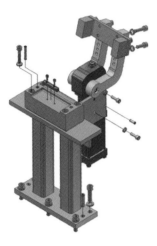

Definition of Presentations

A presentation view is a customized view of an assembly that can be used to create exploded drawing views. Presentation views reside in a presentation file, and you can add as many presentation views as necessary to create your exploded views. Each new view is added to the browser in succession as Explosion1, Explosion2, and so on.

When creating a presentation view, you can use view, positional, and level of detail representations as the starting point for view creation. At the time you create a new presentation view you can also choose Manual or Automatic explosion methods. When set to Automatic, components constrained using mate constraints are offset by the distance you specify. When you create a presentation view using the Manual method, you create component movements, or tweaks, by moving or rotating using a specified vector. The final step is to add trails to show the paths along which the components are moved to create the view.

In the following illustration, a tweak is being applied to a component, and the Tweak Component dialog box is visible.

Example of Presentations

You have created a clamp assembly as part of a larger fixture. Your customer wants you to create preventative maintenance manuals to show plant personnel how the unit should be disassembled and reassembled. You create a presentation file that contains an exploded view of the assembly. You then use the presentation view to create an exploded drawing view showing how to disassemble and reassemble the unit.

In the following illustration, an exploded drawing view displays how to disassemble the assembly to replace components.

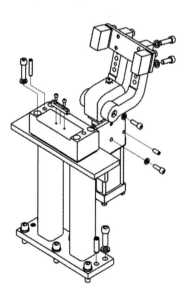

Creating Presentation Views

To create exploded views, you must first create a presentation file. You create a new presentation file using the default template or a custom template. The templates set the file properties for assembly presentations. After you have created the presentation file, you create presentation views from a selected assembly. A presentation file can reference only one assembly.

The following illustration shows the presentation environment.

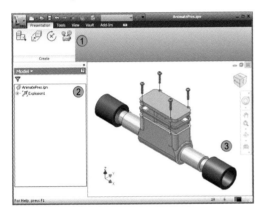

 Presentation Panel

 Presentation browser

 Presentation graphics window

Access

Create View

Ribbon: **Presentation tab > Create panel**

Toolbar: **Presentation Panel**

Select Assembly Dialog Box

When you click the Create View tool, you access the Select Assembly dialog box, where you select the assembly file and design view representation to use when creating the presentation view.

Option	Description
File	Specifies the assembly file to use for the assembly. Available only when placing the first view in the presentation.
Options	Opens the File Open Options dialog box.
Manual	Creates the presentation view without creating an exploded view. You can manually add tweaks to create an exploded view later.
Automatic	Creates the presentation view as an exploded view. Select and then set the tweak distance and trail visibility.
Distance	Specifies the tweak distance for each component when creating an exploded view. Enter the desired distance. Only available when Automatic is selected.
Create Trails	Displays the trails for each tweaked component when creating an exploded view. Available only when Automatic is selected.

File Open Options Dialog Box

When you click the Options button in the Select Assembly dialog box, you access the File Open Options dialog box.

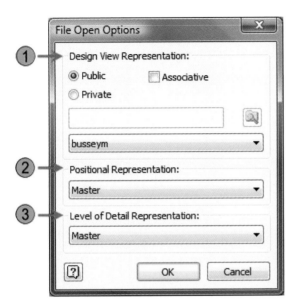

Option	Description
Design View Representations	If the selected file is an assembly, lists the available design view representations. Click Associative if you want the presentation view to update with changes in the assembly.
Positional Representation	Click the arrow to open the file with a specified positional representation.
Level of Detail Representation	Click the arrow to open the file with a specified level of detail representation.

Component Shortcut Menu

When you create a presentation view from an assembly, a node is created in the browser for the assembly. Expanding the assembly node provides access to the individual components that make up the assembly. Right-clicking a component in the browser or in the graphics window displays a shortcut menu with editing options for that component. The image on the left illustrates a component without tweaks, and on the right a component with tweaks.

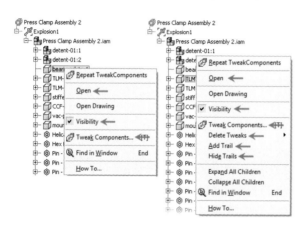

Option	Description
Open	Opens the component in a separate window.
Visibility	Sets the visibility of the component in the active presentation view.
Tweak Components	Opens the Tweak Component dialog box.
Delete Tweaks	Deletes tweaks on the selected component. Only available if the component has tweaks.
Add Trail	Adds trail to the selected component, showing the path of movement for the component. Only available if the component has tweaks.
Hide Trails	Hides trails on the selected component. Only available if the component has tweaks and trails.

Tweak Shortcut Menu

When a tweak is created for a component, it is stored as a node in the Model browser under the component. If you select the tweak, an edit box opens at the bottom of the browser where you can edit the tweak. If you right-click the tweak, a shortcut menu opens with an option to delete the tweak or turn off the visibility of the trail.

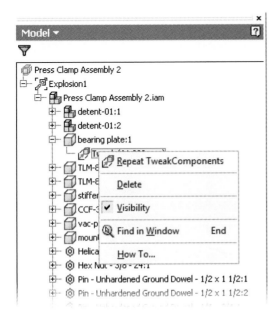

Procedure: Creating a Presentation File

The following steps describe how to create a presentation file. Before you create a presentation view, you must create a presentation file. You store the presentation in an IPN file. Default templates are available for presentation files.

1   On the ribbon, click Create New File. Select the type of file that you want to create.

2   To select a custom template, click Application menu > New and in the New File dialog box, click the desired tab and select the presentation template that you want to use.

The following illustration shows a method for creating a presentation file from a template using the Application menu (left) and the New File dialog box (right).

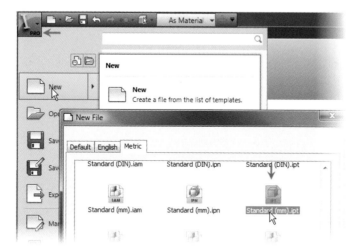

Procedure: Creating a Presentation View

The following steps describe how to create a presentation view.

1   In a presentation file, on the ribbon, click Create View.

2   In the Select Assembly dialog box, select the assembly file and explosion method. If the Automatic explosion method is selected, set the explosion distance and the trail visibility.

3   If the Options button is selected, in the File Open Options dialog box, select the desired design view, positional, and level of detail representations to use.

Creating Tweaks and Trails

After you create the presentation view, you may need to add tweaks to the components to move them to new locations in the exploded view. Even if you have chosen the automatic explosion method, most exploded views require manual tweaks.

When you tweak a component you can move and/or rotate the component in any direction. When the tweaks are created you also have the option of displaying the trails, which represent a path from the component's current location after tweaks have been applied, to its assembled location. Trails help clarify how a component in an exploded view fits into the overall assembly.

In the following illustration, multiple tweaks and trails are shown on this exploded view.

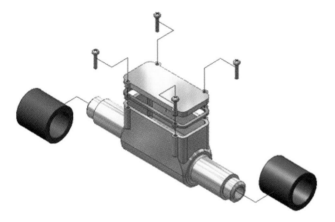

Access

Tweak Components

Ribbon: **Presentation tab > Create panel**

Toolbar: **Presentation Panel**

Tweak Component Dialog Box

The Tweak Component dialog box is shown in the following illustration

Option	Description
Direction	Click the Direction button to define the direction of the tweak. Select a face or edge on any component to display the Triad icon (1). The direction does not have to be defined from a feature on the part you tweak. When the direction triad is displayed, you can select elements of the triad to control the transformation. The blue axis indicates the current transformation axis. You can switch the active direction by: • Choosing another axis in the Tweak Component dialog box. • Selecting the axis on the Triad to make it current.
Components	Click the Components button to select the components to tweak. If you select a component by mistake, deselect it by holding down the CTRL key and reselecting the component.
Trail Origin	Click the Trail Origin button to select a different trail origin.
Display Trails	Select this option to display trails showing the path of the tweak.

Option	Description
Transformations	In the Tweak Component dialog box, under Transformations, you can set the transformation options for the tweak. You can select the option to move or rotate the component.
 ⊙ ╱ [X] [Y] [Z]	This option enables you to move the component along the selected axis. Clicking the X, Y, or Z here is the same as selecting each axis on the triad in the graphics window.
 ○ ↻ [0.000 >] ✓	This option enables you to rotate the component around the selected axis. Enter a distance or angle value for the tweak and click the green check mark button. Note you can use the value field for translational and rotational tweaks. **Note:** When you drag the tweak distance, start dragging the distance with the cursor away from existing components. Inadvertently selecting a point over a component adds that component to the tweak. 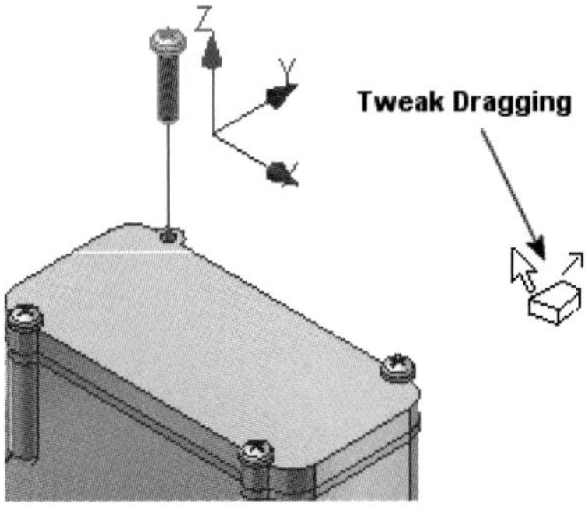 Tweak Dragging
Edit Existing Trail	Click the Edit Existing Trail button to edit an existing trail. You select the trail, then adjust the tweak value.
Triad Only	Select this option to rotate the triad only. This option is available only when the rotational transformation is selected. By rotating the triad, you can tweak the component in different angles. In the same area, click the green check button to finish tweaking the triad.

Option	Description
Clear	Click to apply and clear the current tweak values, and then continue adding tweaks.
Close	Click to close the dialog box.

Procedure: Creating Tweaks and Trails

The following steps describe how to create tweaks and trails in a presentation view.

1   Create a presentation view.

2   On the ribbon, click the Tweak Components tool and select a face or edge to define the tweak direction.

3   Select the components to be included in the tweak.

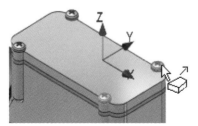

4   Confirm the Transformations settings, then click and drag in a blank area of the screen. Click Clear to apply the tweak and continue.

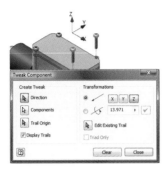

5   Select a face or edge to define the direction.

6   Select the components to include in the tweak, and confirm the transformation direction. Click and drag in a blank area of the graphics window and then click Clear to apply the tweak and continue.

7   Repeat the preceding steps to continue tweaking components. When finished, click Close.

About Animating Presentations

Exploded presentation views show how a group of components should be assembled together. Animating the view changes this process from static to dynamic by adding motion to the tweaks so that you can actually visualize the components coming together or moving apart, as opposed to imagining it. When you record and save the animations in the AVI or WMV format, your animations can be made available to anyone who has a compatible viewer.

In the following illustration, a recorded animation is shown during playback in Microsoft Windows Media Player.

Definition of Animating Presentations

Animating presentations is the process of applying movement to component tweaks in an exploded view. Tweaks can be combined to move at the same time and placed in any order you want so that they move in the sequence that you intend.

In the following illustration, an animation is in the process of being created. You can use the Animation Sequence area to group and reorder tweaks.

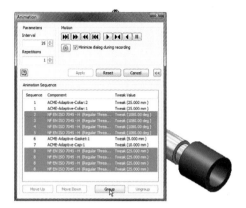

Example of Animating Presentations

You have created maintenance manuals for an important client using exploded drawing views. Although the paper drawings are sufficient, the client is looking for something even better to help their maintenance personnel correctly disassemble and reassemble the components in the proper order. Your solution is to provide animated presentation views on a CD. Using your approach, when the maintenance personnel need to replace components, they can view the animation to see the exact way to take the assembly apart and put it back together again.

In the following illustration, the animation for the presentation view is set and the Record button has been clicked. When the Play button is clicked, an AVI file of the animation is created.

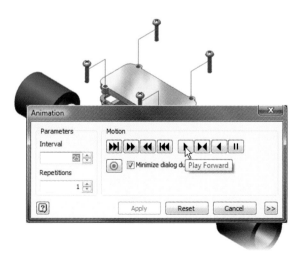

Animating Presentations

You create presentation view animations by clicking the Animate tool on the Presentation Panel. The Animation dialog box contains controls for fine-tuning the creation of your animations, as well as a Record button for saving the animation as an AVI or WMV format file.

In the following illustration, an exploded view is shown with the Animation dialog box open and expanded.

Access

Animate

Ribbon: **Presentation tab > Create panel**

Toolbar: **Presentation Panel**

Animation Dialog Box

When you start the Animate tool, the Animation dialog box is displayed, providing controls and options to fine-tune the animation to your exact requirements.

Option	Description
Interval	Sets the number of intervals in a tweak. The higher the number, the slower the tweak movement, and lower the number, the faster the tweak movement.
Repetitions	Sets the number of times to repeat the playback.
▶▶❘	Steps the animation forward one tweak at a time.
▶▶	Steps the animation forward one interval at a time.
◀◀	Steps the animation in reverse one interval at a time.
❘◀◀	Steps the animation in reverse one tweak at a time.
▶	Plays the animation forward for the specified number of repetitions. Before each repetition the view is set back to its starting position.
▶❘	Plays the animation forward for the specified number of repetitions. Each repetition plays start to finish, then in reverse.

Option	Description
◀	Plays the animation in reverse for the specified number of repetitions. Before each repetition the view is set back to its ending position.
‖	Pauses the animation playback.
◉	Records the specified animation to a file so that you can play it back later.
Minimize Dialog During Record	Minimizes the dialog box while the animation is being recorded. Select the check box to minimize the dialog box. Clear the check box to leave the dialog box active.
Move Up	Moves the selected tweak up one place in the list.
Move Down	Moves the selected tweak down one place in the list.
Group	Groups the selected tweaks to keep them together as you change the sequence. When the tweaks are grouped, the group assumes the sequence order of the lowest tweak number.
Ungroup	Ungroups the selected tweaks so that they can be moved individually in the list. The first tweak in the group assumes a number one higher than the group. The remaining tweaks are numbered sequentially following the first.

Presentation Browser Filters

You can control the Model browser display in a presentation file by clicking the Filter button at the upper left of the browser and selecting the appropriate filter.

	Option	Description
①	**Assembly View**	Sets the assembly and its components as the top of the hierarchy for each view. The tweaks that affect each component are listed under it.
②	**Sequence View**	Sets the tasks as the top of the detail hierarchy for each view. The tweak sequences that make up a task are listed under it. The assembly file used for the presentation is shown at the end of the list for the view.
③	**Tweak View**	Sets tweaks as the top of the detail hierarchy for each presentation view. Components included in each tweak are listed under it. The assembly file used for the presentation is shown at the end of the list for the view.

Procedure: Animating an Exploded View in a Presentation

The following steps describe how to create an animation of an exploded view in a presentation file.

1   In a presentation file, create an exploded view with the necessary tweaks to define component movements.

2   In the Create panel, click Animate.

3   In the Animation dialog box, under Parameters, set the Interval and Repetitions

4   In the dialog box, click the More button to access the Animation Sequence area.

5   Under Animation Sequence, group and ungroup and reorder your tweaks as necessary.

6   Click Apply to accept changes.

7   Click Play to view the animation in the graphics window.

8   After you play the animation, click Reset to reset the sequence back to the beginning.

9   Click Cancel to exit the dialog box.

Procedure: Recording an Animation

The following steps describe how to record an animation and save it as an AVI or WMV file.

1   Create an animation, adjust all the necessary settings, and click Apply.

2   In the Animation dialog box, click the Record button. In the Save As dialog box, set the Files of Type to WMV (*.wmv) or AVI (*.avi) and give the file a name.

3   If you save as a WMV file, the ASF Export Properties dialog box is displayed so that you can set the export profile. If you save as an AVI file, the Video Compression dialog box is displayed so that you can select the codec to compress the video output.

4   In the Animation dialog box, click the Play button to start recording the animation. When the animation ends, click the Stop button. Click Cancel to exit the dialog box.

5   To view your animation file, open the viewer and select the animation file that you created.

Exercise | Create an Exploded Presentation

In this exercise, you create a new presentation file. You then create an exploded view and add tweaks and trails.

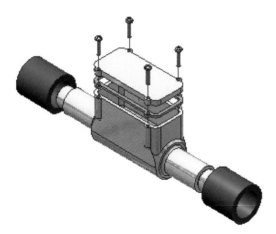

The completed exercise

Completing the Exercise:	*To complete the exercise, follow the steps in this book or in the onscreen exercise. In the onscreen list of chapters and exercises, click Chapter 7: Interacting with an Assembly. Click Exercise: Create an Exploded Presentation.*

1　Create a new presentation file from the default template.

2　Click Presentation tab > Create panel > Create View.

3　In the Select Assembly dialog box:
- Under Assembly, click the Explore Directories button located to the right of the File list. In the Open dialog box, select ExplodedViews.iam. Click Open.
- Under Explosion Method, select Automatic.
- For Distance, enter **25.00 mm.**
- Select the Create Trails check box. Click OK.

4　On the Navigation bar, use the Orbit and Zoom tools to match this view.

5　To edit a tweak:
- In the browser, expand the Explosion1 presentation view to locate the tweak below the ACME-Adaptive-Collar:1 component.
- Select the tweak.
- In the edit box at the bottom of the Browser window, enter **-25 mm** and press ENTER.

The automatic explosion method tweaked the component in the wrong direction based upon its insert assembly constraint. The exploded view is similar to the illustration shown.

6   To select a component to tweak:

- Click Presentation tab > Create panel > Tweak Components.
- For the tweak direction, select the top face of the cap component.

7   To apply the tweak:

- Drag the cap component to a position similar to what is shown in the illustration.
- Click Clear to apply the tweak.

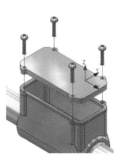

8   To apply a tweak to another component:

- Drag the gasket component to a position similar to what is shown in the illustration.
- Click Clear to apply the tweak.
- Click Close.

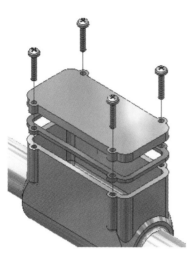

9   Right-click in an open area. Click Save Camera.

10   Save the presentation file. Accept the default name of *ExplodedViews.ipn* and also save all dependents.

Exercise | Animate an Exploded Presentation View

In this exercise, you create an animation of an exploded presentation view, and record and save it as an AVI file.

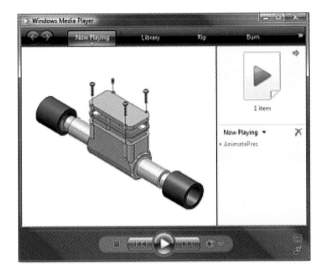

The completed exercise

Completing the Exercise:	To complete the exercise, follow the steps in this book or in the onscreen exercise. In the onscreen list of chapters and exercises, click Chapter 7: Interacting with an Assembly. Click Exercise: Animate an Exploded Presentation View.

1 Open *AnimatePres.ipn*.

2   Click Presentation tab > Create panel > Animate.

3   In the Animation dialog box, under Parameters, set Interval to 15, and Repetitions to 1.

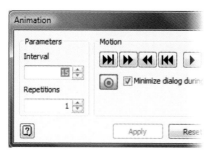

4   In the Animation dialog box, click the button in the lower right corner to expand the dialog box and access the Animation Sequence.

5   Under Animation Sequence, press CTRL and select Sequence 2, 3, 4, and 5, and all four items for Sequence 8. Click Group.

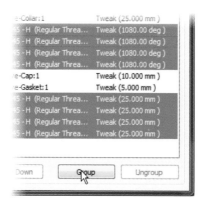

6   Under Animation Sequence, press CTRL and select Sequence 3 and 4. Click Group.

7   Under Animation Sequence, select either item for Sequence 3. Click Move Up.

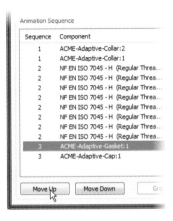

8   In the Animation dialog box, click Apply.

9   In the Animation dialog box, click Play Forward. Confirm that your assembly matches
    the illustration.

10 In the Animation dialog box, click Reset to return the assembly to its previous state.

11   In the Animation dialog box, click the Record button.

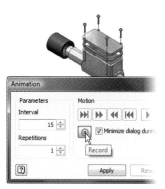

12   In the Save As dialog box, under File Name, enter **AnimatePres**. Under Save as Type, select AVI Files (*.*avi*). Click Save.

13   In the Video Compression dialog box, click OK.
     Note: You may need to select a compressor format that is compatible with your system.

14   In the Animation dialog box, click the Auto Reverse button.

     The dialog box minimizes and the animation plays.

15   Close the Animation dialog box.

16   To view the animation, use an application like Microsoft Windows Media Player that can play AVI files.

17   Close all files. Do not save.

Chapter Summary

This chapter introduced tools and workflows you can use to expedite the assembly design process, validate the integrity of your design, and share those designs with others using animations of exploded views. With knowledge of the fundamentals of part and assembly design, you can use the remaining chapters to learn how to create production-ready drawings of those designs.

Having completed this chapter, you can:

- Use different tools and methods to identify, locate, and select components in an assembly.
- Retrieve important analysis information from the parametric.
- Create animations of exploded views in a presentation file.

Chapter 08
Basic View Creation

Now that you understand the basics of part and assembly design, you need to learn how to create production-ready drawings of those designs. Basic view creation with Autodesk® Inventor® is quite simple when you understand tools and recommended workflows. Within only a few minutes, you can easily create top, front, side, section, detail, and even isometric views of your 3D parts and assemblies.

Objectives

After completing this chapter, you will be able to:

- Navigate the Autodesk Inventor user interface when creating and editing drawing sheets.

- Create base and projected views of 3D parts and assemblies.

- Create and edit section views.

- Create and edit detail views.

- Create and edit cropped views.

- Manage drawing views.

Lesson 26 | Drawing Creation Environment

This lesson describes the main interface components in the drawing environment related to creating production-ready drawings. When you create, annotate, and edit a drawing sheet, you have the same tools that you have when working on an assembly or part. However, the tools and information that display on the ribbon and browser may vary.

Being able to navigate the user interface when creating and editing drawing sheets has a direct impact on your ability to complete your work efficiently.

The following illustration shows the drawing creation environment.

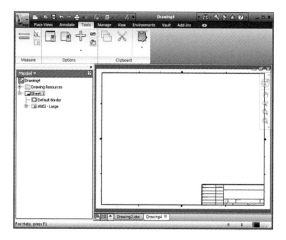

Objectives

After completing this lesson, you will be able to:

- Describe a production-ready drawing and its purpose.

- Describe the process for creating production-ready drawings.

- Recognize the different areas of the drawing creation environment.

- Navigate the drawing creation environment.

About Creating Drawings

A drawing that can be used to produce a part or assembly as specified is referred to as a production- ready drawing. When creating a production-ready drawing, you work in the drawing environment. Within this environment you create the drawing views of the parts or assemblies and add annotations to fully communicate your design requirements and intent.

The following illustration shows a production-ready drawing of a steel die block.

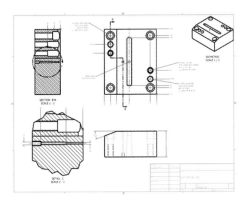

Definition of Production-Ready Drawings

A production-ready drawing contains all the necessary views, annotations, notes, revisions, and title block information, required to manufacture the objects displayed in the drawing.

In the following illustration, the final view, an isometric view, is being positioned to complete the drawing.

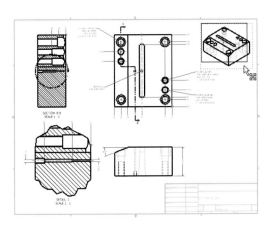

Example of Drawing Views

Production-ready drawings communicate design requirements for manufacturing. To communicate these requirements, a production-ready drawing contains the required combination of views and annotations. A drawing can contain any of the following views:

1   Base views

2   First or third angle projection views

3   Isometric views

4   Section views

5   Detail views

6   Draft views

Example of Annotations

A drawing can also contain the following annotations:

1   Dimensions

2   Hole notes

3   Chamfer notes

4   Centerlines and center marks

5   Notes

6   Parts list

7   Balloons

Creating Drawings

You create drawings to convey information. Depending on the type of parts or assemblies required for production, you create different views and add annotations to define every aspect of the design. A production-ready drawing contains all the necessary views, annotations, and notes to complete the manufacturing or assembly process.

In the following illustration, a section view is created. Because the dimensions to be added would be difficult to locate and read, a detail view is created to simplify the annotation process.

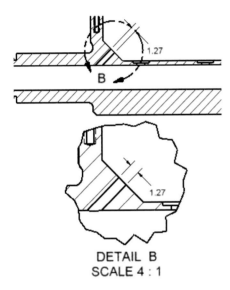

DETAIL B
SCALE 4 : 1

Process: Creating Drawings

The following steps outline the process for creating drawings.

1   Determine the critical aspects of the design.

2   Determine the views required to show the aspects of the design.

3   Create the drawing views.

4   Add drawing annotations.

5   Add any notes or other information needed to manufacture the design.

6   Enter title block data.

About the Drawing Creation Environment

The drawing creation environment enables you to create production-ready drawings by creating the necessary views, annotations, notes, and other information needed to produce a part or assembly. The drawing creation environment has four main areas that you use in the creation of a drawing: drawing sheets, standard tools, panel bars, and the browser.

The following illustration shows the drawing creation environment.

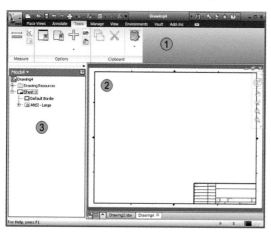

	Option	Description
①	**Ribbon**	The ribbon contain the tools that you use to create views and annotations and the standard tools.
②	**Drawing Sheet**	The primary, and typically largest, area of the drawing environment is the drawing sheet. The drawing sheet represents the paper on which the drawing is created
③	**Browser**	The browser tracks the history of the drawing file and has access to drawing resources such as title blocks, borders, and sheet sizes.

Project Files

When you create designs, each one consists of multiple files and file types. The design and documentation of a single part file require at least two separate files: (a) a part file and (b) a drawing file. The design and documentation of assembly models require a minimum of three different file types: (a) assembly files, (b) part files, and (c) drawing files.

Using separate files for each file type is critical for performance and is common among most parametric modeling systems. By storing path information for each project, the application can search for the required files when opening an assembly, presentation, or drawing file. The need to search in different path locations for files is the primary purpose of project files.

The following illustration represents file dependencies in a typical assembly design.

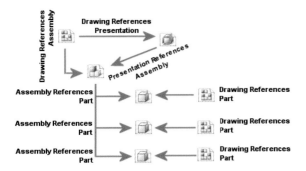

When you open an assembly, drawing, or presentation file, the active project file is used to resolve path locations to the referenced files.

Definition of the Drawing Creation Environment

You use the drawing creation environment to create 2D representations of your 3D models and assemblies.

In the following illustration, the drawing creation environment is used to create the necessary views and annotations for a die block. This part is ready to be manufactured by a die maker.

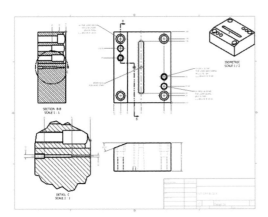

Example of a Production-Ready Drawing

The following illustration shows a valve assembly. The drawing contains the necessary information to select the correct parts and complete the assembly. The parts list identifies the quantity and part numbers. The exploded view shows the assembly order, and the base, projected, and section views show the individual parts in their final location.

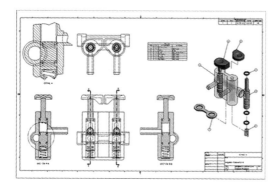

Using the Drawing Environment

The drawing environment contains a number of tools that you can use to create drawing views and add annotations to the view or drawing sheet. The tools on the ribbon are split between the Place Views tab, the Annotate tab, and the browser.

In the following illustration, the ribbon is being switched to the Place Views tab for the addition of drawing views to the sheet.

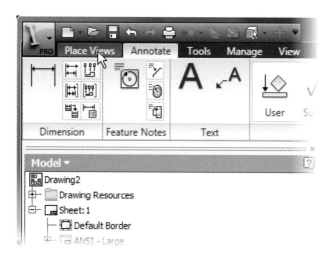

Drawing Tabs

In the drawing environment, on the ribbon, two tabs are available for creating production-ready drawings. You use the Place Views tab to create the various drawing views required to document your parts and assemblies.

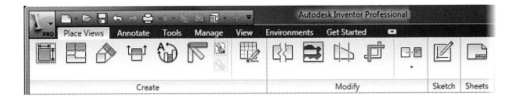

You use the Annotate tab to add dimensions, notes, and symbol annotations to the drawing views. You can switch between the tabs by clicking the tab name on the ribbon.

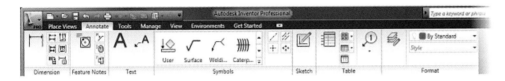

Drawing Environment Browser

In the drawing environment the browser displays the Drawing Resources folder, which contains sheet formats, borders, title blocks, and sketched symbols. It also displays each sheet in the drawing, along with the views that you create for each.

In the following illustration, the cursor is moved to the browser and a new title block is being inserted.

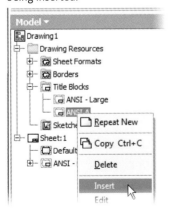

Process: Navigating the Tabs

Navigating the drawing environment is an iterative process. When a drawing has been started, and a base view placed, annotations can be added. Subsequent views can be placed as needed, making additional annotation or even a different sheet size necessary. The following steps outline the general process when navigating the drawing environment.

1   Start or open a drawing file.

2   Select the expected drawing size.

3   Create a base view.

4   Create projected views.

5   Click the Annotate tab.

6   Add drawing annotations.

7   Enter title block data.

Exercise | Use the Drawing Creation Environment

In this exercise you navigate the drawing creation environment to create projected views and change the sheet size.

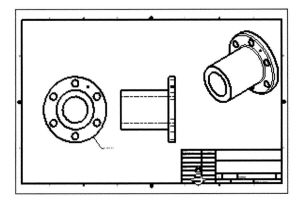

The completed exercise

Completing the Exercise:	*To complete the exercise, follow the steps in this book or in the onscreen exercise. In the onscreen list of chapters and exercises, click Chapter 8: Basic View Creation. Click Exercise: Use the Drawing Creation Environment*

1   Open *Flange.idw*.

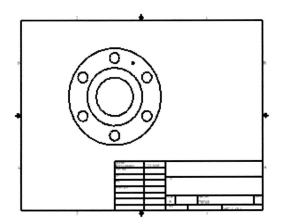

2   Click Place Views tab > Create panel > Projected. When prompted to select a view, click the existing drawing view.

3   To create a projected view, click to the right of the initial view.

4   To create an isometric view, click above the view that you just placed. Your view is outside the border. Right-click above the view. Click Create.

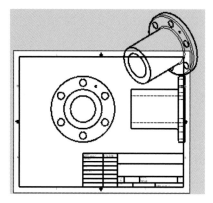

5   Change the sheet size so all the views fit one sheet:
- In the browser, right-click Sheet:1. Click Edit Sheet.
- From the Size menu, select B. Click OK

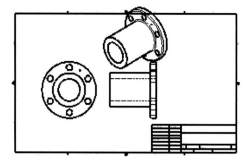

6   Click and drag the border of each drawing view to position them as shown.

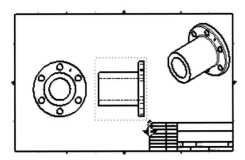

7   To access annotation tools, click the Annotate tab.

8   Click Annotate tab > Dimension panel > Dimension:
    • Click the largest circle in the initial view.
    • Click next to the circle to place the dimension.
    • Right-click above the dimension. Click Done.
    • If the Edit Dimension dialog box appears, click OK.

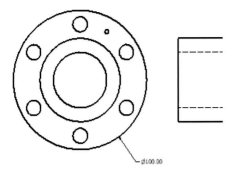

9   Close all files. Do not save.

Lesson 27 | Base and Projected Views

This lesson describes creating projected views of your part or assembly files.

After you complete the 3D design of your part or assembly, manufacturing requires dimensioned drawings in order to build your design. The first step in creating production drawings is to create the required orthographic and isometric views.

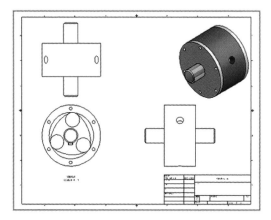

Objectives

After completing this lesson, you will be able to:

- Create base views of 3D parts and assemblies.

- Create and edit exploded drawing views.

- Create projected views.

- Edit orthographic views and describe how other projected views may be affected.

Creating Base Views

You create a base view to begin creating orthographic views. The base view establishes the original view orientation and scale upon which projected views are based. When you create the base view, you specify the file to be used for the view, the view orientation, scale, and style. After you specify this information, the view is placed onto the sheet and an associative link between the drawing and the part, assembly, or presentation file is established. If the part geometry changes, those changes are reflected in the drawing.

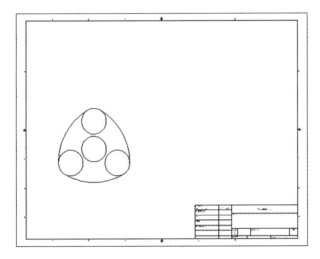

Access

Base Views

Ribbon: **Place Views tab > Create panel > Base**

Toolbar: **Drawing Views Panel**
Shortcut Menu: **Base View**

Drawing View Dialog Box

The following options are available in the Drawing View dialog box.

Option	Description
File	Determines the part or assembly file to create its view. If you have a part, assembly, or presentation file open, it is the default file listed. If multiple files are open, you select them from the drop-down list.
Orientation	Determines orientation for the base view. Move your cursor away from the dialog box to see a preview of the view before it is created. The standard view orientations are based upon the origin planes of the file you select.
Change View Orientation	Opens the model's 3D viewing window. You use standard view tools to define a custom view orientation.
View / Scale Label	Enables you toggle the display of the view and scale label, select a preset scale value, or enter a custom value for the view. Additionally, you can enter a label for the view or accept the default view label. • Scale from Base: Not available when you create a base view. You use it when you edit projected views. • Visible: Displays the scale and view label on the sheet under the view. • Edit View Label: Displays the Format Text dialog box.
Style	Rendering style for the view: • Hidden Line: Hidden lines are displayed. • Hidden Line Removed: Hidden lines are removed. • Shaded: View is shaded using the same colors used in the assembly or part file.

Procedure: Creating Base Views

The following steps describe how to create base views.

1   Create a new drawing file.

2   On the ribbon, click the Base View tool.

3   Enter or browse for the Autodesk Inventor file to create the view, and adjust the options as desired for orientation, scale, and style. Click the sheet to place the view.

4   The base view is placed on the sheet according to the options specified.

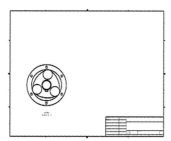

Creating Exploded Drawing Views

One of the main uses for exploded views in presentations is to create exploded drawing views. An exploded drawing view can be used as an pictorial aid to assemble manufactured components. Depending on its complexity, the exploded view can take the place of creating two or three projected views. Finally, the components in the exploded view can be ballooned to document the design and populate the parts list for the assembly.

In the following illustration, an exploded drawing view shows a complete assembly, ready to be ballooned and documented with a parts list.

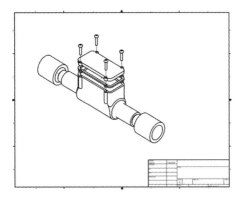

Access

Base View

Ribbon: **Place Views tab > Create panel > Base**

Toolbar: **Drawing Views Panel**

Shortcut Menu: **Base View**

Procedure: Creating an Exploded Drawing View

The following steps describe how to create an exploded drawing view.

1   In a drawing file, on the ribbon, click Base View.

2   In the Drawing View dialog box:
- For File, select a presentation file.
- For Presentation View, select the desired exploded view.
- For Orientation, select the desired assembly orientation.
- Set the scale and display style.
- Click in the drawing sheet to create the view.

Creating Projected Views

The Projected View tool enables you to create projected views from any existing view on the sheet. If you select the Projected View tool you must select a parent view, then position each projected view. All view positions are previewed by a bounding box prior to the views being created.

When you create projected views, the view orientation is automatically determined based on its position on the sheet relative to the base view. If you place the projected view to the right of the base view, it generates a right-side projection of the parent view. If you place the projected view at an angle to the parent view, it generates an isometric view based on the relative position to the parent view.

By default, the following view properties are carried over from the base view:

- Scale
- Style (Orthographic Only)

In the following illustration, the right, top, and isometric views are projected from the lower left base view.

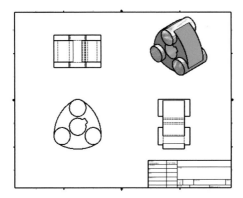

> **Note:** **Drafting Standards Projection Setting** *The description above is based on a Third Angle projection setting in the Drafting Standards dialog box. The First Angle projection method is also available.*

Access

Projected View

Ribbon: **Place Views tab > Create panel > Projected**

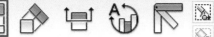

Toolbar: **Drawing Views Panel**
Shortcut Menu: **Create View > Projected View**

Procedure: Creating Views

The following steps describe how to create projected views.

1   On the ribbon, click Projected View.

2   Select the parent view.

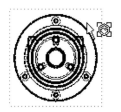

3   Click in the drawing to define the first projected view. Repeat until all views are defined.

4   Right-click in the drawing. Select Create.

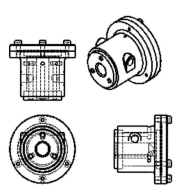

Properties of Editing Base and Projected Views

After you create base and projected views, you can edit the view properties using the Drawing View dialog box. Depending on the type of view, base or projected, different options are available for editing.

When you edit a base view, you can change the scale and style properties. However, while editing a projected view, you can change these properties only if you clear the Scale from Base or Style from Base options. In a projected view, these properties are linked to the base view to ensure the same scale and the same rendering style across views.

Editing a Base View

When you edit a base view, you can edit any option that is not grayed out. If you change the scale factor on the base view, all projected views with the Scale from Base option selected are updated to reflect the new scale factor.

When you edit a projected view, you can edit any option that is not grayed out. Clear the Scale and Style from Base check boxes to change the view scale or rendering style.

Exercise | Create and Edit Base and Projected Views

In this exercise, you create a new drawing and place a base view and three projected views of a rotor assembly as the base for a production-ready drawing.

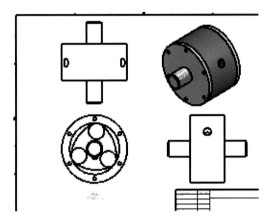

The completed exercise

Completing the Exercise: *To complete the exercise, follow the steps in this book or in the onscreen exercise. In the onscreen list of chapters and exercises, click Chapter 8: Basic View Creation. Click Exercise: Create and Edit Base and Projected Views.*

1   Open *Rotor-Assembly.iam.*

2　At the top of the browser, right-click Representations. Click Representation. The Representation dialog box is displayed.

- Notice the settings under Design View Representation.
- Click Cancel to close the Representation dialog box.

3　On the Quick Access toolbar, click New.

4　In the New File dialog box, select the Metric tab. Double-click the ANSI (mm).*idw* template.

5　In the drawing environment, Click Place Views tab › Create panel Base. Because the assembly is already open, it is automatically selected as the file for the drawing view.

6   In the Drawing View dialog box, adjust the options as shown:

•   From the Representation list, select Housing-Caps-Hidden (1).
•   Under View/Scale label, turn on visibility (2) and select 2:1 (3).
•   Click the lower-left area of the sheet to place the view.

7   Right-click in the base view. Click Create View > Projected View.

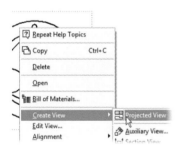

8   Select points on the sheet to position the views as indicated by the bounding box preview
    and isometric preview in the following illustration.

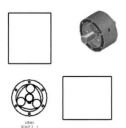

9   Right-click in the graphics window. Click Create to create the projected views.

10   The drawing views are displayed as shown.

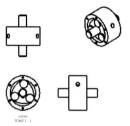

11   Right-click in the base view. Click Edit View.

- In the Drawing View dialog box, under Scale, select 4:1.
- Click OK.

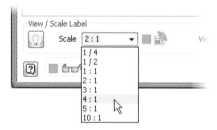

12   The projected orthographic views update to reflect the new scale because they receive their scale value from the base. The projected isometric view is not updated because its scale value, by default, is not based on the base view.

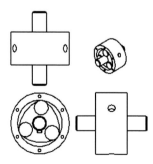

13 Hover the cursor over the projected views, then drag the view border to reposition them as shown in the following illustration.

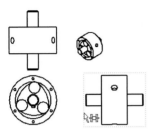

14 Right-click in the isometric view. Click Edit View.
- In the Drawing View dialog box, under Scale, select 4:1 (1).
- Under Style, click Shaded (2).
- From the Representation View list, select Admin (3). Click OK.

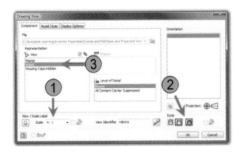

15 The isometric view updates to reflect the new scale factor and the design view with all components visible.
Note: You may need to reposition the isometric view.

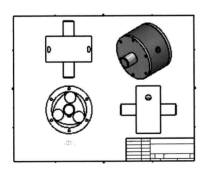

16 Close all files. Do not save.

Lesson 28 | Section Views

This lesson describes creating section views of part and assembly drawings. When you create drawings of parts and assemblies, important internal details are sometimes obscured by other features or parts.

Section views enable you to better visualize these important details by removing the parts or features that are obstructing the view. Features that were obstructed or displayed as hidden lines are drawn with continuous lines with hatch patterns representing the section plane.

In the following illustration, a half section view was created based on the initial view. Then an isometric projection was created from the offset section.

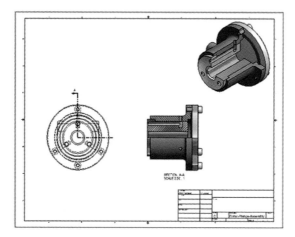

Objectives

After completing this lesson, you will be able to:

- Create section views.

- Edit section views.

- Control hatch and sectioning in section views.

Creating Section Views

In order to create a section view, you must have at least one view on the sheet on which the section line is drawn. After drawing the section line, you choose a side of the current view for the section view. The section view is generated based on the direction of sight relative to the view being sectioned.

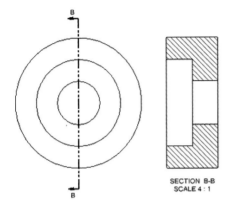

SECTION B-B
SCALE 4 : 1

Access

Section View

Ribbon: **Place Views tab > Create panel**

Toolbar: **Drawing Views Panel**
Shortcut Menu: **Create View > Section View**

Section View Dialog Box

The following options are available in the Section View dialog box.

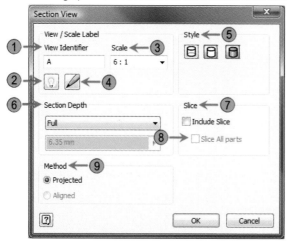

	Option	Description
①	**View Identifier**	Use to specify a view label or accept the default value.
②	**Toggle Label Visibility**	Displays the label and view scale on the sheet
③	**Scale**	Scale factor for the section view.
④	**Format Text**	Access the Format Text dialog box.
⑤	**Style**	Rendering style for the view. • Hidden Line • Hidden Line Removed • Shaded
⑥	**Section Depth**	Section depth for the view. • Full: Section depth is calculated through the entire part or assembly. • Distance: Measured from the section line to calculate the section view. All geometry outside of the calculated distance is ignored and is not displayed in the view.

⑦	**Slice**	Depending on browser settings, when checked, some parts are sliced, and some sectioned.
⑧	**Slice All Parts**	Browser settings are overridden and all parts in the view are sliced according to the section line geometry. Parts not crossed by the section line are not included in the view. Section Depth fields are disabled.
⑨	**Method**	Use the Projected method to project the lines orthogonally to the section views position. The Aligned method projects section geometry perpendicular to each segment of the section line. This option only appears if the section line contains more than one segment.

Section View Projection Methods

The difference between Aligned and Projected section views is visible when the section line cuts through openings in the view at an angle. If you were to add a dimension to an opening in an Aligned section view cut at an angle, the dimension value returned would be identical to a dimension value place on the same feature in the base view. In a Projected view the dimension value returned would be the perpendicular distance from where the section line intersects the opening.

In the following illustration, two section views are created using identical section lines. The differences in the Aligned (1) and Projected (2) Views are as follows. The dimensional value of the feature in the Aligned view matches the same value on the same feature in the base view. In the Aligned view, since you are always viewing the section perpendicular to the section line, you do not see the patterned component in the middle of the view. The projected view is elongated to allow for the increase cross section of the features.

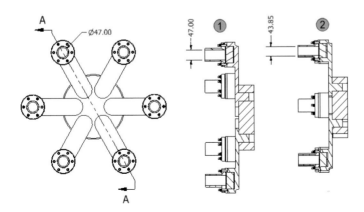

Procedure: Creating Section Views

The following steps describe how to create section views.

1 With at least one view on the sheet, on the ribbon, click Section View.

2 Select the parent view.

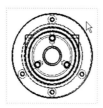

3 Enter the endpoints of the section line.
   - Select the first point of the section line. If necessary, use tracking to align the section line to a feature in the parent view.
   - Click additional endpoints to define the section line. The number of endpoints defined, and their directions, determine the type of section view created.

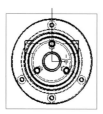

4 Right-click in the graphics window, select Continue.

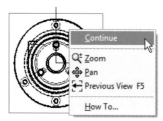

5   In the Section View dialog box, enter the desired values.
     Note: The projected method is used in this step.

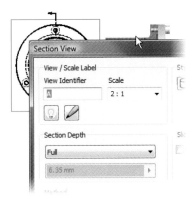

6   Move the preview to the desired location and click to place the section view.

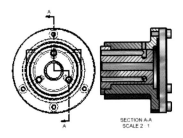

Editing Section Views

The display, style, and scale properties used to create a view can be edited in the section view
in the drawing or browser. The direction, section depth, display, and geometry of the section
line can be edited at the parent view. The hatch patterns applied to the view can be edited in the
section view.

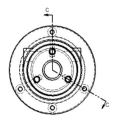

Procedure: Editing a Section View

After you create the section view, you can edit it like other views. You use the Edit View tool to change properties such as scale, label, and style. You can also edit the section view using methods that are specific to section views by selecting the view in the drawing, or by selecting the view in the browser and right-clicking.

1   Right-click in the view. Click Edit View.

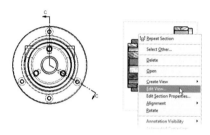

2   In the Drawing View dialog box, make the desired changes to the scale, label, or style.

Procedure: Editing a Section Line

The following steps describe how to edit section lines. You can edit a section line by right-clicking the sketch in the browser, or by selecting the section line in the parent view and right-clicking. You can relocate the section line by dragging it to a new location, or add or delete segments using standard sketch tools.

1   Edit the sketch used for the section line. On the ribbon, the Sketch tab displays, enabling you to edit the sketch geometry in the same way that you would in the modeling environment. You can apply and remove constraints, modify the sketch geometry, and apply dimensions to the sketch geometry.

2   Constraint drag the section line. You can edit the section line by dragging elements of the section line to new positions. You can do this only to elements of the section line that are not constrained to drawing geometry.

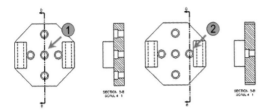

1   Original location of section line

2   Section line dragged to new location

Procedure: Editing the Hatch Pattern in a Section View

The following steps describe how to edit hatch patterns in a section view. After creating a section view, you can edit or hide the hatch patterns applied to the view.

1   To edit a hatch pattern, right-click in a hatch pattern in the section view. Click Edit. This action displays the Edit Hatch Pattern dialog box.

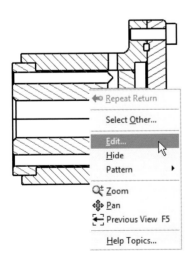

2   In the Edit Hatch Pattern dialog box, you can edit the pattern, scale, angle, shift, line weight, and color of the hatch. You can also cross-hatch the pattern by selecting Double.

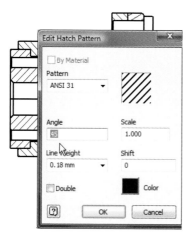

3   To hide a hatch pattern, right-click the pattern to hide. Click Hide.

Properties of Assembly Section Views

When you create section views of assembly drawings, each part in the assembly section view is hatched with different properties for visual clarity as the section plane passes through each part. You can also control which parts are sectioned. By default, parts from the standard parts library are not sectioned; however, you can manually turn on sectioning for standard parts.

In the following illustration, two sections views have been created from the same parent view. In the first view (1), all parts except the shaft are sectioned. In the second view (2) the visibility of the end caps has been turned off.

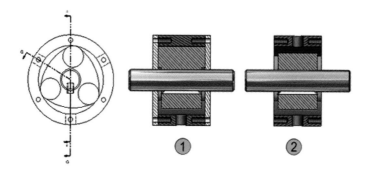

Controlling Component Sectioning

When you create views of an assembly in the drawing, parts are listed under the view in the browser. A gray icon indicates that the part's visibility is turned off.

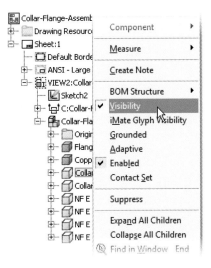

After the contents of the assembly are displayed in the drawing browser, right-clicking a component in the drawing browser opens the shortcut menu. To prevent a part from being sectioned, click Section Participation > None.

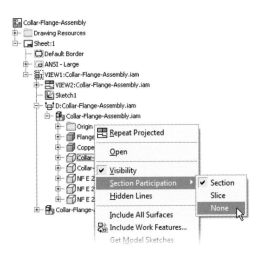

Exercise | Create and Edit Section Views

In this exercise, you create section views of an assembly. After creating the section view, you turn off sectioning for some components. You edit the section by moving the section line and changing the hatch pattern applied to some components.

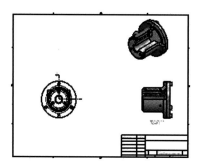

The completed exercise

Completing the Exercise:	To complete the exercise, follow the steps in this book or in the onscreen exercise. In the onscreen list of chapters and exercises, click Chapter 8: Basic View Creation. Click Exercise: Create and Edit Section Views.

1   Open *Collar-Flange-Assembly.idw.*

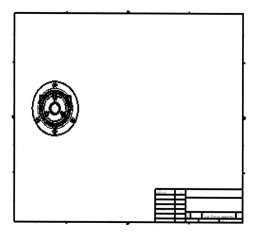

2   Click Place Views tab > Create tab > Section. Select the view on the sheet as shown.

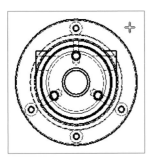

3   Touch one of the inside circles with your cursor, but do not click, then move toward the center of the circle until you see the green dot inferring the center point. Do not select this point.

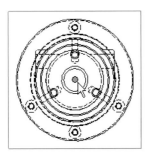

4   With the center point highlighted, move the cursor upward to the top of the view. You should see the dotted line indicating the point is being projected as shown. Left-click near this point to start the section line.

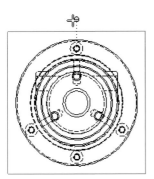

5   Move the cursor back to the center of the view and click when you see the center point indicator. This action constrains the section line to the center of the circle.

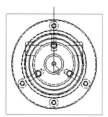

6   Move the cursor to the right and position it outside of the part but over the lower right hole so that the center point indicator for that hole appears. Click when the center point indicator appears.

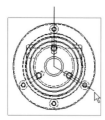

7   Right-click in the graphics window. Click Continue.

8   Define the label and create the section view.

   • In the Section view dialog box, under Method, select the Aligned option.
   • Move the cursor down and notice that the position of the view aligns to the base view as shown.

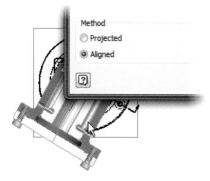

- In the Section View dialog box, for Method, select Projected.
- For View Identifier, enter **A**.
- Move the cursor to the right, and click to position the section view as shown.

9   Validate that the section view displays as shown.

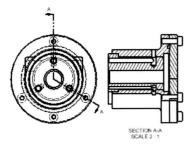

10   Right-click in the section view (away from any geometry). Click Edit View.

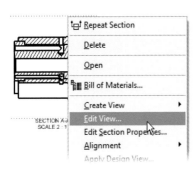

11   Click the Shaded Style button in the Drawing View dialog box. Click OK.

12   Right-click in the hatch pattern indicated in the following illustration. Click Edit.

13   In the Edit Hatch Pattern dialog box, under Pattern, enter the following values:
      - Select ANSI 32.
      - In the Angle field, enter **45**.
      - Click OK.

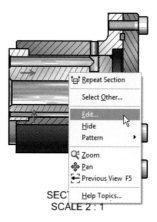

14   Prevent components from being sectioned:

- Expand the section view in the browser.
- Hold down the CTRL key, select the *Copper- Gasket:1* and *Collar-End-Cap:1* components.
- Right-click one of the selected components and click Section Participation > None.

15   Notice the change in appearance in the section view.

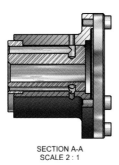

SECTION A-A
SCALE 2 : 1

16   Right-click the section line. Click Edit.

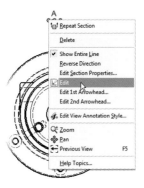

17   To delete coincident constraints to edit the section line position:

- Click the angled line in the sketched section line.
- Right-click, click Delete Coincident Constraint to delete the first constraint.
- Right-click, click Delete Coincident Constraint to delete the second constraint.

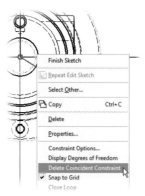

18   You can now click the end of the sketch line and drag it upward until you see the perpendicular constraint glyph. Click to reposition the sketch line perpendicular to the first sketch line.

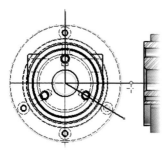

19   Right-click in the graphics window. Click Finish Sketch. Notice the difference in the section view.

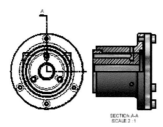

20 Edit the view:

- On the ribbon, click the Projected View tool.
- Create a projected view of the section as shown.

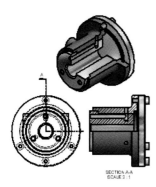

21 Reposition the views on the sheet as shown.

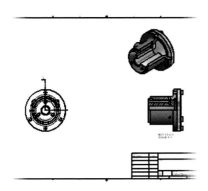

22 Close all files. Do not save.

Lesson 29 | Detail Views

This lesson describes creating detail views. As you create 2D drawings for manufacturing, it may be necessary to magnify areas of the drawing. A detail view shows congested areas of a drawing clearly.

In the following illustration, detail views have been created to magnify congested areas of the main view.

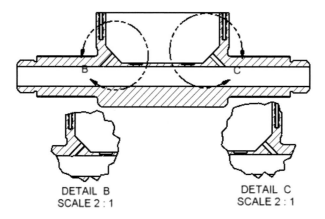

DETAIL B
SCALE 2 : 1

DETAIL C
SCALE 2 : 1

Objectives

After completing this lesson, you will be able to:

- Describe the purpose of detail views.

- Create detail views in drawings.

- Edit the size and location of detail views.

About Detail Views

Before learning the tools, processes, and specific settings to create and edit detail views, you should first become familiar with the function and purpose of detail views.

Definition of Detail Views

When you create a detail view, you draw a specific area of an existing drawing view at a larger scale. The existing drawing view where the detail view originates is referred to as the parent view to the detail view. A detailed view is associated with the main view and any changes that affect geometry within the main view are reflected in the detail view automatically.

The detail view magnifies the specified area, enabling you to add the dimensions to the detail view, or thereby not requiring the same dimensions in the parent view. Although the detail view is scaled, as is true of other scaled views, when you place dimensions on geometry within the view, the dimensions reflect the actual geometry size. By having the dimensions in the detail view, the placement and readability of dimensions in the original drawing are simplified.

Example of a Detail View

Detail views are often used when a part design has small features that require them to be identified and defined. In the following illustration, a detail view border (1) identifies where a detail view (2) originates from. Compared to the parent view, in this detail view, it is easier to identify what the dimension refers to and easier to identify an important slot in the part.

In this example, the dimension in the parent view was included for comparison purposes. In practice, the dimension would only be added to the detail view because that is where the focus on that feature is.

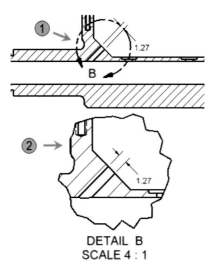

DETAIL B
SCALE 4 : 1

Creating Detail Views

You use the Detail View tool to create detail views of an existing view in the drawing. When you use Detail Views, you define the detailed area by specifying a center point and a rectangular or circular fence. All geometry contained within the detail view rectangle or circle is included in the detail view.

When you create a detail view, you magnify an area of the drawing while creating an associative link between the original view and the detail view. If the geometry being magnified changes in the original view, those changes are reflected in the detail view. Also, the placement and readability of dimensions in these areas of the drawing are simplified.

A detailed view is associated with the main view, and any changes that affect geometry within the main view are reflected in the detail view automatically. Although the view is scaled, as is true of other scaled views, when you place dimensions on geometry within the view, the dimensions reflect the actual geometry size.

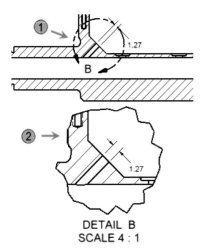

 Detail view circle

 Scale detail view with dimensions

Access

Detail View

Ribbon: **Place Views tab > Create panel**

Toolbar: **Drawing Views Panel**
Shortcut Menu: **Create View > Detail View**

Detail View Dialog Box

The following illustration shows the Detail View dialog box.

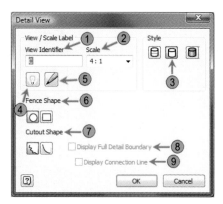

The following options are available in the Detail View dialog box.

	Option	Description
(1)	**View Identifier**	Use to specify a view label or accept the default value.
(2)	**Scale**	Use to specify the scale factor for the detail view. Select from the list or manually enter a custom value.
(3)	**Style**	Determines a rendering style for the view. • Hidden Line • Hidden Line Removed • Shaded
(4)	**Toggle Visibility**	When selected, the view scale label is visible on the sheet.
(5)	**Edit View Label**	Use to access the Format Text dialog box.
(6)	**Fence Shape**	Determines a fence shape for the view. • Circular • Rectangular

	Option	Description
(7)	**Cutout Shape**	Specify the cut line as Jagged or Smooth.
(8)	**Display Full Detail Boundary**	If Smooth cutout shape is selected, select this option to have a boundary drawn around the detail view.
(9)	**Display Connection Line**	If the Display Full Detail Boundary option is selected, select this option to have a line drawn between the detail view boundary in the parent view and the boundary around the detail view.

Procedure: Creating Detail Views

The following steps describe how to create detail views.

1   With at least one view on the sheet, on the ribbon, click Detail View.

2   Adjust the options in the Detail View dialog box as required.

3   Select the center point of the fence.

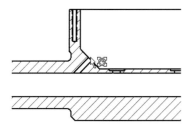

4   Select the endpoint of the fence.

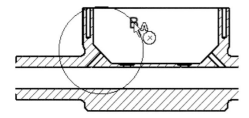

5   Specify a location for the view.

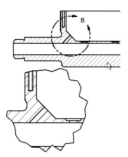

Moving and Editing Detail Views

You can edit detail views in the same way that you would edit other types of views. When you create a detail view, you magnify an area of the drawing while creating an associative link between the original view and the detail view. If the geometry being magnified changes in the original view, those changes are reflected in the detail view. Also, the placement and readability of dimensions in these areas of the drawing are simplified.

You can also edit the detail view by editing the fence circle that defines the area of the detail view. If you select the detail view fence and label on the main view, grip points are displayed, as shown in the following illustration.

In the following illustration, the original fence for the detail view on the left is selected and dragged to a larger diameter. The resulting detail view, on the right, is larger and contains more geometry from the parent view.

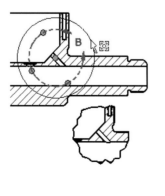 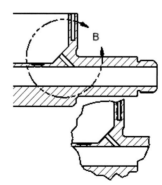

Selecting the center grip point enables you to move the fence circle. By selecting anywhere on the fence circle, you can change the size of the circle and alter the geometry that is included in the detail view. You edit a rectangular fence in the same manner as a circular fence. Selecting the fence alters the size. Selecting one of corner grips enables you to edit the fence uniformly. In the following illustration, the detail view is moved to a different area and resized.

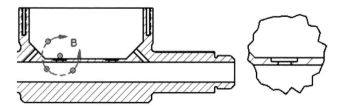

It is also possible to edit the location of the view label that is located on the detail view circle. Movement of the label is restricted to the diameter of the circle.

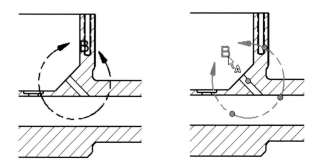

Procedure: Moving Detail Views

The following steps describe how to move detail views.

1   Move your cursor to the fence that defines the detail view.

2   Select the grip in the center of the fence.

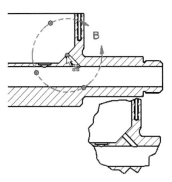

3   Drag the fence to the desired location.

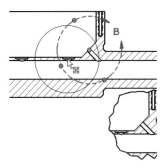

Procedure: Editing Detail Views

The following steps describe how to edit detail views.

1   Move the cursor to the fence that defines the detail view.

2   Click the letter that defines the label. Drag to the desired location to move the label.

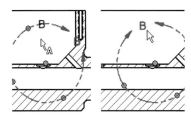

3   To change the amount of geometry displayed in the detail view, click anywhere on the fence.
     Drag to a new size.

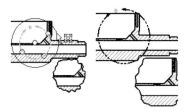

Exercise | Create and Edit Detail Views

In this exercise, you create and edit detail views to magnify critical features of a hydraulic reservoir.

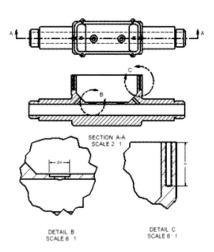

The completed exercise

Completing the Exercise :	*To complete the exercise, follow the steps in this book or in the onscreen exercise. In the onscreen list of chapters and exercises, click Chapter 8: Basic View Creation. Click Exercise: Create and Edit Detail Views.*

1   Open *Detail-Hyd-Res-Housing.idw*.

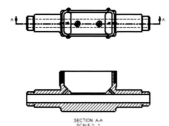

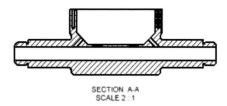

SECTION A-A
SCALE 2 1

2   Zoom in on the section view.

SECTION A-A
SCALE 2 : 1

3   To begin to create a detail view from the parent view.
    • Click Place Views tab > Create panel > Detail View.
    • Select the section view.

4   In the Detail View dialog box, verify the following values:
    • For Label, Enter **B**.
    • For Scale, Enter **4:1**.
    • For Style, Click Hidden Line Removed.

5   For the center point of the fence, select a point near (1). For the endpoint of the fence, select a point near (2).

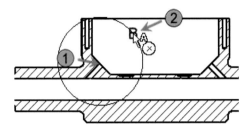

6   When prompted to select a location for the view, select a point as shown in the following illustration.

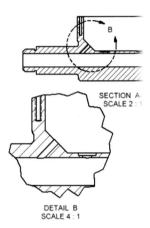

7   Activate the Detail View tool again. Create another detail view as shown.

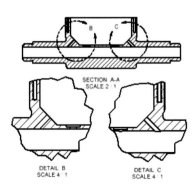

8   Select each detail view circle. Using the grip points, resize and move the detail view fence circles and fence labels as shown.

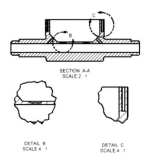

9   To place dimensions in the detail views:

- Click Annotate tab > Dimension panel > General Dimension.
- Place the dimensions as shown.
- Press ESC to exit the General Dimension command.

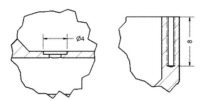

10 To change the scale factor of the detail views:

- Right-click in each detail view. Click Edit View.
- Enter **6:1** in the list.
- Click OK.

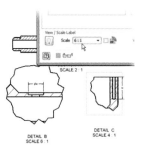

11 Close all files. Do not save.

Exercise | Create and Edit Detail View Edge Shapes and Connections

In this exercise, you create and edit detail views with different cutout edge shapes.

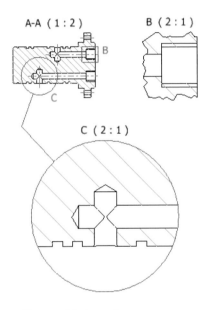

The completed exercise

Completing the Exercise:	*To complete the exercise, follow the steps in this book or in the onscreen exercise. In the onscreen list of chapters and exercises, click Chapter 8: Basic View Creation. Click Exercise: Create and Edit Detail View Edge Shapes and Connections.*

1   Open *DetailView_P-540.idw.*

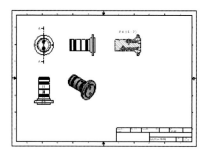

2   Begin to create a detailed view of the thread area of the section view:

   • Click Place Views tab > Create panel > Detail.
   • In the graphics window, select the section view.

3   In the Detail View dialog box, set the following options:

   • Scale = 2:1
   • Fence Shape = Rectangular
   • Cutout Shape = Jagged

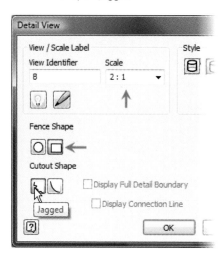

4   To set the area for the detail view, in the graphics window:

- Click a point near the center area of the top thread area (1).
- Click a point above and to the right of the hole (2).

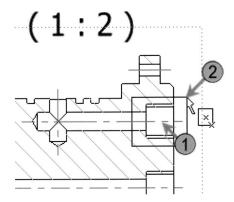

5   Click to place the detail view to the right of the section view.

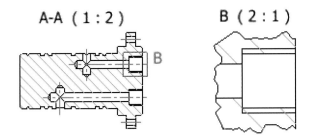

6   Press SPACEBAR to start the Detail View tool again. Select the section view for the detail view's parent view.

7   In the Detail View dialog box, select a scale of 2:1 and select the other options identified in the following illustration.

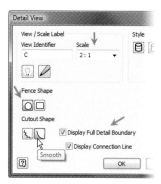

8   To set the area for the detail view, in the graphics window:

- Click a point near the intersection of the two lower holes (1).
- Click a point down and to the right of the hole (2).

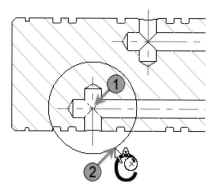

9 Click to place the detail view below the section view and first detail view.

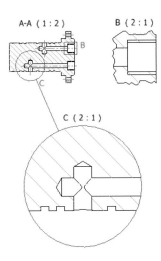

10 To add a vertex to the connection line:

- In the drawing, right-click the connection line.
- Click Add Vertex.
- Click a point near the midpoint of the connection line.

11 In the drawing, click and drag the new connection line vertex to the left as shown.

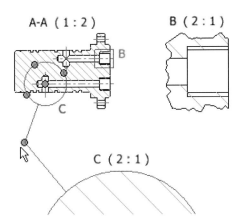

12 To change the rectangular detail view from jagged to smooth:

• Right-click the B detail view border in the section view.
• Click Options > Smooth Cutout Shape.

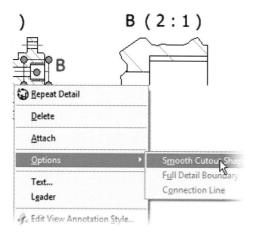

13 To display the full detail boundary and connection line:

• Right-click the B detail view border in the section view.
• Click Options > Full Detail Boundary.

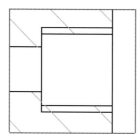

14 To display the connection line:
- Right-click the B detail view border in the section view.
- Click Options > Connection Line.

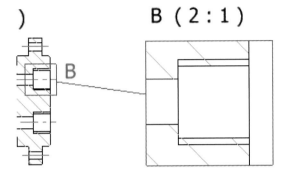

15 To toggle the rectangular detail view back to a jagged cutout edge:
- Right-click the B detail view border in the section view.
- Click Options > Smooth Cutout Shape.

16 Close all files. Do not save.

Lesson 30 | Crop Views

As you create complex drawings, the need to crop view geometry to show only certain areas arises. To display only an area of a drawing view, you need to understand the process for using different boundary shapes to crop drawing views.

The Crop tool provides a straightforward method to show only the area of information that you require.

In the following illustration, the initial view before cropping is shown on the left. The middle image shows the view cropped using a circular default boundary, while the right image shows the view cropped using a closed loop sketch.

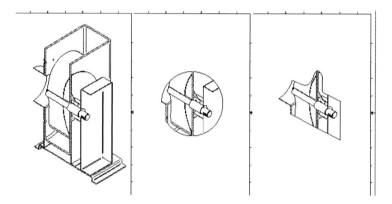

Objectives

After completing this lesson, you will be able to:

- Describe the types of views that can be cropped and the supported display options.

- Crop a drawing view using a circular or rectangular boundary shape.

- Crop a drawing view using a sketched boundary shape.

Supported View Types and Displays

Instead of showing all aspects of a drawing view, you can use the Crop tool to have only the geometry within a defined boundary display on the drawing sheet. To crop a view, you must first begin with a view that supports cropped view creation, then define the boundary by using a default rectangular or circular shape or by using a closed sketch.

In the following illustration, is cropped to show only the detail of the knurled area of the section view.

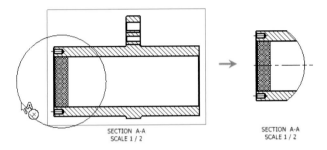

Supported View Types

The following table list the Inventor view types that can be used as foundations for creating cropped views.

- Part and assembly base views

- Projected views

- Isometric views

- Section views

- Detail views

- Slice operations

Crop View Options

You have two different workflows you can follow to crop a view. You can use a default shape of circular or rectangular to crop the view, or you can create a closed loop sketch that is associated to the view and select it to crop the view.

If you want to use one of the default cropping boundaries, after you start the Crop tool and select the view, you initially default to cropping a drawing view using a rectangular shape. You can change to using a circular shape by clicking Circular in the shortcut menu. By clicking Crop Settings on the shortcut menu, the Crop Settings dialog box opens, enabling you to change the default boundary type between Circular and Rectangular. In the Crop Settings dialog box, you can also toggle on or off the display of the cropping cut lines for newly cropped views.

After you crop a view, you can toggle on and off the display of the crop cut lines by right-clicking the crop view in the browser and then clicking Display Crop Cut Lines. By editing the sketch nested below the crop view entry in the browser, you can modify the location or size of the cropping boundary.

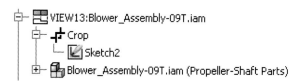

Annotations and Cropped Views

Cropped views support the addition of drawing annotations. After creating a cropped view, you can add dimensions, centerlines, and other drawing annotations to the view. However, if you crop a view that has had annotations already applied, you may orphan the annotations if their anchor points are outside the crop boundary.

In the following illustration, the effects of cropping a view with annotations in place are shown. On the left, the view with annotations is shown. The image on the right illustrates the cropped view. The arrows indicate the annotations that are orphaned due to their anchor points being located outside the cropped view boundary.

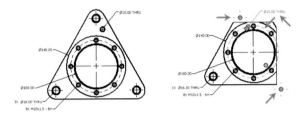

Creating Quick Cropped Views

To create a quick cropped view, you must first have a view on the drawing sheet that supports cropped views. After starting the Crop tool, you select the view to crop and choose a rectangular or circular boundary. You then define the location and size of the boundary.

In the following illustration, the isometric section view is in the process of being cropped on the left. The results of cropping this view with a rectangular boundary is shown on the right.

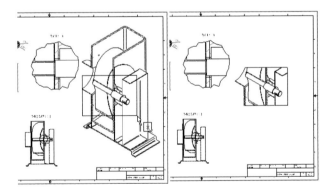

Access

Crop

Ribbon: **Place Views tab › Modify panel**

Toolbar: **Drawing Views Panel › Crop**
Shortcut Menu: **Create View › Crop**

Process: Cropping a View Using a Default Boundary Shape

The following steps give an overview and example of cropping a drawing view using a default boundary shape of circular or rectangular.

1   Start the Crop tool.

2   Select the view to crop.

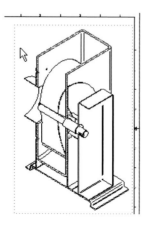

3   If the default boundary type (circular or rectangular) is not what you want, select another crop boundary type.

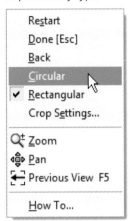

4   Draw the cropping boundary at the location and size that you require. Use opposite corners for a rectangular boundary or the center and radius for a circular boundary.

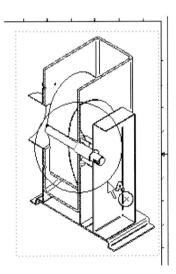

Creating Cropped Views with Sketches

To create a cropped view using a sketch, you must first have a view on the drawing sheet that supports cropped views. You then create a closed loop sketch associated to the drawing view to be cropped. After starting the Crop tool, you select the sketch and the view is cropped.

In the following illustration, a sketch is created in an isometric view. That sketch is then selected using the Crop tool to create the resulting view on the right.

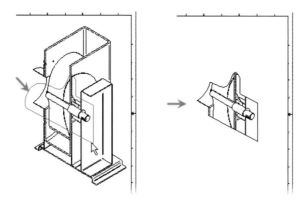

Process: Cropping a View Using a Sketch

The following steps give an overview and example of cropping a drawing view using a closed loop sketch.

1   Click inside the drawing view that you want to crop. Click > Place Views tab > Sketch panel > Sketch to create a sketch associated to the drawing view.

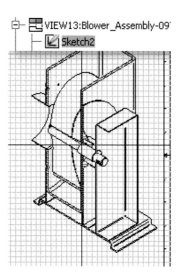

2   In the sketch, create a single closed loop shape using line, arc, or spline segments.

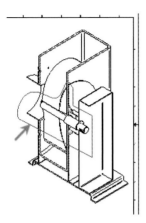

3   Click Place Views tab > Modify panel > Crop.

4   Select the associated sketch.

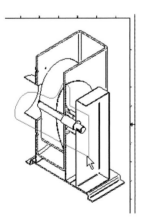

Exercise | Create and Edit Cropped Views

In this exercise, you create cropped views using default and sketch boundaries. In addition, you edit the display of a cropped view.

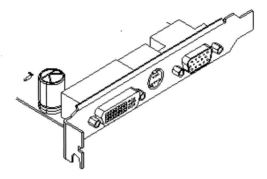

The completed exercise

Completing the Exercise:	To complete the exercise, follow the steps in this book or in the onscreen exercise. In the onscreen list of chapters and exercises, click Chapter 8: Basic View Creation. Click Exercise: Create and Edit Cropped Views.

1   Open *Graphics Card.idw*

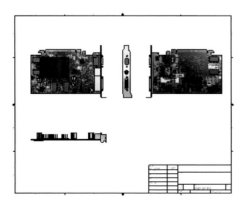

2   To create a rectangular cropped view:
   - Click Place Views tab > Modify panel > Crop.
   - Click the bottom left view.
   - Click and drag a rectangle over the right section of the drawing, as shown.

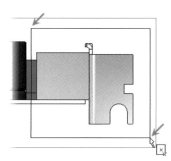

3   The view is cropped to show only the objects inside the defined boundary.

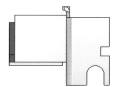

4   Pan to the end view of the graphics card.

5   To create a circular cropped view:

- Start the Crop tool. Click inside the end view.
- In the graphics window, right-click, click Circular.
- Click near the center of the round connection on the card.
- Move the cursor away from the center and click, as shown.

6   In the browser, double-click Sheet:2.

7   To create a sketch based on the view:

- Click inside of the isometric view.
- Click Place Views tab > Sketch panel > Sketch.
- Using standard sketching tools, sketch a closed shape similar to what is shown.
- Finish the sketch.

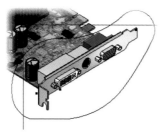

8   To create a crop view using the sketch:

- Start the Crop tool.
- Select the sketch.

9 To edit the display of the view:

- Double-click inside the isometric view.
- In the Drawing View dialog box, click Shaded.
- Click OK.

10 To edit the display of the crop cut lines:

- In the browser, expand *View5:Graphics Card.iam*.
- Right-click Crop.
- Click Display Crop Cut Lines.

11 Review the isometric view in the graphics window.

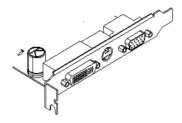

12 Close all files. Do not save.

Lesson 31 | Managing Views

In this lesson you learn to manage your views by moving, aligning, and editing them. When you create a drawing, it is often difficult to know how many views or sheets will be required, and what the best position or orientation of the views will be. As you begin to apply dimensions and other annotations to the drawing, the views may need to be moved, copied, or deleted.

The ability to move, align, and edit drawing views has a direct impact on the quality of production-ready drawings.

In the following illustration, drawing views have been created on a sheet and the orientation of the views has been set.

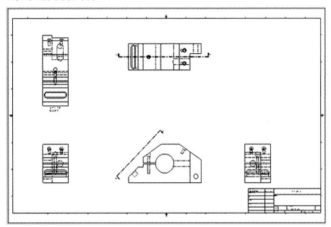

Objectives

After completing this lesson, you will be able to:

- Explain how the browser organizes drawing resources and views.

- Describe moving, aligning, and editing views.

- Move, align, and edit drawing views.

- Identify areas to control line visibility.

- Control line visibility.

About View Organization

In drawing views, the browser stores resources and organizes information related to the current drawing. Access to features that are not directly related to the 3D geometry is contained in the Drawing Resources folder.

In the following illustration, a typical browser tree view shows the contents of the Drawing Resources folder and the first sheet.

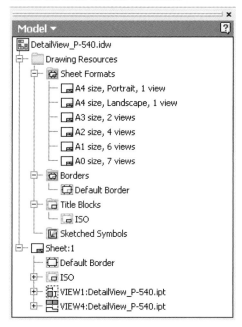

Definition of View Organization

In the Drawing Resources folder, you access standard items such as title blocks and borders, and store and access your custom resources. Each time a view is created, it is listed in the browser under the sheet folder in which it is created. Typically the base view is the first view created, then subsequent or dependent views are added. The browser organizes views based on their dependency to other views.

Example of Organized Views

The following illustration shows a typical browser hierarchy for a production-ready drawing. The Drawing Resources folder is expanded to show the resources available. The base view is expanded and displays a nested view and the features of the part.

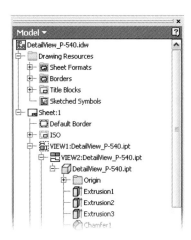

About Moving, Aligning, and Editing Views

Manipulating drawing views is necessary to provide a layout that conveys the information needed to manufacture or inspect a part or assembly. To obtain the best possible layout, you may need to move views to other locations on the layout or even to other drawing sheets. Views may need to be realigned or altered to organize the information.

In the following illustration, the section view is moved to another sheet and enlarged.

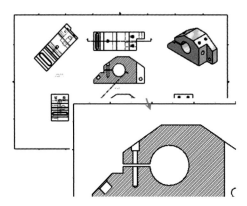

Definition of Moving, Aligning, and Editing Views

Any drawing view that has broken the alignment association with the parent view is considered to have been moved. Any drawing view that is not in the orientation where it was originally placed is considered to have been aligned. A view that has broken its association with the parent view to change the style, or that has had line segments moved or altered, is considered to have been edited.

Example of Moving, Aligning, and Editing Views

In the following illustration, the properties of a pierce hole in a die block are altered to draw attention to the feature. The color is changed and the linetype thickness increased. Nonessential hidden lines are also removed for clarity.

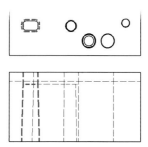

Moving, Aligning, and Editing Views

After you have created drawing views, you can move and copy them between drawing sheets. You can also rotate views, align them with other views on the sheet, delete views, and resolve dependent views.

In the following illustration, the auxiliary view is rotated to horizontal and then aligned to the view below it.

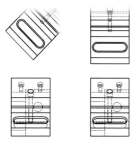

Moving Views

When a projected view is created on a sheet, the style of the view is based on the parent view. When a projected view is moved to another sheet, the style connection is broken. To change the style of the moved view, you edit the view directly.

Procedure: Moving a View on the Current Sheet

The following steps describe how to move a drawing view on a sheet.

1   Click the view and drag it to a new location.

2   Edit the view if movement of the view is restricted. For example, a section view, by default, can only move perpendicular to the parent view.

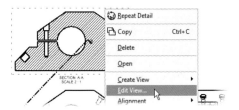

3   Clear the Align to Base check box.

Procedure: Moving a View Between Sheets

The following steps describe how to move a drawing view between sheets.

1. In the browser, select the view to be moved.

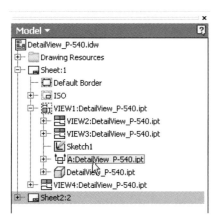

2. Drag the view to the new sheet.

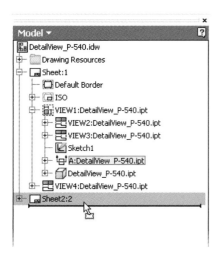

3   The sheet that you moved the view to becomes active. In the browser, right-click the
    A:DetailView_P-540.ipt view that you moved. Use the Go To option to find where the view
    has been moved to. Click Go To. The moved view is displayed with a shortcut icon in the
    browser. The icon for the view and shown below indicates that the view was moved.

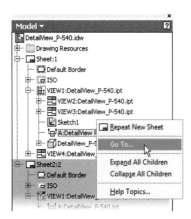

Procedure: Finding a View Moved to a New Sheet

The following steps describe how to locate a view moved to a new sheet.

Aligning Views

As you create drawing views, they automatically align to the parent view from which they were
projected. You may sometimes need to change the alignment of drawing views to make better use
of the available area on the sheet.

There are four options for aligning drawing views.

Option	Description
Horizontal	Aligns views horizontally.
Vertical	Aligns views vertically.
In Position	Aligns views In Position
Break	Breaks the alignment between views, enabling you to move the view in any direction.

Procedure: Aligning Views Horizontally

The following steps describe how to align views horizontally. The Horizontal alignment option aligns the selected view horizontally with another view on the sheet. In this procedure the alignment between the two views has been broken.

1 To realign the two views horizontally, right-click in the view to be aligned.
   Click Alignment > Horizontal.

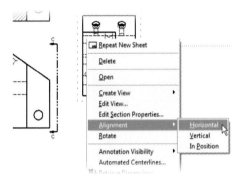

2 Click the parent view for the alignment.

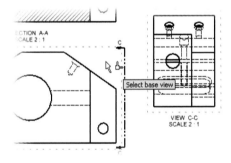

3 Establish the horizontal view alignment.

Procedure: Aligning Views Vertically

The following steps describe how to align views vertically. The Vertical alignment option aligns the selected view vertically with another view on the sheet. In this procedure, the alignment between the two views has been broken.

1   To realign the two views vertically, right-click the view to be aligned and click Alignment > Vertical on the shortcut menu.

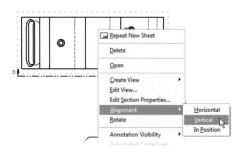

2   Click the parent view for the alignment.

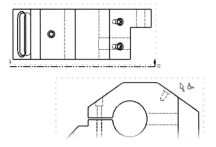

3   Establish the vertical view alignment.

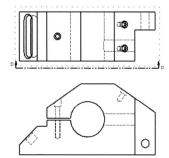

Procedure: Aligning Views in Position

The following steps describe how to align views in position. The In Position alignment option aligns the selected view based on an axis that is neither vertical or horizontal. In this procedure, the alignment between the two views has been broken.

1   To realign the two views in position, right-click in the view to be aligned.
    Click Alignment > In Position.

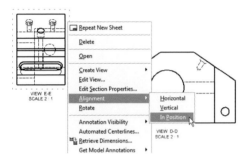

2   Click the parent view for the alignment.

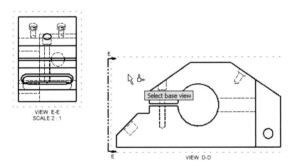

3   Establish the In Position view alignment.

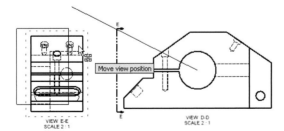

Procedure: Copying Views Between Sheets

The following steps describe how to copy drawing views between sheets.

1   Right-click in the drawing view. Click Copy.

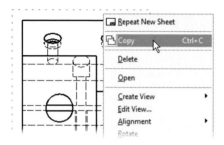

2   In the browser, double-click the destination sheet.

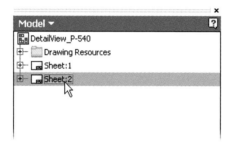

3   Paste the view into the destination sheet.

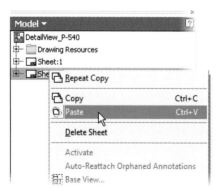

Procedure: Deleting Views

The following steps describe how to delete views.

1. On the sheet or in the browser, right-click the view to be deleted.

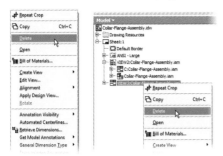

2. If the deleted view is a parent of other views, open the Delete View dialog box and specify whether the dependent views are to be deleted. Delete the view.

About Line Visibility

In this part of the lesson, you learn to control line visibility. When a view is placed on a drawing sheet, every line in the view is calculated based on the style indicated. You may sometimes need to alter or remove individual lines from a drawing view.

In the following illustration, the color and linetype thickness properties of a hole are altered.

Definition of Line Visibility

Line visibility controls the display properties of the geometry calculated in the view. The display properties can be controlled at the individual, feature, or component level.

Example of Line Visibility

In the following illustration, the clarity of a drawing view has been improved by removing hidden and visible lines. On the left, the initial view is displayed. On the right, individual lines have been removed from the drawing view to increase clarity when dimensioning the hole.

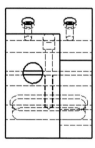 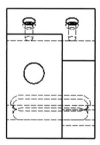

Controlling Line Visibility in Drawings

The visibility of lines in views can be controlled either in the view itself or in the browser. In the view, visibility can be controlled at the segment, feature, or part level. In the browser, visibility can be controlled at the feature or part level. For both the view and the browser, your selections are based on the selection priority that is set on the Quick Access toolbar.

The following illustration shows access to the editing properties of lines in drawing views and the selection priority. Left: Access to a feature in the browser. Center: Setting Feature Priority enables you to select the entire feature in the drawing view, as shown on the right.

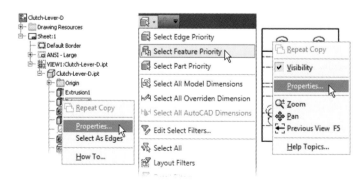

Procedure: Removing Lines in Views

The following steps describe how to remove individual lines from a view.

1   Set the selection priority to Edge Priority.

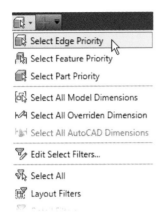

2   Select the line to be removed. Use CTRL+click to select multiple lines.

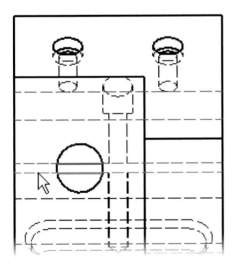

3   Right-click and clear the Visibility check mark.

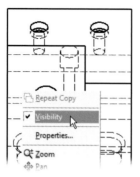

4   The selected lines are removed from the view.

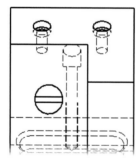

Procedure: Changing Line Visibility in Views

The following steps describe how to change line visibility in drawing views.

1   Set the selection priority to Feature Priority or Part Priority.

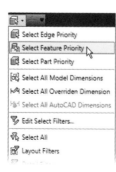

2   Right-click in the feature or part to be changed. Click Properties.

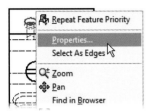

3   In the Feature Properties dialog box, adjust the features to be changed. Clear the By Layer
    check box to edit the line weight and linetype.

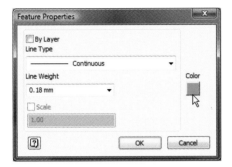

4   Update the drawing view.

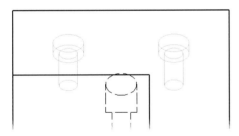

Procedure: Changing Line Visibility in the Browser

The following steps describe how to change line visibility in the browser.

1   Set the selection priority to Feature Priority or Part Priority.

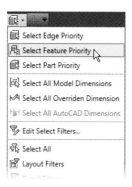

2   Expand the folders in the browser until the features of the part are displayed.

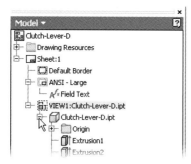

3   Select the feature to change. Press CTRL+click to select multiple features. Right-click the selected features. Click Properties.

4 In the Feature Properties dialog box, adjust the features to be changed. Clear the By Layer check box to edit the line weight and line type.

5 Update the view.

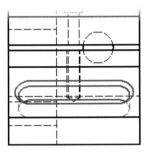

Exercise | Manage Views

In this exercise you navigate the drawing creation environment to create projected views and change the sheet size.

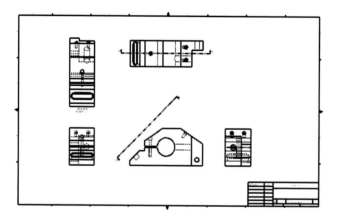

The completed exercise

Completing the Exercise:	*To complete the exercise, follow the steps in this book or in the onscreen exercise. In the onscreen list of chapters and exercises, click Chapter 8: Basic View Creation. Click Exercise: Manage Views.*

1   Open *Clutch-Lever-D.idw*.

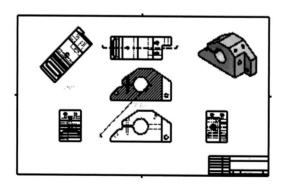

2   Create a new sheet:

- Right-click in a blank area of the browser.
- Click New Sheet.
- A new D size sheet is created and becomes the active sheet.

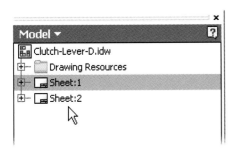

3   In the browser, double-click Sheet:1 to activate the sheet. Expand Sheet:1.

4   Move a view from Sheet:1 to Sheet:2:

- In the browser, expand VIEW1 to display the other views associated with it.
- Drag and drop the section view A:Clutch-Lever-D.ipt to Sheet:2.

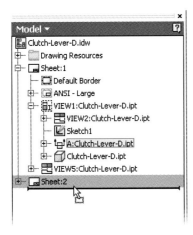

5   Change the scale of the section view:

  - On Sheet:2, double-click the section view.
  - In the Drawing View dialog box, select 4:1 from the Scale list. Click OK.

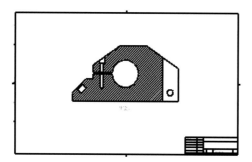

6   Rotate the auxiliary view:

  - In the browser, double-click Sheet:1.
  - In the browser, expand View2.
  - Right-click the auxiliary view. Click Rotate.
  - Select the lower-left diagonal line. In the Rotate View dialog box, click Counter Clockwise. Click OK.

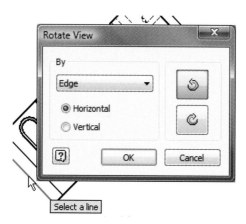

7   Align the auxiliary view to the left view:

   • Right-click in the rotated auxiliary view.
   • Click Alignment > Vertical.
   • Click the left view.

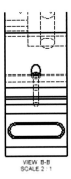

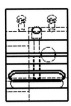

8   Copy the isometric view to a new sheet:

   • Right-click in the isometric view. Click Copy.
   • Right-click in a blank area in the browser. Click New Sheet.
   • Right-click in the new sheet. Click Paste. Move the view to the center.

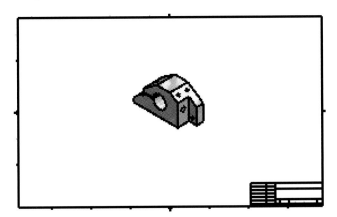

9   Change the scale of the isometric view:
- Right-click in the isometric view. Click Edit View.
- In the Drawing View dialog box, in the Scale list, select 4:1. Click OK.

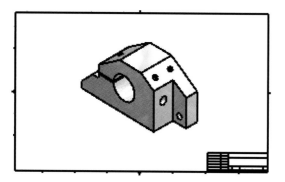

10   Delete the isometric view from Sheet:1:
- In the browser, double-click Sheet:1.
- Right-click in the isometric view. Click Delete. Click OK.

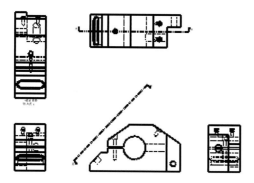

11   Close all files. Do not save.

Chapter Summary

In this chapter, you learned how to quickly and easily create drawing views of your 3D designs. Learning how to create and edit drawing views is the first step in creating production-ready drawings. In the next chapter, you learn how to annotate your drawing views with dimensions, hole and thread notes, centerlines and symbols, and even add revision tables to your drawings.

Having completed this chapter, you can:

- Navigate the Autodesk Inventor user interface when creating and editing drawing sheets.

- Create base and projected views of 3D parts and assemblies.

- Create and edit section views.

- Create and edit detail views.

- Create and edit cropped views.

- Manage drawing views.

Chapter 09
Dimensions, Annotations, and Tables

After creating drawing views, you can annotate those views with dimensions, hole and thread notes, centerlines, and symbols. Production-ready drawings also typically include revision tables and tags. While traditional annotation methods can be quite tedious, you can quickly and easily include these elements in your drawings using the annotation tools available in Autodesk® Inventor®.

Objectives

After completing this chapter, you will be able to:

- Dimension drawings with automated techniques.

- Dimension drawings with manual techniques.

- Create and edit hole and thread notes in drawings.

- Add centerlines, center marks and symbols to your drawings.

- Configure, add, and edit revision tables and revision tags.

Lesson 32 | Automated Dimensioning Techniques

This lesson describes using model dimensions in a drawing. In a typical workflow, a 3D model is created in the modeling environment. This model is composed of sketches and features; dimensions are used to numerically define and constrain these sketches and features. By using these dimensions, you can annotate the drawing views in less time and with fewer steps than if you placed the dimensions manually.

In the following illustration, the dimensions in the two views are retrieved from the dimensions applied during the modeling process. The dimensions are retrieved and then moved into location for readability.

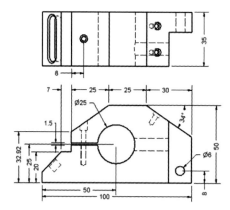

Objectives

After completing this lesson, you will be able to:

- Describe the use and function of retrieved dimensions.

- Retrieve model dimensions for use in drawing views.

- Position model dimensions, add text and symbols, and edit model dimension values.

Dimensions are used extensively in the modeling process. Dimensions can be retrieved from the model and reused in drawing views. Retrieved dimensions can be added to or deleted from drawing views at any time, without affecting the model. However, if the default option of enabling part modifications from drawing views is selected at the time the program is installed, editing the value of retrieved dimensions *will edit the model.*

In the following illustration, the model is created and the drawing view shown. During the process of applying dimensions, an engineering change is received. The designer updates the changed dimension, and the part is updated in the drawing view.

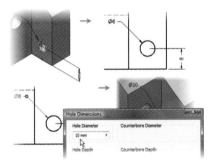

Definition of Automatically Placed Dimensions

Automatically placing a dimension in a drawing view is the process of retrieving a dimension that has been applied in the modeling environment and using it to annotate the drawing view in the drawing environment. Because the retrieved dimension is displayed as applied in the modeling environment, it can be edited to meet your drawing standards.

In the following illustration, model dimensions are retrieved from the modeling environment and used to dimension a drawing view in the drawing environment. The appearance of the dimensions is then edited to convey the correct information for manufacture and inspection.

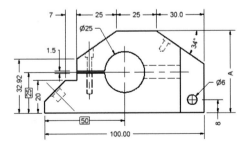

Example of Automatically Placed Dimensions

In the following illustration, three dimensions were retrieved from the modeling environment. The three dimensions establish the relationship of the hole to the lower-left corner of the part.

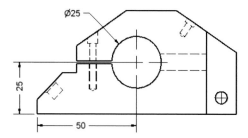

Retrieving Model Dimensions

When you create your 3D model, you place parametric dimensions on sketches and features. Whenever possible, you should use these dimensions on the drawing.

You use the Retrieve Dimensions tool to retrieve dimensions from the model for use in the drawing. When you start the tool, you can select the dimensions that you want to retrieve, while ignoring others. You can do this on both part and assembly drawing views.

When you retrieve model dimensions, you select a view for the dimensions. You can retrieve only those dimensions that were created on the same plane as the selected view.

In the following illustration, the front view of a clutch-lever is dimensioned by using dimensions from the modeling process.

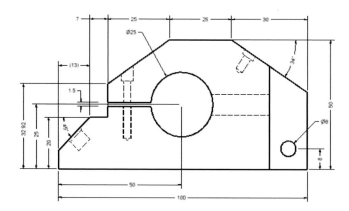

Access

Retrieve Dimensions

Ribbon: **Annotate tab > Dimension panel**

Toolbar: **Drawing Annotation Panel**
Shortcut Menu: **Retrieve Dimensions**

Retrieve Dimensions Dialog Box

The Retrieve Dimensions dialog box is displayed when you start the Retrieve Dimensions tool.

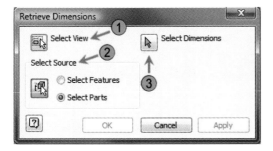

The Retrieve Dimensions dialog box contains the following options.

Option	Description
Select View	Select the view to retrieve the model dimension into. Only required when you start the Retrieve Dimensions tool from the panel bar.

Option	Description
Select Source	• Select Features: Select this option to retrieve dimensions from selected features. • Select Parts: Select this option to retrieve dimensions from the entire part
Select	Select the dimensions in the drawing view to retrieve. Only those dimensions that are selected are retrieved.

Procedure: Retrieving Model Dimensions

The following steps describe how to retrieve dimensions from a model and apply them to a drawing view.

1   Open or create a drawing with drawing views.

2   Start the Retrieve Dimensions tool.

3   Select the view from which you will retrieve dimensions.

4   In the Retrieve Dimensions dialog box, select the source for the dimensions.

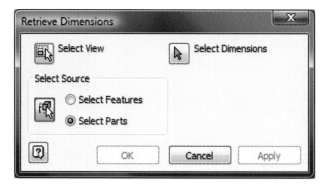

5   Select the part or features in the view to dimension.

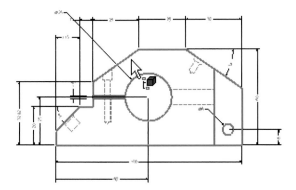

6   Retrieve the desired dimensions from the dimensions displayed.

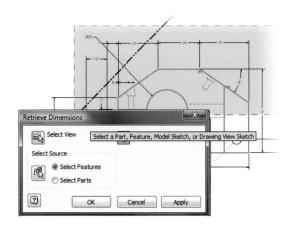

7   Arrange the dimensions as needed.

Note: *Model dimensions can be retrieved at any time. Even if a model dimension has been deleted from the view, it has not been deleted from the model. Executing the Retrieve Dimensions tool displays all dimensions that are parallel to the view and that are not already displayed.*

Editing Model Dimensions

After retrieving the model dimensions, you may need to edit the dimension's position or add information to the dimension. You can edit the dimension and the text, notes, or symbols, or you can hide the dimension value.

In the following illustration, dimensions have been retrieved from the model and placed in a drawing view. The dimensions are edited to add text in place of the numerical values, and to add symbols to define basic dimensions.

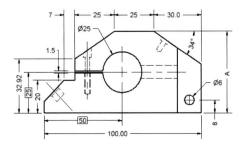

Procedure: Moving Model Dimensions

The following steps describe how to move model dimensions.

1   Place the retrieved dimensions.

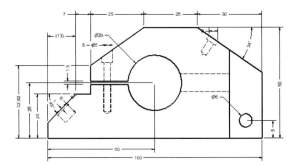

2   Click and drag the dimension text to the desired location.

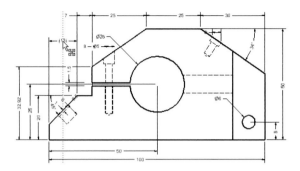

3   Use the Arrange Dimensions tool to select multiple dimensions and edit them together. Press CTRL and select the dimensions. On the ribbon, click Annotate tab > Dimensions panel > Arrange Dimensions. Move the dimension selection set and click to place them.

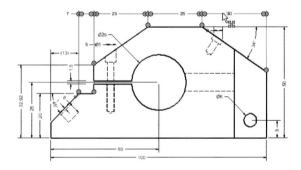

4   The dimensions are moved.

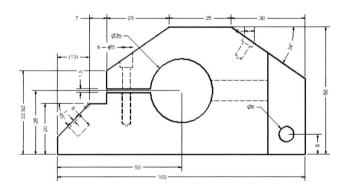

Procedure: Changing Model Dimension Values

The following steps describe how to change the model dimensions from the drawing view.

1   Right-click in the model dimension to edit. Click Edit Model Dimension.

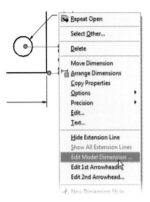

2   In the Edit Dimension dialog box, enter a new value.

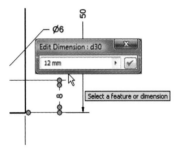

3   The model and the drawing views are updated.

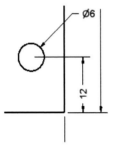

Note: **Proceed with Caution!** *When you edit model dimensions in the drawing, remember that you are changing the parametric dimension of the model. Changing the dimension in the drawing environment has the same effect as changing the dimension in the modeling environment. Constraints are reevaluated and the geometry is updated in the 3D model and in the drawing to reflect the new value.*

Procedure: Editing Dimension Text

The following steps describe how to add standard text and symbols to dimensions.

1   Right-click the dimension to be edited. Click Edit.

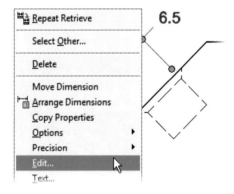

2   In the Edit Dimension dialog box, add the desired text or symbol.

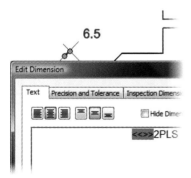

3   To enter a prefix for the dimension, move the cursor to the left side of the brackets.

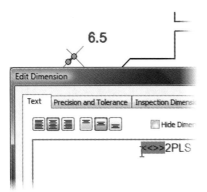

4   In the Edit Dimension dialog box, add the desired text or symbol.

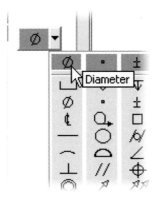

5   The text and symbols entered are displayed in the dimension.

Exercise | Dimension a Drawing View

In this exercise, you dimension a view by retrieving the dimensions that were used to create the model. You then edit one of the dimensions to update the drawing and the model.

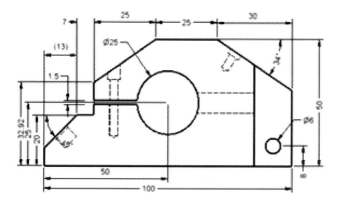

The completed exercise

Completing the Exercise: To complete the exercise, follow the steps in this book or in the onscreen exercise. In the onscreen list of chapters and exercises, click Chapter 9: Dimensions, Annotations, and Tables. Click Exercise: Dimension a Drawing View.

1   Open *Dimensioning-Clutch-Lever.idw*.

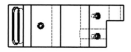

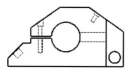

2   Retrieve the dimensions that were used during the model creation:

- Click Annotate tab > Dimension panel > Retrieve.
- Select the front view.
- In the Retrieve Dimensions dialog box, under Select Source, click Select Parts.

3   Apply the dimension to the drawing view:

- Select any segment in the front view.
- In the Retrieve Dimensions dialog box, click Select Dimensions.
- Select all the dimensions in the front view. Click OK.

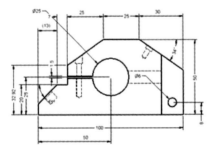

4   Arrange the dimensions in the front view.

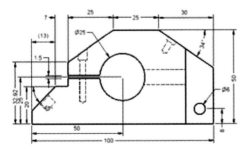

5   Edit a dimension and the model:

-   Right-click the 6mm dimension in the lower right corner of the view.
-   Click Edit Model Dimension.

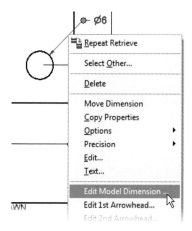

6   In the Hole Dimensions dialog box, change the hole diameter to **10 mm**. Click OK.

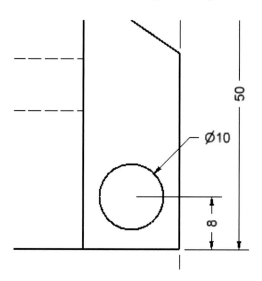

Note: Remember that changing model dimensions from the drawing environment also changes the 3D model geometry.

7   Close all files. Do not save.

Lesson 33 | Manual Dimensioning Techniques

This lesson describes the manual application of dimensions. Dimensions define the size and location of the objects being designed. They are the most important annotation applied to a drawing. Therefore, the application of dimensions is critical to the success of the project.

Dimensions manually applied to drawing views are associated with the object that defines them. Manually placed dimensions provide documentation of the model in the drawing environment. The application of manual dimensions uses general, baseline, and ordinate dimensions.

In the following illustration, the dimensions have been added manually to define features on the part.

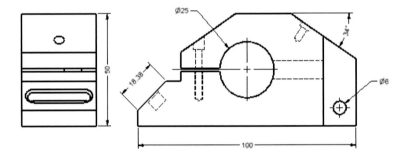

Objectives

After completing this lesson, you will be able to:

- Describe general, baseline, and ordinate dimensioning techniques.

- Place general dimensions on drawing views.

- Place baseline dimensions on drawing views.

- Place ordinate dimensions on drawing views.

About General, Baseline, and Ordinate Dimensioning

Several options are available for placing dimensions in drawings. General dimensions include different options for placing dimensions; this is the most commonly used dimensioning tool. Baseline and ordinate dimensions have more specific applications.

In the following illustration, general dimensions are placed on the drawing as the first step in creating a production-ready drawing.

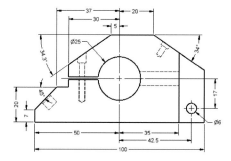

Definitions of General, Baseline, and Ordinate Dimensions

Term	Definition
General dimensions	Placed on a drawing view one at a time. The type of dimension placed depends on the geometry selected to define it.
Baseline dimensions	Each dimension in the set has a common origin and is displayed from the origin in the form of a conventional horizontal or vertical dimension. Multiple segments of geometry can be selected at one time to define the baseline dimension set.
Ordinate dimensions	Each dimension in the set has a common origin, shows the distance from the origin, and uses a leader to define the dimensioned point.

The following illustration shows general dimensions (on the left); baseline dimensions (in the middle), and ordinate dimensions (on the right).

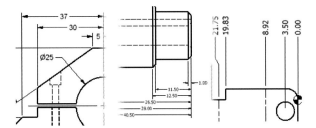

Example of Baseline and Ordinate Dimensioning

The type of dimensioning applied to a drawing is dependent on the objects being designed and the manufacturing process used to create them. Baseline and ordinate dimensioning is most effective when all or most features can be based off a single point or edge of the part. In the following illustration, a stamped part is dimensioned using ordinate dimensions, and a shaft is dimensioned using baseline dimensions.

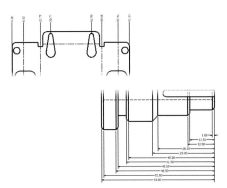

Creating General Dimensions

The General Dimension tool can place many different types of dimensions, depending on the geometry selected. Selecting two parallel lines results in horizontal, vertical, or aligned dimensions; selecting two nonparallel lines results in angle dimensions; and selecting an arc or circle results in radial or diameter dimensions. To obtain a horizontal or vertical dimension between two nonparallel lines, you select one line and the endpoint of the other line, or select two endpoints.

In the following illustration, general dimensions are placed on the drawing to define the part.

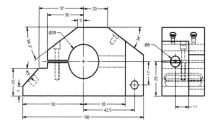

Access

General Dimension

Ribbon: **Annotate tab > Dimension panel**

Toolbar: **Drawing Annotation Panel**
Keyboard: **D**

Option	Description
Horizontal	Creates a horizontal dimension based on the points or segments selected.
Vertical	Creates a vertical dimension based on the points or segments selected.
Aligned	Creates a linear dimension perpendicular to the points or segments selected.

Procedure: Placing General Dimensions

The following steps describe how to place general dimensions on a drawing.

1   Start the General Dimension tool.

2   Select two points or line segments in the drawing view.

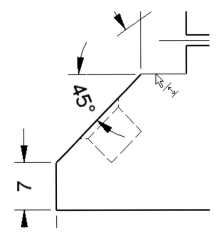

3   Place the dimension.

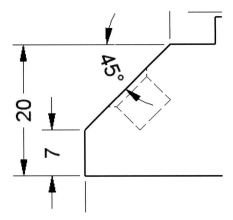

Creating Baseline Dimensions

Baseline dimensions are useful when you have a primary point or edge as a point of origin for the dimensions. You can dimension multiple points in a single selection. You can add or delete members of the dimension set at any time.

In the following illustration, baseline dimensions define a shaft.

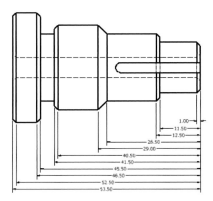

Access

Baseline

Ribbon: **Annotate tab > Dimension panel**

Toolbar: **Drawing Annotation Panel**

Access

Baseline Set

Ribbon: **Annotate tab › Dimension panel**

Toolbar: **Drawing Annotation Panel**
Keyboard: **A**

Procedure: Placing Baseline Dimensions

The following steps describe how to place baseline dimensions.

1   Start the Baseline Dimension Set tool.

2   Select the geometry to be dimensioned. You can select the geometry individually or by using a selection window.

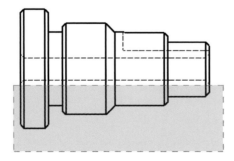

3   When all the geometry is selected, right-click in the drawing. Click Continue.

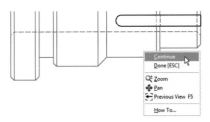

4   Place the dimensions.

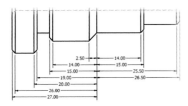

5   Right-click a line, point, or dimension extension line and click Make Origin to set the origin for the baseline dimensions.

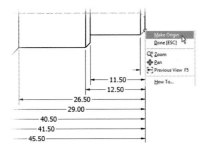

6   Create the baseline dimension set.

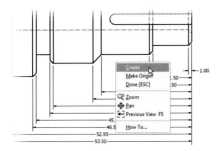

Creating Ordinate Dimensions

Ordinate dimensions are useful when you have a primary point or edge as a point of origin to dimension from. You can use ordinate dimensions when you have limited space to place dimensions.

In the following illustration, ordinate dimensions are used to define the layout of a flat pattern of a sheet metal part.

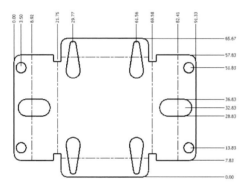

Access

Ordinate Dimension

Ribbon: **Annotate tab › Dimension panel**

Toolbar: **Drawing Annotation Panel**

Access

Ordinate Dimension Set

Ribbon: **Annotate tab > Dimension panel**

Toolbar: **Drawing Annotation Panel**
Keyboard: **O**

Procedure: Placing Ordinate Dimensions

The following steps describe how to place ordinate dimensions on a drawing.

1   Start the Ordinate Dimension Set tool.

2   Select a point or segment to define the origin.

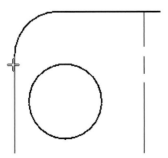

3   Click Continue and place the zero dimension.

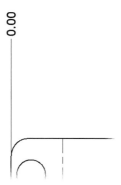

4   Select additional points to apply ordinate dimensions.

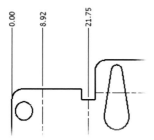

5   When all the locations are selected, create the ordinate dimension set.

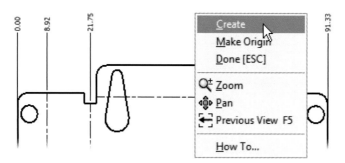

6   To add ordinate dimensions to the set, move the cursor to any dimension in the set and right-click. Click Add Member.

7   Select additional points.

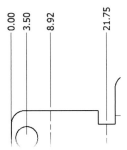

Exercise | Create General Dimensions

In this exercise, you add horizontal, vertical, diameter, and angle dimensions to a drawing. You also create a radial dimension and convert it to a diametric dimension.

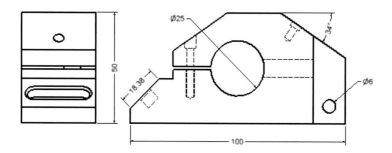

The completed exercise

Completing the Exercise

To complete the exercise, follow the steps in this book or in the onscreen exercise. In the onscreen list of chapters and exercises, click Chapter 9: Dimensions, Annotations, and Tables. Click Exercise: Create General Dimensions.

1   Open *Dimensioning-Clutch-Lever2.idw.*

2   Create a horizontal dimension:
   - Click Annotate tab > Dimension panel > Dimension.
   - In the front view, click the two vertical lines at each end of the part.
   - Place the horizontal dimension below the part.

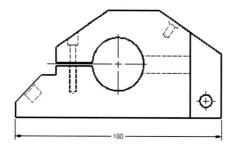

3   Create a vertical dimension:

- With the General Dimension tool still active, select the bottom line in the left view.
- Select the top line in the left view.
- Place the vertical dimension next to the view.

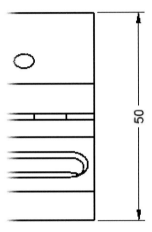

4   Create an angle dimension:

- With the General Dimension tool still active, select the top horizontal line in the front view, then select the line to the right.
- Place the angle dimension.

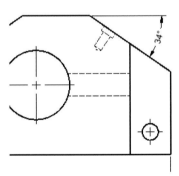

5   Create a diameter dimension:

- With the General Dimension tool still active, select the circle in the front view.
- Click to place the dimension.

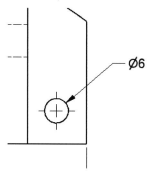

6   Create a radial dimension and change to a diameter dimension.

- With the General Dimension tool still active, click the large circle in the center of the view.
- Right-click and click Dimension Type > Diameter.

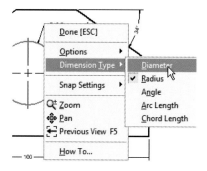

7   Place the dimension in the drawing.

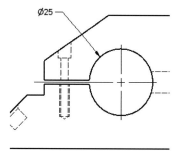

8   Create an aligned dimension:

   • With the General Dimension tool still active, select the angled line on the left side of the front view.
   • Position the cursor as shown to automatically orient the dimension to be an aligned dimension.

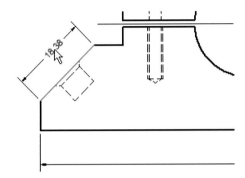

9   Click to place the aligned dimension.

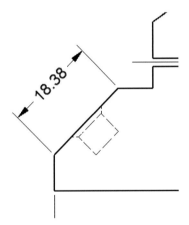

10   Close all files. Do not save.

Exercise | Create Baseline Dimensions

In this exercise, you create baseline dimensions. You then edit the dimensions by adding a member to the baseline dimensions set and arrange the appearance of the dimensions.

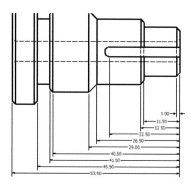

The completed exercise

Completing the Exercise:

To complete the exercise, follow the steps in this book or in the onscreen exercise. In the onscreen list of chapters and exercises, click Chapter 9: Dimensions, Annotations, and Tables. Click Exercise: Create Baseline Dimensions.

1   Open *Dimension-Shaft.idw.*

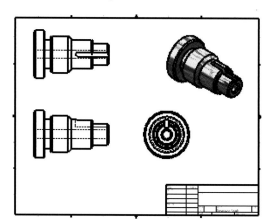

2   Define the location for placement of baseline dimensions.

- Zoom in the top left view.
- Click Annotate tab > Dimension > Baseline Dimension Set.
- Select the geometry as shown in the following illustration.

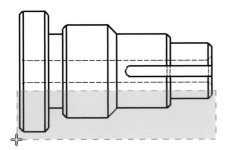

3   Position the baseline dimensions.

- Right-click in the graphics window and click Continue.
- Click below the view to place the dimension set.

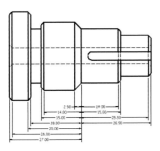

4   Define the zero point for the baseline dimension set.

- Right-click the rightmost extension line. Click Make Origin.
- Right-click in the graphics window and click Create.

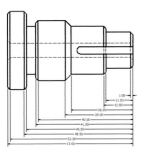

5   Add a member to the baseline dimension set.

*   Move the cursor to any dimension in the set.
*   Right-click and click Add Member.
*   Select the endpoint of the line for the keyway.
*   Right-click, click Done.

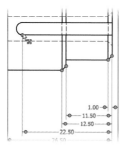

6   Delete members from the set.

*   Right-click the 52.50 dimension. Click Delete Member.
*   Repeat for the 46.50 dimension.

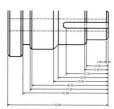

7   Uniformly arrange the dimensions.

*   Right-click any dimension.
*   Click Arrange.

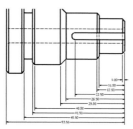

8   Close all files. Do not save

Exercise | Create Ordinate Dimensions

In this exercise, you add ordinate dimensions to the flat pattern of a stamped part.

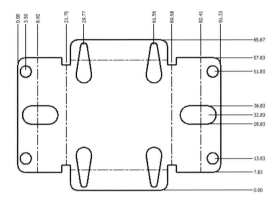

The completed exercise

Completing the Exercise : To complete the exercise, follow the steps in this book or in the onscreen exercise. In the onscreen list of chapters and exercises, click Chapter 9: Dimensions, Annotations, and Tables. Click Exercise: Create Ordinate Dimensions.

1   Open *Dimension-Flat-Pattern.idw.*

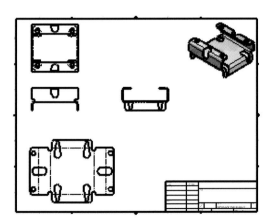

2   Define the zero point for the ordinate dimension set:
- Click Annotate tab > Dimension panel > Ordinate Set.
- Click in the far-left edge of the flat pattern.
- Right-click. Click Continue.
- Click above the view to place the dimension as shown in the following illustration.

3   Place ordinate dimensions on the bend lines:
- Select the four lines indicating the bend lines and the far right line.
- Select the centers of the two slots. Right- click and click Create.

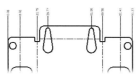

4   Add an ordinate dimension to the set:
- Move the cursor to any dimension in the ordinate set.
- Right-click and click Add Member.
- Select the left hole.

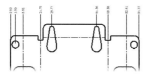

5   Define the zero origin for the ordinate dimensions in the Y direction:
- Click Annotate tab > Dimension panel > Ordinate.
- Select the Flat Pattern view.
- Select the bottom line in the view.

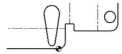

6   Specify the features to apply to the ordinate dimensions:

- Click the line at the origin.
- Click each line and feature as shown in the following illustration.

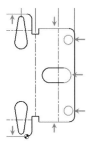

7   Place the ordinate dimensions:

- Right-click in the graphics window and click Continue.
- Place the ordinate dimensions to the right of the view.
- Right-click. Click Done.

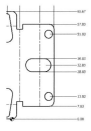

8   Hide the origin indicator:

- Move the cursor to the origin indicator.
- Right-click and click Hide Origin Indicator.

9   Close all files. Do not save.

Lesson 34 | Annotating Holes and Threads

This lesson describes using hole notes, thread notes, and hole tables to create associative annotations to hole and thread features in a drawing. When you create hole or thread features on a part, their parameters are stored in the feature. The Hole/Thread Notes and Hole Table tools extract this information from the hole feature and other types of created holes, and place it in the drawing in the form of a note or table.

When annotating holes in a drawing, you add specific information about the hole and its location on the part. With hole tables, you can efficiently annotate both location and size for all the holes in a drawing view, instead of separately placing location dimensions and hole notes.

In the following illustration, both hole notes and hole tables are used to annotate a drawing. In the upper view, hole notes call out the specifications of the two hole types in the view. In the lower view, a hole table describes the hole specifications, and the location from the center hole.

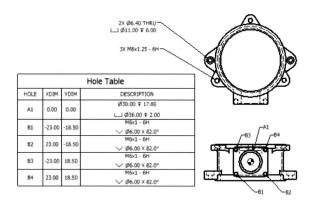

Objectives

After completing this lesson, you will be able to:

- Describe hole notes and their properties.

- Create and edit hole and thread notes.

- Add a thread note to a drawing view so that the note displays as a linear dimension.

- Explain the use and function of hole tables and identify the characteristics of a hole table.

- Create and edit hole tables.

About Hole and Thread Notes

When you create production drawings for manufacturing, you must annotate holes and threaded features on the part. A hole or thread note is an annotation object that references a hole or threaded feature to specify that feature's defining parameters.

The following illustration shows holes with typical hole notes.

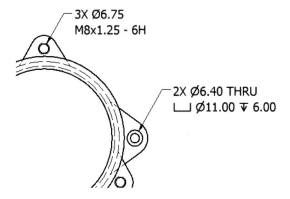

> **Note:** **Hole Notes Are Associative** *When you create hole notes, the notes are associative. Hole parameters are retrieved automatically when you create the note. If the hole feature changes, the hole note reflects the latest values.*

Definitions

Hole Note or Thread Note: An annotation on a drawing view consisting of symbols and text describing a feature. A leader line points to the hole or threaded feature being described.

Hole Parameters: The different characteristics, terms, and values that explain a hole textually and symbolically.

Example of Hole and Thread Notes

The purpose of a hole note or thread note is to communicate information about a hole or threaded feature. The information is used not only by the person building the part, but by the person validating the final quality of the part.

In the following illustration, hole notes are used to define the type, quantity, and style of various holes in the part.

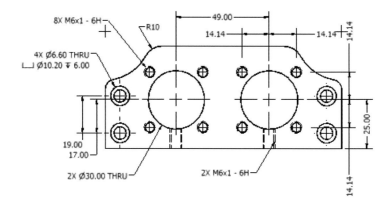

Working with Hole and Thread Notes

Holes in production drawings are defined by the notes attached to them. A part may contain several holes of the same size; however, because of their functions, different processes may be required to create them. Hole and thread notes define the process to create the holes, and therefore the quality and function of the part. The procedure for adding and editing a hole note is very similar to the procedure for adding and editing diameter dimensions.

How Dimension Style Affects Note Appearance

The initial data contained in a hole and thread note depends on the settings in the template for the type of hole selected. The dimension style stores the templates for all major hole types. You can edit the hole note templates by editing the dimension style. Changing the hole note templates to reflect your typical requirements should help you avoid having to edit individual hole notes placed on the drawing.

Editing Hole and Thread Notes

You can control format, content, and other attributes of an individual hole note by changing the dimension style, editing the data in the Edit Hole Note dialog box, or making changes and additions in the Format Text dialog box.

Edit Hole Note Dialog Box

You use the options in the Edit Hole Note dialog box to edit the selected hole note. You can use the text box to add static text in the note, to add specific symbols, or to add dynamic value codes. You can also change the display options to include the tap drill information; the precision, tolerance, and unit type; and the method for displaying the quantity of holes.

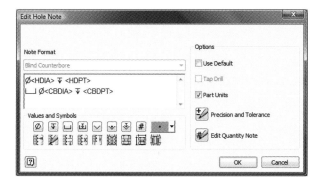

Note: *When you use the Edit Hole Note dialog box to edit a hole note, the changes apply only to the selected note. They do not affect the other hole notes in the drawing, even if they are on the same types of holes.*

Access

Hole / Thread Notes

Ribbon: **Annotate tab > Features panel**

Toolbar: **Drawing Annotation Panel**

Procedure: Creating a Hole and Thread Note

The following steps describe how to create hole and thread notes.

1   Start the Hole/Thread Note tool.

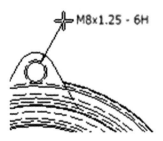

2   Select the hole in the drawing.

3   Continue placing additional hole notes.

4   Right-click in the drawing and click Done.

Procedure: Editing Hole/Thread Notes

The following steps describe how to edit hole and thread notes.

1   Right-click a hole note. Click Edit Hole Note. (Alternatively, double-click a hole note.)

2   In the Edit Hole Note dialog box, add or remove values and symbols to edit the hole note parameters or to add standard text.

Guidelines

Use the following guidelines to work with hole and thread notes.

- You control the symbols and text contained in a hole note with the Dimension Style settings.

- You can include a variety of note data on a hole based on the combination of hole type and thread type.

- In order for the Hole/Thread Notes tool to add annotations to a drawing view, the hole must have been created using one of the specified methods.

- You can change the display of an existing hole note by changing its dimension style.

- You can modify the annotation information within the hole note using the Edit Hole Note dialog box.

- You can add text characteristics and additional text and symbols to a hole note using the Format Text dialog box.

- Editing a hole note in a drawing does not change the initial standard on which that note was based.

Holes You Can Annotate with Notes

You can select the following types of holes for annotation:

- Features created with the Hole tool

- Extrude-cut circles and circular sheet metal cuts

- Voids in extrude-join operations

- Sheet metal features

- Holes in iFeatures

Information about tapped holes and external threads is called out in a drawing by placing a note on the end of a leader line or within a linear dimension. To have the note appear as a linear dimension instead of with the default leader line, you must be able to add it as a linear note.

In the following illustration, the same drawing view is shown with the thread notes as leader lines and as linear dimensions.

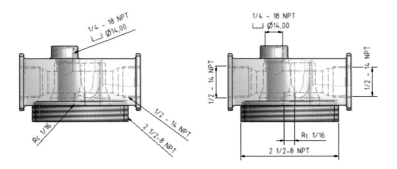

Creation and Settings

When you want to add a thread note to a drawing view where the tapped hole or external threads are seen from the side, you can retrieve and display the thread information with the use of the Hole/ Thread Notes tool. By selecting the pair of lines that identifies the hole or threads instead of just one of the lines, you can add a note that has the thread information while representing it in a linear dimension.

The display of the linear dimension thread note is controlled by a combination of settings within the dimension style. The Notes and Leaders settings control this dimension's text value, while the linear dimension and text property settings are controlled by the rest of the dimension settings.

Procedure: Creating Linear Dimension Thread Notes

The following steps describe how to add a thread note to the side view of a hole feature, so that it displays as a linear dimension.

1   Start the Hole/Thread Notes tool.

2   In the view where the tapped hole threaded feature is shown from the side, select one of the lines representing the hole or threads.

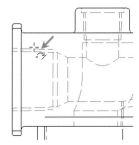

3   Select the matching representative line on the opposite side.

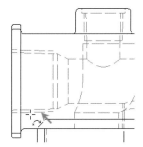

4   Position the linear thread note dimension as appropriate for the drawing view.

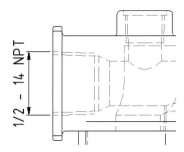

About Hole Tables

A hole table contains the hole identifier, the location of the hole relative to a specified origin, and the hole parameter information. You can export the data in a hole table to a text file or to an Excel CSV file.

When you place a hole table on your drawing, you work with three main elements:

	Item	Description
①	**Origin indicator**	Identifies the 0,0 location from which the hole locations are measured
②	**Hole tags**	Tags placed next to each hole
③	**Hole table**	Rows for data including hole tag, hole position, and size of hole

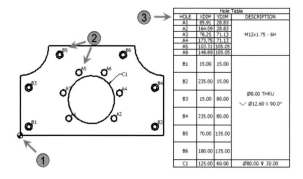

Definitions of Hole Table Features

The following definitions describe the different components involved when a hole table is added to a drawing.

Term	Definition
Hole table	A chart with rows and columns that includes the hole tag value, the hole position relative to the origin indicator, and a description of the hole.
Hole tag	A unique identifier for each hole. Hole tags are displayed in the table and with each hole on the drawing view.

Term	Definition
Origin indicator	Sets and identifies the 0,0 location in the drawing view. Hole position values are relative to this location.
Hole parameters	The characteristics, terms, and values that describe a hole textually and symbolically.

Characteristics of Hole Tables

- Hole table description values are associative to the part. If the hole changes on the part, the hole description reflects the latest value.

- When you move the origin indicator in the view, the position values in the table are automatically updated.

- The settings in the hole table style of the active standard control the initial appearance of the hole table.

- You can export hole table data to a text file or to an Excel CSV file.

Hole Table Editing Options

The following table describes the hole table editing options.

Option	Description
Edit Hole Table	Displays the Edit Hole Table dialog box, in which you can use the Formatting and Options tabs to override standard hole table styles.
Precision	Options from 0 to 8 decimals. Overrides the precision for the X or Y positional dimension.
Table	• Resort Table - Sorts the table in numeric, and then in alphabetic order of values in the Hole column. When a hole value changes, you must sort the table again. • Split Table - Splits the table into two parts, which you can move to different locations. • Export Table - Writes the data in the table out to a text file or to an Excel CSV file.

Option	Description
Row	• Add Hole - Selects and adds to the hole table a hole not previously included in the table. • Delete Hole - Removes a hole from the table and removes the hole tag from the drawing view.
Visibility	• Origin - Turns display of the origin indicator on or off. • Tag - Turns display of the hole tag on or off for the selected hole. • Hide All Tags - Turns off display of all hole tags. • Show All Tags - Turns on display of all hole tags.
Edit	• Edit Tag - Displays the Format Text dialog box in which you can edit the tag annotation for the selected item. • Edit Hole Note - Displays the Edit Hole Note dialog box, in which you can edit hole note data in the selected Description column. • Edit Description Text - Displays the Format Text dialog box, in which you can edit the selected information.

Editing the Origin Indicator

You can edit the origin indicator in the following ways:

• When the position of the origin indicator changes on the view, the X and Y dimension values in the hole table automatically change to reflect the new distance from each hole to the origin indicator.

• To specify relative offset distances for the X and Y directions, you can edit the origin indicator. This change affects only the values displayed in the table and does not change the position of the origin indicator on the view.

Editing the Hole Tags

Repositioning a hole tag generates a leader from the tag text to the hole that it references.

Display the Edit Tag, Hide Tag, Show Leader, and Hide Leader options on the shortcut menu. The Edit Tag option displays the current tag's text in the Format Text dialog box, and you can change the text as required. Use the other three options to hide the hole tag and show or hide the leader.

Example of Uses of Hole Tables

Using hole tables to document the position and parameters of holes on a part can benefit users of the final drawing. For parts that contain a large number of holes, hole tables help to create an easy-to-read and fully informative drawing. Hole tables assist in manually programming or validating parts created using a computer numeric controlled (CNC) machining process. They also help quality assurance to conduct part evaluations with a coordinate measuring machine (CMM).

Working with Hole Tables

You place hole tables in your drawing based on views, type, or manual selection of the holes. You define an Origin for the table, then place the table on the drawing sheet. At any time after placing the hole table, you can edit the format or the contents of the table.

The hole table maintains a parametric relationship with the model. Any edits to the location or type of hole in the model result in change to values in the table. You can also relocate the origin of any hole table.

In the following illustration, a hole table is used to describe the type and location of holes in the part. The use of the hole chart greatly reduces the number of dimensions required on the drawing, improving readability. This information can also be exported for CNC programming.

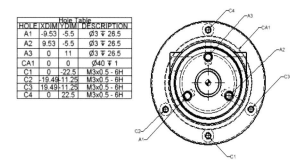

Hole Table

HOLE	XDIM	YDIM	DESCRIPTION
A1	-9.53	-5.5	Ø3 ▼ 26.5
A2	9.53	-5.5	Ø3 ▼ 26.5
A3	0	11	Ø3 ▼ 26.5
CA1	0	0	Ø40 ▼ 1
C1	0	-22.5	M3x0.5 - 6H
C2	-19.49	-11.25	M3x0.5 - 6H
C3	19.49	-11.25	M3x0.5 - 6H
C4	0	22.5	M3x0.5 - 6H

Access

Hole Table - Selection

Hole Table - View

Hole Table - Selected Feature

Ribbon: **Annotate tab › Table panel**

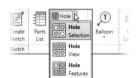

Toolbar: **Drawing Annotation Panel**

Tool	Definition
Hole Table - Selection	Creates a hole table based on the holes that you select in the view.
Hole Table - View	Creates a hole table based on all holes in the view.
Hole Table - Selected Feature	Creates a hole table based on only the holes that are identical to the hole that you select.

Preconfigured Appearance of Hole Tables

The type and layout of data displayed in a hole table depends on the settings for hole table styles. The data in the hole table's Description field is based on the configuration on the Notes and Leaders tab for the dimension style. On the Standard toolbar, you can set the hole table style active. In the Hole Table Style dialog box, you can edit the hole table style or create a new hole table style. Changing the hole table style before adding hole tables to a drawing eliminates most of the need to edit each individual hole table.

You use the Formatting tab in the Style and Standard Editor dialog box to specify the hole table title, the text style, the header position, the columns displayed, and the table line format for all hole tables created within a drawing.

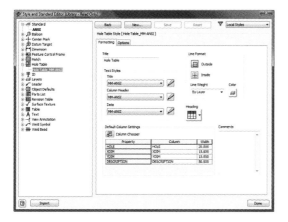

You use the Options tab in the Style and Standard Editor dialog box to control data merging, hole tag order, and the features and hole types that are automatically selected when using the Hole Table - View tool for all hole tables created within a drawing.

Methods for Editing Hole Tables

You can edit the style of an existing hole table in two ways. You use the Style and Standard Editor to edit all hole tables within the current drawing. To override the Style and Standard settings for a specific hole table, you can right-click in the hole table and click Edit Hole Table. This displays the Edit Hole Table dialog box, and depending on the type of hole table created, the same options in the Style and Standard Editor dialog box are available for editing.

To edit the text within the hole table, double-click the specific text to edit. Depending on how the table data was populated, a dialog box is displayed, enabling you to edit the text. When you double- click standard text, the Format Text dialog box is displayed, which enables you to change text or basic formatting options. When you double-click Description text, the Edit Hole Note dialog box is displayed, and you can then change specific options.

You can also switch the style of a hole table. When you select the hole table, the current style is displayed on the Standard toolbar. To change the style, you can select a different style from the list.

In the following illustration, the hole table has been selected for edit.

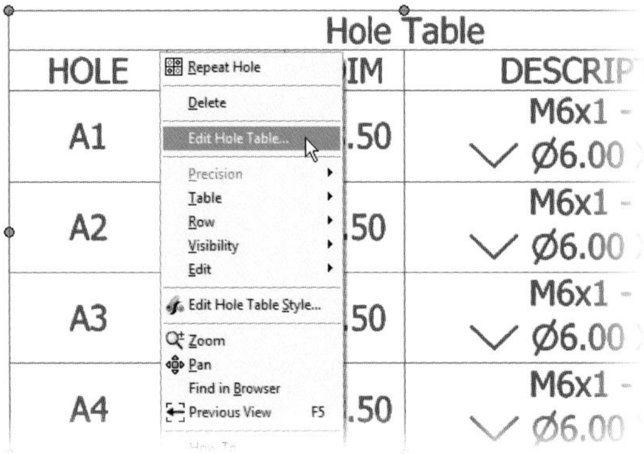

Procedure: Creating Hole Tables - Selection

The following steps describe how to create a hole table using the Hole Table - Selection tool.

1   Start the Hole Table - Selection tool. Select the view that contains the holes that you want to include in the table.

2   Move the cursor to the origin location. When the coincident constraint is displayed, click to
    position the origin indicator.

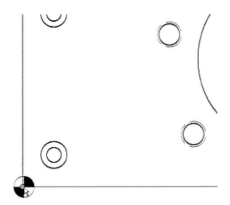

3   Select the holes to include in the table. You can select the holes individually or by dragging a
    selection window around the holes to include.

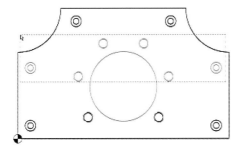

4   Right-click the selection area. Click Create.

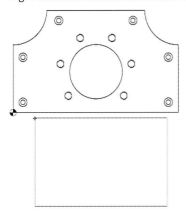

5　Position the hole table on the drawing. The hole table and hole tags are displayed on the drawing.

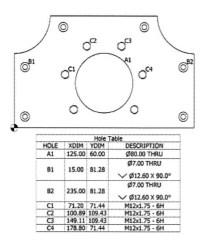

Hole Table			
HOLE	XDIM	YDIM	DESCRIPTION
A1	125.00	60.00	Ø80.00 THRU
B1	15.00	81.28	Ø7.00 THRU
			∨ Ø12.60 X 90.0°
B2	235.00	81.28	Ø7.00 THRU
			∨ Ø12.60 X 90.0°
C1	71.20	71.44	M12x1.75 - 6H
C2	100.89	109.43	M12x1.75 - 6H
C3	149.11	109.43	M12x1.75 - 6H
C4	178.80	71.44	M12x1.75 - 6H

Procedure: Creating a Hole Table with the View Method

The following steps describe how to create a hole table using the Hole Table - View tool.

1　Start the Hole Table - View tool. Select the view that contains the holes that you want to include in the table.

2　Move the cursor to the origin location. When the coincident constraint is displayed, click to position the origin indicator.

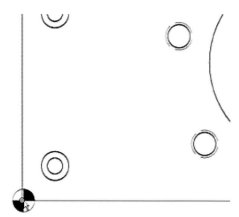

3   Position the hole table on the drawing. You do not need to select the holes because all of the holes in the view are displayed in the hole table.

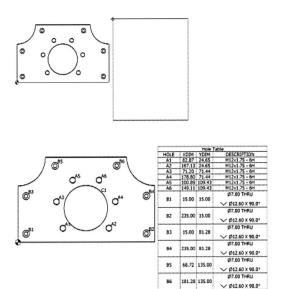

Hole Table			
HOLE	XDIM	YDIM	DESCRIPTION
A1	82.87	24.65	M12x1.75 - 6H
A2	167.13	24.65	M12x1.75 - 6H
A3	71.20	71.44	M12x1.75 - 6H
A4	178.80	71.44	M12x1.75 - 6H
A5	100.89	109.43	M12x1.75 - 6H
A6	149.11	109.43	M12x1.75 - 6H
B1	15.00	15.00	Ø7.00 THRU ∨ Ø12.60 X 90.0°
B2	235.00	15.00	Ø7.00 THRU ∨ Ø12.60 X 90.0°
B3	15.00	81.28	Ø7.00 THRU ∨ Ø12.60 X 90.0°
B4	235.00	81.28	Ø7.00 THRU ∨ Ø12.60 X 90.0°
B5	68.72	135.00	Ø7.00 THRU ∨ Ø12.60 X 90.0°
B6	181.28	135.00	Ø7.00 THRU ∨ Ø12.60 X 90.0°
C1	125.00	60.00	Ø80.00 THRU

Procedure: Creating a Hole Table with the Selected Feature Method

The following steps describe how to create a hole table using the Hole Table - Selected Feature tool.

1   Start the Hole Table - Selected Feature tool. Select the view that contains the holes that you want to include in the hole table.

2   Move the cursor to the origin location. When the coincident constraint is displayed, click to position the origin indicator.

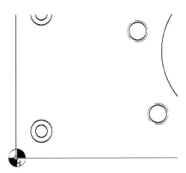

3   Select one hole of each type that you want to include in the hole table.

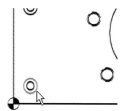

4   Right-click in the drawing. Click Create and position the hole table on the drawing. The hole table is displayed, showing only the holes of the same type as the one that you selected.

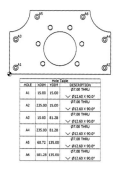

Procedure: Changing Hole Table Style Settings

The following steps describe how to change the hole table style settings of an existing hole table.

1   Right-click the hole table. Click Edit Hole Table.

2   In the Edit Hole Table dialog box, Formatting or Options tab, change the settings as needed.

Procedure: Editing Text Information in a Hole Table

The following steps describe how to edit the description of a hole in a hole table.

1   In the hole table, double-click the text string to be edited.

Hole Table			
HOLE	XDIM	YDIM	DESCR
A1	-9.53	-5.5	Ø3 ▼
A2	9.53	-5.5	Ø3 ▼
A3	0	11	Ø3 ▼

2   For standard text, in the Format Text dialog box, edit the text or formatting options available.

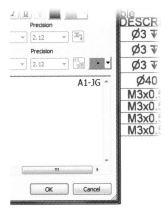

3   For description text, in the Edit Hole Note dialog box, edit the options available.

Procedure: Changing the Style of a Hole Table

The following steps describe how to change the formatting style of the hole table.

1   Click a hole table to select it.

2   Select a hole table style from the Hole Table Style list on the ribbon.

Guidelines

Use these guidelines to work successfully with hole tables.

- You set and control hole table appearance in the Style and Standard Editor dialog box.

- Changes you make to hole tables in the Style and Standard Editor dialog box are for all tables within the current drawing file.

- To override the format of a specific hole table, right-click the hole table and select Edit Hole Table.

- To reposition the origin indicator, drag to other geometry in the view. You can also right-click and select Edit, or double-click and then enter offset values relative to the current position.

- Double-click text in the hole table to change text using the Format Text or Edit Hole Note dialog boxes.

Exercise | Create and Edit Hole Notes

In this exercise, you create and edit hole notes to supply the machine shop with data for CNC programming.

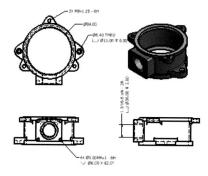

The completed exercise

Completing the Exercise: *To complete the exercise, follow the steps in this book or in the onscreen exercise. In the onscreen list of chapters and exercises, click Chapter 9: Dimensions, Annotations, and Tables. Click Exercise: Create and Edit Hole Notes.*

1   Open *Hole Notes.idw*.

2   To add a hole note:

- Zoom in on the front view.
- Click Annotate tab > Feature Notes > Hole/ Thread Notes.
- Select and place the hole note for lower right hole as shown.
- Right-click, click Done.

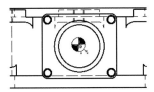

3   To access the hole note editor:

- Right-click the M6x1 - 6H hole note.
- Click Edit Hole Note.

4   To add the tap drill data at the beginning of the note, take the following actions:

- Position the cursor at the beginning of the first line.
- Under Values and Symbols, click the # icon (1).
- Click the down arrow (2) to the right of the Values and Symbols icons.
  Click Diameter.
- Click Tap Drill Diameter Value (3).
  The dialog box now appears as shown.

5 Click OK. The note is modified as shown.

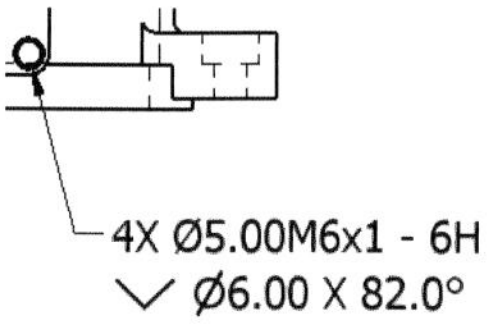

4X Ø5.00M6x1 - 6H
Ø6.00 X 82.0°

6 Add the three notes as shown in the illustration. Exit the tool after placing the third note.

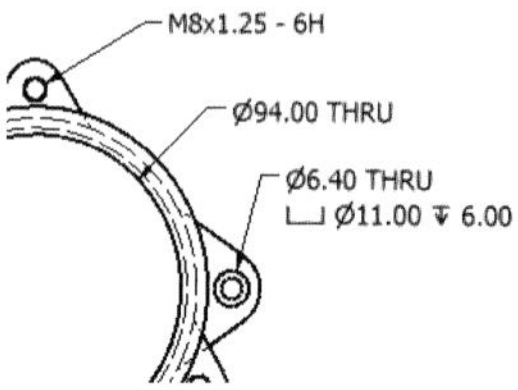

M8x1.25 - 6H
Ø94.00 THRU
Ø6.40 THRU
Ø11.00 6.00

7 Right-click the hole note at the top labeled M8x1.25 - 6H. Click Edit Hole Note.

8 In the Edit Hole Note dialog box:

- Under Options, click Edit Quantity Note.
- In the Quantity Note dialog box, select Number of Like Holes in View (Normal).
- Click OK.

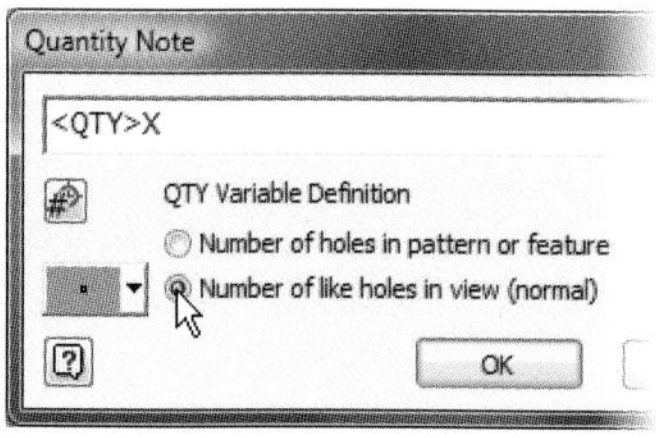

Quantity Note
<QTY>X
QTY Variable Definition
Number of holes in pattern or feature
Number of like holes in view (normal)
OK

9 Next, edit the hole note to have the quantity of like holes displayed in the note.

- Position the cursor to the left of the text in the Edit Hole Note dialog box.
- Click the # icon in the Values and Symbols category.
- Click OK.

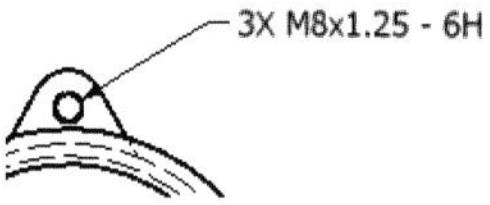

3X M8x1.25 - 6H

10   Delete text from the hole note.

- Click the hole note labeled 94 THRU.
- Right-click in the graphics window. Click Edit Hole Note.
- In the Edit Note dialog box, delete THRU. Click OK.

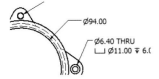

11   Zoom in on the side view.

12   To begin to add a linear hole note:

- Click Annotate tab > Feature Notes > Hole and Thread.
- Select one edge of the threaded inlet, as shown.
  Notice the leader and the hole note text.

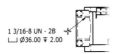

13   To complete the linear hole note:

- Click the lower edge of the threaded hole.
- Click to place the hole note.

14   Close all files. Do not save.

Exercise | Create and Edit Hole Tables

In this exercise you create and edit hole tables.

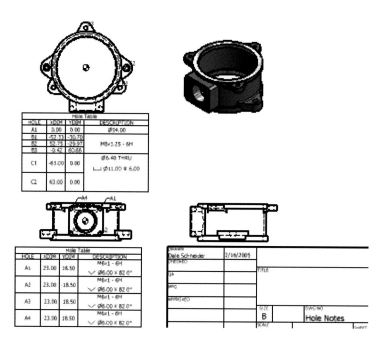

The completed exercise

Completing the Exercise: *To complete the exercise, follow the steps in this book or in the onscreen exercise. In the onscreen list of chapters and exercises, click Chapter 9: Dimensions, Annotations, and Tables. Click Exercise: Create and Edit Hole Tables.*

1   Open *Hole Tables.idw.*

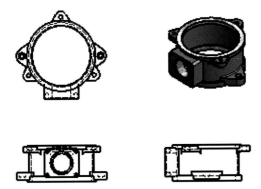

2   Zoom in on the front view.

3   Place the origin locator.
     - Click Annotate tab > Table panel > Hole Selection.
     - Select inside the front view.
     - Hover your cursor over one of the larger circles to acquire it.
     - Move the cursor to their approximate centers.
     - When a coincident constraint glyph is displayed, click to place the origin indicator.

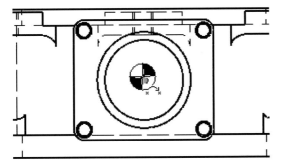

4   Create the hole table.

- When prompted to select an edge, select the four smaller holes.
- Right-click the holes. Click Create.
- When prompted to click in a location, position the hole table below the front view.

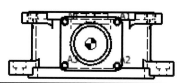

Hole Table			
HOLE	XDIM	YDIM	DESCRIPTION
A1	23.00	18.50	M6x1 - 6H ∨ Ø6.00 X 82.0°
A2	23.00	-18.50	M6x1 - 6H ∨ Ø6.00 X 82.0°
A3	-23.00	-18.50	M6x1 - 6H ∨ Ø6.00 X 82.0°
A4	-23.00	18.50	M6x1 - 6H ∨ Ø6.00 X 82.0°

5   Relocate the hole tags.

- Move the cursor over the top left hole tag.
- When the green grip appears, click and drag the hole tag above the view.
- Repeat for the top right hole tag.

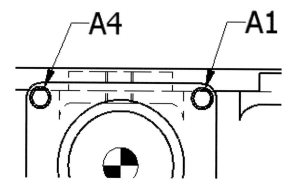

6   Place a hole table on the top view.

- Pan to the top view.
- Click Annotate tab > Table panel > Hole Table - Selection flyout > Hole Table - View.
- Select the top view.
- Place the origin indicator at the center of the large circle.
- Place the hole table in the drawing.

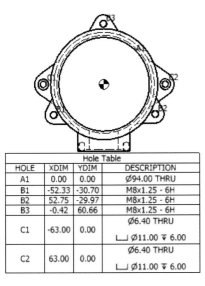

Hole Table			
HOLE	XDIM	YDIM	DESCRIPTION
A1	0.00	0.00	Ø94.00 THRU
B1	-52.33	-30.70	M8x1.25 - 6H
B2	52.75	-29.97	M8x1.25 - 6H
B3	-0.42	60.66	M8x1.25 - 6H
C1	-63.00	0.00	Ø6.40 THRU ⌴ Ø11.00 ▼ 6.00
C2	63.00	0.00	Ø6.40 THRU ⌴ Ø11.00 ▼ 6.00

7   Delete the B1 tag.

- Move the cursor over the B1 tag.
- With the tag highlighted, right-click. Click Delete.

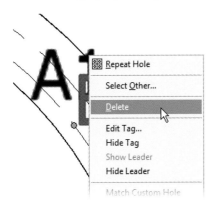

8   With the tag deleted, review the hole note table.

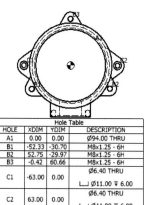

Hole Table			
HOLE	XDIM	YDIM	DESCRIPTION
A1	0.00	0.00	Ø94.00 THRU
B1	-52.33	-30.70	M8x1.25 - 6H
B2	52.75	-29.97	M8x1.25 - 6H
B3	-0.42	60.66	M8x1.25 - 6H
C1	-63.00	0.00	Ø6.40 THRU ⌴ Ø11.00 ▼ 6.00
C2	63.00	0.00	Ø6.40 THRU ⌴ Ø11.00 ▼ 6.00

9   Edit the hole note table.

- Double-click the text in the Description column for hole A1, 94.00 THRU.
- In the Edit Hole Note dialog box, delete THRU.
- Click OK.

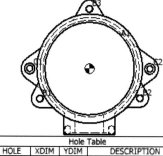

Hole Table			
HOLE	XDIM	YDIM	DESCRIPTION
A1	0.00	0.00	Ø94.00
B1	-52.33	-30.70	M8x1.25 - 6H
B2	52.75	-29.97	M8x1.25 - 6H
B3	-0.42	60.66	M8x1.25 - 6H
C1	-63.00	0.00	Ø6.40 THRU ⌴ Ø11.00 ▼ 6.00
C2	63.00	0.00	Ø6.40 THRU ⌴ Ø11.00 ▼ 6.00

10 Merge common data in the hole table.

- Right-click the hole table.
- Click Edit Hole Table.
- In the Edit Hole Table: View Type dialog box, on the Options tab, click Combine Notes.

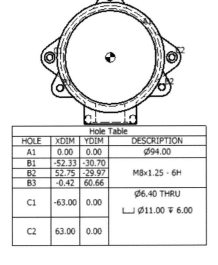

Edit Hole Table: Selection Type

| Formatting | Options |

Row Merge Options

○ None
   ☑ Reformat Table on Custom Hole Match
   ☐ Numbering

○ Rollup
   ☐ Delete Tags on Rollup
   ☐ Secondary Tag Modifier on Rollup

◉ Combine Notes
   ☑ Reformat Table on Custom Hole Match
   ☐ Numbering

Hole Tag Options
☑ Preserve Tagging

Tag Order
○ Arrange by Position

11 Click OK.

Hole Table			
HOLE	XDIM	YDIM	DESCRIPTION
A1	0.00	0.00	Ø94.00
B1	-52.33	-30.70	M8x1.25 - 6H
B2	52.75	-29.97	
B3	-0.42	60.66	
C1	-63.00	0.00	Ø6.40 THRU ⌴ Ø11.00 ▼ 6.00
C2	63.00	0.00	

12 Close all files. Do not save.

Lesson 35 | Creating Centerlines, Symbols, and Leaders

This lesson describes how to add centerlines, center marks, symbols, and leaders to your drawings. These tools help define features and conditions on production-ready drawings relating to the manufacturing process.

The use of centerlines and center marks is critical in the interpretation of symmetrical and cylindrical features in drawings. Symbols aid in defining the manufacturing processes used in creating parts and assemblies. Leaders provide information about the text, symbol, or dimension attached to specific areas on a feature or object.

In the following illustration, centerlines and center marks define symmetrical features.

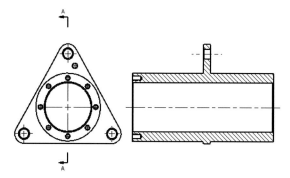

Objectives

After completing this lesson, you will be able to:

- Identify areas in which to use centerlines and center marks.

- Create centerlines and center marks.

- Describe symbols.

- Apply symbols to drawing views.

- Describe leaders and text.

- Add leaders and leaders with text to drawings.

- Edit leaders, text associated with leaders, and standard text.

About Centerlines and Center Marks

Centerlines and center marks are added to a drawing to define axes of symmetrical objects or features. Typically, they provide a visual reference to features that may not appear symmetrical in the view. Centerlines and center marks also aid in placing dimensions in drawings.

In the following illustration, the center of a locator hole uses a center mark for dimensioning.

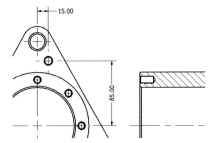

Definition of Centerlines and Center Marks

Centerlines define axes of symmetrical objects or features in a drawing. Center marks define the center point of an arc or circle.

In the following illustration, a centerline defines the cylinder as a symmetrical feature even though the overall part is not symmetrical.

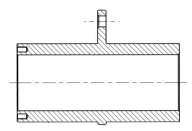

Example of Centerlines and Center Marks

A typical production-ready drawing contains a number of displayed objects. At times it can be difficult to determine the true nature of the geometry when looking at a cylindrical or other symmetrical feature in a side view. A centerline between two lines indicates a symmetrical feature or object.

Dimensions to arcs or circles can be misinterpreted due to the gap between the definition point and the extension line of the dimension. Center marks can locate a dimension to the center of the arc or circle.

In the following illustration, the centerline indicates that the part is symmetrical. The center marks indicate a radial transition between two flat faces that may not be apparent when viewing the geometry.

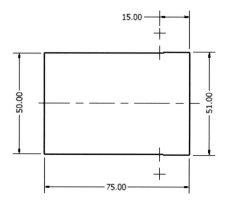

Creating Centerlines and Center Marks

You add centerlines and center marks to drawings to define symmetrical features and to simplify dimensioning. Several tools are available to annotate your drawing with centerlines and center marks. You can place these annotations manually, or place them automatically using the Automated Centerline tool.

In the following illustration, centerlines were automatically placed on each cylindrical feature in the view.

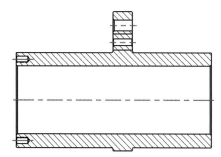

Access

Centerline

Ribbon: **Annotate tab > Symbols panel**

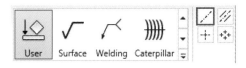

Toolbar: **Drawing Annotation Panel**

Access

Center Mark

Ribbon: **Annotate tab > Symbols panel**

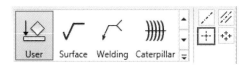

Toolbar: **Drawing Annotation Panel**

Access

Centerline Bisector

Ribbon: **Annotate tab > Symbols panel**

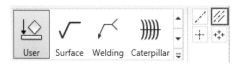

Toolbar: **Drawing Annotation Panel**

Access

Centered Pattern

Ribbon: **Annotate tab > Symbols panel**

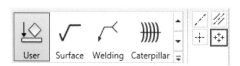

Toolbar: **Drawing Annotation Panel**

Procedure: Adding Centerlines Manually

The following steps describe how to manually add centerlines to drawings.

1   Start the Centerline tool. In the graphics window, click to place the start point of the centerline.

2   Click to place the end point of the centerline.

3   Right-click on the centerline and click Create.

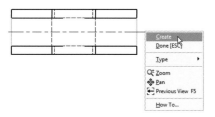

4   Right-click in the graphics window. Click Done.

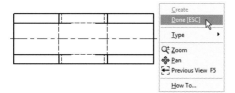

Procedure: Manually Adding Center Marks

The following steps describe how to manually add center marks.

1   Start the Center Mark tool.

2   Move the cursor to an arc or circle. When the coincident constraint glyph is displayed, click the arc or circle.

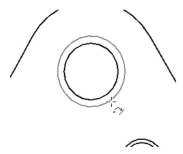

3   The center mark is added to the hole.

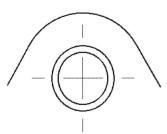

Procedure: Adding Automated Centerlines

The following steps describe how to add automated centerlines to a view.

1   Determine the view to which to add centerlines.

2   Right-click in the view. Click Automated Centerlines.

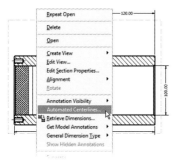

3   Select the desired options in the Automated Centerlines dialog box.

4   The centerlines are added to the view.

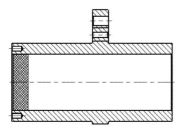

Procedure: Using the Centerline Bisector Tool

The following steps describe how to add centerlines to your drawing views with the Centerline Bisector tool.

1   Start the Centerline Bisector tool and select the first edge to bisect.

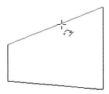

2   Select the second edge.

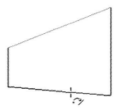

3   The centerline is calculated and drawn by bisecting the angle of the two edges selected.

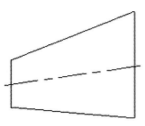

Procedure: Using the Centered Pattern Tool

The following steps describe how to place centerlines on your drawing view with the Centered Pattern tool.

1   Start the Centered Pattern tool.

2 Click the location representing the center of the pattern.

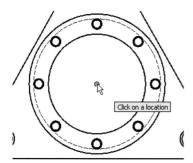

3 Select the features of the pattern in a sequential order around the center. The centerline is displayed when you have selected the second feature.

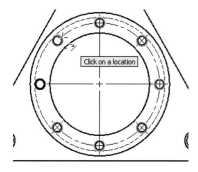

4 Continue selecting features as required. To make a full circle, select the first feature a second time, then create the pattern.

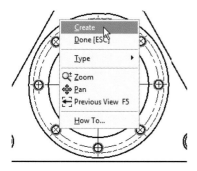

About Symbols

Symbols in drawings define a specific condition about the feature or object they are attached to. Applying symbols to features is critical in determining the proper manufacturing processes.

In the following illustration, symbols are placed in different areas in the drawing to convey critical manufacturing and inspection requirements.

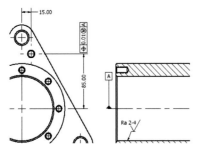

Definition of Drawing Symbols

Symbols are graphical images that are used to convey critical information about features or objects. A graphical image minimizes the amount of text required on a drawing and is often more universally understood than text. Symbols are important in the manufacturing and inspection processes of objects.

Example of Symbols

Symbols are used in numerous places in production-ready drawings. Surface texture symbols are used to define the smoothness of a surface. Feature control frames are used to define the location of features. Symbols can indicate where a hole could be drilled, reamed, or jig ground to perform the intended function.

In the following illustration, a surface texture symbol is placed on the inside wall of a cylinder.

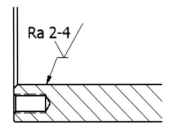

Documenting Views with Symbols

Symbols are key elements in the creation of production-ready drawings. Once you have determined the symbol needed to define the drawing, you select the tool and apply the symbol. There are many different symbol tools, but they typically follow a similar procedure.

In the following illustration, symbols are used throughout the view to define the part.

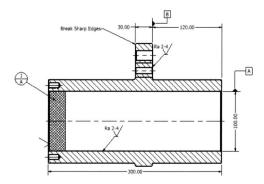

Access

Surface Texture

Ribbon: **Annotate tab > Symbols panel**

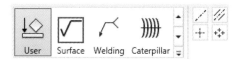

Toolbar: **Drawing Annotation Panel**

Access

Feature Control Frame

Ribbon: **Annotate tab > Symbols panel**

Toolbar: **Drawing Annotation Panel**

Access

Datum Identifier

Ribbon: **Annotate tab > Symbols panel**

Toolbar: **Drawing Annotation Panel**

Access

Datum Target

Ribbon: **Annotate tab > Symbols panel**

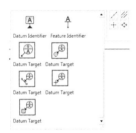

Toolbar: **Drawing Annotation Panel**

Procedure: Documenting Views with Surface Texture Symbols

The following steps describe how to document a view with a surface texture symbol.

1 Start the Surface Texture Symbol tool.

2 Select a location for the leader.

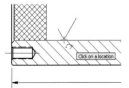

3   Locate the surface texture symbol.

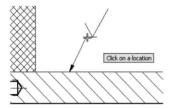

4   Select another vertex location or continue.

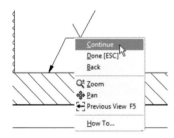

5   In the Surface Texture dialog box, enter the required data.

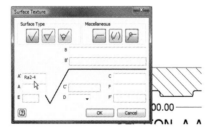

6   The surface texture symbol and data are added to the view.

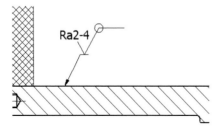

Procedure: Documenting Views with a Feature Control Frame

The following steps describe how to document a view with a feature control frame.

1   Start the Feature Control Frame tool.

2   Select a location for the endpoint of a leader or the Feature Control Frame.

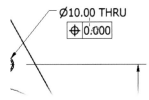

3   Select another vertex location or Continue.

4   In the Feature Control Frame dialog box, enter the required data.

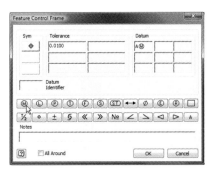

Procedure: Documenting Views with Datum Identifier Symbols

The following steps describe how to document a view with a datum identifier symbol.

1   Start the Datum Identifier Symbol tool.

2   Select a location for the leader.

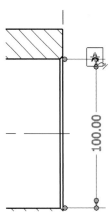

3   Locate the datum identifier symbol.

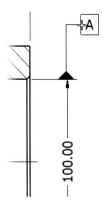

4   Right-click, click Continue.

5   In the Format Text dialog box, enter the required data.

Procedure: Documenting Views with Datum Target-Leader Symbols

The following steps describe how to document a view with datum target-leader symbols.

1   Start the Datum Target-Leader tool.

2   Select a location for the leader.

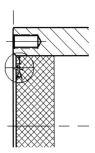

3   Locate the Datum Target-Leader symbol.

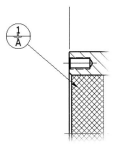

4   Select another vertex location or Continue.

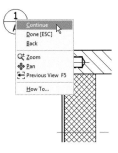

5   In the Datum Target dialog box, enter the required data.

About Leaders and Text

Text is placed on drawings in many different areas to present information that cannot be represented by other annotation methods. Leaders, used in conjunction with text or other annotation symbols, focus the attention of the annotation on a specified feature, object, or area.

In the following illustration, leaders are combined with other annotations such as dimensions, hole notes, and revision tags. Combining leaders with these annotations moves the text or symbols away from the drawing geometry, providing a clearer view of the drawing geometry.

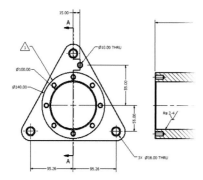

Definition of Leaders and Text

Leaders are pointers or indicators linking annotation such as text or other symbols to a specific feature, object, or location on a drawing. Text is words used to describe specific information on a drawing. Dimensions, revision blocks, title blocks, and labels are just a few of the areas on a drawing where text is located.

In the following illustration, leaders and text are combined to specify surface finish and datum features.

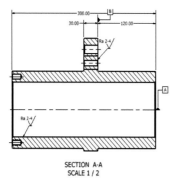

Example of Leaders and Text

In the following illustration, a production-ready drawing has text and leaders. Leaders define dimension locations and revisions. Text is used in the dimensions, title and revision blocks, and symbols.

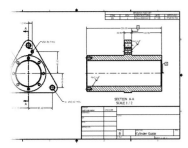

Adding Leaders and Text

You use a leader with text to define a certain condition or specification that cannot be defined with a standard symbol. Leaders are associative to the feature that they are attached to. If that feature changes location, the leader will change location also. If the feature is deleted, the leader will be deleted from the view.

In the following illustration, a leader with text is added to inform the manufacturer to break all sharp edges at this particular corner of the part. Adding a radius dimension to this area would add manufacturing and inspection costs to the part.

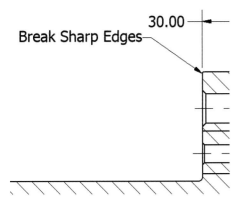

Access

Text

Ribbon: **Annotate tab › Text panel**

Toolbar: **Drawing Annotation Panel**
Keyboard: **T**

Access

Leader Text

Ribbon: **Annotate tab › Text panel**

Toolbar: **Drawing Annotation Panel**
Keyboard: **Ctrl+Shift+T**

Notes and Leaders

You use the Text and Leader Text tools to add notes and leaders to drawing views. When you use the Text tool to place paragraph-style text on the sheet, the Leader Text tool attaches a leader with text to the geometry within the view.

The following illustration shows the Format Text dialog box, which you use to add text to your drawings.

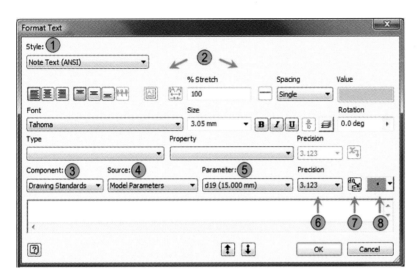

	Option	Description
①	**Style**	Select a text style for the text or accept the default text style listed.
②	**Text Formatting**	Adjust the text formatting options such as justification, text size, color, and width as required.
③	**Component** (Optional)	Select the component to be used for parameters.
④	**Source** (Optional)	Select Model Parameters or User Parameters.
⑤	**Parameter** (Optional)	Select the parameter to use in the text.
⑥	**Precision** (Optional)	Enter a precision for the parameter value.
⑦	**do Button** (Optional)	Click to add the selected parameter to the text window.
⑧	**Symbols Flyout**	Select a special symbol to insert into the text.

Procedure: Adding Text to a Drawing

The following steps describe how to add text to a drawing.

1   Start the Text tool. Define the text boundary.

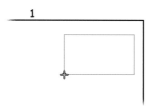

2   In the Format Text dialog box, enter the text, and select options.

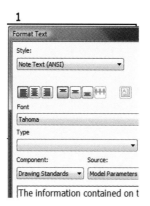

3   The text is displayed in the drawing.

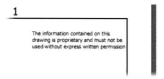

Procedure: Adding Leader Text to a Drawing

The following steps describe how to add leader text to your drawing.

1. Start the Leader Text tool. Select a start point and a second point for the leader.

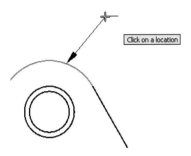

2. Right-click in the graphics window. Click Continue on the shortcut menu.

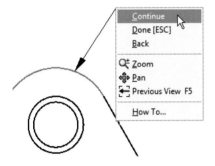

3. Enter the text for the leader.

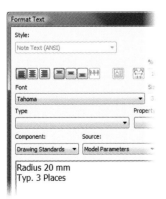

4　The leader text is attached to the drawing geometry.

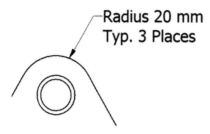

Editing Leaders and Text

Editing leader text in drawings is similar to editing standard text. You edit text in the Format Text dialog box, where you can also change fonts and formatting. The menu for editing leaders contains applications for leaders such as units, arrowheads, and adding a vertex.

The following illustration shows the menu for editing standard text in a drawing (on the left) and for editing leader text (on the right).

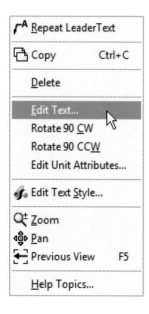

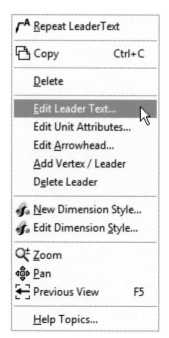

Procedure: Editing Text

The following steps describe how to edit text.

1   Right-click the text to be edited. Click Edit Text.

2   In the Format Text dialog box, enter the new text or edit the formatting of the existing text.

Procedure: Editing Leaders with Text

The following steps show you how to edit leaders with text.

1   Move the cursor to the leader text to be edited.

2   Right-click and click Edit Leader Text.

3   In the Format Text dialog box, enter the new text or edit the formatting of the existing text.

Exercise | Add Centerlines, Center Marks, and Symbols

In this exercise, you annotate a drawing of a cylinder rod guide with centerlines, center marks, and symbols.

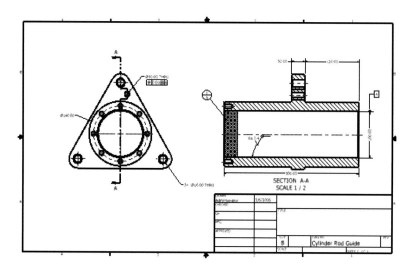

The completed exercise

Completing the Exercise: To complete the exercise, follow the steps in this book or in the onscreen exercise. In the onscreen list of chapters and exercises, click Chapter 9: Dimensions, Annotations, and Tables. Click Exercise: Add Centerlines, Center Marks, and Symbols.

1 Open Cylinder *Rod Guide.idw.*

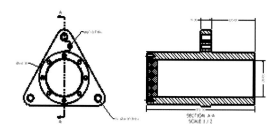

2   Add centerlines to the section view.

- Click Annotate tab > Symbols panel > Centerline Bisector.
- In the section view, select the outer symmetrical lines for the cylinder.
- Select the symmetrical lines defining the bolt and guide pin holes.
- Right-click and click Done.

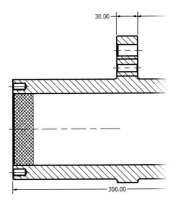

3   Adjust the centerline length.

- Move the cursor to the end of the centerline.
- Select the grip and drag past the end of the part.

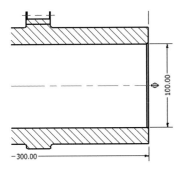

4   Add center marks to the bolt holes and guide pin hole.

- Pan to the view on the left.
- Click Annotate tab > Symbols panel > Center Mark.
- Select the three bolt holes and the guide pin hole.
- Right-click. Click Done.

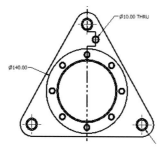

5   Add a centered pattern of center marks to the front view.

- Click Annotate tab > Symbols panel > Centered Pattern.
- Select the cylinder opening to define the center.
- Select the eight mounting holes in order.
- Select the first hole a second time to complete the pattern.
- Right-click. Click Create. Right-click. Click Done.

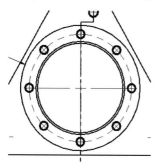

6   Locate and define a surface texture symbol on the inner diameter of the cylinder.

- Click Annotate tab > Symbols panel > Surface Texture.
- In the section view, click the inner diameter of the cylinder.
- Click a location up and away from the first point. Right-click and click Continue.

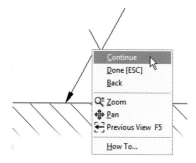

7   Define the Surface Texture symbol.

- In the Surface Texture dialog box, under Miscellaneous, click All-around.
- In the A' field, enter **Ra 2-4**.
- Click OK.
- Right-click in the graphics window, click Done.

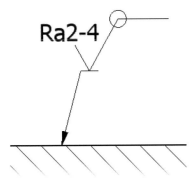

8   Add a Datum Identifier symbol.

- Click Annotate tab > Symbols panel > Datum Identifier. (Expand the available options).
- Click the arrow point on the 100mm dimension.
- Click a point above the first point.
- Right-click and click Continue.

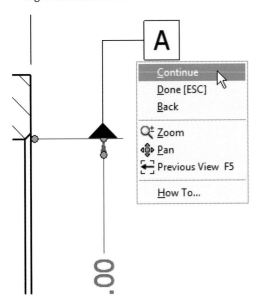

9   In the Format Text dialog box, click OK. Right- click in the graphics window and click Done.

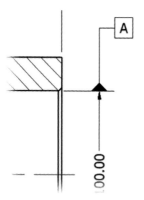

10 Add a feature control frame.

- Click Annotate tab > Symbols panel > Feature Control Frame.
- Click a point below the 10.00 THRU dimension. Right-click and click Continue.
- In the Feature Control Frame dialog box, enter the following data as illustrated.

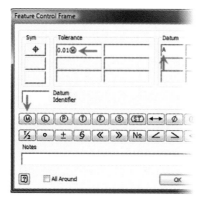

11 In the Feature Control Frame dialog box, click OK. Right-click in the graphics window and click Done.

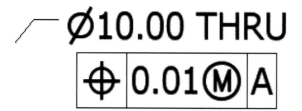

12   Add a datum target-leader to indicate an area for inspection.

- Click Annotate tab > Symbols panel > Datum Target-Leader.
- In the section view, click in the cross- hatched area.
- Click a point up and away from the hatch. Right-click, click Continue.

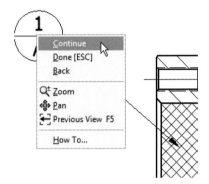

13   In the Datum Target dialog box, click OK. Right- click in the graphics window and click Done.

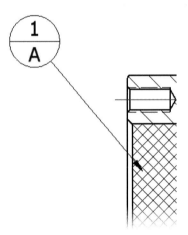

14   Close all files. Do not save.

Lesson 36 | Revision Tables and Tags

This lesson describes the configuration of revision tables and tags, how to add them to a drawing, and how to edit them after they are in a drawing.

Using revision tables and revision tags, and being able to add and edit them, you can record current changes made to a drawing, and review past changes and where those changes occurred.

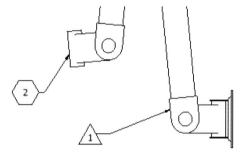

Objectives

After completing this lesson, you will be able to:

- Explain the purpose of revision tables and tags on a drawing.

- Describe the overall process of working with revision tables and tags.

- State where the settings for revision tables and revision tags are preconfigured and what settings can be preconfigured.

- Describe the process and options for adding a revision table to a drawing sheet.

- Explain the types of edits that can be made on an existing revision table in a drawing.

- Add and edit revision tags.

About Revision Tables and Tags

Before learning how to add and edit revision tables, you should first be able to explain the function of revision tables and tags in a drawing.

The following illustration shows a typical revision table.

ZONE	REV	DESCRIPTION	DATE	APPROVED
B3	1	Changed Diameter	2/26/2006	Administrator
B4	2	Added Holes	2/27/2006	Administrator

REVISION HISTORY

4

The following illustration shows revision tags attached to features in a drawing.

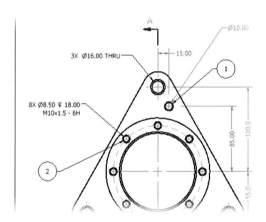

Definition of Revision Tables and Tags

You add revision tables and tags to a drawing to document and identify changes made on the drawing sheet or within model views on the sheet. The revision table becomes a historical record that helps you track changes through the life of a design. Some of the common information tracked in a revision table includes the revision number or letter, a brief description of the change, when the change occurred, who made the change, and where on the drawing sheet the change was made. A revision tag identifies the feature in the drawing that has been changed. It is a callout inserted at the location of the change and includes the revision number or letter that is listed for that change in the revision table.

Depending on a company's standards and revision documentation requirements, revision tables may track the changes for multiple drawing sheets within a single design, or they may track only changes to a single drawing sheet.

Example of Revision Tables and Tags

When a change is necessary in a production-ready drawing, the change is tracked using revisions. Revision tables are placed on drawings to track the changes and centralize the information.

In the following illustration, a drawing is revised and the changes are recorded in the revision table and identified with revision tags.

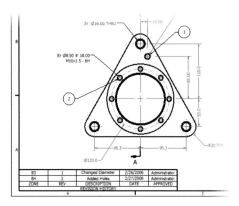

Process of Working with Revision Tables and Tags

Before learning about the individual steps and aspects of any process, you should understand the steps involved in the total process. Thus before learning how to add and edit revision tables and tags, you first learn about the overall process of working with revision tables and tags.

Process: Working with Revision Tables and Tags

The following steps give an overview of working with revision tables and tags in a drawing.

1   Configure the style settings for the revision table and revision tags.

2   Add a revision table to at least one drawing sheet.

3   Add a revision tag identifying the location of the revision.

4   If required, edit table properties, rotation, or values of the revision table.

5   Add a row to the revision table when a revision occurs.

6   Repeat adding tags, editing values, and adding rows as design changes occur.

Guidelines for Revision Table Styles

For consistency between drawings and for efficient use of your time, you should make and save the style configuration for revision tables and tags in the template file or Styles Library. This way, the first step of configuring the style only occurs once. After the style is configured and available in the template or Styles Library, you need to ensure only that the proper revision table style is active before adding a revision table or tags into the drawing.

Revision Table Styles

If your drafting standards or drawing documentation requirements dictate different information or appearances from the default revision table style, you must know where and what settings can be preconfigured to ensure compliance and efficiency.

In the following illustration, two different revision table configurations are shown. The upper table consists of the default settings, while the lower table has settings custom to a company's unique documentation requirements.

REVISION HISTORY				
ZONE	REV	DESCRIPTION	DATE	APPROVED
B3	1	CHANGED DIA.	1/25/2007	Administrator

1	07-10073	DRS	1/25/2007
REV	ECO	REV BY	DATE
REVISION			

Access Style for Configuration

To configure the initial settings for a revision table or to create and configure multiple revision table styles, you first access the Style and Standard Editor dialog box and then the Revision Table element. To access the editor, on the ribbon, Manage tab, click Styles Editor. As for the other elements in the standard, you can modify existing styles or create new ones. If you want to save the style setting changes to the Style Library instead of only saving them in the current drawing, the Use Styles Library option in the active project file must be set to Yes.

If you need to use a revision table from a different standard, or the active standard has more than one Revision Table style to select from, along with configuring the style, you must select the appropriate object style for the object type. You set this in the Object Defaults style element for the active standard. In the following illustration, the Company ABC object style is being selected for the Revision Table object type.

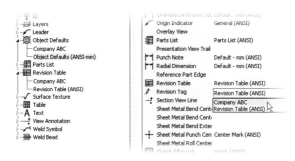

Options for Revision Tables

After you select a style under the Revision Table element, the settings for the style appear on the right section of the Style and Standard Editor dialog box. The initially active tab is the Revision Tables tab. On the Revision Tables tab you have the following options:

- Turn on or off the title for the table, or enter a new title.

- Set the display of the horizontal and vertical lines of the table.

- Individually set which text styles to use for the title, column header, and data.

- Enter row and header gap and the spacing for each line of data.

- Set the display of the column headings.

- Select which direction the rows are added to the table.

- Choose which iProperty or custom property to include as a column in the table, its column title, and default column width.

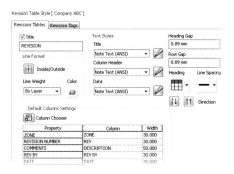

Options for Revision Tags

For revision tags, you select which leaders and text styles to use and the shape that should be drawn around the revision number or letter. The four shapes you can select are circle, hexagon, triangle, and square.

You can choose to have the leader line for the revision tag display with or without a horizontal shoulder. The image on the left shows an example of a revision tag's leader line when the option is selected, and the image on the right shows the same revision tag leader line with the option deselected.

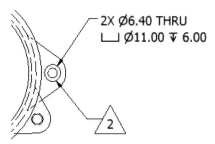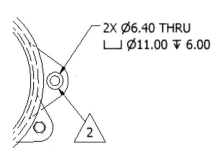

Adding a Revision Table

Depending on your documentation procedures and standards, revision tables you add to the drawing may reflect the revision information for the entire drawing file or just the revisions of that sheet. To insert revision tables that adhere to your requirements, you need to understand the process and options for adding a revision table to a drawing sheet.

Revision Table Options

You use the Revision Table tool to add a new revision table to the active drawing sheet. As part of the process of adding the revision table, you have the option of setting the table to display the revision information for the entire drawing or for the active sheet.

If you select to add a revision table that is based on the revisions for the entire drawing and one does not already exist, you also have the option to set revision indexing to occur automatically, along with its associated property. If a table for the entire drawing already exists on one of the sheets in the drawing, the revision table takes on the properties assigned to the existing table. When you add revision tables to different sheets and the revision table's information applies to the entire drawing, those revision tables display the same information.

 By selecting to insert a revision table for the active sheet, the table indexing and contents are unique from all other tables in the drawing file. If a revision table already exists on the active drawing sheet and it was created uniquely for that sheet, the new table becomes an exact duplicate of the original revision table.

Access

Revision Table

Ribbon: **Annotate tab > Table panel**

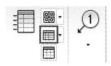

Toolbar: **Drawing Annotation Panel**

Revision Table Dialog Box

After you execute the Revision Table tool, the Revision Table dialog box is displayed, enabling you to select the settings appropriate for the revision table that you are adding to the active drawing sheet.

① Set the new table to apply to the entire drawing file or to be unique for the active drawing sheet.

② Specify whether the revision value should be automatically incremented, if it should be a letter or number, and which value to start with.

③ Select if you want the revision value in the active table row to update the drawing file's Revision iProperty value or the sheet's Revision property value. If not selected, revision index value changes in the active table row do not update the values in the property fields.

Process: Adding a Revision Table

The following steps give an overview of adding a revision table to a drawing sheet.

1   Start the Revision Table tool and ensure that the required revision table style is active.

2   Select the scope for the revision table to be either for the entire drawing or for the active sheet.

3   Specify the revision indexing options and properties.

4   Set the update relationship between the active row value and the revision value for the drawing's iProperty or the sheet's property.

5   Position the table on the drawing sheet.

About Editing Revision Tables

The types of edits that you are required to make on an existing revision table can vary from drawing to drawing and sheet to sheet. You may need to add a row to a revision table, edit a displayed value, change the size of a column, or rotate the entire revision table. By knowing the types of edits that can be made on an existing revision table and how or where to make those changes, you can achieve the revision table edits that you require.

In the following illustration, the default values for a newly inserted revision table are shown above that table after adding rows and changing values.

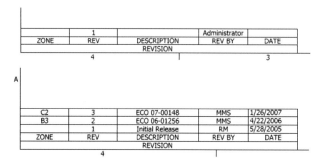

Resizing Tables

While the settings in the Revision Table style control the initial row and column size, you can change the width and height of columns and rows by clicking and dragging the vertical and horizontal lines in the table. The size of the table can also be adjusted by clicking and dragging the grip points at the outer edges of the table.

In the following illustration, in the upper revision table, the column width for the Description column is being adjusted. The lower table shows the results of this column width adjustment.

Rotating a Table

When you insert any type of table into a drawing sheet, the table is inserted so that the rows go horizontally across the sheet. For revision tables, parts lists, and general notation tables, you can rotate the table in 90 degree increments either clockwise (cw) or counterclockwise (ccw).

To rotate an inserted table, you right-click the table in the drawing and then click Rotate > Rotate 90 CW or Rotate 90 CCW.

In the following illustration, a revision table is shown in the default horizontal position and then again after being rotated 90 degrees counterclockwise.

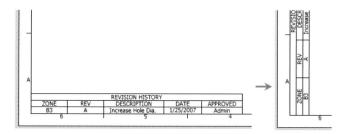

Properties to Values

As part of the configuration of a revision table style, you select which columns of information to display. If an iProperty is selected as a column, the active revision table row receives its information from that iProperty. By changing the iProperty value, the active revision row value also changes.

Because the application programming interface (API) for revision tables and iProperties is available, external applications like Autodesk® Productstream® can automatically update revision data and edit revision tables.

The following table lists the columns that are in the default revision table style, and which property you edit if a column's value can be driven by a property.

Column Name	iProperties Tab	Field on the Tab
ZONE	Not Applicable (NA)	NA
REV	Project	Revision Number
DESCRIPTION	Summary	Comments

Column Name	iProperties Tab	Field on the Tab
DATE	Project	Creation Date
APPROVED	Status	Eng. Approved By

Where you edit the number or letter of the revision depends on the scope of the revision table. You change a revision table with a scope of the entire drawing by editing the iProperty field Revision Number located on the Project tab.

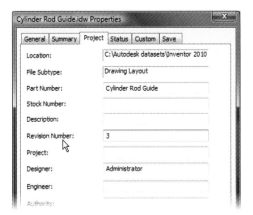

For revision tables with the scope of the active sheet, you edit the Revision value in the Edit Sheet dialog box. You open the Edit Sheet dialog box by right-clicking the sheet name in the browser and clicking Edit Sheet.

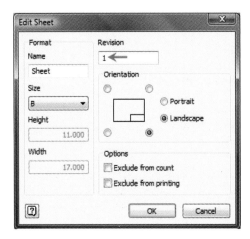

Edit Revision Table Dialog Box

Along with editing the contents of a revision table by changing the iProperties of the drawing, you can also edit the revision table by selecting a different style table, adding or removing rows, entering a static value for a cell, adding or removing columns, overriding the style's table layout settings, and splitting the table at specific rows into multiple sections.

The majority of these edits take place or are initiated in the Edit Revision Table dialog box. You open this dialog box by either double-clicking the revision table in the drawing window or the browser, or right-clicking the revision table in the drawing window or browser and then clicking Edit. On the title bar after the title of the dialog box, the text indicates the scope of the revision table as being for the entire drawing or for the active sheet.

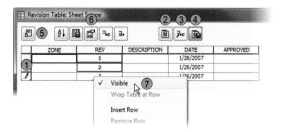

① The current revision row is indicated with the edit pencil icon. Changes to the iProperty values affect the associated values in this row.

② Use to access the iProperties dialog box to change the properties without having to first exit the Edit Revision Table dialog box.

③ Add a new revision row to the table.

④ Toggles on and off the setting to update the revision iProperty or sheet property value when the Rev value in the current revision row is edited.

⑤ Use to access the Revision Table Column Chooser dialog box to add, remove, or reorder the columns in the revision table.

⑥ Use these options to sort, export, add empty rows, remove a selected row, or override the style's table layout settings.

⑦ Right-click a cell to access the options to toggle the row's visibility, wrap the table at that row, set a cell to a static value or reset a cell to use the property value instead of a static value, or insert and remove rows. Cells that have static values appear in bold blue text with a blue rectangle around the cell. The values in the Zone column are static values.

Adding and Editing Revision Tags

After adding a revision table to the drawing, you typically want to identify on the drawing where the revision occurred. You make this callout by adding revision tags to the drawing that include the corresponding revision value. To add and edit revision tags to your drawings, so they meet your documentation requirements, you need to know how to add revision tags to a drawing and edit them to reference a different revision or use a different shape.

When you add a revision tag to a drawing, you can add it with or without a leader line. During the creation, the clicks and pick are the same as any other type of symbol, including surface texture symbols, feature control frames, and datum identifiers, among others.

In the following illustration, a revision tag has been placed on a drawing to locate the change defined in the revision table.

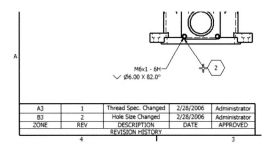

Access

Revision Tag

Ribbon: **Annotate tab › Table panel**

Toolbar: **Drawing Annotation Panel**

Assign Tag Revision

When you add a revision tag to a drawing, its value is initially set to the current revision value. If you want the revision tag to refer to a different revision after it has been added to the drawing, right-click it. Then click Tag and the required revision value.

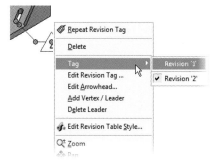

Edit Revision Tag

If you want a specific revision tag to appear in a different shape, you override the current style for the revision tag. You override the shape by selecting a different shape in the Edit Revision Tag dialog box. To access this dialog box, in the drawing window either double-click the revision tag, or right-click it and then click Edit Revision Tag.

Within this dialog box, you can also change the revision value. When you change it in the Edit Revision Tag dialog box, the revision table automatically updates to reflect this change.

Exercise | Configure, Add, and Edit Revision Tables and Tags

In this exercise, you configure a revision table style, add multiple revision tables to different drawing sheets with different scopes, edit the revision tables, add revision tags, and edit the revision tags.

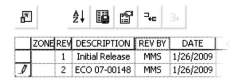

	ZONE	REV	DESCRIPTION	REV BY	DATE
		1	Initial Release	MMS	1/26/2009
		2	ECO 07-00148	MMS	1/26/2009

The completed exercise

Completing the Exercise: *To complete the exercise, follow the steps in this book or in the onscreen exercise. In the onscreen list of chapters and exercises, click Chapter 9: Dimensions, Annotations, and Tables. Click Exercise: Configure, Add, and Edit Revision Tables and Tags.*

Configure a New Revision Table Style

In this portion of the exercise, you create a new revision table style, make configuration changes to that new style, and set that style as the default style to use.

1   Open *Revision Tables.idw.*

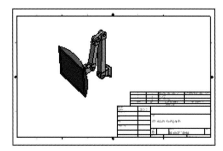

2　　Begin to create a new revision table style. Click Manage tab > Styles and Standards panel > Styles Editor.

3　　In the Style and Standard Editor dialog box list of styles:
- Right-click Revision Table (ANSI), located below the Revision Table category.
- Click New Style.

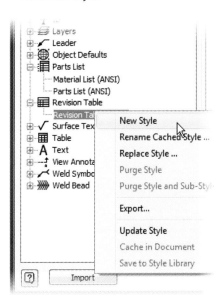

4　　To specify a name for the style:
- In the New Style Name dialog box, enter **Company ABC**.
- Click OK.

5   To modify the revision table title:

- Verify that the revision table style Company ABC is selected.
- On the Revision Tables tab under Title, change from REVISION HISTORY to **REVISION.**

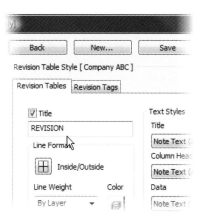

6   Under Heading, select the option to have the heading at the bottom, and the direction of the numbers to start at the bottom and go up.

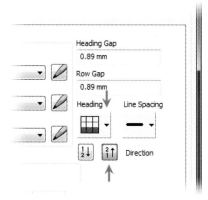

7   To change which iProperty date field is used, in the Default Columns Settings area, click Column Chooser.

8   In the Revision Table Column Chooser:

  • In the list of Available Properties, select ENG APPROVAL DATE.
  • Click Add.
  • In the list of Selected Properties, select DATE.
  • Click Remove. The Selected Properties list now displays as shown.
  • Click OK.

9   Under Default Columns Settings, make the following changes in the table.

  • For DESCRIPTION width, enter **50**.
  • For the column title for the ENG APPROVED BY property, enter **REV BY.**
  • For the approval date column, enter **DATE.**
  • For DATE width, enter **30**.

	Column	Width
Y	ZONE	30.000
R	REV	30.000
	DESCRIPTION	50.000
Y	REV BY ←	30.000
ATE	DATE ←	30.000

10   Click the Revision Tags tab.

11   In the Revision Tag Formatting area, Shape list, select Hexagon.

12   Click Save.

13   In the list of styles under Object Defaults, click Object Defaults (ANSI-mm).

14   In the Object Defaults Style list, for Object Type Revision Table and Revision Tag, select the Object Style Company ABC.

15   Click Save. Click Done.

16   Continue to the next exercise or save and close all files.

Add and Edit Revision Tables

In this portion of the exercise, you add a revision table to three different drawing sheets in the previously configured drawing, add rows to the tables, and edit the values the tables display.

1   Click Application menu > iProperties.

2   On the Summary tab in the Comments field, enter **Initial Release**. Click OK.

3   To add a revision table to sheet:1:

- Click Annotate tab > Table panel > Revision.
- In the Revision Table dialog box, click OK to accept the default settings for a table scope of Entire Drawing.
- Click to position the revision table in the lower left corner of the drawing sheet.

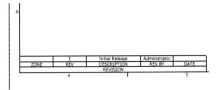

4   In the browser, double-click Sheet2:2 to make it active.

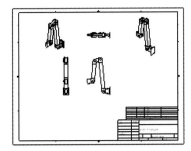

5   To add a revision table with a scope of the entire drawing:

- Click Annotate tab > Table panel > Revision.
- In the Revision Table dialog box, with Entire Drawing selected, notice that the Revision Auto-Index options are unavailable because an entire drawing table already exists.
- Click OK.
- Click to position the revision table in the lower left corner of the drawing sheet.

6   In the browser, double-click Sheet4:4 to make it active.

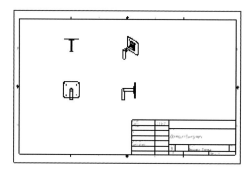

7   To add a revision table with a scope of the active sheet:

- Click Annotate tab > Table panel > Revision.
- In the Revision Table dialog box, under Table Scope, select Active Sheet.
- Under Revision Index, select Auto-Index, for Start Value, enter **5**.

8 Click OK. Click to position the revision table in the upper right corner of the drawing sheet.

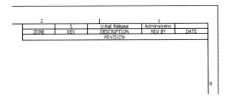

9 In the graphics window, double-click the revision table.

10 In the Revision Table: Sheet Scope dialog box, under Description, enter **Inventor Model Release**. This description helps indicate the design is now based on the 3D model instead of the previous 2D CAD drawing.

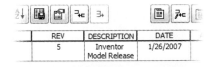

11 In the Revision Table: Sheet Scope dialog box, click iProperties.

12 On the Status tab,
- For Eng. Approved By, enter **MMS**.
- For Eng. Approved Date, select today's date.
- Click OK.

13 In the Revision Table dialog box, click OK. Notice the new revision table values that you specified.

14 To change the reading orientation of the revision table so its readability is different when the paper print is folded, in the graphics window, right-click the revision table, click Rotate > Rotate 90 CW.

15 Repeat the same rotation again and then move the revision table back inside the upper right corner.

		2		
				REVISION
DATE	REV BY	DESCRIPTION		
1/26/2007	MMS	Inventor Model Release		

16 In the browser, double-click Sheet:1. Review the values of the revision table compared to the one just edited. Notice the REV BY and DATE fields updated to the same value because they are referencing the same iProperty, but the REV value is unique.

17 In the browser under Sheet:1, right-click REVISION. Click Add Revision Row.

18 In the Edit Revision Table dialog box, click iProperties.

19 On the Summary tab, Comments field, enter **ECO 007-00148**. Click OK.

20 With the Revision Table values appearing as shown, click OK.

	ZONE	REV	DESCRIPTION	REV BY	DATE
		1	Initial Release	MMS	1/26/2009
		2	ECO 07-00148	MMS	1/26/2009

21 Activate Sheet2:2 and Sheet4:4 to review the similarities and differences to the data in the different revision tables.

22 Continue to the next exercise or save and close all files.

Add and Edit Revision Tags

In this portion of the exercise, you add two revision tags and edit one to refer to a different revision number and different symbol shape.

1   Set Sheet2:2 active.

2   Click Annotate tab > Table panel > Revision Tag.

3   In the front view of the assembly, click the line and then move the cursor toward the left as shown.

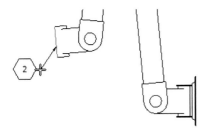

4   Click to specify the second point of the leader line. Right-click anywhere in the drawing. Click Continue. Press ESC.

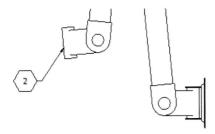

5   Repeat the process again to add another revision tag located as shown.

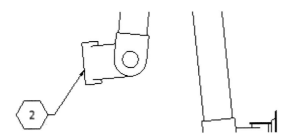

6   Right-click the second revision tag. Click Tag > Revision '1'.

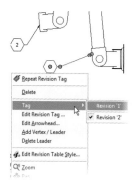

7   Double-click the second revision tag.

8   In the Edit Revision Tag dialog box, under Revision Tag Type:
  • Select Override Shape (by Style).
  • Click the Triangular shape.
  • Click OK.

9   Review the changes to the revision tag.

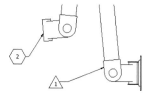

10   Close all files. Do not save.

Chapter Summary

Autodesk Inventor offers a wide variety of tools for automating the process of annotating your drawings. While this chapter focused on annotations that you can use on part and assembly drawing views, the next chapter focuses on the tools and workflows you use to annotate assembly drawings.

Having completed this chapter, you can:

- Dimension drawings with automated techniques.
- Dimension drawings with manual techniques.
- Create and edit hole and thread notes in drawings.
- Add centerlines, center marks and symbols to your drawings.
- Configure, add, and edit revision tables and revision tags.

Chapter 10
Annotating Assembly Drawings

Assembly drawings typically include annotations that identify and describe the components in the assembly. You can include balloons in your drawing views to identify specific parts, and then add a parts list to your drawing that includes a quantity and description for each component. In this chapter, you learn how to add balloons and a parts list to your assembly drawings, and how the bill of materials (BOM) is used to manage this type of information.

Objectives

After completing this chapter, you will be able to:

- View and edit bill of materials data.

- Create and customize parts lists to document the components in your assembly.

- Review balloons and their purpose in the drawing annotation process.

Lesson 37 | Assembly-Centric Bill of Materials

This lesson describes the Bill of Materials editor in an assembly. A bill of materials is a table that contains information about the parts within an assembly. This can include quantities, names, costs, vendors, and all the other information someone building the assembly might need.

Reviewing and editing bill of materials (BOM) data is an important step toward communicating a completed design. Knowing where and how to edit BOM data and being able to view just the right amount of data helps you in this review and edit process.

In the following illustration, the Bill of Materials editor is shown after enabling and editing the view of the Structured data to show all levels of the assembly's data. The Outsourced and Material columns were added to the display so that their data could be viewed and edited from this single location.

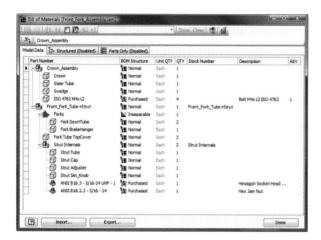

Objectives

After completing this lesson, you will be able to:

- Describe the bill of materials and its uses.

- Use the bill of materials to document assemblies.

- State how to renumber, lock, and set the view properties for item numbers.

About the Bill of Materials

The bill of materials plays a significant role in collecting and managing the data that is displayed in a parts list on a drawing, or used by other software applications.

In the following illustration, a portion of the Bill of Materials dialog box displays some of the many columns with component information. You can specify which columns you want to view. For columns that display specific component iProperty data, you can change the value in the cell and have the value change for the component as though you made the change in the iProperties dialog box.

Definition of a Bill of Materials

The concept of a bill of materials (BOM) means you have a single location where the data for the BOM such as part number, item number, quantity, material, and so on, is stored. From that single location, you can edit the values in a BOM, use its data and structure to populate the information in balloons and parts lists placed on a drawing, and populate the data and structure for a material acquisition and resource planning program. The data stays synchronized between the balloons and parts lists on drawings and the assembly bill of materials.

Because the BOM makes all the data for the assembly accessible in a single location, you need different ways to interact with and present the data. When viewing and editing the data in an assembly, the Bill of Materials dialog box has three tabs that have different purposes for viewing, editing, and presenting the data. These three tabs are:

- **Model Tree:** Always active for display. This view is similar to the browser except each component is listed only once for each assembly or subassembly it may be used in. You use it to edit properties including some editing functions that cannot be done in one of the other tabs, like changing properties for components whose BOM structure is set to Phantom or Reference.

- **Structured:** Use to display either just the top-level BOM data or all levels of BOM data. When displaying all levels of data, the data displays in a hierarchy structure. Each component has a unique item number and the components within a subassembly display the item number of the subassembly as a prefix to their item number. You have the option of including a delimiter between the numbers. The hierarchy of components and item numbers is used in the parts lists and balloons that you place on the drawing sheet. An exported copy of this same data and structure can also be created.

- **Parts Only:** Use to display the BOM data for parts only. All subassemblies are ignored and the parts in those subassemblies are promoted to display as though they were directly placed in the top- level assembly instead of in a subassembly. Each part is also assigned a unique item number. You can use this display configuration for the parts list and balloons on the drawing sheet. This same data can also be exported for use by other software applications.

Only the Model Tree tab is enabled at all times for selection and viewing of data. The Structured tab and Parts Only tab can be enabled or disabled. By enabling only the tab you require, the amount of information to collect and the ways of presenting it in the Bill of Materials dialog box are less than if you enabled both tabs.

Editing Tasks in the Bill of Materials

In the Bill of Materials dialog box, you have the option to change the BOM data in many different ways. Some of the changes you can make include but are not limited to:

- Changing the order in which the components are displayed.

- Changing the order in which the columns of information are displayed.

- Changing which columns of information are displayed.

- Creating columns for custom iProperty data.

- Remembering the item numbers.

- Locking the item numbers so they cannot be changed.

- Changing the material property.

- Creating conditions for the merging of row data based on the same part numbers.

Example of Bill of Materials Display

In the following illustration, the display of the BOM is currently set to display only the parts used in the assembly. A list of these parts and the parts' information can be displayed on the drawing or exported for use in other software applications. Displaying and organizing the BOM data in this manner is especially useful if you only order and manufacture parts and do not require the listing of subassembly components.

Using the Bill of Materials

The information for the bill of materials is automatically collected from the iProperties of the components in the assembly. You access the bill of materials by clicking the Bill of Materials tool on the Assembly Panel or the Tools menu.

You have many ways that you can modify a component's data and display that data in the BOM. By adding the columns of properties you need to modify for the components, you can make those changes for the component file directly from within the Bill of Materials dialog box. When components have the same part number, you can control whether and under what condition those components merge together and display on the same item row.

The following illustration shows the synchronization between iProperties and the bill of materials.

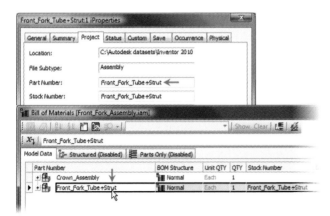

Access

Bill of Materials

Ribbon: **Assemble tab › Manage panel**

Toolbar: **Assembly Panel**
Browser shortcut menu on an assembly or subassembly in a drawing file: **Bill of Materials**

Procedure: Using the Bill of Materials

The following steps describe how to access the Bill of Materials dialog box to view and manipulate the data.

1   In the assembly file, on the ribbon, click Bill of Materials.

2   In the Bill of Materials dialog box, select a view and change properties and settings for the components to fit your requirements.

3   Click Done.

Editing iProperty Data

When you change the data in any cell for a component, except in the QTY column, that change is written back to the iProperty value in that component file. Using this editing method, making changes from within the assembly BOM is a powerful and efficient way to change data for many components. However, use caution when making your edits because those changes actually reside in the component file. Thus any place that the component is used, the information changes there as well.

You can add any property column to the display of the BOM by dragging and dropping the property column name from the Customization dialog box onto a column heading. You display the Customization dialog box by clicking Choose Columns on the toolbar. This dropped column is then added before the column it was dropped on. By adding the Material property column to the BOM, you can display and change the material property for a component. Just like the other properties, the material property changes in the part file when it is changed in the BOM. You can also assign a material value to a virtual component. In these cases, the material change is stored in the assembly file where the virtual component resides.

Note: *After you assign a material and enter a volume for a virtual component, the mass of the component is calculated and available for reporting in the Mass property column.*

In the following illustration, a new column is being added to the Bill of Materials editor.

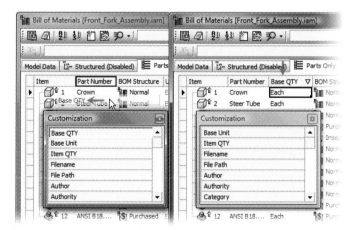

The left image shows the new column being dragged into position. The right shows the Bill of Materials editor with the new column in place.

To add a column for data that does not pertain to a preset property, on the toolbar, click Add Custom iProperty Columns. When you click this, the Add Custom iProperty Columns dialog box is displayed, where you enter a name for the property and select the type of data to be stored in the property. The custom iProperty column is then added to the far right end of the BOM. Like the other columns in the table, you can reorder its display by clicking and dragging its heading to the left or right.

By specifying the name and data type of an existing custom iProperty, the existing data is automatically displayed in the cell. If the custom iProperty name does not exist in a component, and you add data to this custom property column for the component, the custom iProperty is automatically added to the component file.

Row Merging for Same-Part-Numbered Components

When you have different part files with the same iProperty part number, you can control whether they are merged into a single item entry in the BOM. You turn on or off this functionality in the Part Number Row Merge Settings dialog box by checking or clearing the Enable Row Merge option in the Part Number Match dialog box. You access this dialog box by clicking Part Number Merge Settings on the toolbar. In this same dialog box, you can create a list of different exclusion strings. Enter the part number as the exclude string so that components with that part number are not merged together.

When row merging has occurred, the icon to the left of that item number row is displayed as a blue rectangle stacked on top of a red rectangle. In the following illustration, the same BOM is shown. The upper-left image shows the BOM without merging and the lower-right image shows it with merging.

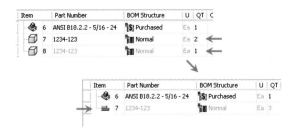

Item Number Manipulation

Editing and arranging the item numbers in the bill of materials enables you to establish the configuration in one location and have it appear with those same numbers and order wherever it may be referenced. To have component item numbers display the way you want them to, you need to learn how and where to make those changes.

In the following illustration, the structured view of the assembly has been set to view all levels and have a hyphen appear in the item numbers for components nested in a subassembly.

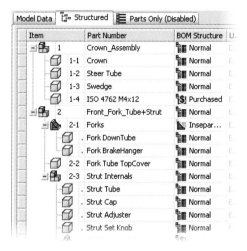

Item Number View Properties for Structured and Parts Only

After you have enabled the BOM view for Structured or Parts Only, you can change the appearance of the item values listed in the Item column for each component. To change the appearance, you use the View Properties tool. You access this tool by clicking View Properties on the shortcut menu when you right-click anywhere on that tabbed page. To access it on the toolbar, click View Options button > View Properties. The available options in the properties dialog box depend upon which tab is active when you execute the tool.

For the viewing property options for Structured, you select First Level or All Levels. When you select First Level, your BOM lists only the components referenced directly into the assembly. Components referenced into subassemblies are not displayed. When set to First Level, you also set the number of minimum digits the item numbers display. For example, when set to 1, all item numbers less than 10 do not have a 0 as a prefix. If you set the minimum digits to 01, then all numbers less than 10 would have a 0 prefix. Thus for example, instead of item number 6, you would see item number 06. When you select All Levels, your BOM lists all components for any expanded nested level. The item numbers for nested levels have the previous level's item number as the prefix for all components in the nested level. When you select the All Levels option, you can also specify a delimiter character to appear between the level of item numbers. For example, if a hyphen is selected as a delimiter and a subassembly has an item number of 2, when you expand the display for that subassembly, the components in that subassembly have item numbers of 2-1, 2-2, 2-3, and so on. If 2-3 is a subassembly and that level is expanded, the first component has an item number of 2-3-1.

For the viewing property options for Parts Only, you select between having the item value appear as a numeric value or as an alpha character. After selecting Numeric, you can set the minimum number of digits to display just like you can for the Structured tab. After selecting Alpha, you set the character to appear in either upper or lower case.

Renumbering Item Values

When renumbering item values, you can renumber:

- One component row at a time.

- A range of selected components.

- All components based on their order in the list.

To change the item number for a single component, click the item number and enter the required number. To renumber a selected range or all components, you use Renumber Items from the toolbar or right-click the Item number and click Renumber Items from the shortcut menu.

To select a range of components, first click the square to the left of the icon on that component's row. After you select the first row, you select a range of rows by pressing SHIFT while clicking the last row in the range that you want to select. Pressing and holding CTRL enables you to select the component rows in any order and skip some rows. Regardless of the order in which you select them, the item numbers are always incremented from the top of the list to the bottom of the list. In the Item Renumber dialog box, you also have the option to specify an increment value where you can have the numbers increase by any whole number other than zero.

Because the Renumber Items tool renumbers the components based on the order in which they are listed, you should first arrange the components in the list prior to renumbering. To reorder the rows, in the table listing, click and drag the component icon up or down the list to set the order.

In the following image, a range of rows is being selected. Notice where the cursor is positioned to click to select the row.

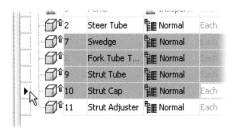

Locking the Item Value

After editing the item value for a component, lock the value so it cannot be changed until you first unlock it. You lock item values by selecting the row or rows, right-clicking the item value, and clicking Lock Items. Follow the same procedure to unlock the items. Item numbers that are locked are displayed in a light gray color.

In the following illustration, item number 8 has been locked based on its display in light gray.

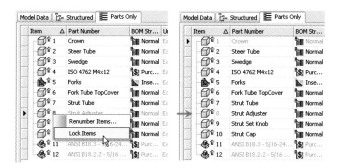

Exercise | Edit an Assembly Bill of Materials

In this exercise, you edit an assembly bill of materials so that it displays the assembly data in the way you need it to appear. You also edit component properties by changing the values in the Bill of Materials dialog box.

The completed exercise

Completing the Exercise: *To complete the exercise, follow the steps in this book or in the onscreen exercise. In the onscreen list of chapters and exercises, click Chapter 10: Annotating Assembly Drawings. Click Exercise: Edit an Assembly Bill of Materials.*

Edit BOM Views and Item Numbers

In this portion of the exercise, you change the display of the bill of materials, change the order in which the items display, and renumber the items.

1   Open *Front_Fork_Assembly.iam*.

2 Click Assemble tab > Manage panel > Bill of Materials.

3 To review the available information, on the Model Data tab, click to expand the display of all the subassemblies.

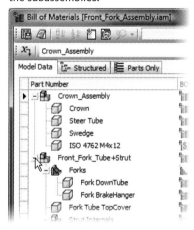

4 Click the Structured tab to make it active.

5 To enable the BOM view:
   • Right-click the Structured tab.
   • Click Enable BOM View.
     Notice that it is displaying only the first level of the structure and you cannot expand the structure.

6 Right-click the Structured tab. Click View Properties.

7 To change the display of the structured data to show all components, in the Structured

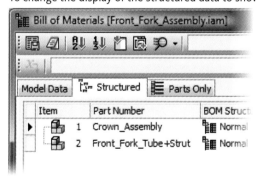

Properties dialog box:

- Under Level, select All Levels.
- Under Delimiter, select - (hyphen).
- Click OK.

8 Expand the display of the subassemblies.
Notice the item numbers and the nesting of subassemblies under Item 2.

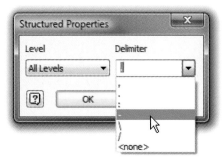

9 Change the subassembly Front_Fork_Tube+Strut from being a Normal BOM structure item to Phantom:

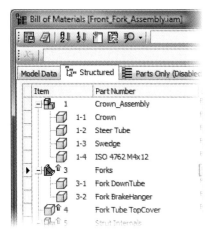

- In the column BOM Structure for Front_Fork_Tube+Strut, click Phantom.
- Press ENTER. The structured display now appears with the previous nested items at the top level.

10 To renumber the Strut Internals subassembly:

- Click in the item number cell for that subassembly.

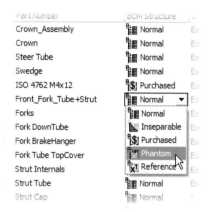

- Enter **2** and press TAB.
- Review the change in the structure. The components nested under Strut Internals automatically change to have the number 2 as the prefix before their unique item numbers.

11 Click the Parts Only tab to make it active.

12 Right-click the Parts Only tab. Click Enable BOM View.

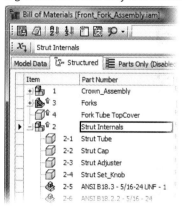

13 Change the display order of the items:

- Click and drag the Weldment icon for Forks and drop it on the top row.

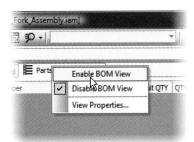

- Click and drag the library icon for Item 12 and drop it on the top row.

14 To renumber the items:
- On the toolbar, click Renumber Items.

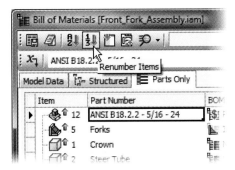

- In the Item Renumber dialog box, click OK.
- Click the Item column header to sort the items.

15 Right-click the Item 7 cell. Click Lock Items. The information in this row now is displayed as light gray.

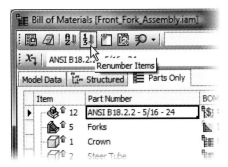

16 To select a range of components to renumber their Item numbers:

- Click the cell to the left of Item 6.

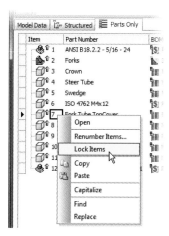

- Press and hold SHIFT. Click the cell to the left of Item 9.

17 On the toolbar, click Renumber Items.

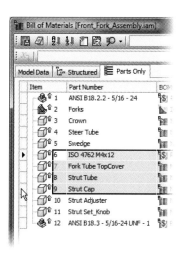

18 In the Item Renumber dialog box, for Start Value, enter **20**. Click OK.

19 In the Locked Row Message box, click OK.

20 To reorder by item number:

- On the toolbar, click Sort Items.
- In the Sort dialog box, under Sort by, select Item.
- Click OK.

21   Review the current Parts Only display.

Add Columns and Change Properties

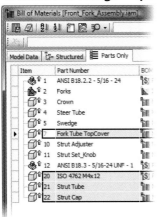

In this portion of the exercise, you add the Material column and a custom iProperty column to the BOM. After adding the columns, you also change the property values for some of these components.

1   Click the Structured tab.

2   On the toolbar, click Choose Columns.

3   In the Customization (Choose Columns) dialog box:

- Click and drag the Material row to the heading row. Release when positioned on top of the Description column.
- Close the dialog box.

4   To change the material:

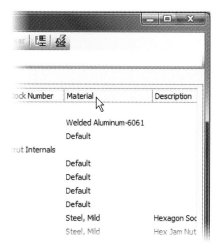

- Under item, expand the contents for Item 1.
- For item 1-1, double-click the Material column.
- From the list, select Titanium.

5   On the toolbar, click Add Custom iProperty Columns.

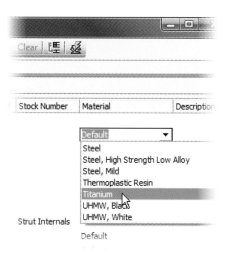

6   To add a custom iProperty, in the Add Custom iProperty Columns dialog box:

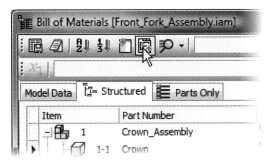

- Click the row labeled <click to add iProperty column>.
- Enter **Outsourced**.
- In the Data Type column, click Yes or No.
- Click OK.

7   Click and drag the Outsourced column to the top of the heading for the Stock Number column.

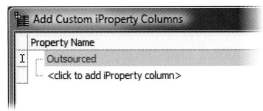

8   To enter a property value for multiple rows:

- Click the cell to the far left of Item 1-1.
- In the Outsourced column for Item 1-1, click Yes.
- Repeat for Items 1-3, 2-1, and 2-3.
- Press ENTER.

9   Click Done.

10   In the browser, under Crown_Assembly:1, right-click Crown:1. Click iProperties.

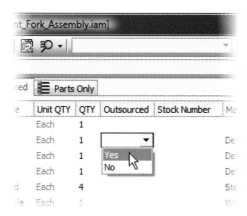

11 To view the iProperty:

- In the Crown:1 Properties dialog box, click the Custom tab.
- Under Name, click Outsourced.
- Notice that the custom iProperty was automatically added to the part.
- Close the iProperties dialog box

12 Close all files. Do not save.

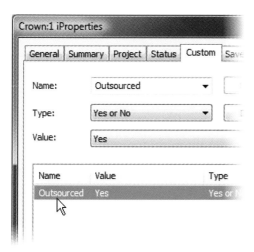

Lesson 38 | Creating and Customizing Parts Lists

This lesson describes how to create and customize parts lists to document the components in your assembly. The parts list is generated from a bill of materials (BOM) and shows all or only certain parts and subassemblies in the BOM database.

Parts lists play a vital role in the assembly documentation process by displaying the components that make up the assembly, and their quantities, materials, and any other properties that you wish to convey.

In the following illustration, an exploded assembly drawing is shown with the associated parts list.

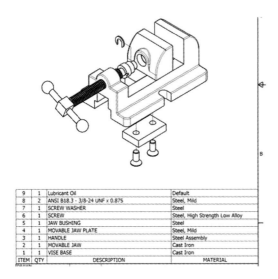

ITEM	QTY	DESCRIPTION	MATERIAL
9	1	Lubricant Oil	Default
8	2	ANSI B18.3 - 3/8-24 UNF x 0.875	Steel, Mild
7	1	SCREW WASHER	Steel
6	1	SCREW	Steel, High Strength Low Alloy
5	1	JAW BUSHING	Steel
4	1	MOVABLE JAW PLATE	Steel, Mild
3	1	HANDLE	Steel Assembly
2	1	MOVABLE JAW	Cast Iron
1	1	VISE BASE	Cast Iron

Objectives

After completing this lesson, you will be able to:

- Describe parts lists and their role in documenting components in assembly drawings.

- Create parts lists in drawings.

- Use the Edit Parts List dialog box to modify your parts lists.

About Parts Lists

The parts list is generated from the bill of materials database and can be customized to show the columns and information needed to complete the assembly. Formatting such as table layout, column width, and heading names can be customized to give the parts list the exact look that you want.

Parts lists can display four types of information:

- Structured

- Parts only

- Structured (legacy)

- Parts only (legacy)

Legacy drawings are from versions prior to Autodesk® Inventor® Release 11 and can be left in their original format or converted to the new format.

The following illustration provides a comparison between the parts list and bill of materials database for an assembly.

Definition of Parts Lists

A parts list is a table in an assembly drawing that contains information about the assembly. The parts list can include component information such as quantities, names, costs, vendors and other associated information that someone building the assembly might need. Information such as quantities are updated automatically when parts are added or removed from the assembly, while other data can be edited in the Edit Parts List dialog box or in the Properties dialog box.

In the following illustration, the Parts List dialog box is displayed, ready for input to create and place the assembly parts list.

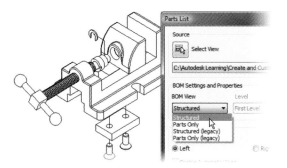

Example of Parts Lists

You have designed a drill press vise and created a presentation file to create an exploded view to use in the assembly drawing. After the drawing file is created and you have placed the exploded view in the drawing, it is time to document the parts and subassemblies that make up the assembly. The first step toward creating the parts list is to open the bill of materials database to confirm that all of the information for the columns that you will use are filled in with the correct information and to make any necessary edits. You can now use the Parts List tool to choose the source view, BOM settings, and define the placement of your parts list. If the standard parts list style is not to your standard, you can edit column widths, headings, text justification and other parts of the parts list layout as necessary to achieve the look that you want.

In the following illustration, view (1) shows the parts list as originally created. View (2) shows the parts list after customization.

Parts List

ITEM	QTY	PART NUMBER	DESCRIPTION
9	1	VISE BASE	
2	1	MOVABLE JAW	
3	1	MOVABLE JAW PLATE	
4	1	JAW BUSHING	
6	1	SCREW	
7	1	SCREW WASHER	
5	1	HANDLE	
8	2	ANSI B18.3 - 3/8-24 UNF x 0.875	Hexagon Socket Flat Countersunk Head Cap Screw
1	1	Lubricant Oil	

ITEM	QTY	DESCRIPTION	MATERIAL
1	1	VISE BASE	Cast Iron
2	1	MOVABLE JAW	Cast Iron
3	1	MOVABLE JAW PLATE	Steel, Mild
4	1	JAW BUSHING	Steel
5	1	HANDLE	
6	1	SCREW	Steel, High Strength Low Alloy
7	1	SCREW WASHER	Steel
8	2	ANSI B18.3 - 3/8-24 UNF x 0.875	Steel, Mild
9	1	Lubricant Oil	Default

Creating Parts Lists

You create parts lists by clicking the Annotate tab > Table panel > Parts List. The Parts List dialog box is displayed to reveal the following controls for creating your parts list.

	Option	Description
①	**Source**	This area specifies where to pull the parts list data from, an existing view or a file (IPT, IPN, IAM).
②	**BOM Settings and Properties**	The options in this area dictate how to represent subassemblies and their parts. When the selected view is Structured, the subassemblies show as line items. When the selected view is Parts Only, the parts within the subassemblies show as line items with their Item value containing the delimiter character specified.
③	**Table Wrapping**	In Table Wrapping, set the wrap direction. If you select Enable Automatic Wrap, you can set the maximum number of parts list rows, or number of parts list sections.

Access

> **Parts List**
>
>
>
> Ribbon: **Annotate tab > Table panel**
>
>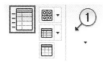
>
> Toolbar: **Drawing Annotation Panel**

Procedure: Creating a Parts List

The following steps describe how to create a parts list in a drawing file.

1   In a drawing file, click Annotate tab > Table panel > Parts List.

2   Select a drawing view and make the appropriate settings in the Parts List dialog box.

3   Position the parts list on the sheet. The parts list is displayed.

Configuring the Parts List Style

By default, the parts list contains four columns of information that are associated with every Autodesk Inventor file. You can configure all properties displayed in the parts list. These properties can include both standard and custom properties and are configured in the parts list style.

The following illustration shows the default parts list style in the Style and Standard Editor dialog box.

	Option	Description
①	**Heading and Table Settings**	In this area, specify the title for the parts list, the spacing between the text and the cell frame for the heading row, the text style to use, the vertical spacing between the text and the cell frame for the parts list rows, the output direction of the parts list, the heading position for the parts list, and the line spacing for each row.
②	**Default Columns Settings**	In this area, you select and define the columns of data to display in the parts list and any special settings for that property. The Column Chooser enables you to add and remove columns to and from the parts list, while you can change the actual title for the columns in the fields under the Column table heading. You adjust the width of the column in the values under the Width column. Additional formatting values for the columns are accessed by clicking the name of the property under the Property table heading.

Editing Parts Lists

Unless your drawing template already has a parts list style that meets your specifications, you probably need to edit your newly created parts list. In the Parts List dialog box, you can make the changes to the data and layout of your parts list so that it meets your requirements.

In the following illustration, the Parts List dialog box is shown. Here you can change values for components and if necessary write the changes back to the bill of materials.

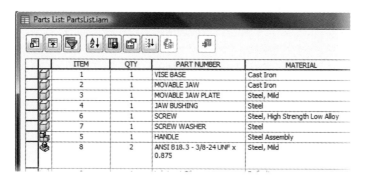

Access

Edit Parts List

Shortcut Menu: **In the graphics window, right-click the parts list and select Edit Parts List**
Shortcut Menu: **In the Model browser, right-click the parts list and select Edit Parts List**
Object: **In the graphics window, double-click the parts list**

Procedure: Editing a Parts List

The following steps describe how to edit a parts list to suit your requirements.

1. Access the Parts List dialog box.

2. Using the controls and options in the Parts List dialog box:
   - Modify the parts list layout.
   - Format columns.
   - Choose the columns for the parts list.
   - Change the information in the individual cells of the parts list.

3. If the changes you make affect the bill of materials (BOM), you can save the edits to the BOM in the assembly file.

4. Click OK to display changes in the parts list.

Edit Parts List Tools

The following tools are available at the top of the Parts List dialog box.

		Option	Description
①		**Column Chooser**	Opens the Column Chooser dialog box. You can add, remove, or change the order of the columns for the selected parts list. Affects all parts lists which use the same source file.
②		**Group Settings**	Opens the Group Settings dialog box. You select parts list columns to be used as a grouping key, and group different components into one parts list row.

		Option	Description
③	🔽	**Filter Settings**	Displays the Filter Settings dialog box. Enables you to define and apply parts list filters.
④	↕️	**Sort**	Opens the Sort Parts List dialog box. You can sort the parts list by applying primary, secondary, and tertiary sort criteria. Sorting affects only the edited parts lists.
⑤	💾	**Export**	Saves the selected parts list to an external file. Click the button and specify the file name and format.
⑥	📋	**Table Layout**	Opens the Table Layout dialog box. You can change the title text or heading location for the selected parts list. You can change the row height, table direction, and the table wrapping settings.
⑦	↕️	**Renumber Items**	Renumbers parts list rows consecutively according to the current order of rows in the parts list. Affects the item renumbering of all parts lists with the same source as the edited parts list.
⑧	🔧	**Save Item Overrides to BOM**	Saves Item column override entries back to the assembly bill of materials.

Column Editing Options

In the Parts List dialog box, you can right-click a column heading to access the following menu options.

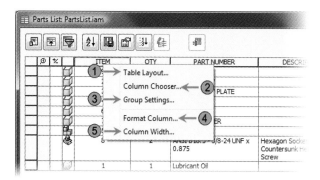

	Option	Description
(1)	**Table Layout**	Opens the Table Layout dialog box. Changes the title, location of the heading, row spacing, table wrap preference, and sort order.
(2)	**Column Chooser**	Opens the Parts List Column chooser dialog box. Selects columns to include in the parts list.
(3)	**Group Settings**	Opens the Group Settings dialog box. Groups several parts list rows into one row according to selected sorting keys.
(4)	**Format Column**	Sets the column name, alignment of text, and formatting properties.
(5)	**Column Width**	Sets the width of one or more selected columns.

Row Editing Options

In the Parts List dialog box, you can right-click a row or a cell to access the following shortcut menu options.

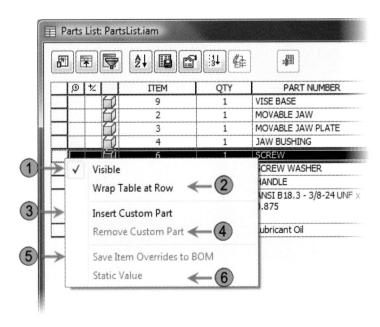

	Option	Description
①	**Visible**	When checked, shows the rows or columns in a parts list. When cleared, hides the rows or columns in a parts list.
②	**Wrap Table at Row**	Manages the length of a parts list by dividing it into sections extended to the left or the right of the main table.
③	**Insert Custom Part**	Creates a new parts list row so that parts that are not contained in the model can be added. The row is added to all parts lists with the same source.
④	**Remove Custom Part**	Removes one or more rows that were manually added with Insert Custom Part.
⑤	**Save Item Overrides to BOM**	Saves item overrides back to the assembly bill of materials (BOM).
⑥	**Static Value**	Sets the selected parts list cells as static values. When a cell is static, it does not update if the corresponding value in the parts list source changes.

Exercise | Create and Customize a Parts List

In this exercise, you create a parts list and customize its look by choosing and formatting columns, changing column widths, changing column headings, adding static values, and saving edits to the bill of materials (BOM).

ITEM	QTY	DESCRIPTION	MATERIAL
9	1	Lubricant Oil	Default
8	2	ANSI B18.3 - 3/8-24 UNF x 0.875	Steel, Mild
7	1	SCREW WASHER	Steel
6	1	SCREW	Steel, High Strength Low Alloy
5	1	HANDLE	Steel Assembly
4	1	JAW BUSHING	Steel
3	1	MOVABLE JAW PLATE	Steel, Mild
2	1	MOVABLE JAW	Cast Iron
1	1	VISE BASE	Cast Iron

DRAWN			
Engineering	7/24/2006		
CHECKED			

The completed exercise

1   Open *PartsList.idw*.

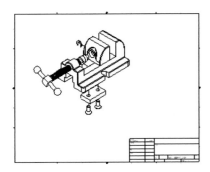

2   Click Annotate tab > Table panel > Parts List.

   • Select the Exploded View.
   • In the Parts List dialog box, click OK.

3   In the graphics window, click just above the title block to place the parts list.

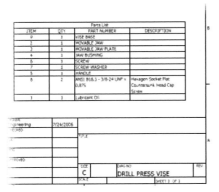

4   In the graphics window, double-click the parts list to open the Parts List dialog box.

5   In the Parts List dialog box, click Table Layout.

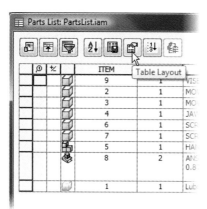

6   In the Parts List Table Layout dialog box:

- Clear the Title check box (1).
- Under Direction, select Add New Rows to Top (2).
- Under Heading, select Heading Placement: Bottom (3).

7   To change a column width:

- In the Parts List dialog box, right-click the Item column heading.
- Click Column Width.
- In the edit box enter **12.7**.
- Click OK.

8   Using the same method, edit the following column widths:

- Qty = **12.7**
- Part Number = **101.6**

9   In the Parts List dialog box, click Column Chooser.

10 To remove a column from the parts list:

- In the Parts List Column Chooser dialog box, under Selected Properties, select Description.
- Click Remove.

11 To add a column to the parts list:

- In the Parts List Column Chooser dialog box, under Available Properties, select Material.
- Click Add.
- Click OK.

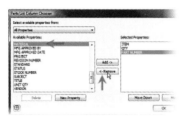

12 Change the column width for Material to **69.85.**

13 To format a column heading:

- Right-click the Part Number column heading.
- Click Format Column.
- In the Heading edit box, enter **DESCRIPTION**.
- Click OK.

14 In the Parts List dialog box, click OK.

15 To relocate the parts list:
- In the graphics window, move your cursor over any of the text in the parts list, and it changes to a four-way arrow.
- Click and drag the parts list to line up with the top edge of the title block.

16 Note the order of the Item quantity.

ITEM	QTY	
1	1	Lubricant Oil
8	2	ANSI B18.3 - 3/8
5	1	HANDLE
7	1	SCREW WASHER
6	1	SCREW
4	1	JAW BUSHING
3	1	MOVABLE JAW
2	1	MOVABLE JAW
9	1	VISE BASE

17 In the graphics window, right-click the parts list. Click Edit Parts List. Note the order of the Item column matches the Parts List order.

18   In the Parts List dialog box, click Sort.

19   To define the sorting order:

- In the Sort Parts List dialog box, under Sort By, select Item in the list.
- Select Ascending for the direction of sorting.
- Click OK.

20   Notice in the Parts List dialog box that the components are now reordered by item number.

In the Parts List dialog box, click the blank cell in the Material column and enter **Steel Assembly**. Click Apply.

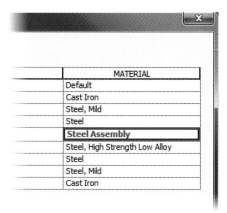

To reorder items:

- In the Parts List dialog box, click the Item cell for Lubricant Oil, currently 1, and enter **9**.
- Click the Item cell for Vise Base, currently 9, and enter **1**.
- Sort the components by Item and Ascending orders.
- Click OK.

23 To view the order of components in the bill of materials:
- In the browser, right-click *Parts List:PartsList.iam*.
- Click Bill of Materials. Verify that the Structured tab is selected.
- Observe the order of the components in the bill of material database.
- Click Done.

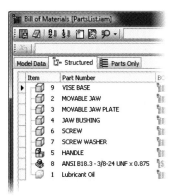

24 To save item overrides to the Bill of Materials:
- In the browser, right-click *Parts List:PartsList.iam*.
- Click Save Item Overrides to BOM.

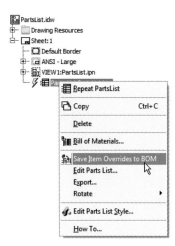

25 To view the updated order in the bill of materials:

- In the browser, right-click *Parts List:PartsList.iam*.
- Click Bill of Materials.
- View the updated order of the components in the bill of material database.
- Click Done.

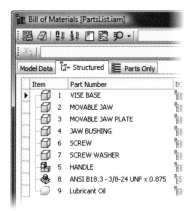

26 Your parts list is complete and up to date. Confirm that your parts list matches the following illustration.

9	1	Lubricant Oil	Default
8	2	ANSI B18.3 - 3/8-24 UNF x 0.875	Steel, Mild
7	1	SCREW WASHER	Steel
6	1	SCREW	Steel, High Strength Low Alloy
5	1	HANDLE	Steel Assembly
4	1	JAW BUSHING	Steel
3	1	MOVABLE JAW PLATE	Steel, Mild
2	1	MOVABLE JAW	Cast Iron
1	1	VISE BASE	Cast Iron
ITEM	QTY	DESCRIPTION	MATERIAL

DRAWN			
Engineering	7/24/2006		
CHECKED			

27 Close all files. Do not save.

Lesson 39 | Creating Balloons

This lesson describes how to add balloons to your assembly drawings. You use balloons to identify components in drawing views to correspond with the information contained in the parts list. You learn how to create balloons automatically and manually, display other component properties in your balloons, and use different shapes depending on your requirements. You also learn how to organize your balloons by aligning them vertically and horizontally or by stacking them.

In the following illustration, an exploded view is shown with balloons placed to identify the components.

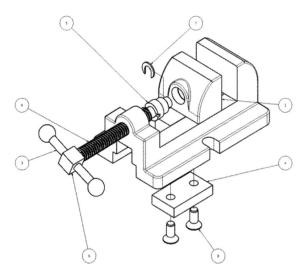

Objectives

After completing this lesson, you will be able to:

- Describe balloons and their use in the 2D drawing process.
- List the steps required to manually place balloons.
- List the steps required to automatically configure and place balloons.
- List the steps required to manually place and edit balloons.

About Balloons

After you create a drawing view, you can add balloons to the parts and subassemblies in that view. A balloon is an annotation tag that identifies an item listed in a parts list. The number in the balloon corresponds to the number of the component in the parts list. If you have a virtual part defined in an assembly, or a custom part defined in the parts list, you can also create balloons for them.

In the following illustration, the exploded view with its balloons is shown with the parts list which supplies the component item numbers.

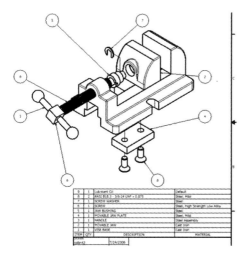

Definition of Balloons

You place balloons on assembly drawings to identify parts in the drawing and relate them to rows in the parts list. When you place a balloon on a part, the item number of the part displays in the balloon. This item number is the same item number used in the parts list.

Balloons and parts lists are associative. If an item number in the parts list changes, the change is also reflected in the balloon. This associativity is unidirectional only. If you override the item number in the balloon, the new value is not reflected in the parts list.

In the following illustration, a balloon is shown being added to a drawing view.

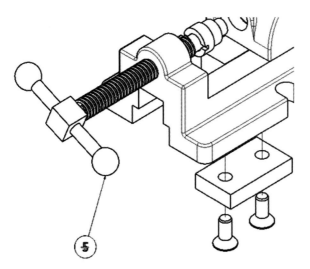

Example of Creating Balloons

After completing the design of a loco screw jack, you need to document the design. After creating a drawing view of the assembly, you create a parts list to document the components that make up the assembly. Using the Auto Balloon tool you quickly place balloons with numbers to correspond to the item numbers in the parts list.

In the following illustration, the Loco Jack Screw assembly drawing is shown with balloons and parts list in place.

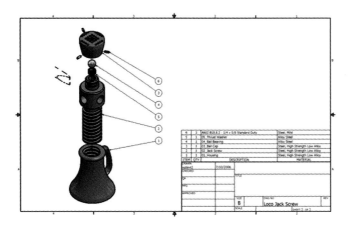

Placing Balloons Manually

You use the Balloon tool to place balloons manually in a drawing view. If you create a parts list before adding balloons, the balloons use properties specified by the parts list. If the view does not have an associated parts list, the BOM Properties dialog box opens so you can set the properties.

The BOM Properties dialog box is shown in the following illustration. You set the properties for balloons in this dialog box when no parts list has been created.

Access

Balloon

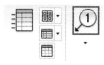

Ribbon: **Annotate tab > Table panel**

Toolbar: **Drawing Annotation Panel**
Keyboard: **B**

Procedure: Placing Balloons Manually

The following steps describe how to place balloons manually in your drawing view.

1   Click Annotate tab > Table panel > Balloon. Select a component in the drawing view. If this is the first balloon, and there is no parts list in the drawing, the BOM Properties dialog box is displayed. Adjust the options as required and click OK.

2   Click to position the balloon, then right-click and select Continue on the shortcut menu.

3   Continue selecting components and placing balloons as required. Right-click in the graphics window and click Done when completed.

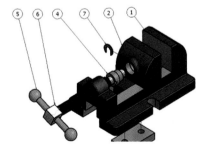

Note: **Adjusting Balloon Location** *After you have placed a balloon, you can adjust its location by clicking the balloon and dragging it to a new location. If you select multiple balloons, click and drag one of them and they all move together.*

Procedure: Placing Balloons for Custom and Virtual Parts

The following steps describe how to place balloons for virtual and custom parts.

1   Click Annotate tab > Table panel > Balloon. Select a component in the drawing view. Right-click in the graphics window and select Custom/Virtual on the shortcut menu.

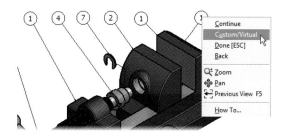

2   Click to position the balloon, then right-click and select Continue on the shortcut menu. The Custom/Virtual Parts dialog box opens. Select the custom or virtual part you want to balloon.

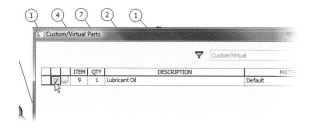

3   Click OK to create the balloon.

Placing Balloons Automatically

Auto ballooning is a process in which all components contained within a single view can be ballooned simultaneously. When you auto balloon a view, you select the components in the view that you would like to balloon, and balloons are automatically placed on the parts that you select. You use the Auto Balloon tool to access options to control the placement of your balloons.

Access

Auto Balloon

Ribbon: **Annotate tab > Table panel**

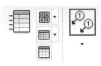

Toolbar: **Drawing Annotation Panel**

Auto Balloon Options

The Auto Balloon dialog box is shown in the following illustration. You use this dialog box to set the properties for view and components, balloon placement, BOM settings, and style overrides.

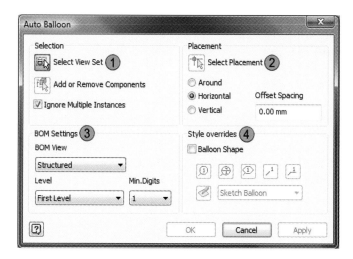

	Section	Description
1	**Selection**	Selects views and components for balloon attachment. • Select View Set sets the source for balloon item numbers. • Add/Remove Components adds components to or removes them from the selection set for balloon attachment. You can use Window select and SHIFT+select to remove components. • Ignore Multiple Instances, when selected, permits placement of balloons on the first selected instance only. Clear the check box to place balloons on all instances.
2	**Placement**	Specifies the placement of balloons in the view. • Select Placement specifies Around, Horizontal, or Vertical placement of balloons. • Offset Spacing sets the distance between balloon edges. The original value is specified in the balloon style.

	Section	Description
③	**BOM Settings**	The BOM view set in the source assembly determines the settings and properties available.
④	**Style Overrides**	Provides style overrides for balloon shapes during creation. Sketch symbols are available when sketch symbols exist in the active document's drawing resources. Select the check box to replace the style-defined balloon shape with a different shape. Click a button to specify the appropriate balloon shape. Clear the check box to use the default balloon style shape.

Procedure: Placing Balloons Automatically

The following steps describe how to place balloons on a view automatically.

1. Create a drawing containing at least one view of an assembly.

2. Click Annotate tab > Table panel > Auto Balloon. Select the view to be ballooned.

3. Select the components in the view to be ballooned. You can select components individually or with a selection window.

4   Select the desired options in the Auto Balloon dialog box, and click the Select
    Placement button.

5   You can preview the position of the balloons by moving the cursor. Click in the sheet to set
    the balloon positions.

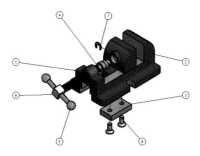

6   Click OK to place the auto balloons.

7   Complete the ballooning process by adjusting the positions of balloons as required.

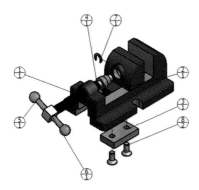

Editing Balloons

Whether created manually or automatically, all balloons are edited by the same method. Using the Edit Balloon dialog box, you can change the balloon style and the value displayed in the balloon. You can also change a balloon's arrowhead, add a vertex to the leader line, attach balloons, and align balloons in a drawing view.

In the following illustration, a balloon for a virtual part has been attached to another balloon.

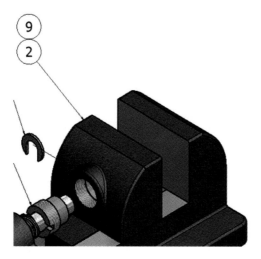

Access

Edit Balloon

Shortcut Menu: **Right-click balloon > Edit Balloon**

Balloon Shortcut Menu

In the following illustration, the shortcut menu shows different balloon editing options.

Edit Balloon Dialog Box

The Edit Balloon dialog box is shown in the following illustration, with options to change the appearance of balloons and their associated values.

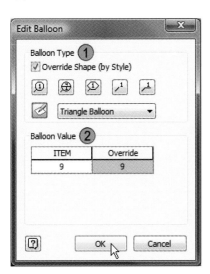

Option	Description
Balloon Type	Sets the balloon type for the selected balloons. • Override Shape (by Style) sets the balloon shape to a style in the active drafting standard. Check the box to override the default balloon style. Clear the check box to use the default balloon style. • User-defined Symbol selects a sketched symbol to use as a balloon. Available only if you have added sketched symbols to the drawing resources. Sketched balloons use all of the properties of the associated balloon style, and by default, display the item and quantity values.
Balloon Value	Override the values displayed in the selected balloons. • Item sets the value for the item in both the balloon and the parts list. Select the value and then enter a new value. • Override overrides the value in the balloon only. If you override the balloon value, it does not update if you make changes in the parts list. Select the value, and then type a new value.

Procedure: Editing Balloons

The following steps show how to edit balloons.

1   In a drawing view with balloons, right-click a balloon and select an editing option on the shortcut menu.

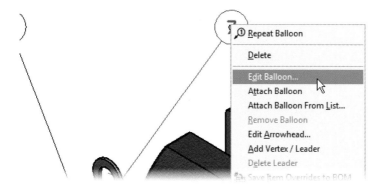

2   Make edits to balloon as required.

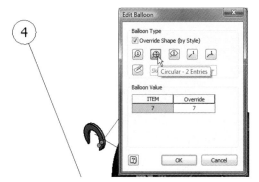

3   Repeat steps 1 and 2 to edit more balloons.

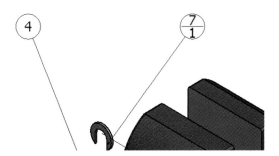

Note: **Selecting Multiple Balloons** *You can select multiple balloons using the window or crossing method, or press CTRL and select the balloons that you want to edit. Right-click in the graphics window to select an editing option.*

Exercise | Create Balloons

In this exercise, you place balloons for a drawing view using the Auto Balloon tool, edit their style, and manually place a balloon for a virtual part.

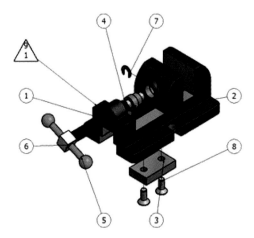

The completed exercise

Completing the Exercise: *To complete the exercise, follow the steps in this book or in the onscreen exercise. In the onscreen list of chapters and exercises, click Chapter 10: Annotating Assembly Drawings. Click Exercise: Create Balloons.*

1   Open *Balloons.idw.*

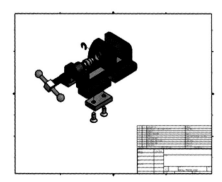

2   Click Annotate tab > Table panel > Auto Balloon. In the graphics window, click in the exploded view.

3   The Add or Remove Components button is activated automatically. Use a crossing window, by clicking at Point 1 and then Point 2, to select all of the components in the exploded view.

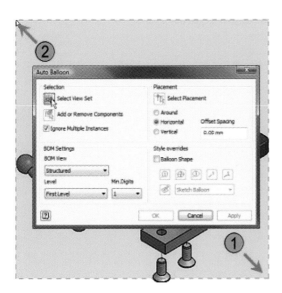

4   In the Auto Balloon dialog box:

- Click Select Placement.
- Under Placement, click Around. Under Offset Spacing, enter **6.00 mm**.
- Under Style Overrides, select Balloon Shape. Select Circular - 2 Entries.

5   Move your cursor to set the preview as shown in the following illustration. Click in the graphics window to place balloons. In the Auto Balloon dialog box, click OK.

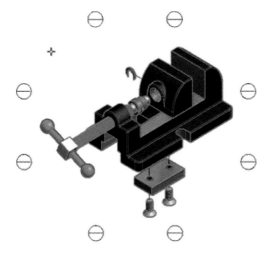

6   Confirm that your view matches the illustration.

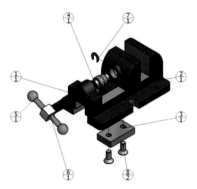

7   You now add a balloon for the virtual part. Enter **B** to access the balloon tool. Select the part as shown.

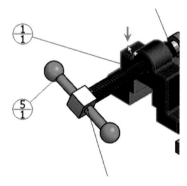

8   Right-click in the graphics window. Click Custom/Virtual.

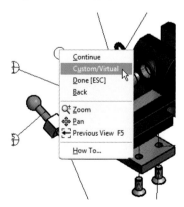

9   In the graphics window:

- Click to place the balloon.
- Right-click in the graphics window. Click Continue.
- The Custom/Virtual Parts dialog box is displayed. Check Item 9.
- Click OK.

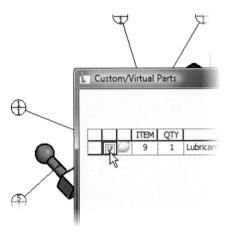

10   Right-click in the graphics window. Click Done.

11   In the graphics window, CTRL+click all of the split balloons. Right-click in the graphics window. Click Edit Balloon.

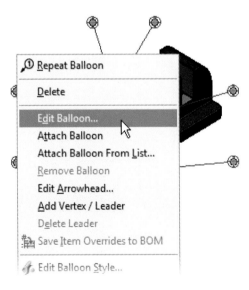

12 To remove the override:

- In the Edit Balloon dialog box, under Balloon Type, clear the Override Shape (by Style) check box.
- Click the same box again. Verify that the options below are grayed out.
- Click OK.

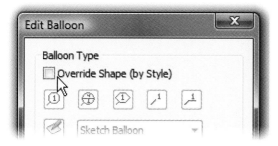

13 The balloons update to the default style. Confirm that your view matches the following illustration.

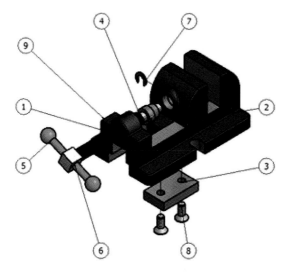

14   In the graphics window, right-click the balloon for Item 9. Click Edit Balloon.

15   In the Edit Balloon dialog box, under Balloon Type, change the settings as shown:
- Select Override Shape (by Style).
- Click the User-defined Symbol button.
- Select Triangle Balloon from the list.
- Click OK.

16   The Item 9 balloon updates to the Triangle Balloon sketched symbol, and displays the item number and the item quantity. Confirm that your view matches the following illustration.

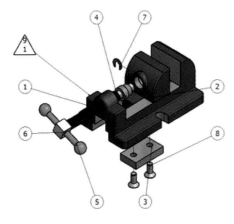

17   Close the file. Do not save.

Chapter Summary

Annotating assembly drawings typically requires the identification and description of components using balloons and a parts list. This type of information is managed in the bill of materials. With your understanding of these tools and workflows, you can create production-ready assembly drawings.

Having completed this chapter, you can:

- View and edit bill of materials data.
- Create and customize parts lists to document the components in your assembly.
- Review balloons and their purpose in the drawing annotation process.

Chapter 11
Drawing Standards and Resources

Previous chapters focused primarily on how to create and annotate drawing views of your part and assembly designs. You also need to understand how to control the appearance of your drawings so that they follow your company standards. This chapter focuses on the tools and resources that help you to define and follow drawing standards and styles, distribute your drawing views across multiple sheets, and create title blocks and borders that meet your specific documentation needs.

Objectives

After completing this chapter, you will be able to:

- Set drafting standards to control the appearance of drawing features.

- Use drawing resources to create multiple sheets and add borders and title blocks to your drawings.

Lesson 40 | Setting Drawing Standards

In this lesson you learn how to use drafting standards to control the appearance of drawing features. The ANSI, BSI, DIN, GB, ISO, JIS and GOST drafting standards are supported. You use these standards to control the appearance of drawing features such as dimensions, balloons, weld symbols, and parts lists. The default standard is determined by the option you select during installation and can be changed for each drawing.

The following illustration shows the Style and Standard Editor dialog box. From the styles list on the left side of the dialog box, you can see the different options for setting styles and standards.

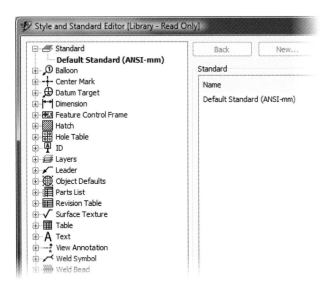

Objectives

After completing this lesson, you will be able to:

- Describe styles and their role in drawing standards.

- Create styles in the Style and Standard Editor dialog box.

- State the use and function of drawing standards.

- Describe the drawing styles and standards editor environment and the options available.

- Define styles in the active standard.

- Identify how layers can be used to logically organize geometry in drawings.

About Styles

Styles provide an efficient way to control the appearance of your drawings and define your company standards. Each style is a subset of a standard. As you are defining your styles, you are also defining your drawing standards.

In the following illustration, the styles list is displayed.

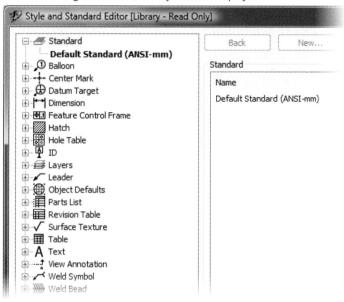

Definition of Styles

A style is a collection of settings that defines an annotation theme. Styles are used to control the appearance of a production-ready drawing. A style applies a common theme to common features on a drawing. If applied properly, this theme will be used throughout the design and manufacturing processes.

In the following illustration, a dimension style is being updated to reflect the company standard.

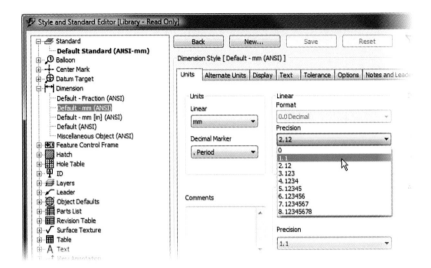

Examples of Styles

A feature on a drawing is defined by the annotations applied to it. For instance, the tolerance on a dimension may determine the method used to create the hole when manufactured. Each of these annotations is defined in a style. Dimension styles, balloon styles, layer styles, and text styles are just a few of the styles available. A company will define styles to best match the products it designs and manufactures, and the manufacturing processes available.

Creating Styles with the Style Editor

Styles are created or modified in the Style and Standard Editor dialog box. The procedure for other styles is similar.

In the following illustration, the Hatch style is being edited to add and remove patterns from the active style.

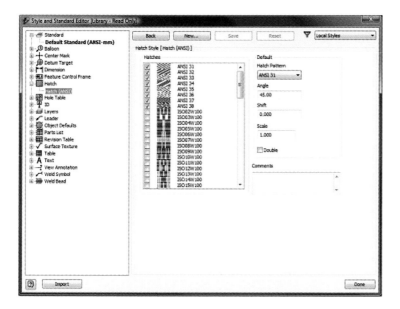

Procedure: Creating Dimension Styles

The following steps describe how to create a dimension style in the Style and Standard Editor dialog box.

1   Click Manage tab > Styles and Standards > Styles Editor. In the Style and Standard Editor dialog box, expand the Dimension Style list.

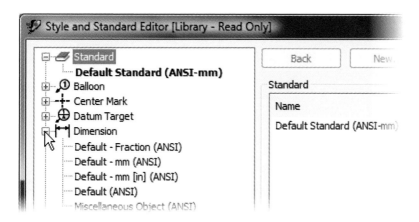

2   Create a new dimension style based on the dimension style that is closest to your standards.

3   Adjust the values of the new dimension style.

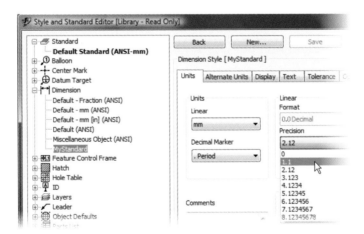

Procedure: Creating Text Styles

The following steps describe how to create a text style in the Style and Standard Editor dialog box.

1   Click Manage tab > Styles and Standards > Styles Editor. In the Style and Standard Editor
     dialog box, expand the Text list.

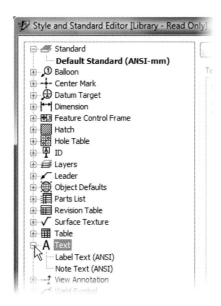

2   Select Note Text and create a new text style.

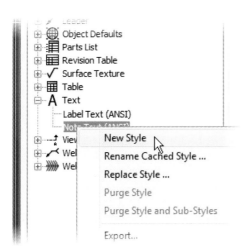

3   Assign a unique name to the style.

4   Adjust the values of the new text style.

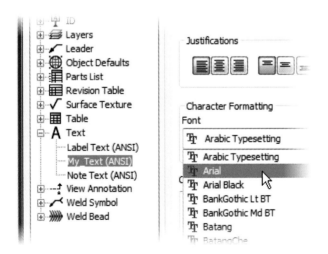

Procedure: Creating Layer Styles

The following steps describe how to create layer styles in the Style and Standard Editor.

1   Click Manage tab > Styles and Standards > Styles Editor. In the Style and Standard Editor dialog box, expand the Layers list.

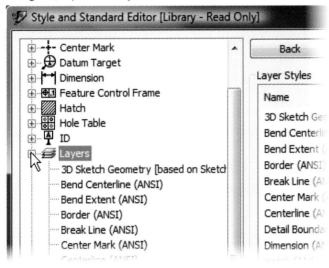

2   Create a new layer based on the layer that is closest to your new values.

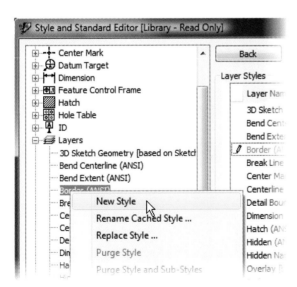

3   Adjust the values of the new layer.

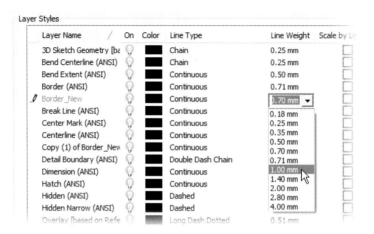

Procedure: Creating Balloon Styles

The following steps describe how to create balloon styles in the Style and Standard Editor dialog box.

1   Click Manage tab > Styles and Standards > Styles Editor. In the Style and Standard Editor dialog box, expand the Balloon list.

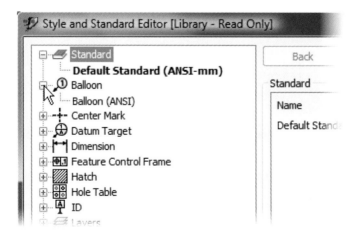

2   Create a new balloon style.

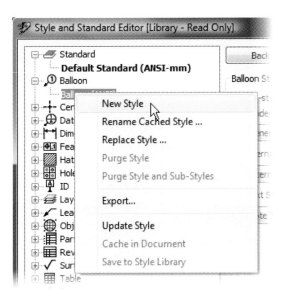

3   Adjust the values of the new balloon style.

About Drawing Standards

The Style and Standard Editor dialog box contains the options required to implement existing standards or to create your own company standards. You define standards to control the appearance of your drawings. You can change the default values, select an existing standard, or import standards from a DWG file.

In the following illustration, the Style and Standard Editor dialog box displays the options for Feature Control Frames.

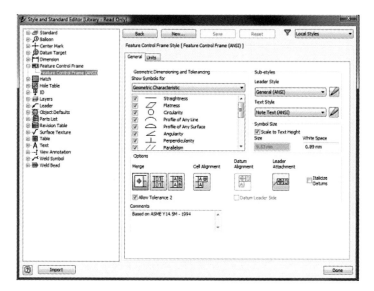

Definition of Drawing Standards

A standard is a compilation of styles under a title. Each style is edited to define an accepted practice that is followed by everyone involved in the project, and then the style is added to the standard. Drawing standards provide an efficient and consistent means to communicate designs to the many groups that work on a project.

In the following illustration, the settings for hole tables are adjusted to define company drawing standards.

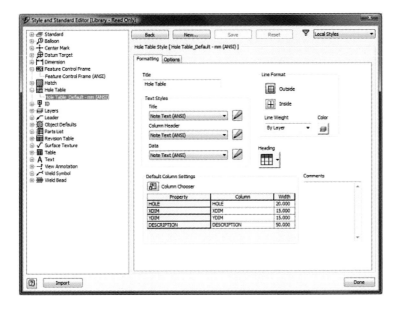

Example of Drawing Standards

In production-ready drawings, standards are used to communicate to everyone on the production team. A company typically adopts an existing standard, modifies an existing standard, or creates its own styles. Using standards, the design team applies specific annotations to a design. Referencing the same standards, the production team defines the manufacturing processes required to produce the design.

Properties of Drawing Standards

You use the Style and Standard Editor dialog box to control the drawing feature properties. When you create a new drawing, the default drafting standard is determined by the options chosen during installation. You can create a new standard or modify an existing standard for the current drawing. When you create or modify drafting standards, the changes apply only to the current drawing. If you want the changes to be available to all new drawings, you must save the standard to the styles library.

In the following illustration, a new drawing standard is created based on a default standard.

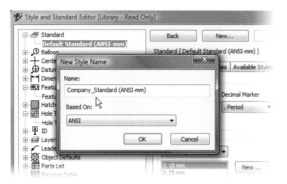

Style and Standard Editor Dialog Box

In the following illustration, the list of available standards is displayed, along with a standard created from one of the existing standards.

The Style and Standard Editor dialog box consists of two areas:

Area	Description
Standards and Styles List	Select a standard or style to edit. Double-click a standard to activate it. The active standard appears bold.
Editing Pane	The editing pane changes to reflect substyles and properties of the selected style or standard.

Default Drafting Standards

The following list summarizes the available default drafting standards. You can use these standards as they are, modify them, or create a new standard based on one of the default standards.

- ANSI

- BSI

- DIN

- GB

- GOST

- ISO

- JIS

Style and Standard Editor Dialog Box

In the following illustration, the current values of the new standard are being reviewed in the Style and Standard Editor dialog box.

Drawing Standard Properties

When you select an available drafting standard from the list, five tabs display containing the specific properties of the standard. You use the tabs to navigate through the different settings of the standard.

Tab	Description
General Tab	Use this tab to control common drawing properties: units, preset line weights, character exclusion from automatic alphabetical indexing, and global line scale. 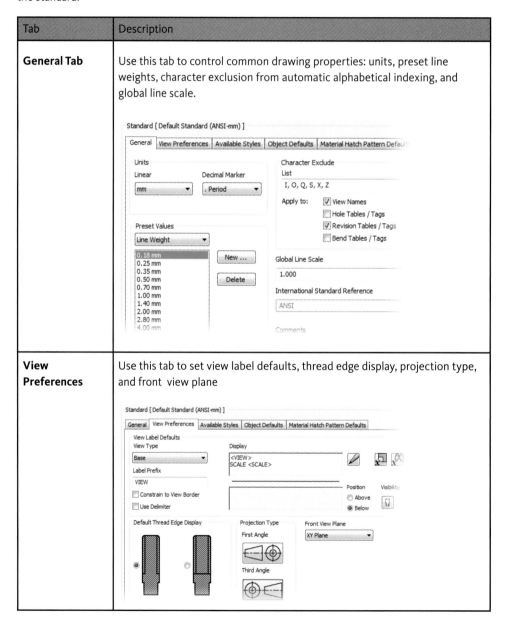
View Preferences	Use this tab to set view label defaults, thread edge display, projection type, and front view plane

Tab	Description
Available Styles Tab	Use this tab to select styles for balloons, center marks, dimensions, and others. Only styles that are selected are available for use in the drafting standard. Make certain the filter setting at the top of the Style and Standard Editor dialog box is set to All Styles in order to view all styles in the style library. 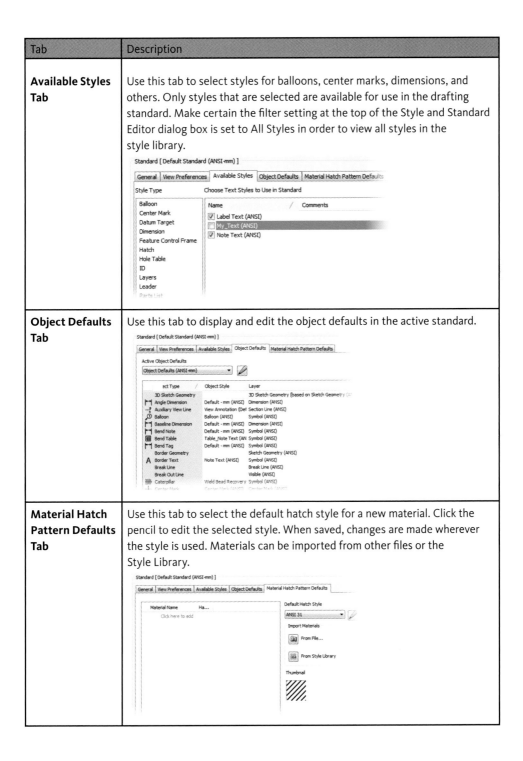
Object Defaults Tab	Use this tab to display and edit the object defaults in the active standard.
Material Hatch Pattern Defaults Tab	Use this tab to select the default hatch style for a new material. Click the pencil to edit the selected style. When saved, changes are made wherever the style is used. Materials can be imported from other files or the Style Library.

Defining the Active Standard

Standards applied to drawings in the Style and Standard Editor are useful for changing the appearance and function of a production-ready drawing. It is important to convey information in a concise manner and for every member of the design and manufacturing teams to interpret drawings in the same way. Defining the proper standard ensures that drawings are interpreted correctly.

In the following illustration, dimension styles are being selected to include in the active standard.

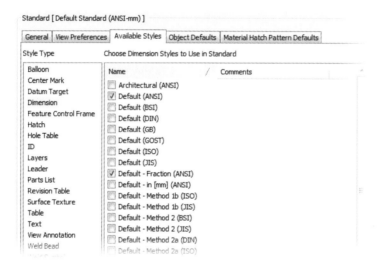

Guidelines for Defining the Active Style

In a typical workflow, you first define the required styles and then incorporate them into the standard. The following procedure is based on that workflow. It is possible to create a standard first and define the styles to be used in the standard later. This method is analogous to updating a standard to incorporate changes once a standard has been established.

Procedure: Defining the Active Style

The following steps describe how to define an active style in a drawing.

1   Click Manage tab > Styles and Standards > Styles Editor. In the Style and Standard Editor dialog box, in the Styles list, create a new standard based on the existing standard that is closest to your standards.

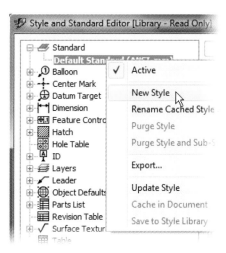

2   Assign a unique name to the style.

3   Click the Available Styles tab. Select the Style Type.

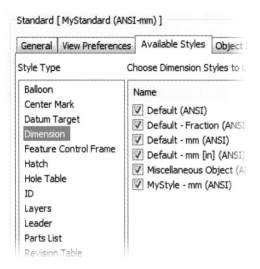

4   Select the styles to be available in this standard.

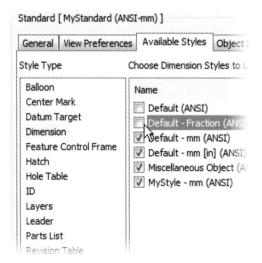

Using Layers

Layers provide a way for you to logically organize 2D geometry in your drawings. They also improve the results of importing geometry from other CAD systems that use layers.

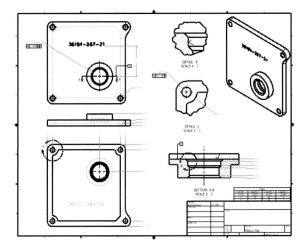

Layers

You can use layers to organize your 2D geometry in a logical manner by separating different types of geometry and grouping them together based on common features, properties, or uses.

When you assign types of geometry to layers, you can control the properties of all geometry on a layer by changing the layer's properties. This approach is more efficient than changing properties on each piece of geometry separately.

Layer Properties

The following properties can be applied to all geometry on a given layer.

- On/Off
- Color
- Line Type

- Line Weight
- Scale by Line Weight
- Plotting

The following illustration shows a typical 2D drawing. The geometry is grouped logically onto layers. For example, visible lines are placed on a different layer than hidden lines, section lines, and annotations.

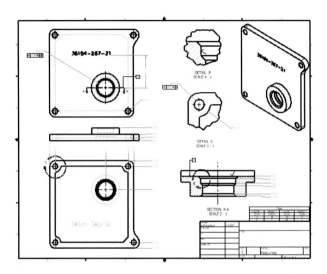

> **Note:** **Automatic Layer Assignment** *When you create geometry and annotations in a drawing, they are automatically created on a specific layer. Unlike other CAD applications that assign new geometry to the current layer, Autodesk® Inventor® uses settings in the active standard to determine layer assignment for geometry and annotations.*

Creating and Managing Layers

You use the Style and Standard Editor dialog box to create and manage layers. The default layers are stored within the style library and are edited and managed using the same tools as other kinds of styles. Because layers are stored as styles within a style library, you have the same advantages of management and portability that other style-based properties have.

Layer Styles in the Style and Standard Editor Dialog Box

The following options are available for editing layer styles.

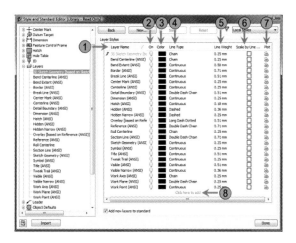

	Option	Description
(1)	**Layer Name**	Click to edit the layer name. If you rename a layer, object types assigned to the original layer name are updated to reflect the new layer name.
(2)	**On/Off**	Click the light bulb icon to toggle the layer on or off. When a layer is off, geometry on that layer is not displayed.
(3)	**Color**	Click the color swatch button and select a new color in the Color dialog box.
(4)	**Line Types**	Select a linetype from the list.
(5)	**Line Weight**	Select a line weight from the list or enter a new one.
(6)	**Scale by Line Weight**	Select this option to scale the linetype based on the line weight.
(7)	**Plot**	Controls whether the selected layer is plotted. Select the icon plot to toggle On/Off.
(8)	**Click Here to Add**	Select to add a new layer to the layer style. The properties of the currently selected layer are copied to the new layer by default.

Object Defaults and Automatic Layer Mapping

When you create geometry and annotations in a drawing, they are automatically placed on specific layers. This process is controlled by the Object Defaults style that is currently in use. After you select the Object Defaults style in the Style and Standard Editor dialog box, you can use the following options to configure the object default styles and layer mappings.

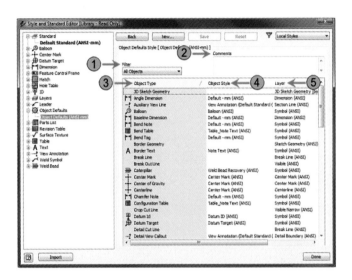

	Option	Description
1	**Filter**	Select a filter in the list to filter the object types that are displayed.
		• All Objects - All objects types are displayed.
		• Dimension Objects - Only dimension objects are displayed.
		• Leader Objects - Only leader objects are displayed.
		• Model/View Objects - Only objects related to the view geometry or view annotation (such as labels) are displayed.
		• Text Objects - Only sketch text and note text objects are displayed.
2	**Comments**	Optionally enter comments related to the object styles and layer mapping.

	Option	Description
③	**Object Type**	This column indicates the specific object type to which to apply a default style and layer assignment.
④	**Object Style**	Select the default object style to be used for the selected object. Not all objects can be assigned an object style.
⑤	**Layer**	Select the layer assignment from the list. If a layer is assigned and its name is changed later, the layer mapping takes on the new layer name automatically.

Procedure: Creating and Using Layers

The following steps describe how to create and use layers.

1 Open a drawing containing views and annotations.

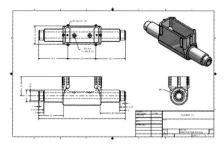

2 Click Annotate tab > Format panel > Edit Layer.

3 In the Layer Styles pane, click the Click Here to Add area and create a new layer by assigning a name, color, linetype, and line weight. Click Save to save the new layer.

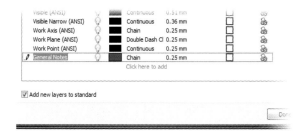

4   In the Style and Standard Editor dialog box, click the Object Defaults style and assign the appropriate object types to the new layer. Click Save, then click Done.

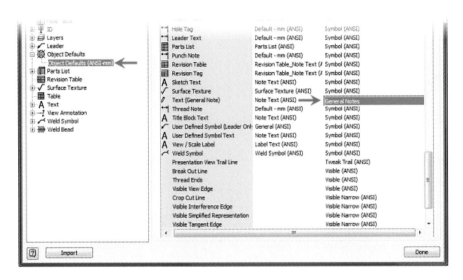

5   As you create new objects, they are automatically assigned to the correct layer.

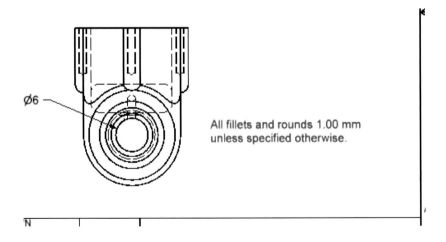

Ø6

All fillets and rounds 1.00 mm
unless specified otherwise.

6   To change the layer of objects in the drawing, select the objects, then select the new layer in the layer list on the ribbon.

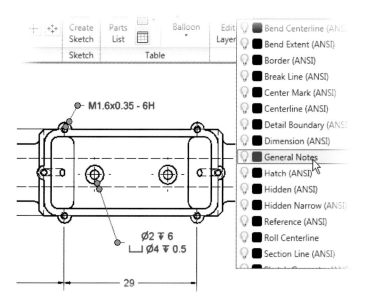

Tip: **Edit Layers Tool** *The Edit Layers tool is location on the Annotate tab > Format panel > Edit Layer.*

Exercise | Set Drawing Standards

In this exercise, you define a new drafting standard, text, and dimension style.

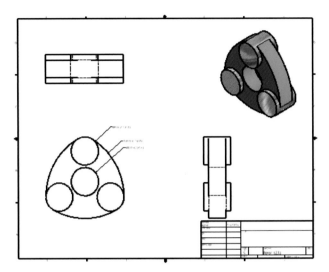

The completed exercise

Completing the Exercise:	*To complete the exercise, follow the steps in this book or in the onscreen exercise. In the onscreen list of chapters and exercises, click Chapter 11: Drawing Standards and Resources. Click Exercise: Set Drawing Standards.*

1   Open *Drawing Standards.idw.*

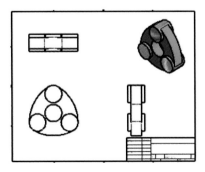

2 Create a custom standard:

- Click Manage tab > Styles and Standards panel > Style and Standard Editor.
- In the Style and Standard Editor dialog box, click Default Standard (ANSI-mm). Click New.
- In the New Style Name dialog box, enter **My-Standard.** Click OK.

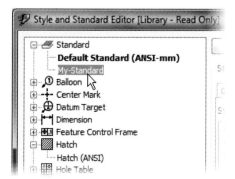

3 Select the dimension styles to use in My- Standard:

- In the Style and Standard Editor dialog box, click the Available Styles tab.
- Under Style Type, click Dimension.
- Clear the Default - Fraction (ANSI) check box.
- Click Save.

4 Set the linear precision:

- In the Styles list, expand Dimension.
- Click Default (ANSI).
- Click the Units tab. Select 3.123 from the Linear Precision list.
- Click Save.

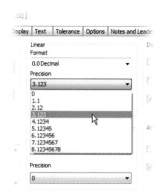

5   Repeat these settings for Default - mm (ANSI) and Default - mm [in] (ANSI). When prompted, click Yes to Save Edits. Click Save.

6   Create a new text style:
- In the Style list, expand Text.
- Move the cursor to Note Text (ANSI).
- Right-click Note Text. Click New Style.
- In the New Style Name dialog box, enter **Gen-Dim-Text.** Click OK.

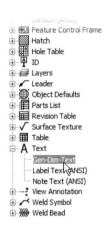

7   Set the font for the new text style:
- In the Style and Standard Editor dialog box, under Character Formatting, select Arial from the font list.
- Under Comments, enter **General Dimension Text.**
- Click Save.

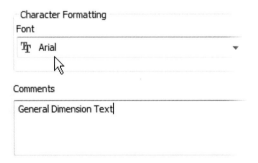

8   Assign text to the Gen-Dim-Text style:

- From the Standards list, select My-Standard.
- Under Standard, click the Available Styles tab.
- From the Style Type list, select Text. Select the Gen-Dim-Text check box.
- Verify that Label Text (ANSI) and Note Text (ANSI) are selected. Click Save.

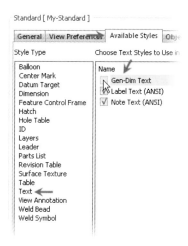

9   Assign Gen-Dim-Text to a dimension style:

- In the Styles list, expand Dimension. Click Default (ANSI).
- Under Dimension Style, Text tab, in the Primary Text Style list, select Gen-Dim-Text. Click Save.
- Repeat for Dimension Styles: Default - mm (ANSI) and Default - mm [in] (ANSI).
- Click Yes when prompted to Save Edits. Click Done.
- Click Yes to Save Edits.

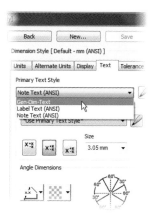

10   Assign My-Standard to the drawing:

- Click Tools tab > Options panel > Document Settings.
- In the Drawing Standard.idw Document Settings dialog box, on the Standard tab, select My-Standard from the Active Standard list.
- Click OK.

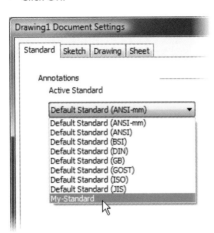

11   Apply dimensions to the front view:

- Click Annotate tab > Dimension panel > General Dimension.
- Place dimensions as illustrated. Right-click in the graphics window, click Done.

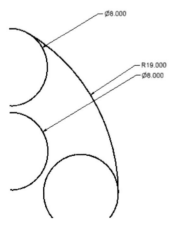

12   Change the dimensions to a new dimension style:

- Press CTRL and select the three dimensions.
- On the Annotate tab > Format panel > select Default -mm [in] (ANSI) from the Style list.

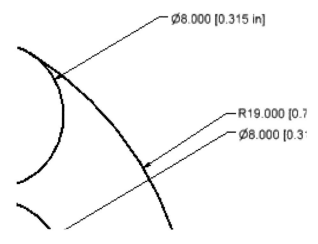

13   Close all files. Do not save.

Lesson 41 | Drawing Resources

In this lesson, you learn how to use the various drawing resources that are available in the drawing environment. A typical drawing contains several features that are not directly related to the 3D geometry they are used to represent. Features such as sheets, title blocks, borders, and views are all used to present information that meets typical drawing standards.

Drawing sheets provide an efficient way to translate 3D designs into a 2D format for communication with customers, vendors, and the production team.

In the following illustration, a custom title block is used on a production-ready drawing to comply with company standards.

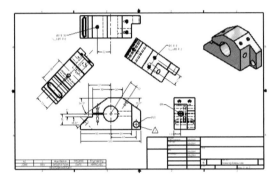

Objectives

After completing this lesson, you will be able to:

- Describe drawing sheets.

- Create drawing sheets.

- Describe custom border and title blocks.

- Create custom borders.

- Create custom title blocks.

About Drawing Sheets

When you are working in the 3D environment, you still need to document your design in 2D. Drawing sheets are the foundation for creating 2D production-ready drawings.

In the following illustration, a sheet shows typical drawing resources. A drawing border and a title block containing basic drawing information are the beginning for creating a production-ready drawing.

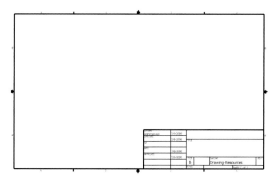

Definition of Drawing Sheets

You create a drawing sheet that contains all the standard elements required to communicate the information needed to manufacture a design. By default, a new drawing sheet contains a border and a title block. You add drawing views and annotations to complete the production-ready drawing.

In the following illustration, a production-ready drawing is created on a B-size sheet. The drawing sheet provides the foundation for essential information for production drawings: the title block, drawing views with annotations, and a revision block.

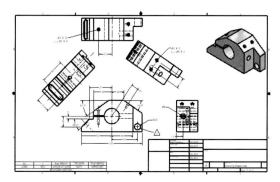

Example of a Drawing Sheet

In the following illustration, a basic production-ready drawing is created on an A-size sheet. The drawing contains the essential information for a production drawing: title block, border, and orientation (portrait).

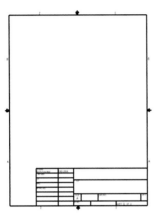

Creating Sheets

Although each new drawing is created with a single sheet, the number of sheets that can be included in a single drawing is not limited.

When you create a new sheet in the drawing, depending on the method chosen, either the New Sheet dialog box appears or the sheet size and properties are duplicated from the current sheet.

The following illustration shows multiple sheets in the browser. You can view only one sheet at a time. In this illustration, Sheet:2 is being viewed. To activate a sheet, double-click the sheet in the browser.

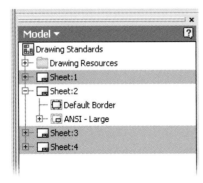

Access

New Sheet

Ribbon: **Place Views tab > Sheets panel**

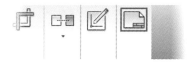

Toolbar: **Drawing Views Panel**
Browser: **Right-click in a blank area, click New Sheet**
Keyboard: **CTRL+SHIFT+N**

New Sheets

New Sheets are created based on the active sheet. To create a new sheet, right-click in the browser and click New Sheet.

The New Sheet dialog box is displayed when you add a new sheet from the Insert menu. When you add a sheet from the panel bar or the shortcut menu, the format and orientation of the new sheet are based on those of the current sheet.

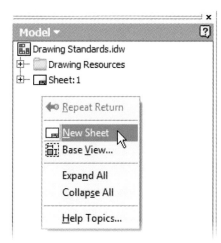

Edit Sheet Dialog Box

After you create a sheet, you can edit that sheet by right-clicking on it in the browser and clicking Edit Sheet. The Edit Sheet dialog box is shown here.

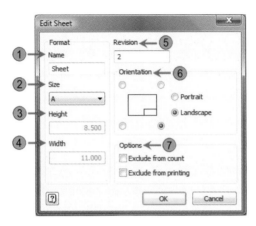

The New Sheet dialog box contains the following options.

	Option	Description
(1)	**Name**	Displays the name of the sheet. Enter a new name to rename the sheet.
(2)	**Size**	Select a predefined sheet size, or select Custom to enter a custom sheet size.
(3)	**Height**	(Available only when Custom is selected from the Size drop-down list.) Enter a height for the sheet.
(4)	**Width**	(Available only when Custom is selected from the Size drop-down list.) Enter a width for the sheet.
(5)	**Revision**	Enter a drawing revision number.
(6)	**Orientation**	Select an orientation option, either Portrait or Landscape.
(7)	**Options**	Use the Exclude from count option to prevent the total sheet count from including this sheet. Use the Exclude from printing option to exclude the sheet from print jobs

Sheet Format for Sheet Layout

For each drawing, a Sheet Formats folder is located in the Drawing Resources folder in the drawing browser. You can expand this folder to display predefined sheet formats to automatically create predefined drawing views.

A sheet format is defined for most common sheet sizes. Double-click a sheet format to create a new sheet using the predefined sheet size and views. Each sheet format consists of one view based on a predefined orientation, such as Front, and other projected views. The view scale is set to 1 and may require editing after placement.

Procedure: Creating New Sheets from the Browser

The following steps describe how to create drawing sheets.

1   Move the cursor to the browser and right-click.

2   Click New Sheet.

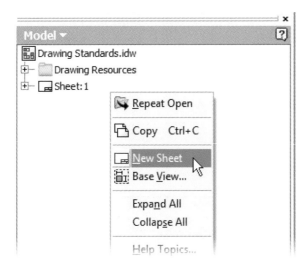

Procedure: Using Sheet Formats

The following steps describe how to use sheet formats.

1   In the browser, expand the Drawing Resources folder.

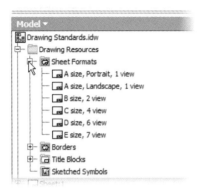

2   Double-click the desired layout.

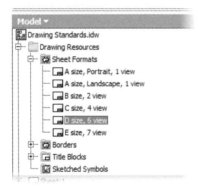

3   In the Select Component dialog box, navigate to the desired part or assembly file.

About Custom Borders and Title Blocks

If the default borders or title blocks do not meet your design needs, you can create custom borders that are updated automatically if the sheet size changes. You can create custom title blocks to match your company standards for information contained in a drawing.

In the following illustration, an A-size border is modified to add more drawing zones. The title block is customized by adding fields to meet company standards.

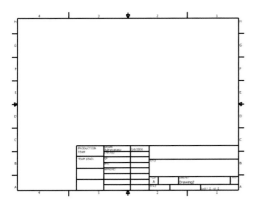

Definition of Custom Borders and Title Blocks

Custom borders contain zone specifications, and are updated to match the sheet size. You can add text and sketched elements to custom title blocks to match your company standards.

In the following illustration, a border was created for use on an A-size drawing sheet. That same border is now used on a B-size print. The border is automatically updated to the drawing sheet size.

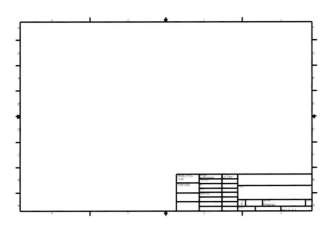

Example of Custom Borders and Title Blocks

The following illustration shows a drawing sheet with a custom border and title block. Both the border and the title block were created by modifying existing drawing resources and adding sketched elements based on the company standards for design information.

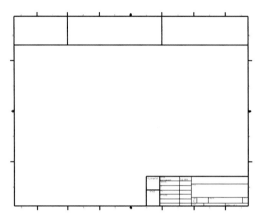

Creating Custom Borders

If the default borders do not meet your design needs, you can create custom borders that are updated automatically if the sheet size changes.

In the following illustration, a custom border block has been created and inserted on the sheet.

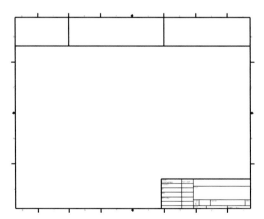

Define New Zone Border

You can use the Default Drawing Border Parameters dialog box to create custom zone borders by specifying zone indicators, text styles, and sheet margins.

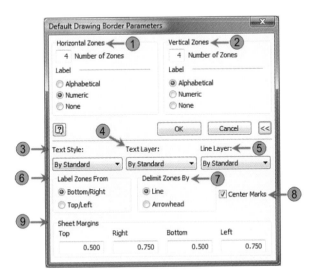

	Option	Description
①	**Horizontal Zones**	• **Number of Zones:** Enter the number of horizontal zones for the border. • **Label:** Select a zone label option.
②	**Vertical Zones**	• **Number of Zones:** Enter the number of vertical zones for the border. • **Label:** Select a label option.
③	**Text Style**	Select the text style to be used for zone labels.
④	**Text Layer**	Select the layer to which to assign the zone labels.
⑤	**Line Layer**	Select the layer to which to assign the border lines.
⑥	**Label Zones From**	Select a direction from which to start the zone labels.
⑦	**Delimit Zones By**	Select a zone indicator (Line or Arrowhead).

	Option	Description
8	**Center Marks**	Select to place arrowheads at the vertical and horizontal midpoints of the border.
9	**Sheet Margins**	Enter sheet margin values to adjust the spacing between the border and the edge of the sheet.

Creating Custom Title Blocks

Each drawing template contains at least one default title block that is placed on each new sheet in the drawing. In most cases the default title block requires only minimal modifications to include information required by your company.

Like other drawing resources, title blocks are stored in the current drawing. Saving the drawing as a template ensures access to the revised title block at a later date.

When you add text elements to the title block, use the Text tool on the Sketch Panel bar to include property fields or prompted entry items.

The following illustration shows two ways to access editing title blocks.

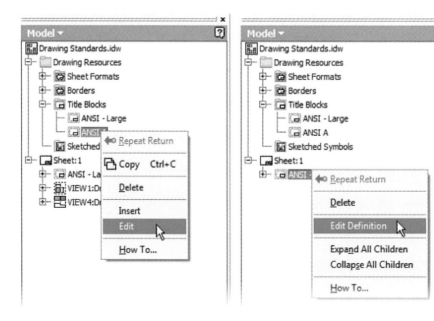

Procedure: Customizing Title Blocks

The following steps describe how to customize a title block by adding text and sketched segments.

1   In the Title Blocks folder, right-click a file. Click Edit.

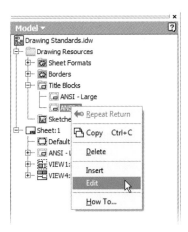

2   Click Sketch tab > Draw panel > Text.

3   Select a location on the drawing for the text.

4   In the Format Text dialog box, select Properties - Drawing from the Type list.

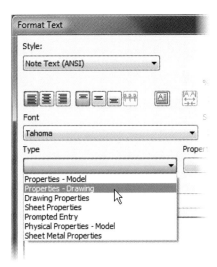

5   Format and enter the text.

6   Using standard sketch tools, add any additional sketched items. Save the title block edits.

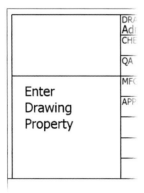

Exercise | Use Drawing Resources

In this exercise, you use the Drawing Resources folder features to perform common tasks in the drawing environment.

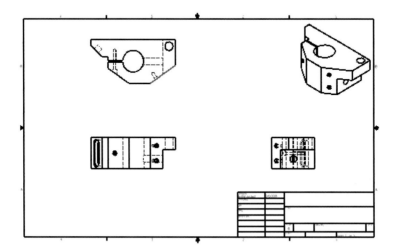

The completed exercise

1. Create a new drawing based on the *ANSI (mm).idw template*.

2. Define the views for the sheet:
   - In the browser, expand the Drawing Resources and Sheet Formats folders.
   - Double-click the C size, 4 view sheet format to create a new sheet with predefined views.

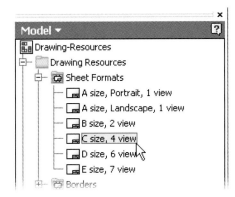

3. Locate the *Drawing-Resources.ipt* file:
   - In the Select Component dialog box, click Browse.
   - Navigate to the *Drawing-Resources.ipt* file. Click Open.
   - Click OK.

4   Create a B size sheet:

- In the browser, right-click Sheet:2. Click Edit Sheet.
- In the Edit Sheet dialog box, select B from the Size list.
- Click OK. Arrange the views as shown in the following illustration.

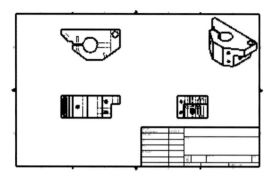

5   Replace the title block:

- In the browser, expand Sheet:2. Right-click ANSI-Large. Click Delete.
- In the browser, under Drawing Resources, expand Title Blocks.
- Right-click ANSI A. Click Insert.

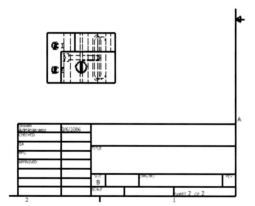

6   Create a sheet format:

- In the browser, right-click Sheet:2. Click Create Sheet Format.
- In the Create Sheet Format dialog box, enter **B Size, 4 view.**
- Click OK. The new sheet format is displayed in the browser under Sheet Formats.

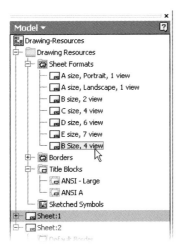

7   Test the new sheet format:
   - In the browser, double-click B Size, 4 view.
   - In the Select Component dialog box, navigate to *Drawing-Resources.ipt*. Click Open.
   - Click OK. Sheet:3 is displayed in the browser.

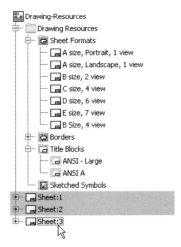

8   Delete Sheet:1 and Sheet:2:
   - In the browser, right-click Sheet:1. Click Delete Sheet.
   - Click OK. Notice that Sheet:3 is missing from the list. Sheet:2 was labeled Sheet:1.
   - Repeat step one and delete Sheet:2.

9   Close all files. Do not save.

Exercise | Customize a Title Block

In this exercise, you customize a title block.

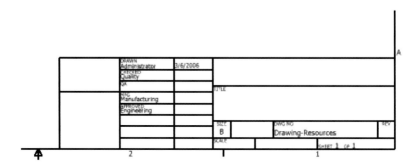

The completed exercise

Completing the Exercise:	*To complete the exercise, follow the steps in this book or in the onscreen exercise. In the onscreen list of chapters and exercises, click Chapter 11: Drawing Standards and Resources. Click Exercise: Customize a Title Block.*

1   Create a new drawing based on the *ANSI (mm).idw* template.

2   To change the sheet to B size:
   • In the browser, right-click Sheet:1. Click Edit Sheet.
   • In the Edit Sheet dialog box, under Size, select B. Click OK.

3   To replace the title block:
   • In the browser, under Sheet:1, right-click ANSI-Large. Click Delete.
   • In the browser, expand Drawing Resources. Expand Title Blocks.
   • Right-click ANSI A. Click Insert.

4   To customize the title block:

  - In the browser, under Sheet:1, right-click ANSI A. Click Edit Definition.
  - Using standard sketching techniques, add the four lines and one dimension, as shown.

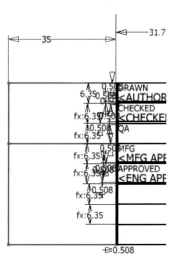

5   To save the custom title block:

  - Right-click in the graphics area. Click Save Title Block.
  - In the Save Edits dialog box, click Yes.

6   To edit the iProperties of the drawing:

- In the browser, right-click the Drawing node. Click iProperties.
- In the Properties dialog box, click Status.
- Enter the values shown in the Checked By, Eng. Approved By, and Mfg. Approved fields.
- Click OK.

7   To view the new title block:

- Zoom in on the title block area.

DRAWN Administrator	6/9/2009
CHECKED QA	
QA	
MFG Manufacturing	
APPROVED, Engineering	
2	

8   Close all files. Do not save.

Chapter Summary

In this chapter, you learned about the tools and resources that help you to define and follow drawing standards and styles, distribute your drawing views across multiple sheets, and create title blocks and borders that meet your specific documentation needs.

Having completed this chapter, you can:

- Set drafting standards to control the appearance of drawing features.
- Use drawing resources to create multiple sheets and add borders and title blocks to your drawings.

Index

Notes